CONNECTIONS:
REFLECTIONS ON SIXTY YEARS
OF BROADCASTING

Mary C. O'Connell
Oral Historian

NBC SIXTY YEARS

Here you will find a sampling of personal recollections recorded by some of the people—affiliates, programmers, stars, news correspondents, sportscasters, executives of various stripe—who were part of the 60-year history of NBC. There is no way for us to push the clock all the way back to 1926 when David Sarnoff, with 189 employees, created the National Broadcasting Company. A national network broadcasting company had never existed before. So there we find the first of many firsts achieved by NBC in all the years leading to the present, robustly healthy, sexagenarian organization.

Some of the first "recollectors" I taped in the fall of 1985 were part of network radio's heyday; not a few of them had to invent good things to do with television after television itself was invented. Our panel makes clear that in 60 years many of the problems and challenges of network broadcasting have changed hardly at all in size but merely come in different wrappings. One thread runs throughout these accounts: a considerable pride in having worked for NBC, or in having the special links claimed by the network's affiliates.

This mosaic is not, strictly speaking, an oral history of NBC. The history of the company would be a very different book. But taping our random sampling has yielded enough firsthand, funny, and, indeed, fascinating stories to fill NBC's 60th birthday book.

There is no way we could have included all the stories of all the people who played important roles in the company's first 60 years. This small volume, however, can be dedicated to all those who have added distinction to the NBC call letters, including the few whose accounts are here, and the many more, sung or unsung, who have been part of this great company.

Mary C. O'Connell   January 3, 1986

CONTENTS

Affiliate Broadcasters

NBC Executives

Network News

Network Sports

Network Entertainers

Harold (Hod) Grams is a former Vice President of the Pulitzer Publishing Company and former President of KSD-TV in St. Louis. He was Chairman of the NBC Board of Delegates from 1967 to 1971.

"Later that night, I went up to Harry Truman's suite with Pete Brandt. We went into a bedroom and had a private talk with Truman. I'll never forget it. He sat on the bed and tears actually came to his eyes, and he said, 'I don't want to be Vice President. I just want to be the Chairman of the Senate Preparedness Committee.'"

I was born in Rock Island, Illinois, which was, at the time, the center of farm equipment manufacture. The International Harvester Company's plant and John Deere's corporate headquarters were there, and the Rock Island Arsenal, which was very important during World War I. *And* the Mississippi River, the big river.

I got a football and basketball scholarship at St. Ambrose College in Davenport, Iowa. During high school and college I was always interested in dramatics and in speech and debating. I was in the dramatics course class at St. Ambrose when a fellow from General Motors asked the head of the department to recommend two young men who could be "pitchmen" at the auto show at the Davenport Coliseum. She selected Dick Stengel and me. The Program Manager of the radio station, WOC, "Moon" Reagan, heard me there one evening and came up to me afterwards and offered me a job as a vacation replacement announcer, which I took. In the fall, I was asked to stay on full-time. I dropped out of school and went into announcing.

"Moon" Reagan, at WOC, was President Reagan's brother, J. Neal Reagan. "Dutch" Reagan was the sports announcer at WHO. Both stations were owned by the Palmer Broadcasting Company of the Palmer School of Chiropractic. WOC stood for the "Wonders of Chiropractic." A year later, I was promoted to WHO in Des Moines. "Dutch" Reagan was just leaving to go to Hollywood, and I, after a year, was politely fired by Harold Fair, the Program Manager, who said, "Hod, WHO is a station that appeals to the rural listeners, and your voice is more of a metropolitan voice. I think you'd be better off in a metropolitan area."

I was recommended to Ed Hamlin, Manager of KSD in St. Louis. He wrote me a letter and invited me to come down and audition at KSD, which I did. He hired me as an announcer, and I went to work with KSD thinking I would be there for a year or two. I stayed for about 41 enjoyable years.

"Moon" Reagan subsequently went to Hollywood and headed up the McCann-Erickson office. Recently, I sent him a film clip that I had kept for many, many years which featured his brother, "Dutch" Reagan, who made it when he was head of the Screen Actors Guild. He was M.C. at the Golden Globe Awards when Jayne Mansfield announced an award for Cantinflas. She wore one of her revealing gowns, and when Mickey Rooney accepted the award for Cantinflas, he stood there on the stage looking directly at Jayne, and the crowd just roared because he was looking directly at her bosom. When they quieted down, Mickey said, "Who said it was nice to be tall?" I sent this to "Moon" who sent it on to his brother, because I had read that Nancy was looking for a copy of the film. I got a very nice note from President Reagan, dictated on Air Force One.

KSD was one of the original NBC radio affiliates in 1926. The station was owned by The Pulitzer Publishing Company, publishers of *The St. Louis Post-Dispatch*. It was an ideal ownership. Mr. Joseph Pulitzer let management run the radio and subsequently the TV station with absolutely no interference at all. It would be on a very rare occasion if you heard from him. When I joined the company, the one who brought me along was the second Mr. Pulitzer (The third Joseph Pulitzer is presently running the operation. His grandfather instituted the Pulitzer Prizes). He was a true gentleman and just as nice a man as you could ever hope to work for, but still a regular guy. He loved to hunt and fish, and he loved his martinis.

The Pulitzers have always had a reputation for being willing to experiment in their field. When radio came along, Mr. Pulitzer, being a man of vision, thought it was a part of the communications field, and formed KSD. The radio station was regarded as a sideline. It was in the same building as the newspaper. George Burbach, the General Manager, ran the station for a good long time.

Earlier, George had worked at the newspaper as Advertising Manager. Ed Hamlin followed him as Ad Manager. As the radio station grew, Burbach left the newspaper and became a full-time manager at KSD.

At the time I was hired, KSD was 12 years old and was a very good radio station. I was doing sports and news at the same time I was a staff announcer. (Eventually, I became Program Manager, and then Station Manager.) I called the action on the football games on radio. We did the Notre Dame, Illinois, and Missouri football games. We divided our schedule among those three teams because we felt the people in St. Louis were interested in the Illinois team; there was a very pronounced interest in Notre Dame, *and* in Missouri, three games at each of the schools. In those days, Notre Dame had great teams, Illinois was not so good, Missouri was great! Describing the games was a matter of familiarizing yourself with the team, and then we'd have charts with the names of the players, as well as a "spotter." A spotter was someone provided by the team who was familiar with the players, and he would point to the name of the ball carrier or the tackler on the chart.

One time, Illinois was playing at Northwestern. The booths up there had very thin walls, very rudimentary, and there I was on the end, and on my left was Ted Husing of CBS, and on his left was Bill Stern of NBC. We got going, and I noticed that Ted Husing was yelling so loud that he fed into our microphone, and I had to turn so the microphone faced the other way and do my broadcast in a cramped position to avoid having his voice feed into my microphone. After the game was over, Husing said, "I want to apologize to you. I had to talk as loud as I did because I had that Bill Stern shouting on the other side of me, and I couldn't let his voice feed into my microphone."

One of the great games that I broadcast was the final game between Army and Notre Dame. There used to be a great rivalry when Army and Notre Dame had some fine football teams. They played in South Bend and in New York at Yankee Stadium. There was a good deal of rowdyism in connection with the games in New York, and so they decided to discontinue the series. The final game in the series was going to be played in South Bend. Bill Stern, once again, was right next to me in the booth. Army kicked off to Notre Dame, and the Notre Dame

man who received it was Terry Brennan, number 37. (He subsequently was a coach at Notre Dame.) I could hear Bill Stern in the booth next to me saying that Sitko had received the kickoff. Well, ordinarily in the days of radio, that's no big problem because nobody would have seen the play. In this case, it soon became evident that Brennan was going to go all the way for a touchdown, so Stern said, "At the 15-yard line, Sitko laterals to Terry Brennan who goes for the touchdown." Typical of Stern.

On Thanksgiving Day following his election, President Reagan had agreed to be interviewed at half-time during the pro-football game. The announcer said, "Now, Mr. President, I'm going to play a little game with you. I'll say a word and you tell me what flashes first in your mind." And he said, "Sports announcer." And Reagan went on to tell the story which I just told you without mentioning Bill Stern's name. But then he added a twist and told the story about Clem McCarthy broadcasting the Preakness Race the following spring, and he had the wrong horse winning the race. Someone said to Clem "How could you *do* that?" Clem said, "Well, you can't lateral a horse."

It was a very heavy schedule, but I had a great time broadcasting the games. During the 40's when I was promoted to Program Manager, I continued to announce. I had a daily sports program with J. Ray Stockton who was Sports Editor of *The St. Louis Post-Dispatch*. We did a news and sports show at 6 o'clock every evening.

We carried a heavy schedule of NBC radio programs, and the principal local activity in radio, much like television today, was in the area of news, and some public service programs, although we did have a live one-hour program with an orchestra. Prior to that, we had a daily 15-minute program with a full studio band. Those programs gradually disappeared. I'll always remember the "Vic and Sade" program out of Chicago, sponsored by Crisco; and, of course, "Fibber McGee and Molly," "Amos 'n' Andy," the "Kraft Music Hall" with Ken Carpenter and Bing Crosby, and the "Lucky Strike Hit Parade." All the great, *great* old shows.

The station had become profitable in the late 30's. Before that, we were operating at a loss because there wasn't that volume of advertising in those days. We were 5,000-watts day, 1,000-watts night.

Was I very ambitious? Not really. I found myself at KSD in a situation where I admired the Pulitzer Publishing Company, and I admired what the Pulitzers stood for. They were progressive liberals. This goes back, of course, to the days when Roosevelt was President, although Pulitzer at one point thought Roosevelt should not have run for a third term, and he supported the Republicans. His editorial choice for President got clobbered, but basically, the *Post-Dispatch* and the Post Publishing Company were liberal in their outlook, and they fought for all of the things that I believed in. I more or less dedicated myself to becoming a part of an organization that I admired very much.

Because of the newspaper ownership, KSD had a pretty heavy focus on news. And had a rather strict policy of commercial acceptance which we inherited from the newspaper. They had a man at the newspaper called Doc Pritchard, who had to approve all advertising and all advertising claims. He worked with us at KSD also, and so there was a good deal of advertising that we couldn't accept. For instance, we had a hassle about Geritol and their claims about iron-poor blood. There were many other radio commercials that we turned down because we insisted on verifiable claims and good taste. We had very high standards.

In 1946, I had an interesting experience. KSD Radio decided to broadcast Winston Churchill's speech at Westminster College which President Truman had arranged. As a routine thing, we notified NBC that we were going to pick it up and asked if they would like to have a feed, and NBC said no. I went up to Fulton, Missouri, with an engineer and when we were checking the line back to the station early in the afternoon (the speech was scheduled for 4:45 p.m.), they said NBC had just sent word they'd changed their mind. They read a copy of the speech, and they wanted a feed. I had never fed the network, and I was petrified because I knew, hav-

ing covered events, that things never go according to schedule, and you have to fill and ad lib, and I thought, my God!, I'll be on the network ad libbing.

I told the guys at the station, "Churchill's coming on the train from Kansas City, and I'll bet there's someone from NBC on the train." At the train station, I saw Pete Brandt, head of the Washington Bureau of the *Post-Dispatch*, and asked if there was anyone on the train from NBC. He said, "Yes, it's some new guy, a young fellow, a David Brinkley." He pointed out a skinny fellow. I went over to David, introduced myself and told him what my problem was. I said, "I wonder if you would work with me and help me out. I have to do some ad libbing." David looked me right in the eye with those clear blue eyes of his and said, "That's your problem." And he turned and walked away. I was disappointed, but I got along fine by myself.

KSD-TV went on the air in 1947 as a result of General Sarnoff's address at the affiliates' meeting. Mr. Pulitzer was there with George Burbach. Unfortunately, I wasn't there. David Adams tells the story about one affiliate who ran out of the meeting, went to a pay telephone, called his ownership and said, "Start ordering the equipment." Pulitzer was equally gung ho. Jack Harris told me that he was sitting near Mr. Pulitzer and every once in a while, Pulitzer would clench his fists and say, "You tell 'em, Dave." In any event, "Dave" did a good selling job, and that's why KSD Television became the *first* post-war television station on the air. There were five experimental stations around the country on the air during the war, but KSD-TV, St. Louis, was the *first* commercial station to go on the air after the war. February 1947. We were the sixth station on the air.

I would like to give you a little background on KSD-TV. Four or five companies in St. Louis applied to the FCC for television licenses before the FCC froze everything during the war. Three companies had been granted licenses, Pulitzer, CBS, and the *St. Louis Star-Times* newspaper. When the war was over, the FCC lifted the freeze and CBS and the *Star-Times* said they were not going to put a television station on the air; they were going to wait for color to come. CBS was working on a color system; it eventually worked out and the FCC gave it tentative approval and then withdrew it. The FCC then approved the RCA compatible system. In any event, the CBS station here did not go on the air and the *Star-Times* did not go on the air, and then the FCC, in 1948, put on another freeze to take a look at the allocations. The CBS people and the *Star-Times* people tried to talk us into not going on the air, but Pulitzer said, "Hell, no, we're going." Then Burbach started fighting with Harry Bannister up in Detroit to see who would get the first RCA transmitter because Harry was on the same time schedule we were on. Burbach was successful. Then Harry went and bought a Federal Transmitter which gave him nothing but trouble. We went on the air in February, and they went on the air about June or July.

Burbach and I ran both radio and television. When television first went on the air, it was just one crisis after another. Every day was a crisis. I went through a period when I finally had to get to a doctor and get sedated. I was under sedation for a year. We didn't know what we were doing because nobody had done it before. No ten easy lessons! To keep going on radio and working on television was exhausting, but we lived through it. We were working 18 hours a day. It was great fun really, a great challenge.

We'd go on the air from 3 to 5 p.m. and then sign off and then come back around 7 to 9 p.m. We had news and on Sunday night we had a fellow, Calvin Ringgenberg, who played the organ and had a group of people who sang *hymns*. Can you imagine that at 8 o'clock on Sunday nights?! People watched anything and *everything*. Betty Grossman did a 15-minute program from the Art Museum every Sunday night. She'd bring down little objects from the museum and talk about them. You look at those old schedules, and you just can't believe that was the start of television.

How many people bought sets originally? When we started out, the RCA distributor, Dale Neiswander of Interstate, brought in 50 sets. They were costly. We kept a count of the sets because the only sets that were coming into St. Louis were sold by Interstate. There was a slow accumulation, and then, all of a sudden, all hell broke loose.

We set TV rates in comparison to radio rates really, and we got what we thought we could get. There was no rhyme nor reason, although in the early days of our active association with NBC, network money was always part of the discussion. The Manager of NBC Television back in those really early days was an engineer named Nick Kersta. I remember being in New York and talking with Nick who said, "Now, Hod, we're not going to handle television like we handled radio. We're not going to take all the risks; we're not going to spend all the money to mount these programs and then be satisfied with making less money than Macy's department store. We're going to get the lion's share of the income out of television."

That was Nick's pitch. That was before anyone was interconnected, and before we knew what the hell was going to happen. Later, Bill Hedges came along with his rate plan based on the number of sets. That never did get off the ground, but *if* it had, then it would have been the greatest thing in the world for stations because of the astronomical growth of the number of sets. That was always a battle—how to set the relationship between the network and the affiliates. I felt the network was very fair with the stations in the matter of compensation. A very good deal.

When we invited Mr. Pulitzer to come over for the first time to take a look at television, we put a 15-minute film program on the film chain and piped it up to Mr. Burbach's office. Mr. Pulitzer sat there very intently watching it all. He had difficulty with his eyes, and he had to be up very close to the set. I'll never forget after the film was finished, he leaned back and said, "Well, that is the death of radio." It wasn't, but that was a popular conception at the time. There was a period when there was a co-relationship between the revenue on radio and the revenue on television. The network revenue from radio gradually diminished, and the network revenue on television gradually increased. The local station programming reflected the manager's tastes, the emphasis they would give to news or to public affairs or whatever. Management (Louis Read and Jack Harris and others), in those early days, had very positive ideas about what television should be, as we did at KSD-TV.

Among other things, KSD Radio had the policy of covering the national political conventions, and the one that I remember most clearly was one in 1944 when Truman was nominated to be Roosevelt's Vice President. The convention was held in Chicago, Bob Hannegan of St. Louis was the chairman of the convention, and, of course, he was *very* interested in getting Harry Truman accepted as the Vice Presidential nominee. Hannegan went down to see President Roosevelt, who came through Chicago during the convention in his special railroad car which was pulled into the stockyards. He told Roosevelt how he felt about the Vice Presidential nominees. Hannegan came away from that meeting with a list of just three names that Roosevelt said would be okay with him, and Hannegan said the first name on the list was Harry Truman's. Whether that was true or not, I don't know.

When Hannegan got back to the convention hotel, he called Ed Harris, a Washington correspondent for the *Post-Dispatch*, who also worked with us on our pickups from the convention, and Hannegan told Ed that he had been to see President Roosevelt, and that Roosevelt had told him that Harry Truman was the man he would like to have on the ticket as his running mate. I was having dinner with Pete Brandt, the head of the Washington Bureau of the *Post-Dispatch*, when Ed Harris came dashing in and told us what Hannegan had told him about Truman. We went right back to the hotel where we had our broadcast lines, went on the air and announced the great scoop that President Roosevelt had selected Harry Truman as his choice for Vice President. We were the first on the air with it.

In looking at it later, I knew that Hannegan had used us to get Harry Truman on the ticket and to get the steam roller going. At the convention when the nominations were made for Vice President, I can see Hannegan up on the podium as clearly as if it were last night. He couldn't see or hear *anyone* who wanted to nominate

someone from the floor other than the person who nominated Harry Truman. It was a real example of putting power to use. Later that night, I went up to Harry Truman's suite with Pete Brandt. We went into a bedroom and had a private talk with Harry. I'll never forget it. He sat on the bed and tears actually came to his eyes, and he said, "I don't want to be Vice President. I just want to be the Chairman of the Senate Preparedness Committee." He was the chairman of the committee which was investigating our national mobilization for war and war production profits. Bob Hannegan, the Democratic Party Convention Chairman, wanted Harry in there for his own reasons. The rest is history. Harry wound up as President, an excellent President, a good man.

Before the network was interconnected, and back in the very early days of television, NBC News had a damn good operation under Davidson Taylor, and then Bill McAndrew came along and did an excellent job. Julian Goodman, in those days, was in the Washington Bureau of NBC News, and he was put in charge of syndicating the film of President Eisenhower's press conferences. As you know, Jim Hagerty, Eisenhower's Press Secretary, got President Eisenhower to agree to have his press conferences filmed, with the proviso that Hagerty would have the right to check out the film. If there was anything on the film embarrassing or incorrect, changes could be made. Julian called and told me that the films were going to be available, and, if we would like to have a print, it would cost us $25. I said, "Julian, that seems awfully high to me." And we went back and forth. Finally, I got him to agree that they would charge us $15 for this film, and we would have the right to show it twice, and after we showed it twice we could give it over to the educational station here, and they could show it any number of times! Julian has always been a considerate man.

I want to tell you that back in the early fifties, Mr. Paley went to work on

Mr. Pulitzer about switching from NBC to CBS. We were the only station on the air in St. Louis. CBS would have preferred to have KSD-TV their affiliate in St. Louis, and then they could have applied or bought a television station in a larger market.

Paley was doing a selling job on Mr. Pulitzer, and Mr. Pulitzer was receptive because he had great admiration for CBS News, particularly Ed Murrow. They were riding high at the time. Mr. Pulitzer asked Mr. Burbach and me to come out to his home one Sunday morning, and we spent three hours discussing the pros and cons of staying with NBC or going with CBS.

Burbach and I both took the position that we should remain with NBC. Back in those days, CBS had an edge on NBC in the news. We took the position that CBS was a good company, very alert and aggressive, but they didn't have the strong financial backing NBC had with RCA. We were also helped by a friend of Mr. Pulitzer's, Bernie Baruch. Pulitzer had talked to him about switching to CBS and about the excellence of CBS News, and Baruch said, "Well, Joe, you must remember that no one has a monopoly on excellence." It was that close.

My moving into the actual job of General Manager wasn't a change in my responsibilities. For a number of years I had been doing the work. Burbach and I had worked very closely together. I pretty much handled the day-to-day operation, and he oversaw it. KSD-TV became profitable very early. We were on the air by ourselves for six years, and so we were serving four networks— NBC, CBS, DuMont and ABC. In those days, we used to meet every 13 weeks in the Johnny Victor Theatre in New York with a fellow named McFarland of AT&T to allocate time on the cable, because there was only one cable going from east to west. The allocation would be based somewhat on what we would schedule here in St. Louis because we were at the end of that one coaxial cable line. Every hour of the week had to be negotiated for 13 weeks. There would be Carleton Smith of NBC, Bob Wood of CBS, Ed Jamieson of DuMont and Lee Jahncke for ABC.

First of all, there was a Mid-West network which was hooked up a year or so before it hooked up from the east, and we originated the program here in St. Louis that dedicated the Mid-West NBC Network, fed out of St. Louis into Chicago, Milwaukee, Buffalo, and Detroit. Jinx

Falkenberg was the M.C. of a program which was made up of vaudeville acts. I remember a fellow named Peg-Leg Bates, who did a dance with his peg leg, and then there were two black dance performers, who had a knack of pushing a piano around the stage. Jinx Falkenberg kept giving plugs to the Schlitz Brewery, which didn't go over very well here in St. Louis, but she had some contract with Schlitz in Milwaukee, and she was using her appearance on the NBC Mid-West Network to plug the brewery.

Speaking of proud moments, we always worked with the NBC News Department trying to get coverage of the Veiled Prophet Ball. It's a high social event when all the debutantes are introduced to society, an elaborate ceremony. It was a very popular TV show in St. Louis because the average person never expected to see a Veiled Prophet Ball. We were never successful in getting the network to take any coverage. I got a call one afternoon from Don Mercer. He said, "Hi, do you folks have any programming that you could feed us this evening? Someone with a bulldozer ran into the coaxial cable in Indiana and we're out of commission, but we can take west to east feed through the Mid-West Network." I said, "Well, you're lucky. The Veiled Prophet Ball is on tonight." So that night KSD fed the Ball from 8 o'clock to 10:30 on the NBC Television Network. We finally made it!

In 1967, I became Chairman of the NBC Board of Delegates. When Jack Harris was Chairman of the Affiliates Committee, we had a meeting in New York. The affiliates were really complaining about all the money NBC's President, Bob Kintner, was spending on news. Kintner was determined to create a first-class news operation, and he did. Jack was loaded for bear, and we met up on the sixth floor in that little conference room. At the appointed time, Jack got into his pitch and was talking about the money that was being spent on remotes and special programs, and how the affiliates felt. About that time, someone came in and handed Bob Kintner a note. He read it and he said, "Jack, do you mind if we have a slight interruption here? There's something that's going to come on the air that I'd like to watch."

We were there on the day that the astronaut, Alan Shepard, who had done the first orbit, was honored with a big parade in New York, and NBC, of course, was covering it with I don't know how many remote units. On that same day, a commercial airliner crashed out in Jamaica Bay on Long Island. One of the remote units swung away from the parade, went out to Jamaica Bay, and had a direct on-the-scene pick up of this airplane crash. Boom! Kintner turns on the switch, and that's what comes up on the air. You may remember there was a fellow on board named Jones from Cities Service, a friend of Eisenhower's, who was carrying a huge sum of cash when the plane went down. In any event, we all watched that dramatic scene. Bob finally switched it off and said, "Now, Jack, is that the type of thing you're talking about? Is that the sort of thing you don't want us to do?" That was the end of that.

I had no quarrel with the Station Relations men over the years; they had been great, very fair with us. I thought they were good executives, good representatives of NBC. I still consider Don Mercer and Paul Hancock my friends. NBC was a quality company, particularly when David Sarnoff was around. After he left, there was a change. His influence was so vast.

I once told David Adams that back when NBC was having their problems with radio, one problem was that people still had an idea that General Sarnoff started— that they are the network of high quality programming, and this means programming that does not have mass appeal. David disagreed. I still feel that NBC did establish the reputation of high quality programming, and I attribute it directly to David Sarnoff. Later, Pat Weaver, Mort Werner, and Dick Pinkham really created some excitement in programming. They came up with the "Today" show, the "Tonight" show, "Home," and "Wide, Wide World," which really was ahead of its time.

My God, "Wide, Wide World" almost broke our backs because they'd do all these damn remotes. They came out to St. Louis most, and they wanted to do a remote with the cameras on land and sea and in the air! On a barge out in the Mississippi River and on land, and in a damn airplane. In those days, that was something! Whenever they came out, it was a great challenge to the engineering department. They would tell us what they wanted, and then the producers would come out. When the nation was united with coaxial cable from West Coast to East Coast "Wide, Wide World" put one camera on the Atlantic Ocean, put another camera on the Pacific Ocean, and melded the water of the two oceans together as a symbol of the tying together of the United States with the coaxial cable.

From the standpoint of programming, Weaver was great, and, of course, Mort Werner was very helpful. Mort was instrumental in putting together the concept, and deciding the direction it would go.

George Frey, head of sales, was always one of my favorites. Walter Scott was another. You couldn't ask for a nicer man. He was talented, and he was a good man, the perfect gentleman. I was very disappointed when Don Durgin resigned. NBC lost the opportunity to use his considerable talents to the fullest. I was pleased when Julian became President because I had known him in the News Department. It was unusual for someone from the News Department to take over a job of that sort. Very unusual. However, I had been in the news and sports area, and I had taken over administrative work and it worked out okay. I knew that Julian could do the same thing, and I think he did. Julian is a prince of a guy. I have always enjoyed talking to David Adams; he's a fascinating man.

I remember when I was Chairman of the Affiliates Committee there was one thing I did that I was very proud of. I appointed Doug Manship of Baton Rouge to head up the affiliates' committee for negotiations with NBC at a time when there was to be a readjustment of compensation because of a significant increase in the cost of interconnection, the coaxial cable charges. NBC was going to give us more announcement positions, and we were going to agree to some cut in compensation, and Doug Manship handled that and worked with David Adams. We finally reached an agreement at the meeting in Jamaica. Doug and David Adams really worked out the final details of the compromise. Included in the compromise was, we thought, a firm agreement that in the event satellite interconnection became possible and interconnection costs came down, there would be a reimbursement or readjustment with the affiliates to make up for what they had given up during that period. When that day came along, NBC said no, there was no firm agreement on any readjustment.

The reason I remember that is because it was a time when Vice President Agnew gave such a threatening speech against our industry in Des Moines. Pat Buchanan wrote that speech. They sent a copy of it over the teletype to Jamaica, and it was a shock to read what Agnew had said.

Jack Harris took over from Walter Damm and Louis Read took over from Jack, and I took over from Louis Read. The outgoing head went on the little nominating committee. Just a little incest going on there. We, Jack and Louis and my successor, Bob Ferguson, became fast and good friends.

The Post Dispatch Company started buying stations, and, by coincidence, the stations we bought were ABC affiliates, and I would go to ABC affiliate meetings, but there was never any real discussion about KSD switching. We now have seven stations, five VHF, two UHF, and two radio stations.

In 1974 I became President of KSD/KSD-TV, something I never dreamed would happen when I started in 1938. People have helped me. I've been very fortunate in my career. And I had a strong constitution. I believed in managing with a loose rein, a style that perhaps is still successful in certain cases, but now management by loose rein is not too popular. Pulitzer managed with a loose rein, which I loved, and that's the way I managed. It made for a much easier and pleasanter life. Whether it maximized profit, I sometimes wonder. I was not primarily a bottom line guy except when dealing with NBC. That was something of a game. I was fortunate because I was in television at a time when you couldn't help but improve your performance because rates were going up and circulation was going up, and we just rode the wave. The station won many awards. One was a national Emmy in '64, and there were three regional Emmys. Those were proud moments.

Throughout the years, but especially in the seventies, we knew NBC should be supported, they were doing a good job. They were not having any luck in some cases wih the programming, but they were in there trying. I've followed Grant Tinker's career with great interest. Obviously, he is doing all of the right things.

My 60th birthday wish for NBC? I wish that a group of talented producers and reporters would give NBC a weekly news program in the top ten and follow that with a Monday-Friday early evening hour of news.

September 18, 1985

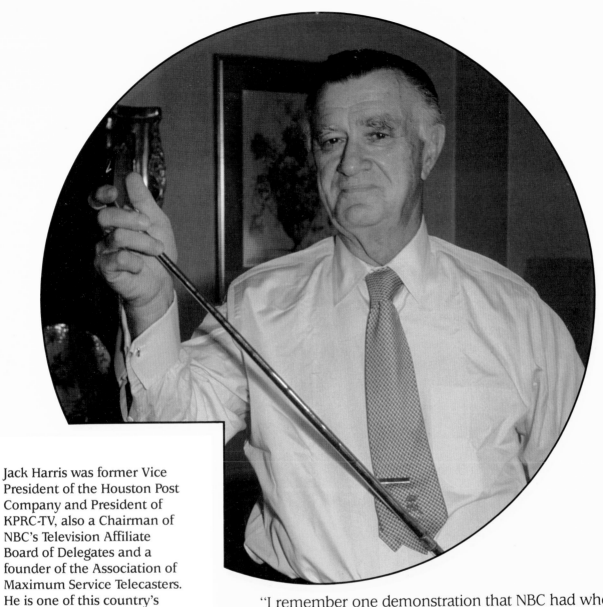

Jack Harris was former Vice President of the Houston Post Company and President of KPRC-TV, also a Chairman of NBC's Television Affiliate Board of Delegates and a founder of the Association of Maximum Service Telecasters. He is one of this country's pioneer broadcasters.

Jack Harris

"I remember one demonstration that NBC had when they were promoting color. They reproduced a *Vogue* ad, a beautiful girl in color frozen on the screen...the video started...she got up, walked around and demonstrated and talked. The effect was just overwhelming. I was sitting in the theatre at the right of one of the large magazine publishers, who also owned television stations. He was with his broadcaster, and I heard him gasp, 'Ohhhh, my God, that will kill magazines.'"

I was born in Nashville, Tennessee, went to Vanderbilt University for a Liberal Arts degree and went on to complete a Master's in political science. In the aftermath of the Depression, the job opportunities were very limited. The best offer I had was to be a trainee for manager of an A&P grocery store. I had had some extra-curricular activities which kept me in school for that extra year. I worked as a cub reporter on the *Nashville Tennessean* morning newspaper when I was going to school, and I was also Editor of the *Hustler*. (The school paper.) The Editor and the Business Manager split the profits.

I had a chance to do some special shows with WSM Radio and also some commercials. WSM, at that time, had a number of local programs sponsored by the National Life and Accident Insurance Company. I helped to write some of those, acted in some and announced in others. I also had some very good commercials, largely refrigerators and Lawndale Cemetery, over at WLAC, a CBS station. Apparently they felt that my voice was funereal and I made $25 per program from Lawndale, all live. That was a high fee in Nashville in radio at that time.

After Vanderbilt, I was offered a reporter's job at the *Tennessean*, but I found out that the managing editor, who was my idol at that time, was making $75 a week, and that was the job I aspired to in about 10 to 12 years! I was offered jobs at that time at both WLAC and WSM. I felt that WSM was a "class" station and accepted slightly less money for the opportunity to work there at a salary of $70 per week, which was very high in those days. I was hired by Edwin Craig, a member of the family and Executive Vice President of the National Life Insurance Company that owned the station.

When I joined WSM there were basically on staff just announcers and engineers. I started out straight announcing, but I also did sports, because I had written sports on the *Tennessean*. I was particularly interested in sports. I worked in almost every department of WSM until I could hire somebody to replace me. I started the Continuity Department, the Publicity Department, Talent Coordination. I never tried to do the farm reports. I went out and hired John McDonald, a farm director who, this very summer, is still at WSM.

Parenthetically, when I later tried to counsel announcers, I found many of them wanted to put their hand behind their ear and speak in a very deep voice to sound like Harry Von Zell. There was so much imitating going on. I used Franklin D. Roosevelt as an example. I'd say the two things that made Roosevelt so effective were his naturalness and sincerity. I told them when they used the microphone to assume they were talking to one person.

I worked with Ed Kirby a great deal in developing programs for the National Life on radio. When I first went to work there I spent half a day, mornings, in the insurance company planning and writing shows for radio, then went upstairs and worked on radio until I did the 10 o'clock news. Saturdays, I broadcast football games. I never thought about it, but you see I never had the privilege of working on hours. By the time they put wages and hours in, I was exempt. But I never thought about how many hours I'd worked because I loved the work.

WSM, an NBC affiliate, became very successful. We competed with WLW, "the nation's station." National Life was not that interested in the bottom line, it was interested in doing a good job. I thought NBC was *the* network.

I joined the War Department as a civilian in April 1941, before Pearl Harbor. I helped organize the first radio branch of the War Department. Before WWII, Ed Kirby joined the National Association of Broadcasters. He asked the War Department what would happen to radio if we got into a war. Having no answers, they finally said, "Ed, why don't you come over here and help us find out. You've got all the questions, help us find the answers." Once there, about February of 1941, he began to think of building a small staff. Major General C. Richardson was head of Public Relations at that time, and Ed mentioned my name to General Richardson, who asked, "Is that the fellow who does the news?" He had heard me in Birmingham, Alabama, and okayed Ed's choice.

When Ed called me, I said, "Well, I think we're going to get into war." I wanted to be a part of it, but I also was only a couple of years into my career then, and I was concerned about financial security. Mary and I were married and had our first child, less than a year old. It was a hard decision because I wasn't worried about an early draft. I suggested that he get General Richardson to ask for a leave of absence for me from National Life.

General Richardson did better than that and had Henry L. Stimson, the Secretary of War, write Edwin Craig requesting that I be given a leave. With that, I trotted off to Washington.

Ed and I built a small staff at the War Department but we had to grope along to find out what we were going to do. One of the first things we did was to tackle a problem that radio could help on. Relatively small communities had burgeoned with Army posts near them. For example, Fayetteville, North Carolina, was near Fort Bragg, with 100,000 soldiers there. Relations between the military and the community were frequently strained, and we persuaded the radio stations to put on some programs involving the military. It was very successful. We began to get some writers to send the stories back to local radio stations, where they could participate as the new, small community newspapers had been doing.

We also had troops stationed in Alaska, Iceland, Panama, wherever, even though war had not been declared. In Iceland, a Colonel Boeing, General McNair's deputy (McNair was in charge of all the Army ground forces), said, "General McNair demands that you get some radio entertainment to those troops in Iceland." We weren't in the entertainment business or the short-wave, but there was no one else in the Army to do it—so started the first overseas broadcast to troops. We were searching for a name for it; we'd gotten all the Hollywood and radio personnel to take part and we hit upon "Command Performance" (produced by Pat Weaver). The name came from Colonel Boeing saying, "McNair commands you to do this." In effect we said to the stars of radio and Hollywood, "This is a command performance, from the GI's to you." "Command Performance" survived to the end of the war.

Another program that I did was "Your Grandstand Seat," the sports news of the week plus interviews and comments by the two top radio sportsmen. I got Bill Stern from NBC and Ted Husing from CBS involved; Bill and Ted alternated weekly. They recorded it at NBC. I was particularly impressed with Ted Husing. There were times they'd call me from the studio and say, "We can't find Stern." And I would call Husing who'd say, "Tell them I'll be there in 30 minutes." And he'd grab a bunch of notes and do the show.

I had been trying to get out of Washington to do anything that would take my grade. By this time I was a Lieutenant Colonel. I started as a civilian mainly because I could not afford at my age to take the pay of First Lieutenant. But right after Pearl Harbor I became a Captain. In 90 days I was promoted to the rank of Major. The War Department sent me on a PR mission to all the Pacific islands under our command at that time. Abe Schechter had been sent out to MacArthur. Abe had been News Director of NBC radio, one of the finest and greatest newsmen. I think Schechter and Paul White were the founders of broadcast news. I don't think Abe has ever gotten the credit that he deserves.

Abe found the job was not quite as glamorous as he had expected, nor did he have many people doing all manner of jobs for him, and he was overage in grade and wanted out. I met him in Leyte with General Diller. General Diller told him he'd let him out if he could get an adequate replacement. So I said, "Would you consider me adequate?" He said, "Yes." And I said, "Well, if you will have General MacArthur request me by name, I don't think they'll turn it down." And that's the way I became the Press and Radio Communications Officer. This was 1944.

When we took Manila, Pat Flaherty, who later when I went to Houston was my news director, was an NBC correspondent in the Pacific. When we freed Manila the first thing he did was to go to Santo Tomas prison, and there he found Bert Silen, who had been an NBC correspondent in Manila. Bert Silen was literally broadcasting from the rooftops of Manila when the Japanese came in, and everything went off. He was interrupted right in the middle of the radio broadcast. On Pat's first broadcast for NBC out of Manila, he introduced Bert Silen. And Bert's opening line was, "As I was saying when I was so rudely interrupted three-and-one-half years ago...."

Abe Schechter told me another story about Bert. Bert Silen was a stringer for NBC for years because at that time Manila was not a main news city. News organizations were not as far reaching as they are now. Before Manila fell, Bert had been on NBC radio a number of times. At that time, the News Department of NBC was under the Program Department, and the Vice President of Programs, Clarence Menser, came to Abe and said, "Why are you paying so much money to this guy out in Manila?" I don't know whether they paid $50 a spot or $75 or whatever it was, but if a spot was on a number of times, he may have made $1,200 that September, and maybe $1,700 for October. So Abe explained, "Well, a year ago he may have made $150, it all evens out." Clarence said, "We'll have none of that. We're not going to pay a stringer this kind of money. You will put him on staff immediately." So Bert was put on staff less than 30 days before he was captured, and when he got out, he had three-and-one-half years of NBC pay waiting for him.

I became head of press communications and radio for General MacArthur. I am convinced that General MacArthur had only a very few days' knowledge of the dropping of the atomic bombs, because we had all sorts of contingency plans for the occupation of Japan, all predicated on an invasion. After the bombs were dropped, MacArthur was made the Supreme Commander and it became our role to go in for the occupational surrender.

There were all sorts of different plans devised over the 24, 48 hours they had, and, finally, MacArthur decided we didn't have enough troops or ships for a landing, and you're not supposed to have combat troops until the formal surrender, so about 50 C-54's took the staff in to Atsugi airport.

We had arranged when the Japanese delegation came to Manila for preliminary planning to have them set up studios and facilities in Yokohama so we could do our broadcasting there. So when we got into Yokohama, I had a plan with the Signal Corps. Colonel Auchincloss had the

facilities at the airport at Atsugi. What we did was to have all bulletins pre-recorded in Manila, and as soon as we landed, we had those bulletins for the networks, the AP, UP and INS, and *The New York Times* and a few other papers released from Manila.

We went from Atsugi to the Yokohama studio and then started calling RCA in San Francisco. There had been no communications all during the war between Japan and RCA, and one of the great thrills I got was to hear a voice from San Francisco coming in as if he were in the same room with us. "We hear you loud and clear. This is RCA, San Francisco."

General MacArthur, who understood the oriental mind better than any American, had planned to have the surrender ceremony at the U.S. Embassy in Tokyo, and his rationale was that he would then repossess that piece of real estate from which we had been thrown out, and that would mean something to the Japanese. Well, Colonel Auchincloss and the Signal Corps laid the lines, and two days before the ceremony General Diller told me that the Chief wanted to see me. MacArthur read a message from President Truman directing that the broadcast take place aboard the USS Missouri. MacArthur asked, "Can that be done?" I said, "General, our plan is *far* superior." He said, "That's not the question. Can it be done?" I said, "Well, if we have to do it aboard ship, the USS Iowa out there has much better facilities." Again, "Can it be done?" I said, "Sir, if we have to, it can be done." So he said, "Very well, we will comply. After all, we may be lucky that little man didn't tell us to come back and have it in the lobby of the Muehlebach Hotel in Kansas City."

It was a very complicated broadcast because President Truman not only directed it be aboard the USS Missouri, but that, as soon as the surrender ceremony ended, a cue be given to him at the White House for his remarks. He would then return to us for Nimitz's remarks, to be followed by MacArthur's remarks. There was no way that we could have everybody standing for 20 minutes, since we would hear nothing on the Missouri while President Truman was talking. We could not relay live from the Missouri, so what we did was to record in advance Admiral Nimitz's and General MacArthur's remarks, and then we recorded the surrender ceremony.

We timed the trip back to Yokohama on a destroyer. We would start the broadcast either on the hour or the half-hour. We didn't have tape, but we had disk and wire recordings. So when we got back, we got our recording ready of the surrender ceremonies, which ended up with a cue to President Truman. We were ready about four minutes before the hour. I told RCA we would go on the hour, and they gave us the cue, and everything turned out perfectly. At that time, we were supposed to say, "The preceding is an electrical transcription." I decided that for an historical event like that, the hell with the FCC. As far as the public was concerned, and even the networks, everyone thought the event was live. It started 28 minutes after the Japanese finished. Truman was live but he was the only one.

When we discussed with General MacArthur which network would do the narration, I said, "Well, General, we have always tossed a coin." The General regarded the Mutual correspondent, Don Bell, as not suitable, and he said, "Well, if you toss a coin, it's possible that Don Bell might get it." I said, "He's got one chance in four." So he said, "Find another means." What I actually did was to pick "Red" Mueller of NBC, who I felt was the best of all of our correspondents. Then I asked Admiral Miller over at Guam for the Navy to pick another network representative, excluding NBC, and Webley Edwards of CBS was picked. Those two did the narration of the surrender ceremonies without giving their names or their network affiliation.

The other network correspondents at our headquarters were furious at me and General Diller. They fired off wires to the networks demanding they go to the White House and complain. We still had censorship, and General Diller didn't want to let the wires out, but I told him they'll never pay any attention to it. I said, "Abe Schechter is back at Mutual. I know the guy at NBC. I know the CBS guys, and you'll never hear a word from any of them as long as we do a good job." We got wires from all of them saying what a good broadcast it was.

I figured I could never top that event, so everything else had to be downhill. I had gone back to WSM with high hopes, and when I'd gotten back I learned what Wolfe said—that you can't go home. There wasn't anything wrong with WSM, it was just that I had had very broad experiences during the war.

When I worked at the Pentagon, I met Mrs. Oveta Culp Hobby (the first Commander of the WACS) and her husband, Governor Hobby, the Houston Post Company owners. They needed a manager at their radio station. I was Station Manager at WSM when I left, and I went down as General Manager of KPRC. It was a good but small station; we didn't have staff musicians; we had the Texas Quality Network, which was Dallas, Houston, San Antonio, and Corpus Christi. We fed more than two programs a week to them.

KPRC was situated in the Lamar Hotel. The facilities were a little primitive, and Houston was not the boom town it later became, but I loved Houston from the time we moved there. The radio station had great potential, and we did well with it. Because the Hobbys were leaders in the community and the state, and the *Houston Post* had prestige, they and I wanted a first-class radio station. We needed the profits from the radio because the newspaper was struggling. We built our audience and KPRC became a very good station; it was not a big-time station. It was affiliated with NBC, and we had the best, not the biggest, news operation under Pat Flaherty, the News Director. It was a responsible station which was a strong influence in the community.

Niles Trammell, then President of NBC, was "Mr. Personality." He knew the station owners as well as the managers. However, I think Niles was responsible for the underpricing of radio. When I got to Houston, there had been a freeze on rates because of the war. KPRC was terribly underpriced at its network rate, but the network was selling out and everything was fine at 30 Rockefeller Plaza. CBS was second, and they couldn't move rates if NBC didn't, but Niles would not raise the rates. Niles did many great things and was one of the most popular men that ever headed NBC. When he retired, he, for a brief time, owned a television station in Miami. He flew over to Houston to see me, and after an hour or two, he said, "You know, for the first time I'm beginning to appreciate some of the problems that you damn station managers...."

KPRC carried most of NBC's network scheduling. We had some programs on TQN with the other markets as additional stations, depending on the advertising. We had a School of the Air public service program at all times, and we developed some morning disc jockey programs. We had one entertainment program in the early evening with singers and a nice musical unit that was fed to the TQN network. We had the only News department in town, but very small; the others had announcers taking news off the ticker.

In 1947, in Texas City, there was a chemical explosion aboard a tanker which ignited all the chemicals in a chain reaction. It was almost like an atomic bomb. We had a tip on it from a Western Union man who called our news department and told Pat Flaherty, "I'm getting all sorts of messages for Red Cross and ambulances. There's something happening in Texas City." We were able to go on with the first bulletin about 22 minutes before AP did. Pat and several of his people started out for Texas City. We didn't have the kind of equipment we have in radio and television now, but we were able to give it coverage.

After the event, Mrs. Agnes Meyer, publisher of the *Washington Post*, was commissioned by the President to make a study of communications during that period. She gave the station the highest mark for strength and accuracy. Literally we controlled the NBC network that evening. When they would start the program a minute late, we were doing bulletins into the evening, and we'd say, "We would need 40 seconds." The next day, NBC sent Morgan Beatty down. By the time he got there, he was the mop-up reporter. Pat said to him, "All right, Morgan, take over, tell us what you want." He said, "No, you guys are doing a great job." Pat Flaherty did a great, great job. The next year the coverage of the Texas City disaster won the Headline Award—for Morgan Beatty. He forgot to thank Pat Flaherty and KPRC.

The man responsible for many, many stations getting into television was Brigadier General Sarnoff. In 1947, the NAB was held in Atlantic City. Paley had advised the CBS affiliates to wait for color, but General Sarnoff said, "If you're in radio or own a newspaper, you'd better get into television because it's going to be bigger than both of them." I went back to Houston and proposed to Governor and Mrs. Hobby that we apply for a television license. One man, not in broadcasting, had just gotten a radio license, and had already applied for a television license and got it within 30 days. The FCC was just granting them upon request. As soon as we applied, the other network radio stations in Houston applied immediately, making four applicants for three channels.

At that time, the FCC put applicants in what they called a consolidated hearing. While we were waiting for a hearing, they decided they had allocated wrong, and they put a freeze on licenses. But then we had the opportunity in late '49 because Albert Lee, who had gotten the license, was losing so much money with it that he had to sell. Over the years, I reminded a lot of my associates among the affiliates that, "You know, the network owes you, and you owe the network, but we all owe General Sarnoff everything for his advice at that time."

The second station in Houston didn't get on until 1953, after the freeze was lifted. We bought in '49 and went on the air in early 1950. Our facilities consisted of a small tower, a transmitter, and a lot of leased equipment. Albert Lee had operated the station for a little over a year and there were 20,000 sets in the market. He did not have the resources, so when he had to sell, Mrs. Hobby and I both talked to him. The Governor was very reluctant to buy. Some of our political friends said, "Don't pay that outrageous price of $750,000 for a television station. We'll get you one." They couldn't guarantee that at all, and I told Governor Hobby, "When you own a newspaper you've got one strike against you, maybe two." So the Hobbys bought it from Lee, who was losing about $35,000 a month, a lot of money in those days.

The paper and the radio station were doing well. We figured to spend another $250,000. (We talked in terms of an outlay of $1 million because I thought it would take a while to turn the corner.) When we took over the station, for the first year all we did was to try to sell sets. It was a way to pay the General back a little bit and we sold a lot of RCA sets! The distributors, the source of our circulation, gave us the monthly sales figures. In a year we had close to 100,000 sets. The General's prophecy was coming true.

I remember one demonstration that NBC had when they were promoting color. They reproduced a *Vogue* ad, a beautiful girl in color frozen on the screen, and then the video started, and she got up, walked around and demonstrated and talked. The effect was just overwhelming. I was sitting in the theatre at the right of one of the large magazine publishers, who also owned television stations. He was with his broadcaster, and I heard him gasp, "Ohhhh, my God, that will kill magazines." The TV ad was 100 times as effective as the magazine ad. I never had any doubt about that, and I was lucky that Mrs. Hobby was willing to take the risk.

Nobody really knew much about television. We all learned together. We'd go on the air about 3:30 in the afternoon, and I'd go out to the station at 1:30 to tell them everything that went wrong the night before and try to anticipate everything that was coming up. Finally, I told them we couldn't anticipate everything. An old Dorothy Parker story was illustrative. She had hired a new maid for a party she was having one night. Before she left for her office, she opened her mailbox to find a little box with a little alligator in it. She ran upstairs and put the alligator in water in the tub. She got home about 5 o'clock and found her apartment in a shambles. No maid. She found a note, "Dear Miss Parker: I quit. I cannot work in any place that keeps alligators in the bathtub. I would have told you this before but I didn't think the subject would ever come up." To this day we still call our "boo-boos" alligators.

We had four networks, NBC, CBS, ABC and DuMont. There wasn't much daytime television. We went on around 3 o'clock with a local show, and then we'd go on till 1 a.m., delaying some of the better network shows till 11:30, 12:00. With 100,000 sets, we were then profitable. From an operating point of view, we never used all the money that we had allocated, and our radio audience had not yet started to decline.

I became, in 1958, Chairman of the Affiliate Board of Delegates, but I'd been a member of the Board for the preceding five or six years. I had two things that I wanted to do in this new television age. Walter Damm had been the Chairman of the Affiliates Committee since its inception. I wanted to prove that Walter wasn't indispensable. The other thing was to prove that nobody was, and put a term to the office.

Walter Damm was very difficult for the network. He spent most of his time watching television during the day, and he nitpicked all the time. One of my favorite stories has to do with the middle break in "Howdy Doody." He opened every meeting by saying, "Well, Mr. President at NBC, the affiliates want to know when are we going to get a middle break in 'Howdy Doody?'" The fact of the matter was that Bob Smith, who produced that, put a little film right across the mid-break time, so you couldn't have a break. Bob Smith was so popular that NBC couldn't do anything with him anyway. He wasn't going to let anything interrupt his program.

NBC's answer was, "Well, we'll look into it, and we'll let you know." When Joe McConnell became President of NBC, Walter hit him with this. I don't think Joe knew what a station break was, let alone "Howdy Doody." Pat Weaver was head of programming at that time, so Joe turned to Pat and Pat said, "We'll look into it and let you know." By the next year, Pat Weaver was President, and Walter said, "Well, Mr. new President of NBC, the affiliates want to know when are we going to get a mid-break in 'Howdy Doody?'" And Pat replied, "Walter, just as soon as you get a new President of NBC." After a long pause he said, "Well, fellows, I guess we finally got an answer." There is a postscript to this.

At a meeting in Chicago after Pat was gone and Bobby Sarnoff had taken over I said, "Bob, I want to remind you of a commitment that was made to us by the former President of NBC. Walter Damm and the affiliates have been trying to get a middle break in 'Howdy Doody.'" By this time, it had long since gone off the air. I thought I was being pretty funny. I said, "We had a commitment that we could get a middle break in 'Howdy Doody' when we got a new President of NBC." Bob Sarnoff is not noted for his sense of humor. He looked at me and said, "Jack, I will not be bound by any commitments of prior administrations."

I was urged by NBC to run for Chairman. I wasn't reluctant to do it because my two objectives were to get it organized right and to draw up by-laws to specify that a chairman could only serve two terms of two years each.

I was delighted to work with David Adams who I admired so greatly when he was Chairman of a tremendous undertaking, the Economic Study of Radio. We met out at the Westchester Country Club for a week. Charlie Denny was Chairman of the Network and I was Chairman for the Affiliates in Radio. The purpose was to find a way to price radio with the uneven penetration of television in some markets. Some markets didn't have television at all. It may be unfair, but I would say the final draft was a creation of David Adams. The rest of us didn't know how to proceed. It would have been an equitable way to price radio on a sliding scale where no one would be hurt too much. I was all for it. The book was well researched but very complicated. Some markets would have gotten tremendous increases and some, very large decreases. Charlie Denny was going to present it at the Boca Raton meeting.

I came back to New York and told McConnell and Denny and the network people that I felt I could not sell this rates and compensation plan to the affiliates. It needed to be pre-sold. NBC had to go out and go over this book with them. They couldn't vote without knowing more about it. When I had gone back, I had called in Martin Campbell of WFAA in Dallas and Hugh Halff at WOAI in San Antonio and showed them how advantageous it was to them. They were 50,000-watt clear-channel stations; they would have done great on it.

NBC sent a few people out, but when we got to Boca Raton, it had not been pre-sold well. Denny made a presentation, whereupon it was voted down by the affiliates. I think that was one reason Joe McConnell got out of broadcasting. I don't think Joe McConnell ever understood what an affiliate was. He called us outlets, always referred to us as outlets. Outlets! He thought we were like an RCA distributor, an outlet for NBC's products. Never understood the unique relationship of an affiliate. Jack Herbert would call us partners at the same meeting. Joe just didn't want to be part of a business where a bunch of outlets could tell him what he couldn't do. That plan was dead.

The relationship between the affiliates and the network is unique. We're competitors in one area and partners in another. An affiliate cannot hurt the network without hurting himself, and, in the same way, the network can't hurt the affiliate without hurting itself. A station can't just look at this year's bottom line, because when we preempt, we hurt the network and ourselves. We may make a few more bucks, but that's not the way a partner acts.

Pat Weaver is a legend. Pat Weaver has been the most creative man in television. And if you ask me who was Number 2, I wouldn't know. He is so far ahead of everyone else. Pat Weaver created the "Today" show, "Tonight," "Wide, Wide World" (which we don't have any more), "Home," the "Show of Shows," and the spectaculars. He was going to have three-hour shows, "An Evening with Leland Hayward," "An Evening with Frank Capra." There will never be another one like him. His imprint on television programming is still there.

I wasn't surprised when he left. One of General Sarnoff's primary aims was to have his son succeed him, and Pat was in the way. Contrary to what was said, Pat maintains that profits were good. I wasn't privy to that. He told me a funny story. When General Sarnoff was berating him about the network profits not being as juicy as the O&O's, he said to the General, "If you will permit me to do one thing, I'll let you name the amount of profit you want." And the General said, "What is that?" Pat said, "Allow me to affiliate with any stations I want to." The General asked, "What would that do?" Pat said, in New York, instead of WNBC-TV, he'd go over to WPIX or WNEW, and, instead of paying them $2.5 or $3 million in compensation, he should *get* $5 million. And he added, "That's a turn around of $8 million there, then I'd go to Los Angeles and Chicago and drop those O&O's."

I told that story to the affiliates many times because the relationship between the network and the affiliate is very much in the favor of the affiliate. They really inherited a very favorable deal. If, when television came along, if they'd known everything then that they know now, they wouldn't have adopted the radio formula.

I don't mean NBC necessarily would have charged us for the programs, but I don't think there'd ever been any compensation.

I think I came away from the chairmanship with the affiliates' respect and the network's respect. I don't engage in "B.S.," and I say what I think. The network people and the affiliates knew there wasn't any hidden meaning in what I said. I was sincere whether right or wrong. That's the only way I ever knew how to operate. I never tried to run a popularity contest, but morale was high at NBC and in our group.

Louis Read followed me, and we worked well together. I always believed that the greatest form of government was benevolent despotism, that if you leave it to chance, something could happen. Louis is one of my close friends. I said, "Louis, I'm going to push you for Chairman on one condition: that I be Chairman of the Nominating Committee." I wanted guys who operated stations and knew what the heck was going on and were not on the committee just to make trips. I said, "Not only that, Louis, but when you go off after four years, you can be on the Nominating Committee, and I can be on the Nominating Committee, and so forth." The result is: I think the NBC Affiliates Committee has been far superior than those of the other networks.

I knew the top brass at NBC over the years starting with Trammell. Adams was one I admired greatly. McConnell not so much. Frank White was just a little blip. Weaver was just tremendous. *Broadcasting* magazine interviewed me before I got the Distinguished Service Award, and I said one of the most effective presidents of NBC was Bob Kintner. He and I tangled frequently. One time, I tried a little sweetness. "Bob, you have really brought this network up in the news area. The next thing that Robert E. Kintner ought to do is go after CBS in the entertainment field. Let that be your next achievement." It worked pretty well.

Walter Scott is Mr. Sweetness. He was a very, very effective chairman and one of the most likeable men ever at NBC. Julian Goodman is a prince. Julian and I first met during World War II in Washington. I did "The Army Hour" at NBC's WRC studios on NBC radio. And Julian and David Brinkley were at WRC. Carl Lindemann sometime back thought NBC was not aggressive enough in getting the baseball package, including the World Series. He asked me if I would put in my nickel's worth. At that time Lyndon Johnson didn't want to be the first president to lose a war (the Vietnam war). I said, "Julian, you don't want to go down as the President of NBC who lost the World Series." And he said, "Well, let me ask you something, Jack. It's going to take a lot of money. How much will the affiliates chip in?" And I said, "I can't speak for all of them, but west of the Mississippi, not one nickel."

Harry Bannister was Mr. Mysterious. With Harry everything was a big deal. He'd call from a pay phone, "I have to come down to Houston." We'd go to the Shamrock, and he'd send his suit out for pressing and sit there in his BVD's and we'd play gin rummy. When his suit came back, he caught his plane, and he'd go to play with Walter Damm in Milwaukee. Tom Knode was difficult to deal with, but I loved him. I've always felt that the war affected Tom, and he was a difficult friend. He was destroying himself, and nobody could help him.

Every Chairman of the Board of Delegates has had to handle the affiliates' perception of NBC News. Everybody thinks the news is either left or right of them, and I was presiding one time when an affiliate, Fred Beard from Jackson, Mississippi, had a proposal. His station lost its license because he literally would not let blacks on. They would zip in, edit and blip out the news items. He wanted the affiliates to insist that NBC have two feeds; the second couldn't be any farther North than Charlotte, North Carolina, so that the stations in the South could put on their own news!

I've been loyal to NBC through good times and bad. We've had two other stations, one affiliated with CBS and one with ABC. We now have two CBS stations. I sincerely believe that an affiliation with a network is like a marriage. Not lightly entered and not lightly severed. Popularity is cyclical. I'm not knocking my friends who have changed. Ours is a very long-term relationship. We'd owed NBC something from General Sarnoff way back there. You don't just go for the quick buck. If we'd started out with CBS, I would have felt the same way. When NBC was going through the difficult '70's I was a strong, staunch supporter. We are part of the network.

I was a founder of the Association of Maximum Service Telecasters, one industry organization I'm most proud of. They tapped me to be the first President, and I served for 16 years. The carefully selected Board is by invitation and has broad representation of some of the finest broadcasters in the country. We have a very small staff. Most of the money went for legal and engineering help. Most broadcasters think that it is the most effective trade organization that we've had. I happen to believe that. MST was organized by the real pioneers when the FCC was about to change the structure of broadcasting to have islands of UHF and islands of VHF, which technically would never work. We organized to protect the spectrum and the maximum coverage of stations so we wouldn't get a bunch of drop-ins. Ultimately, our decision was to sponsor the All Channel legislation which we got through the Commission and the Congress to make both VHF and UHF not necessarily equal, but viable in the same market. We had a statesmanlike approach with enlightened self-interest.

I was very pleased to receive the highest award in the broadcast industry in '79, the NAB Distinguished Service Award. I was a critic of NAB over the years, but since Vince Wasilewski took over, I've been supportive.

In Houston, I've been very active in Muscular Dystrophy. I was persuaded to do the first telethon, and by putting my big toe in the water, I drowned. In Houston alone, we have raised over $20 million, and to my great delight, the Jack Harris Research Unit of the Jerry Lewis Neuromuscular Disease Research Center was dedicated in 1977. It's the most lasting and important volunteer work I've done.

I was Vice Chairman of the Board of Radio Free Europe and Radio Liberty combined. I found it fascinating and very rewarding work. Under the Reagan administration, it appeared it was going to be politicized, which I think it has been to some extent, and I resigned about three or four years ago.

That $750,000 investment is now worth somewhere in excess of $400 million, which belongs to the Hobbys. Governor and Mrs. Hobby and others were very, very good to me. I had opportunities to go elsewhere, but I turned them down, and I never regretted it because they gave me the opportunity to run the station in the way that I wanted to. No great pressures to do things that I felt were not good for broadcasting.

I have some heroes: General Sarnoff, who was great on hardware and research but weak on programming,

which is why Paley moved in. Pat Weaver is another. David Adams is far and away the most admirable. Bill McAndrew. There are so many people at NBC I have great respect for. Grant is super. Grant has a desire for excellence; he would like to see television better than it is, and so would I.

As long as the networks strive for excellence and variety, there is no other medium that can ever touch it. The size of the audience may not grow as fast as it has, it may diminish slightly, but I think the networks will be the dominant national force. There is no national medium other than network television. There is no other way for the Commander-in-Chief of the United States to reach the American public except on network television. There's no other way in any kind of an emergency, or any kind of a tremendous event, that this country can be brought together. I think the finest hours of television, when it really reached its promise, was the coverage of the tragic assassination of President Kennedy. We showed a fallen President and a new President taking office with no panic. That could never have happened except for network television.

I wish NBC everything good, and I hope that in the days to come, communications can fulfill its promise even more than it has in the past 60 years.

September 9, 1985

James T. Lynagh became President of Multimedia Broadcasting Company in 1981 and Chairman of the NBC Board of Delegates in 1984.

"I became an NBC affiliate General Manager in 1978 with some trepidation, because NBC had slipped into third place behind ABC. I was afraid there would still be a sense that all wisdom resides at 30 Rockefeller Plaza. There weren't any great signs that NBC was making aggressive, competitive moves…"

I was born and grew up in Birmingham, Alabama. My first job was as an announcer at a Mutual affiliate in Gadsden, Alabama, in 1951, one week after I finished high school. I was 16 and I had wanted to be an announcer since I was six. It never occurred to me that I mightn't have the self-confidence to be an announcer. After all, everybody in the family listened to me more than they wanted to!

I had done a great deal of debating in high school and won a debating scholarship to the University of Alabama in 1951. I intended to major in radio. (Incidentally, I'm on the board of advisors of U. of A.'s School of Communications, now the largest communications school in the country.) I got bored with college. I was working at a radio station in Tuscaloosa as a freshman and knew seniors who couldn't get a job because they didn't have experience. I left and went on about making my career in the business.

After two-and-a half years in radio, I lucked into a job in television, and that's been my love ever since. Early jobs included the ABC affiliate in Nashville, the CBS affiliate in Toledo, and the NBC affiliate in Shreveport.

In 1964, I joined Kaiser Broadcasting, owned by Kaiser Industries Corporation. Henry J. Kaiser's son, Edgar Kaiser, was the Chairman of Kaiser Industries. Dick Block was the President of Kaiser Broadcasting, which consisted of one television station in Honolulu, but when the All-Channel bill was passed by Congress, Kaiser decided to build UHF independent stations in major markets around the country, and the first one they built was in Detroit. I went there as program manager about four months before it went on the air and helped to build it. I became manager of the station two months before it went on the air and learned by doing! Every television station that I worked for, from my first job in television in 1953 until I joined Post-Newsweek in 1968, was with a station that was going on the air. I was involved in building one, two, three, four, five, six stations before going with one that was already on the air.

My first job as a General Manager was at WKBD-TV in Detroit. It was a very small station, and when I asked Dick Block why he chose someone as young and relatively inexperienced as I, he said he couldn't find anyone else who would work as cheaply. He also wanted someone malleable who wouldn't have opinions counter to his.

I learned a great deal from Dick Block, who had the foresight to believe that UHF independents could become significant factors in major markets. Dick had foresight and also believed that if some major corporation didn't support Congress in building UHF television stations, the law might be rescinded. Many television set manufacturers were opposed to including all-channel receivers in their sets because it added to the price.

Dick was one of my first mentors. Another was Walter Windsor, who was my previous General Manager in the first NBC station with which I was associated, KTAL-TV in Shreveport. I was Program Director of that station and Walter was the General Manager, and he certainly was a big help in my career.

I commuted from Detroit to Philadelphia for about six months to help build and manager that Kaiser station, WKBS-TV. Then the Kaiser Board of Directors came up with the money to buy a Boston station, and Dick asked me to build it. That station today is WLVI-TV, but was, at that time, WKBG, a 50-50 partnership between Kaiser Industries and the *Boston Globe*.

Managers have different goals when they run different kinds of stations. The number one goal for a manager at Kaiser was cash flow. We certainly had losses in the early days, and we had to be careful about spending. On the other hand, Kaiser recognized that you couldn't skimp on the signal. A good signal was part of a proper facility. In the long run, you compete with programming. It was a tight budget, but they recognized what had to be done.

I stayed in Boston for two years and loved it. It was a very competitive market because it had three good television stations: WBZ-TV, one of the preeminent NBC affiliates in the country, Westinghouse, plus two independents, one owned by Kaiser and one owned by Storer. It took longer for either independent to make a profit than anticipated, and I left to join Post-Newsweek Stations, Inc., before profitability was attained. I liked programming, sales, promotion and the other things that UHF independents were doing, but I missed the news and journalistic involvement. I wanted to work with network affiliates again, so Post-Newsweek was an absolutely perfect choice for me.

Post-Newsweek had two stations then, and Larry Israel sought me out to be the General Manager of the Jacksonville station. I knew that Jacksonville had a tremendous news image and operation. It had been under the same General Manager for 20 years, from the day it had signed on the air. He was retiring, and it was a great opportunity.

To build a news organization seemed to me the most important and significant thing we did, even back in the early sixties at the NBC station in Shreveport. I like programming overall, but the news interests me most.

Broadcast news has been controversial. Some stations felt it necessary to follow Huntley-Brinkley with their own commentary. I subsequently managed a station which did that during the Vietnam war. I personally feel there are individual reports from time to time which reflect an individual point of view, but, in general, I think we have a terrific history and we've gotten better and better at telling the public what is going on in the country. What we've done is highly defensible.

An hour's nightly network news isn't likely to happen during my broadcast career. I was on the NBC Affiliate Board when it appeared that the FCC would abandon some aspects of the Prime Time Access Rule and permit the networks to expand network news. The Board negotiated a compromise with the network that would have been, at that time, in the interest of the affiliates, the viewers and the network in terms of compensation and advertising inventory. The affiliates, however, rejected it. Conversations with Grant Tinker, Larry Grossman and others in the news business indicate to me that there may well be an expansion of programming by the network News Division, but it is not likely to be an expanded early-evening newscast.

With today's technology, the affiliates can expand the national news presented. The average market has at least an hour-and-a-half of news in the early evening. Major markets have anywhere from two to two-and-one-half hours or more, and I don't think the affiliates are going to give up 30 minutes of news time to let the networks produce it rather than producing it themselves. The networks may look at a cable news service, as NBC is at this point, and other ways of producing more programming, but, again, I don't think it will be on the network in the early evening.

Obviously, we don't provide an in-depth service. We're not the New York Times of the air, but we do a lot of in-depth things, and when the network newscast comes on the air, most of the viewers already know the national news, so the network can and should provide perspective and more detailed stories, and more contextual stories.

The professional critics of television news focus on the 30-minute nightly newscast and say it isn't enough. But that isn't the only way to judge how people in this country get their news from TV. They get it from live coverage of events, like the TWA hostage situation in Beirut. They get it from the "Today" show; from the local station's newscast, from the network newscast, from the late-evening newscast, from "Nightline," as well as from reading newspapers and magazines. This combination of media provides the American public the breadth of information they get. I don't think they look at any medium alone or any one newscast as the single source of all the wisdom, or all of the depth, or all of the context within which they should view a particular story.

I was with Post-Newsweek for 13 years and managed four different television stations for them. After Jacksonville, I went to Miami, Post's most recent acquisition at that time, an ABC affiliate.

In 1974, I went to WTOP-TV in Washington and was there for four years. The station had a very strong news operation but was running second in the market. With a few additions and a terrific staff, including a magnificent News Director and Vice President of News for Post-Newsweek, it moved on up to Number One. It's fun to run a highly-respected local news operation in the news capitol of the world. Congress and the FCC looked at it as a model of what the industry ought to produce. We felt strongly that we had a special obligation being in Washington. While I was there, we won a Peabody and a number of other awards.

I don't think I was just a trouble shooter. Each of my positions was, in fact, a larger opportunity. News was my first focus with Post-Newsweek. Jacksonville and Washington, two of the four stations, already had very fine news organizations, but I had the job of maintaining them and constantly trying to make them better.

My next move presented a choice. The Post Company, with *The Washington Post*, *Newsweek* magazine, Washington's all-news radio station, and the number one television news operation at that time, felt they were fair game because of dominating the news media in that town. In the long run they might face challenges, and the public interest and their own business interest would be best served by diversifying. The Evening News Association in Detroit, with the *Detroit News* and a television station, felt the same way about Detroit, so the two companies arranged to swap. I chose to remain with the Washington Post Company and go to Detroit, where I had lived before when I put WKBD-TV on the air. I like that city, so it was a natural move for me.

I have dealt with all three networks. When you ask me to describe the difference between them, I find it a little tough to characterize them. I like and respect the people who run all three networks. I've managed two CBS stations, but my closest associations were with ABC because I served on the ABC Affiliate Board and was Vice Chairman. As an NBC affiliate for some years now, I have served on the NBC Board and am now its Chairman, so I feel closest to NBC. It's harder to be close to CBS.

Through the years, CBS has had an image of a domineering father relationship with affiliates, and I say that with great respect for everyone there. I never knew Mr. Paley, but I knew people from Bob Wood and John Schneider on. They run a very fine organization and are very buttoned up, but it is a little bit like the Methodist church versus the Presbyterian church; in the Methodist church it all funnels down from the top, and in the Presbyterian church it bubbles up from the bottom.

At ABC, it went both ways. When I was an ABC affiliate,

they were third and striving hard, so that my dialogue and all the experience I had with them was very good. When I became an NBC affiliate, as a General Manager, with previous experience as Program Manager, it was at a time when NBC was struggling, so there was more of a two-way street dialogue going on there and great responsiveness to the affiliates. While I like and respect them all, my best experiences have been as an NBC affiliate manager.

I became an NBC General Manager in 1978 with some trepidation, because NBC had slipped into third place behind ABC. I was afraid there would still be a sense that all wisdom resides at 30 Rockefeller Plaza. There weren't any great signs that NBC was making aggressive, competitive moves at that particular time. Part of the problem was the executive changes going on at the top, and and there was no single, dominant personality above the top executives, as in the days of General Sarnoff.

It was fun to join Multimedia because WLWT, its Cincinnati flagship (through its ownership by Crosley, then Avco, now Multimedia) has a record of innovative, live local television unmatched in America. The station, the second non-owned NBC affiliate in the country, formally went on the air in January, 1948. Andre Kostelanetz made his first television appearance with a symphony orchestra on WLWT, live on January 5, 1949. In August, 1957, WLWT began telecasting its local programs in color. And in 1960, the station produced the first colorcast in the country of a night sporting event, a telecast of a Cincinnati Reds-San Francisco Giants baseball game from Crosley Field in Cincinnati. Through the years, WLWT originated many programs that were seen nationally on NBC-TV.

I believe broadcast companies, whether they are like Multimedia or Post-Newsweek, or networks, are a product of their owners, and NBC, CBS and ABC had the vision that General Sarnoff, William Paley and Leonard Goldenson brought to them. Companies reflect the capital funds and operating support they receive from the top, and General Sarnoff had a vision of what he wanted NBC to be. I believe that Thornton Bradshaw and Bob Frederick have the same kind of vision of NBC. Given that, key executives can achieve a lot.

Grant Tinker was a wonderful choice as Chief Executive Officer for NBC, but he could not have accomplished what he has without the stable, strong, unwavering support that he received from Thornton Bradshaw. Bradshaw gave him time, understanding and support.

As President of Multimedia Broadcasting, with Wilson Wearn in the past and now Walter Bartlett running the parent company, I am responsible for five television stations and eight radio stations. We believe in a lot of autonomy for our managers, and we have good ones. We have an Engineering Vice President and a Financial Department on the corporate level; otherwise, I'm it.

I like to make decisions and I'm not afraid of making decisions. I'm certainly not creative enough to come up with all original ideas, but I like to problem-solve. There are creative people who can write beautiful words or beautiful music or a beautiful play. That kind of creativity I don't have. The other kind of creative people are scientists, inventors, those who see a problem and like to find a solution for it, and I like to be creative in that sense. You can't solve problems without making a decision. You come to forks in the road constantly and you have to say I'm going left or right.

Part of autonomy is insisting on an autonomous environment. As executives we have an obligation to all the individuals who work for us. We are obliged to give them feedback, to tell them what's wrong, what's right, to give them guidance, nor surprise them when they fail. All of us want feedback with lots of love and lots of positiveness. But once having done that, then if a personnel decision has to be made, I don't focus on the one person that I have to let go. I focus on the 200 people who will be hurt if I leave the wrong person in that job and hurt the company. I do have a problem with the sympathy that I have for an individual because I hate to see anyone have to come face-to-face with that kind of situation.

Do I take risks? I don't believe I would have managed seven different television stations and taken on different assignments if I wasn't willing to take risks. In their markets, some of the stations were number one; some were in last place; some were UHF independents in that era before the All-Channel bill had become totally effective.

The NBC executive who has represented the affiliates, the real anchor through much turmoil—and whom I admire for keeping a clear head through all of it and weathering lots of storms—is Ray Timothy. He has been terrific because he understands the affiliates and the station business and has communicated both the emotion and the sense of what the affiliates feel.

I've competed with Bob Walsh in Washington when he was General Manager of the NBC Owned Station there, and I have enormous respect and friendship for him because I've known him a long time. Bud Rukeyser I feel very positively about, and he worked for the Washington Post Company for a while, so we share a common background in a sense there. Brandon Tartikoff has grown in his job. Brad and Grant saw in Brandon that he had the intellect, the capacity, the creativity, the skill. The pressures on Brandon must have been enormous during those years.

As Chairman of the NBC Board of Delegates, I really "lucked in" to the best period in the whole world to be Chairman. However, let me point out the other side of that coin. Ancil Payne and Fred Paxton are two of the smartest people I've ever known, and two of the best; we (NBC and the affiliates) ought to erect monuments to them, because they were Chairmen at a stressful time when NBC was in trouble. NBC's top management had to pay attention to the affiliates. Some defected, unwisely I think, which many now realize, because even when they made a move to a higher-rated network, it didn't pay off for them. At that time, the NBC management had to respond. It is more difficult to go to the number one network having all this success and say, "Wait a minute, the affiliates want this, or the affiliates want that." In the sense of leverage and clout, this is not necessarily the easiest time to be the Chairman of the NBC Affiliates Board.

The affiliates are concerned at this moment about a number of things, including the news situation. The quality of NBC News is certainly excellent, but the News Division has gone through a number of changes in leadership and it needs stability. It is not the number-one rated newscast on the air. NBC has made a great deal of progress with the "Today" show, but it is still second. "NBC Nightly News with Tom Brokaw" is second, sometimes third. NBC and ABC are very close, and a couple of points behind CBS. We're all so intent on being Number One that sometimes we forget we're only talking about two points difference, between number one and number two, or number one and number three. But that still makes a difference to us. NBC has also yet to mount a successful weekly prime-time news program, a documentary product or magazine. "20/20" and "60 Minutes" have been established and are on the air, and NBC has not yet done it.

Larry Grossman is a stable, solid executive. I'm not a clairvoyant when it comes to programming, but I hope "American Almanac" will be successful. It is a real uphill battle. NBC is plowing new ground. There should be a good reason for trying an unproven concept, and I think this is going to be a difficult one. I hope it's successful.

NBC has finally made changes in "Meet the Press," but it was the last of the Sunday morning programs to make a change. ABC with "Nightline" has an extra dimension. We don't want to give up the "Tonight" show with Johnny Carson; we feel that's terrific. But in terms of the overall news image, NBC really has just had the "Today" show and "Nightly News." And the other two network news divisions have had a good deal more programming, which not only get ratings and respect, but, frankly, make a profit. NBC needs that as well.

Daytime is still a very real issue, although NBC has made some progress and we're very pleased with that. The most important single hour of daytime programming to the affiliates is that hour that leads into its local programming. Flow is so important.

NBC has been responsive to many things that we have come to them about, including the need to improve their promotion, which they did several years ago while they were still fixing the programming. And they are very conscious of the daytime need.

Grant Tinker has overcome the problem of instant ratings by saying we're going to stick with a program if we believe it's right. A few programs have already been cancelled by CBS and ABC two weeks into the 1985-86 season.

We are frequently criticized for doing programs which appeal to a mass audience. We *are* a mass medium. I have never wanted to work in public television. I admire what they do and I'm happy that they are there. But I wanted the discipline of being judged, being in competition with other people, and saying if what I do is successful, it will be successful from an economic standpoint. A profit motive is a terrific economic discipline. Certainly some junk programs succeed. With all the programming we produce, local stations or networks, programming 22 hours each a week of just prime time alone, 140 hours sign-on to sign-off, some of it is going to be bad. But some of it is going to be *very* good, and I have no apologies for being in both sides of the business.

As long as it has the economic capability to do it, I think television has a prime responsibility for broadcasting the news. (Because government decreed that there would be so many radio stations, very, very few radio stations have the capacity or funds to be more than readers of wire copy or re-transmitters of network news programs.) I would hate to see a national system of media, be it newspapers or broadcasting. If radio stations can't afford to do local news, and the television stations don't do it, and we have only one newspaper in most cities in the country, then it's going to be pretty sad for our cities.

NBC has already had its 60th birthday present in Grant Tinker. We got him early. We got him as a 56th birthday present!

October 4, 1985

Bruce McGorrill is the Executive Vice President and CEO of the Maine Broadcasting Company, an NBC affiliate since NBC's first radio broadcast on November 15, 1926.

"The radio station was a department of the hotel. Our employees were listed on the payroll sheet with the chambermaids, the garage attendants, and bellhops. Our statements, our affidavits, our monthly bills, for years came out of the hotel's accounting office. All symbols on the statement were hotel symbols. The charge for an announcement had 'RM' next to it, the charge for talent had 'TX', and so forth, and when an agency, particularly a national agency, got the bill from WCSH, they were baffled by those symbols."

I'll begin by describing the Maine Broadcasting System: WCSH-TV in Portland and WLBZ-TV in Bangor. The call letters, WCSH, stand for the Congress Square Hotel, which was owned by Henry Rines. It became not only the largest hotel north of Boston, but the first hotel in America to have a new gadget, a radio, in every room. Henry had a friend who was in the business of selling radios, and he sold Henry on the idea, which led him to founding a radio station.

The heirs of Henry Rines still own the broadcast properties. Same call letters, same ownership, same network affiliation since 1926. The link between WCSH-TV goes back to the beginning of NBC. There's an NBC peacock next to the call letters on the top of our new broadcast facilities. Henry Rines' daughter, Mary Rines Thompson, is the Chairman of the Board. When she retired as President about two years ago, one of her sons, Fred, replaced her.

We probably have the only 360° organizational chart in the business, because Fred is the Program Director here in Portland and reports to the General Manager, who reports to the CEO, but during the day Fred moves to another office where he represents the family as the company's President. Something like that can only work if you have people who want to make it work, and it does. It's a marvelous ownership. Fred's the third generation to represent the family, which is great news to the employees, because that means that the family intends to stay in broadcasting.

The radio station was located in the penthouse of the Congress Square Hotel, and years later, the television station,

WCSH-TV, moved in a floor below in the ballroom, which has a beautiful terrazzo floor. We had a studio with one of the greatest views in America overlooking beautiful Casco Bay. I don't think that there are any years that WCSH missed making a profit in radio. Radio grew very fast, and became very profitable after some lean years. In 1944, the radio station, WLBZ in Bangor, was purchased by the Maine Broadcasting Company. The year that the FCC lifted the freeze on television licenses, WCSH-TV went on the air, December 20, 1953. No one at MBS realized before 1953 that television would eclipse radio and become the powerful medium that it is. It was unforeseen—an absolute surprise. The Rines applied for a television license after that marvelous speech General Sarnoff gave to all the affiliates in Princeton. That message was repeated in this company for years after—get out there and do it!

Television was a very costly enterprise for management. Prior to that, the radio station was a department of the hotel. Our employees were listed on the payroll sheet with the chambermaids, the garage attendants, and bellhops. Our statements, our affidavits, our monthly bills, for years came out of the hotel's accounting office. All the symbols on the statement were hotel symbols. The charge for an announcement had "RM" next to it, the charge for talent had "TX," and so forth, and when an agency, particularly a national agency, got the bill from WCSH, they were baffled by those symbols.

It was fine for the hotel to pay our radio costs because the cost of the equipment was comparable to the price of a piece of equipment for the hotel. *But* with television, you had to spend, in those days, a quarter of a million dollars for transmitters. It suddenly became a *very* expensive toy on the 7th floor of the hotel. The accounting people who had paid us no more heed than they did the chambermaids or the chefs or the waiters suddenly began to wonder why all this money was going into this foolish thing called television. Henry Rines died in the late thirties, and it was his son, Bill, who had to make the hard decisions. I would say the start-up cost was about $2,500,000 in 1953.

There was opposition to this channel from the Rae family in Pittsburgh, who owned a radio station in Portland. The Rines family and the Rae family competed for Channel 6. A man from Bangor had applied for what became the CBS affiliate in this market against the local newspaper. The Raes then joined a group to apply for an FCC allocation in Lewiston, Maine. With its antenna on top of the tallest mountain on the Eastern seaboard, Mt. Washington, New Hampshire, it was to have the widest coverage of any New England station. While the FCC freeze was on, the Raes withdrew their application for Channel 6 in Portland. When the freeze was lifted, the FCC went through the applications, found no opposition, and the Rines got the license. Owning the radio station helped.

The Rae group ultimately became the ABC station. Their hope to be first on the air and to let everybody else compete with them for audience was never realized—they were the last on the air. The problems of transmitting from the top of Mt. Washington, 6,200 feet up, hadn't been thought out technically. All these things happened very quickly. Our transmitter today is about 26 miles away in a little town on top of a large hill, or a small mountain.

I came on the scene in 1953 after I had graduated from Bowdoin as an economics major. I had worked at WCSH during college as well as for the CBS competitor as an announcer. I was summer and weekend relief in those days. In Portland in the late forties, I don't know how glamorous a job in broadcasting was, but at least it was not heavy lifting. My father made me get a different job in a different area every summer, literally. I was a Fuller Brush salesman. I worked in a factory that made wooden boxes for duPont ammunition. It was a marvelous way of forcing me to see other things, other people, to understand other disciplines.

After working as a summer broadcaster, I was hired as a permanent announcer for WCSH, Radio and Television. In those early days, we worked about 60 hours a week. There was one announcing staff; we got the princely salary of $75 a week. I hoped to get talent payments but there weren't that many for a beginner. I had joined AFTRA when I worked in the summer. By the time I was full-time the union had pretty much fallen away. Companies who get unions deserve them because they've done something to cause their employees to unionize. The only union this company had was an announcer's union, and it lasted for a few years and then petered out.

In the summer of 1944, the popular "Dr. I.Q" show—which consisted of an announcer who owned the package, a man he'd hired to play Dr. I.Q., the organist and a secretary—was broadcast from Portland. The man who owned the package rented a summer home on Peak's Island, out in the bay in Portland. He rented the State Theatre, and, for eight weeks, the NBC weekly radio broadcast of "Dr. I.Q." came from Portland, Maine. When that news broke here in Portland, all the announcers thought of the network fees for being out in the audience saying the famous line, "I have a lady in the balcony, Dr." In those days, they were getting about $35 a week, and the network fee for an announcer on that show was $35.

Three or four local announcers were needed, so when "Dr. I.Q." came to town, the announcers they hired were the program directors and the sales managers. Management saw to it that this was *their* break to be on network radio, so, for two months, the announcing staff never got a network fee, never got on network radio, but they did get a union. It was absolutely justified because they said, "The next time the 'Dr. I.Q.' show comes to town, that's not going to happen to us." The show never came to town again, but the company ended up with a union. It learned its lesson, and, by the time television came along, there was an entirely different situation here. The union contract lapsed about 1955 and a new one was never signed. Knock on wood.

I was hired by Jack Atwood, who was General Manager when the station went on the air. He had been managing the company station in Augusta, Maine, before he was brought to Portland by Bill Rines. The company owned stations in Bangor and Augusta, and Manchester, New Hampshire. At one time, it owned four stations and two hotels.

I was an announcer for about two years when Jack Atwood convinced me that I had *no* future in the talent side of the business. He needed someone in sales to go to New York once in a while and deal with something called "national business and the network." In those days, we had to sell the advertiser to get the network program. We were an optional station. In the early days of television, you had the "must" buys in the first 50 markets, and the rest were optional. My first sales call was in Chicago, at Foote, Cone & Belding, because we were not cleared for "Hallmark Hall of Fame." Try to explain to your viewers four times a year, after all the network promotion, that you're not going to carry "Peter Pan."

I went to the buyer's office and found a frail woman with a cardigan over her shoulders, glasses on a cord, a cigarette in a cigarette holder, and she looked over her glasses at me and said, "*God*, you're young." I was, I was 24 years old, but I did get the order. Had to. Jack Atwood said, "Don't come back unless you get the order." I didn't want to spend the rest of my life in Chicago. I continued in national sales and became General Sales Manager, the normal progression.

Jack Atwood and Don Powers, the TV Station Manager (he had been General Manager of our radio properties), really taught me all I know. Atwood taught me the importance of integrity. I owe that man a tremendous amount for that. We all are a part of what we're taught initially, and, after a certain point, we become our own person. I hope that my son is working for people who will teach him the right things to do. Atwood taught integrity; he was a very knowledgeable broadcaster, a pioneer. His philosophy was that a station can print a new rate card every day if it has to, but every day it must offer all of its clients the rates that are applicable that day, and you can never favor one client over another.

I learned from Jack Atwood to have two piles on my desk, a money pile and a no-money pile. You can let the no-money pile go right to the ceiling as long as the money pile is gone by the end of the day.

Don Powers is a good management person in terms of personnel. He taught me patience, to start out with the basic precept that people will disappoint you, so if you start out that way, you're never disappointed. It sounds cynical and he wasn't. It's a management style. You cannot give an assignment and walk away from it assuming your employees are going to do it without checking up on them.

There came a point in time when I had to decide whether I was going to stay in this business, this industry, and decided yes, if I could, I would. Then came the decision of whether to move on from market to market, to bigger markets, bigger stations, bigger opportunities. I was married and had begun to have children. That decision was made one Sunday on a porch in Connecticut. I was being interviewed by Don McGannon to be National Sales Manager for Westinghouse Television, working out of New York. I was 30 years old. It was a very tempting offer. But that Sunday afternoon, Don's wife and my wife were sitting by the pool nursing their most recent babies, and I realized that if I got into that kind of a situation, because I wanted to succeed, it might

cost me my marriage; because my wife was very much a family person, a mother and a homemaker, and my being home was important to her. That day, I decided I would stay in Portland.

Don Powers decided, at age 55, that he would like to retire early at age 60, if his health was good, and if he could afford it financially, because obviously he had only a predictable number of years to live after age 60, and he wanted to enjoy them. He set out to put his financial house in order, and to get himself in the best physical condition by going to the "Y" every working day. He told the ownership about his plans to retire by age 60. I was the General Manager of this station and in the line of succession. In his last year, Don appointed me Senior Vice President here and had Bangor report to me. He put himself on half-time and half-pay. He prepared himself for retirement, and, although he said he was going to do this project and that project, really what he did was watch me for a year to see if I was competent.

Don never set a retirement date. It was his option, and he would arrive at it at whatever moment of truth he thought right. Occasionally he would call me to say, "If you can get away from the desk, I'll buy you a drink after work." We did this for a number of years, and it was a chance to talk. On the first Friday in December of '82, we arranged to meet at 5 o'clock. He arrived in his chinos and the flap jacket, and, as he walked up to the table, he reached in his back pocket, took out a heavy envelope. When I opened it, there were the keys to his office door, keys to his desk, keys to the files, the combination to the company safe, and the key to the company postal box. As he poured these out on the table, he said, "Goodbye, see ya." That was his last day, he didn't want a fanfare, didn't want a farewell. He had mailed letters to NBC and to our rep; he had letters for the staff here and in Bangor the following Monday.

That's the end of the story—almost. There was a slight problem. Don, his brother and their wives were leaving Sunday, January 2, for Florida for three months. On December 31, New Year's Eve, 8 o'clock at night, I had a heart attack, and the next day my wife had to call him and give him the news. He stayed for several weeks, went to an affiliates' board meeting and then went back and forth to Florida until ice caused our tower to fall in

March, 1983. He came back to handle that while I was recuperating. (The following year, the ABC and CBS stations' towers in Bangor were toppled by ice. We thought that was friendly of them.)

Our stations are connected round robin by microwave. We have a satellite studio in Lewiston where we go live. We produce a newscast at 11 o'clock at night that's co-anchored 120 miles apart in Portland and Bangor. The sets are identical, the news director is in charge of both operations. We cover the state. We think we will be successful if we provide that which cable cannot—local news and weather, local commercials (which are news announcements of a business nature), new openings, the price of a car or a suit or the price of lettuce at the supermarket, as well as public service messages. This information our audience can use, they need, and they won't get that from an imported signal from Atlanta or Boston or by satellite.

Stations which have the best news and weather, the most commercial messages, the most diversified clients, and the most informative public service messages will be a signal the public has to utilize, whether they're on cable or not on cable, or no matter how many signals come into the home. A station has to have the staff and equipment to do it, and the Rines ownership is investing in that so that we can compete against the new technology, no matter what it is.

Back in the fifties, WCSH-TV won a national award, the Howard W. Blakesley Award, given by the American Heart Association. We filmed one of the earliest open-heart surgeries in the country in black-and-white.

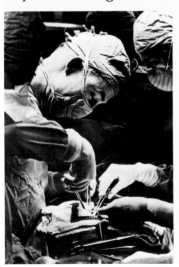

We did it with our fingers crossed that the patient would leave the hospital alive and well; and he did. That was exciting! Another program called "America's Future Award" describes outstanding students nominated by their peers for volunteer efforts. At one school, the high school kids are trained and then run an emergency CPR rescue unit. When the alarm goes off, they leave their class immediately. It's a marvelous, marvelous program.

In Bangor, our Vice President and General Manager, Margo Cobb, has been at that station for 30 years. She came from college right to the station, started typing logs and traffic; she went from traffic to production to local sales, to local Sales Manager, to Station Manager. She has raised four children, gotten a black belt in karate, and is now on the NAB Board. When she was elected, we kept the black belt status quiet. She's a good broadcaster, she's a good person, she's bright. She says that the experience of raising four children helps in managing a station in a small market. Her staff will climb mountains for her, and, literally, a year ago they did. They went on a mountain-climbing trip one weekend, and Margo cooked the chowder.

She's one of many women in our company. Our treasurer is a woman. We have more women on our sales staff than we do men. We hired the first television female salesperson in Maine. In 1958, we did an all-women's newscast one day. All the women on our staff handled anchor, weather, sports, everything else. I realize that was discriminatory because we kept all the men out. Of course, Mary Rines Thompson was our President for many years.

Maine Broadcasting has been a charter affiliate of NBC's since that first broadcast on November 15, 1926. The network/affiliate relationship is totally symbiotic. There is no network without affiliates, that's it, clear and simple. If there is an affiliate that doesn't understand the word affiliate, he'd best get into insurance. It can be adversarial, but we need each other. There could not have been television in Bangor, Maine, without networks. The networks put in the microwave, the networks paid network compensation to these smaller stations, and, many times, that network compensation was the difference between the profit and the loss that kept the stations going until television became more accepted.

In the early days, advertisers were wary of putting money into television. Television sets were expensive, and only the upper middle-class and middle-class had sets. How times change! In the 50's, if a Maine house had a roof antenna, it was a sign that they could afford a TV set. In the 80's, if a house has a roof antenna, it's a sign they can't afford cable!

The networks, including DuMont, built television in this country. We give them all the credit for doing that. In a way, it reminds me of the problems newspapers faced when radio came along, and the government said it's your obligation to build this new technology called radio because you're the purveyors of news, and this is your opportunity to bring America together with radio, and then later with television. Newspapers that had radio stations got into television, and *then* the government said they had a monopoly, so they had to split up. The networks created instant communication throughout America, and now there are those who say the networks are too powerful and something has to be done to provide competition. We wouldn't have television if there hadn't been men like David Sarnoff, with that famous speech, "Get out and do it now. Let's get going. Let's build this system." We wouldn't have moved so quickly. It's amazing that it was done without *any* government interference.

In Don's and my years, we have dealt with many NBC top brass. We heard them at meetings and dealt with them, and I think the fact that we're still an NBC affiliate, with the troubles they went through in the seventies, is a testimony to those who were there and have been there during that time.

We've been approached by other networks during the bad times with very lucrative offers. But what's the fun? If everything is bottom line, then there aren't very many decisions to make—they're made for you. If we changed affiliations during NBC's bad times, it would only be a matter of years before the pendulum would swing. It is cyclical, and it's a lot more fun being down coming up than being up going down. How smart can you be going from the No. 3 network to the No. 1 as an affiliate? There's no guarantee that the audience will follow you. As far as affiliates with NBC, we would rather work to correct the situation than be a part of the problem. We might have made more money, but we would have lost some friends. This is still a company that puts a lot of stock in that.

Maine winters are long and cold, which account for our ratings, too. Sets in use don't go up until Daylight Saving Time ends, when it gets dark by 4:15. In the February rating period, we pray for snowstorms. Our sets-in-use are enormous!

I was very active in community affairs. From these volunteer activities, I developed the McGorrill Law of Economics: "If all you want to do is break even, you will surely end up with a loss." I learned that the hard way.

The switch from landlines to satellites doesn't make any difference to the public. At our station, we see all kinds of possibilities down the line. We're still having equipment failures, but no one is tearing their hair; no one is upset. Its flexibility will provide all kinds of options. A few of us remember the early days at this station when the telephone company's microwave would fail. We became used to steady service, and we tend to forget what the problems were in the beginning.

Jack Atwood did something which was very interesting. In the first two years we were on the air, the telephone company microwave was quite unreliable, so he had a slide made up which said, "The trouble is not your set nor your station, it is AT&T," for whenever it was a network problem. Three weeks later, there was a vice president of AT&T in Jack's office demanding he not do that. He said, "I will stop doing it when you correct your service to us. We do not want our viewers to think that this station is technically deficient or that it's their sets." No "Due to circumstances beyond our control" for him. He'd say, "They're lying. It's in somebody's control."

One of the toughest problems that NBC faces is regulation—Washington. The FCC commissioners perceive television as being NBC, ABC, CBS, period. They really don't go beyond that to the licensees that they're responsible for. Congress and the FCC think of the networks as the gatekeepers, but *we're* the gatekeepers. We decide to carry a program or not. If a network program is not fit or right or whatever, we'll exercise our option not to carry it, and we do, many times. No one understands how the networks developed television in this country, how beholden the country is to the networks.

As a loyal NBC affiliate, I'm delighted to watch NBC's program schedule succeed. Grant Tinker is a mature, secure individual who knows who he is and where he's at. Brandon Tartikoff is a young man who has matured beyond any expectation for a man that age in that environment. During the depths of despair he kept his sense of humor and didn't lash out at the press. Now that he's the toast of the television programming industry, he still has a self-deprecating sense of humor. He has a right to feel confident. He has a right to say, "Hey, I'm proving it." He's balanced. It's a delight to see him at NBC.

My 60th birthday wish for NBC is for all dayparts, all divisions, to achieve their stated goals.

July 29, 1985

Fred Paxton, President of WPSD-TV and President of Paducah Newspapers, Inc. in Paducah, Kentucky, is a former President of the NBC Board of Delegates and current Chairman of MST, regarded by some as the most important board in broadcasting.

"Just as our military establishment is ultimately under the control of civilians, I think our news departments should be supervised by non-news people who have a balanced perspective of what is right, what is needed, what is really happening.... The news people are experts; the front office may not understand the nuances of news and may be tempted by monetary returns, or influenced by advertisers and government figures.... However, a good station manager or network chairman is aware of those pressures, and if he's worth his salt, he will resist them.... True, the stakes are bigger at the network, they've got a network to lose, and I've got a station to lose."

W e like to think of Paducah as a typical grass-roots, middle-of-the-road community with traditional values. It is located at the juncture of the Ohio and the Tennessee Rivers, in largely an agricultural area (though it does have some manufacturing plants), part of the Bible Belt. There's no big city atmosphere in Paducah; it is small enough, about 31,000, for the residents to know each other. This gives WPSD-TV a good sense of their tastes in programming, and what they like to hear on the news. We don't let that dictate the news, but I feel that we are closer to our audience than television executives in bigger cities.

The Paxtons have been in Paducah for generations, and the communications business is a family tradition. My father, Edwin Paxton, Sr., was active in publishing for 60 years, until his death in 1961. He worked for his father in The Citizens Bank of Paducah, and when his father and a group of his associates acquired *The Paducah Evening Sun* in 1900, they needed someone to run it. My father, 23 years old at the time, fell heir to that job. I marveled at his courage when I learned, years later, that he operated the newspaper in the red for the first 18 years. Barter is a big word in our business today, something we think we learned about ten years ago, but in that pre-Depression period, he bartered—traded advertising for suits of clothes and bicycles. He was a role model for all of us, and his family looked up to him at all times.

My father was very interested in what was going on in the community and deplored "stuffed shirts." He wrote a daily column, "Add Your Own Comment," about what was happening in his life, in the community, and

in the world as he saw it. He evoked responses from his readers. He kept close to the people and was admired by his employees, who fondly referred to him as "Boss," never Mr. Paxton.

My father was followed by Ed Paxton, Jr., my half brother, 21 years older than I, who established WPSD-TV. They acquired a radio station license in 1946 for station WKYB. Today, our television market is very competitive, but we don't have local competition for *The Paducah Sun*. The newspaper has been edited by three people: my father, Ed, Jr., and Ed, Jr.'s son, Jack, who had been a correspondent for NBC for ten years. Jack died tragically early this month in an airplane accident. Ed, Jr., is retired now.

I knew that I would go into the family business when I graduated from the University of Notre Dame. My father was editor and Ed, Jr. was destined to succeed him; my other brother, Frank, was Business Manager. The logical place for me was advertising and sales, so I majored in marketing, but never spent a day in the sales side of our business!

My father set high standards for the newspaper, the radio station, and the television station. He insisted on fairness; he was deeply committed to improving the community. Paducah, as a river town, was isolated until the bridges were constructed, and then we were inhibited by tolls on those bridges. My father launched campaigns to lift the tolls, and he succeeded. He was involved in virtually every civic activity that came along, and he encouraged us to do likewise. He was an energetic, open-minded man. He never touched alcohol, yet he took an editorial stand against Prohibition. There was a campaign to vote Paducah dry, and he opposed it because he felt that it just would not work, and, further, would bring criminals and bootleggers to Paducah. And, too, moonshining was not unknown.

I finished college in 1954, married and went into the Air Force. I was on active duty as a pilot on a B-47 bomber in the Strategic Air Command at March Air Force Base in Riverside, California. We carried nuclear weapons, and we had a target behind the Iron Curtain. If they ever blew the whistle, we knew where we were going, and what we were going to do. They told us how to get back, too, but I was never convinced we would make it, or even that we would survive the blast of our own bomb. I haven't really used my pilot training since then, although I occasionally take the controls of our small company plane. But, I think, being at the bottom of such a massive organization as the Air Force, seeing it do some things that were right, and some that were wrong, taught me a lot. I promised myself that I *wasn't* going to make the mistakes the Air Force made if I ever had a position of authority.

To think that whenever a mistake is made, you simply pass a regulation or set a policy, and it will never be made again is just nonsense. People are human beings, and they make mistakes. You must be able to separate the important from the unimportant, the controllable from the uncontrollable. The truly successful organizations are people-oriented and haven't lost the perspective of the person on the bottom looking up.

My father was not authoritarian in running the business. If he had a weakness, it was in being too tenderhearted. In 1946, Ed, Jr., persuaded him to start the radio station—a daytime-only station. Ed wanted to be an NBC affiliate, but NBC about that time had to break up the Red and Blue networks, and they did not have a network affiliation available for a daytime-only station. So Dad and Ed chose Mutual. Several years later, they acquired a full-time frequency, day and night, and got the NBC affiliation.

When I left the Air Force, I came back to be Associate Editor of the newspaper. Ed was running the television station, and my father, who was 80 years old, was looking for help and wanted to groom a replacement. For two years I served as an apprentice under him. The next two years I was there, I was acting editor of the paper. I was 27 years old at the time. If the people on the paper resented my age, they concealed it nicely.

My father and Ed applied for the television license some time prior to 1954. When I was at Notre Dame, one of my professors who had been successful in the advertising agency business said, "You know, no one can make money in television in a market smaller than Indianapolis." And here was my family applying for a license for little old Paducah with 31,000 people! My father was advanced in age; he could have been thinking about retiring. Instead, he invested in something that might have produced zilch. I think he wanted to have something for succeeding generations; he was an entrepreneur, always willing to try something new.

When the FCC began issuing licenses again in 1954, there was a competing application, and it took three years for our case to wind its way through the FCC. We finally won in 1957, the only newspaper applicant to win a contested hearing for many years. The FCC didn't want a media monopoly, so it was an automatic demerit if a newspaper applicant was faced with a competing application. My father's tremendous record of community involvement through the years swung the tide in our favor. I don't recall the initial investment, but I think it was about $1 million, and we spent several hundred thousand dollars on the legal proceedings before we got the application. I'm afraid to ask the value of the station today. At the time we obtained the TV license, we decided to sell the radio station without any pressure from local citizens or government agencies.

We located our tower at Monkey's Eyebrow. According to legend, this site on a bluff in the bend of a river looks like an eyebrow on a topographical map. That name has won us a lot of fame. The tower is 22 miles northwest of Paducah so it can reach a densely populated area in Illinois. We work hard to make the people there feel an integral part of our audience. We have a news bureau staffed with four full-time people in Marion, Illinois. We have a live microwave link, and we report from both studios on our 6 and 10 o'clock newscasts.

The call letters, WPSD, named after the newspaper, *The Paducah Sun Democrat*, were a real problem in the early years. Once, when the Arbitron ratings were not what we thought they should be, we discovered that some of the viewers' diaries which should have been credited to WPSD in Paducah were credited to WSPD in Toledo, Ohio. In the second year, the station made a profit, and it's gone up ever since. It must have been good management!

We are very conscious that owning both a newspaper and a station in the same market is a real "pressure cooker" situation, and if it's abused, something can be taken away from us. One of our guiding principles has been to operate the TV station separately from the newspaper. In the early days, a lot of joint owners used combined news staffs, but we never did. Our news staffs compete vigorously with each other. Our TV people would rather scoop the newspaper than the CBS affiliate in our marketplace, and I think the same thing is true with the newspaper people. The independence of our news organizations is healthy for the people in our area.

Some of our biggest problems are the result of our trying to be very fair and very open. When our nation was adjusting to integration (and it was a difficult adjustment in this part of the country), we gave coverage to the black movement. Some of the white establishment in certain parts of our area were greatly chagrined and resented it. That was never a problem here in the city of Paducah, I'm glad to say.

A lot of broadcasters are concerned with the Fairness Doctrine, but it's never bothered us because we think any citizen's broadcast rebuttal to what we have said acts as a pressure relief valve. We have a very firm policy: we are an information medium, and our goal is to give information about all sides of an issue. We do not play God. We do not try to decide what is true or false, right or wrong, wise or unwise. We respect the people who live in our area and expect them to make the proper judgment. Our mission is to put out as much information as we can, and then let the public decide.

If a voice at one end of the political spectrum produces a strong reaction, we do not suppress it, but give voice to the other side. We quote the excerpt from the Supreme Court cases about robust debate, which, unfortunately, most American citizens are not aware of. They're not really in favor of robust debate, they're in favor of very lucid explanations of their point of view.

We have always had a strong news department because it had roots in a newspaper background. But we still add to it whenever we get a chance. Statistics across the country show that the stations with the leading newscasts generally have the best audiences for their entertainment programs as well. But you can't concentrate on just one; you have to do both well. I don't believe a station can succeed without good entertainment programs. To insure the station's future viability, I think we must continue to enhance the news department. It's true that we are faced with new competition from satellites and cable television. But the people who are bringing in these programs from distant sources cannot serve the local news and information needs of our viewers. Only we can do that, and I believe our fate depends on how well we do it.

As a result of my father's death in 1961, I left the newspaper and came to the television station. I didn't want to make any changes. I was 29 years old, absolutely green in the industry, and I wanted to learn about it. Sam Livingston was an awfully good tutor. Sam started writing sports stories for our newspaper when he was in high school, and became sports editor of *The Paducah Sun Democrat*. My father needed a good solid businessman to watch expenses at the radio station, and made Sam General Manager, later, General Manager of the TV station.

During the next ten years I was Managing Director of the station. At the time Robert Kintner was President of NBC. He appeared to be the opposite of today's management at NBC. I did not know him well. I watched him from afar, but he seemed to be very authoritarian.

Kintner's sucessor, a fellow Kentuckian, Julian Goodman, is an amazing man, brilliant, with a great sense of humor, a nice sense of understanding and caring about people. He had a very balanced perspective. He came up through the news organization, but, for a news person, was very normal. News people sometimes think of themselves as special human beings, and I think that's a real problem. I have the advantage of coming up through the news ranks, so the news director can't tell me that I don't understand news. When I want to use my judgment, he can't say, "Oh, that's front office judgment." Station managers and network presidents are frequently afraid to challenge their news directors or presidents of the news division because the news people claim non-journalists don't understand their profession, and, therefore, are not qualified to criticize it. That's not true.

Fred Silverman didn't necessarily agree with everything Bill Small, President of News, did, but, it seemed to me, he was reluctant to be decisive because he felt he did not have the necessary background and expertise in news. News people are articulate and plead their cases well. They can make you look bad if you challenge some of their judgments, as Fred Friendly did when CBS overrode some of his decisions about what should and shouldn't go on the air. I feel the news people should not be autonomous nor think they cannot make errors in judgment. Unfortunately, some of them do feel that way. It's a *real* problem in our industry and our society.

Handling the news is a very difficult business. Sure, you've got to bring out the warts, you've got to bring out the sordid, but you have to be careful that you don't overdo that. There is a balance. Just as our military establishment is ultimately under the control of civilians, I think our news departments should be supervised by non-news people who have a balanced perspective of what was right, what was needed, what was really happening.

The analogy of the Commander-in-Chief and the military is a good one. The news people are experts; the front office may not understand the nuances of news and may be tempted by monetary returns, or influenced by advertisers and government figures. However, a good station manager or network chairman is aware of those pressures, and if he's worth his salt, he will resist them. I'm not sure the pressures are lesser at the local stations. True, the stakes are bigger at the network, they've got a network to lose, and I've got a station to lose. Here at our station, we're close to our people, and they can lay an eyeball on us across the desk or over a cocktail. That makes the pressures greater and more frequent.

Affiliates confronted the network about news more in the 60's when our whole society was torn apart than they do today. If a newsman does his job right, he will be criticized from at least two sides. The danger is in thinking that if he's being criticized from both sides, he must be right. 'Tain't necessarily so. Both of his critics may have a point. But in most cases, people outside the news areas who criticize it are wrong. They see truth and wisdom from their own point of view. Most of the newsmen I know are professional and objective to the best of their ability. I think they're doing a better job than their critics would do if they were making the decisions. I hope news will always be a subject at the affiliates' meetings. If it's not, the newsmen are not doing the job.

In 1972, I took over the dual role of publishing *The Paducah Sun* and running the station. My brother Frank, who'd been publisher of the paper, went to Chicago to run a photographic supply business we had acquired. The family and my two brothers asked me to be the publisher. I was reluctant because I was *very* happy at the TV station. I had a fulfilling career and a full-time job, but I saw the need, and tried to meet it. There are times I have felt fragmented, but I enjoy both jobs very much. I spend half a day there, and half a day at the newspaper if everything is on schedule. I'm not working 18 hours a day. For my family and my health, I have resolved to try to get home by six o'clock every night. If you set priorities for your activities, you get the important things done. Procrastination *does* pay off. If you set your papers in Must-do, Can-do, and Maybe piles, a lot of the Maybes never need attention and eventually fall off the desk into the waste basket.

You have to delegate, which means giving up some control. I learned that when I was at the newspaper as associate editor working under my father and my brother. If I wrote an edtorial on a controversial subject, there would be three different opinions.

If their opinions prevailed, the consistency of our editorial policy was skewed. I realized the difficulty of having the responsibility for something, and having outside opinions influence it. I resolved again if I had to delegate authority, I would give that person the opportunity to make judgments I disagreed with. If they were minor, I would ignore them so I wouldn't stunt the person and suppress his creativity—the most important element in an executive.

Broadcasting, more than publishing, is a dynamic industry, changing rapidly, and you must be innovative and adapt to those changes or you will be left behind.

I became President of the Kentucky Broadcasters in 1977. I had served on that Board for five years. In 1978, I became Chairman of Television Committee of the Broadcast Rating Council. The Council polices the work of Arbitron and Nielsen, very important work because what they report dictates what is shown. How well they do their job determines how well we serve the needs of the audience.

From 1972 to 1976 I was on the NBC Affiliates Board, and in 1977, I became Chairman of the Sports Committee. Art Watson, President of NBC Sports, is a terrific guy, and he's built such *esprit de corps* in the sports division. It's amazing! Look at the success in getting the Olympics again. I'm thrilled about that. I was Chairman of the Sports Committee when NBC had the 1980 Olympics, and one of the *biggest* disappointments in my life was when they were cancelled. Our Sports Committee had worked hard with the network to divide the inventory between the network and its affiliates. We put together a package which was mutually beneficial, and I was just dying to see how that was going to work out.

If I have a chance to go to the Olympics in Seoul, I probably will. We don't have all the details yet, but Art Watson and his people put together an innovative, creative package in winning the rights. The NBC Sports Committee met with Art, his staff, and other network people recently, and talked a great deal about what NBC's posture should be. All the affiliates wanted NBC to get the Olympics, but not at too great a price, which might undermine their financial resources or the resources of their executives and take the focus off the entertainment programs, the news division, and the daytime programs. Everyone at NBC wanted the Olympics very much,

but only at a fair price. They were determined not to overreach, and Art Watson must have conveyed that effectively in the negotiations with the IOC, as he certainly can. I would not want to be in a poker game with Art Watson! I'd lose; I'd probably have better cards and still lose! He and his people convinced the IOC that there was a price beyond which NBC wouldn't go, and they presented an innovative technique for sharing in the risk and profitability. They listened to the Affiliates Sports Committee.

When I was first on the Affiliates Board, the network left us very little time to talk after their presentations. The network pretty much filibustered at those meetings. They listened politely, but not a lot happened as a result. As the years went by, the network began to listen more and more to the affiliates. That was partly a change in dynamics. When the network was doing well, it didn't need a whole lot of advice. When it began to hit the skids, the affiliates got more irate, more vigorous, and more pointed in their remarks, and, too, the networks needed the affiliates more. As the ratings slipped, some affiliates switched to other networks. To the long term detriment of NBC, some of the affiliates who left NBC were forerunners, leaders in the market, and they still have that distinction.

When NBC came up with a good program or newscast, it did not get as big a rating as it would on another network. NBC didn't want that situation to get any worse, so they began to listen to affiliates more. ABC was out to get any NBC affiliate it could. Our station

resisted the temptation. NBC was mired in third place. Many said, "Oh, the pendulum will swing." But there is no pendulum in broadcasting. Look at how long NBC was in the cellar. That was no pendulum swinging, it was a dead weight down at the end of that shaft. ABC did court us, and made a good point, not just, "Hey, we're number one, and NBC is number three." They cited their strengths, their management team, their momentum. It was impressive.

But we knew the people at NBC, good people, decent people, intelligent people, who were doing everything they could to correct the situation. In those dark days, people in our audience said to me, "Nielsen says NBC is number three, but I don't believe it. NBC is still my favorite network. I like the programs, I like the newscasters." Loyalty built over the years makes it difficult to change an affiliation. It would be a wrenching experience, not only for the station management and the network people, but for the audiences of the stations. Most affiliation switches did not work well. One station in a three-station market would come out well, and that was the station which stayed put.

It was a bolt out of the blue when I was asked to be Chairman of the Affiliates Board. One of the board members, Mike McCormick of Milwaukee and I often talked about spot sales and classified ad lineage because he was also involved in a newspaper (*The Milwaukee Journal*) and TV (WTMJ-TV). I said to him once, "Well, who are you guys thinking about as Chairman?" (There was an unexpected vacancy in the chairmanship of the Affiliates Board.) It was a rugged time for NBC, and they needed a strong Chairman. He said, "I understand they're thinking about you." I was shocked, amazed, floored, flabbergasted and told him I thought that was one of the wildest ideas I'd ever heard. He said, "You're not slamming the door are you?" I said, "No, I never knew the door was open."

At the next NAB meeting, some of the godfathers among the NBC affiliates asked me to do it. I prefer to have other people talk about my tenure, dangerous though that may be. I admire Ancil Payne. I think there's no one quite like him, a magnificent leader of the NBC affiliates at a tough time. Jack Harris' saying that Ancil Payne was the best Affiliate Chairman we had ever had is testimony to that, because Jack was no slouch in that job. I knew I could not be Ancil Payne. I don't have his personality, his style, so I did not try. I tried to be Fred Paxton. I assumed they wanted me to do it my way, and I did. It's the only way I knew how.

The major problem when I came on the board was programming. The schedule was in chaos. NBC was sliding in the ratings, and Fred Silverman was trying desperately to do something about it. When he was first appointed, with his reputation as a programming genius, I thought it was an inspired choice. Fred was a good programmer, but they put him in as head of the network to deal with news, all the mundane things that go on in a network as well as programming. NBC was going downhill, and I know he felt tremendous pressure to arrest that decline. In retrospect, I think he jerked programs around too much. That was bad in building an audience, and it made it impossible for an affiliate to sell the station breaks in between those programs. By the time the order hit the air, the program had been moved. We had no credibility with the advertising agencies. They didn't know what they were buying.

I tried to convey to the affiliates my personal sense of loyalty to the network. My board members were my strongest allies. Ancil and Jack Harris were great supporters too. Affiliates like to take pot shots at networks, particularly when things are bad. They get irate when the network programming is doing poorly, and their bottom line is hurting. They preempt network programming, and you can't blame them. But, in the long run, that's self-defeating. The Affiliate Board, Ancil, and Jack Harris, tried to convey to the affiliates that we're all in the same boat, and if it's leaking, we all sink, unless we plug that leak and hold together. NBC is the only network we've got. Some affiliates can change, but most don't have that option so they're stuck in good times and bad with the network. The Affiliate Board during that time had a twofold job: give good advice to the network to help them regain their momentum, and keep the "natives" on the reservation while maintaining our own credibility. I know now why preachers move every so often!

Ancil was honest when he said it would take 30% of my time. Sometimes it would take all day. The network would pose a question, and I tried to respond for 215 affiliates who don't agree with each other. We had large markets and small markets, different geographical zones, and different time zones. I had to think how we could represent 215 affiliates and answer their questions lucidly. You can't do it yourself, you must use the 11 board members, and it's not easy to contact all of them.

You have to consider polling the affiliates. But it's almost universally true that an affiliate poll is inclusive. We believed that the Affiliate Board was a well-designed structure, a good cross-section of large markets, small markets, West Coast, and East Coast. It might take me two or three days to have enough sense of the Board's feeling to answer a network question. And with no staff, just my own secretary, that was a burden sometimes.

Fred Silverman and Jane Pfeiffer departed fairly quickly. However, I did not think it was a good idea for the affiliates to initiate any of that pressure, and we did not do so.

I never thought NBC was in such bad condition that it couldn't recover, but I knew it was going to be a long haul. I thought Grant Tinker could do it. I had seen him at a conference organized by himself, David Wolper and John Mitchell, who was President of the Academy of Television Arts and Sciences. Its purpose was to talk about and think about the pressures that were put on prime-time programs. There were some network people there. Dick Salant represented NBC. He asked me why I was the only affiliate chosen to attend. I found out later it was because I represented NBC, which, lodged in third place, was feeling more pressure than anybody. The discussion of sex and violence was effective. In fact, the producers moderated what they were doing to such an extent that the pressure went away for a while. Grant Tinker, then head of MTM, was a part of that gathering. We broke into groups to hear reports and make decisions. Grant reported for his group. I was never so impressed with anyone in all life. When I got the telephone call that he had been made Chairman of NBC, I was elated!

I am presently Chairman of the Association of Maximum Service Telecasters, normally referred to as "MST." It is made up of approximately 250 stations. If you would look at its board of directors, I think you would agree that it is a most impressive group. And they are doing some of the most important work in the industry, because the main function of MST is to ensure the continued availability of high quality, interference-free, locally-oriented television service to the American public. We guard the public's access to free, over-the-air broadcasting. Those goals might seem to be obvious, needed, fair and unquestioned. Therefore one might wonder why MST has marshalled such a collection of industry leaders and exerts so much effort in pursuit of these goals. But the fact is there is a limited number of frequencies available, not only for broadcasting our programs, but for radio communications with our news teams, for microwave links to our transmitters, and for relaying live remote coverage to our studios.

There is more demand for these frequencies than there is supply. The temptation of the FCC is to "shoehorn" in additional users of these frequencies, but this can only be done by allowing interference to the present users, which means the public would lose some of its present service. Under most proposals, the public stands to lose more than it would gain. But the pressures on the FCC are unrelenting. Therefore MST must stand ever-vigilant to see that no proposals are adopted which would cause interference to present high-quality television service.

You ask if a change in network structure is likely in the future. The potential for change has been around for a few years. The ability to pick up signals off satellites poses a threat to network-affiliate relationships as we know them, because now an affiliate can point his dish to any one of dozens of birds up there, each with a couple of dozen transponders. If somebody has a good program he wants to offer, he no longer has the complicated and expensive problem of interconnecting a group of stations with telephone landlines. It's very easy to put together an ad hoc network on short order, and this poses a threat to the network.

When I was Affiliate Board chairman I repeatedly emphasized this to network executives and even to the folks at RCA. They needed to realize how easy it was for an affiliate to slip off and pick up one of these programs. And they needed to know that the affiliate could make more money from the satellite program than he could from the network program. This was particularly pertinent when the NBC programs were faring poorly. At the same time, I, along with Affiliate Board members and former chairmen, had to remind our affiliate brethren that every time they slipped off in this fashion they diminished the network and eroded its potential to develop successful new programs. The network is, after all, our main source of programming and is likely to be so forever unless we mortally wound it in pursuit of short-range interests.

My 60th birthday wish to NBC is to be Number One in all dayparts for the next 60 years.

October 15, 1985

Ancil Payne is President of the King Broadcasting Company in Seattle, Washington. He served as the Chairman of the NBC Board of Delegates from 1975 to 1979, a difficult time for the company and its affiliates. He has deservedly won high praise for the way he handled that responsibility.

"We were the first of the television stations on the Coast to open a Washington, D.C., bureau...because...the Northwest had the most powerful Congressional delegation in the nation...the Chairman of the Ways and Means Committee, the Chairman of Senate Appropriations Committee, the Chairman of the House Agricultural Committee, the Chairman of the Budget Committee, the Chairman of the Atomic Energy Committee, the Chairman of the Foreign Affairs Committee...we had to report what these people were doing. It's one thing to talk about agriculture, but, *God*, they've got the power to blow us square to hell."

I was born in Mitchell, Oregon. My family moved to Dalles when I was very young. After graduating from high school in Dalles, I entered the University of Willamette in Salem, and two years later transferred to the University of Oregon. In the fall of 1941, a man came by beating a drum, and I followed him. Three-and-a-half years later, following WWII, I came back to civilization and transferred to the University of Washington, graduating in 1946. I majored in political science and made Phi Beta Kappa, probably because there were so few possible candidates returning early from the war. Later, I took graduate courses at American University in Washington, D.C.

Like many WWII veterans, I became involved in politics and spent four years—1948 to 1952—as assistant to State of Washington Congressman Hugh Mitchell. It was a great experience because it has provided the knowledge and an insight into political life. I find broadcasting not that unlike political life: we have our own constituency which we have to maintain, and we have to warrant their support. As a matter of fact, a main difference is, instead of being elected every two years, as broadcasters we're "elected" every 30 minutes.

My political experience helped me understand the FCC and appreciate politicans' problems, particularly during campaigns when emotions are strong. Candidates are uptight and distraught at election time. As broadcasters, one of our many responsibilities is to help them get their information to the public as fairly as we can. A political background helps generate understanding.

I returned to Seattle in 1952 and ran a small film-production house making experimental television commercials and doing industrial films. After two years, I got out of that business and went to Alaska and ran a trucking company. Both Alaska and the business became so interesting, I stayed there for three-and-a-half years, until the company grew into the largest of all the house-goods transportation companies in Alaska. I also enjoyed political life there, serving as Chairman of the Statehood for Alaska movement.

Returning to Portland, I served as an executive of an investment firm, Frontiers Oregon Ltd., for three years, underwriting timber production, general construction work and housing developments in Alaska, Idaho, Oregon and California.

I was asked to look over some property in Portland owned by the Bullitt family of Seattle. When I reported to Stimson Bullitt, Dorothy's son, that developing the property wasn't feasible, he told me that his mother was looking for someone to take Henry Owens' place as the Financial Vice President of the company, and asked if I would talk with her. I said, "It would be very pleasant to talk with your mother, but I'm not really interested." After a few conversations with Mrs. Bullitt and Mr. Owens, I decided to take the job.

The story of how Mrs. Bullitt got into broadcasting is fascinating. At the end of the war, in 1946, many people were trying to find out how they could help returning veterans, and society in general. Dorothy Bullitt, follow-

ing the deaths of her father and brother, and finally, in the early 30's, her husband, was forced into the management of the family's property holdings. She had long been nominally interested in radio and decided to buy a very small independent radio station, KEVR, the Evergreen station. An early decision was to take off all the paid religion and instead broadcast the Seattle Symphony, which was not one of the best financial moves but gave tone to the station and established her approach to community responsibilities.

Along with many other responsibilities, she ran the radio station, and developed the news, sports and music format, which at that time became very popular.

And then television came along! T.K. Lieberman, who had been a radarman in the Navy, filed on Channel 5. It cost him $50 to make the filing, and he was awarded the construction permit. He built the station and put it on the air in 1947. Their first broadcast (the screens were about 4" x 5") on Thanksgiving Day was the high school football game.

In 1948 he decided to sell the station. Since there were fewer than 600 television sets in Washington state, the big companies weren't interested. He called Mrs. Bullitt and found she was interested because, at the Chicago World's Fair, in the Wanamaker store window, she had seen an exhibition of television, and decided then that it had a great future. Lieberman came to her house for dinner, and, at 4 a.m. the next morning, she bought his license—the first ever sold in the television business—for $500,000. Shortly thereafter the FCC freeze went into effect, and Mrs. Bullitt had a monopoly in Seattle, Everett, and Tacoma for a period of five years. It has not proven to be a bad investment.

She bought KGW Radio in Portland in 1953, and was awarded the Channel 8 TV permit in 1956. Both of these stations were ABC affiliates until 1959 when we shifted to NBC, incidentally, turning over our major audience to ABC. For the next two or three years, NBC had a somewhat difficult time. At the first affiliates' meeting I went to in 1960, Jack Kennedy, NBC's chief Engineer, laughed and said, "Oh, you're our newest station. You sure chose a hell of a time to come aboard."

When I came to King in December 1958, it was as the Assistant Vice President, Business Division, which was responsible for finance, personnel, and labor negotiations. Three years later Mr. Owens retired, and I was elected a Vice President. A year later, in 1964, we ordered an organization and management study by the McKinsey Company. They proposed decentralization, and, as a result, we placed a vice president in each of the cities in which we owned properties. I chose the Portland operation and became responsible for all King Broadcasting properties in Oregon, including KGW Radio, KGW Television, and later KINK-FM. I thought this the best possible assignment since it was a distance away from the home office, and I'm an Oregonian. I remained in Portland for five years and enjoyed it immensely. Station managers have the best jobs in broadcasting.

King has always looked for people who understood the broadcasting business *and* community responsibility. Of course, any manager must also understand people. We don't make shoes or tin cans; the only thing we "manufacture" comes from the heads of our people. Therefore we must have some appreciation for what broadcasting is and *should be*. We think it has a great deal to do with the community, and with society. We want to be leaders in thinking and developing ideas. Many

people in broadcasting don't share this philosophy, so we have to search and find those who do. Now the pioneer generation of broadcasters is relinquishing its power and position; businessmen are buying the stations, and the bottom line is becoming paramount. In my judgment, this is probably the most frightening social change that we've seen inside our business.

I've talked with a number of the old pioneers. Historically, there were three generations of people involved in station ownership. The first generation was divided equally among fine broadcasters who accepted genuine community-service obligations and first-class pirates who considered licenses gold mines and pumped all the money possible out of them. The second generation was made up of management people who grew up in the broadcasting business, and, for the most part, chose to be responsible broadcasters. This was partially due to the leadership of the good early pioneers, and somewhat to the FCC and government regulation that encouraged them to think and act responsibly and in the public interest.

Now we are in the third generation, and we are experiencing the Graduate Business School managers who are looking solely at the bottom line and care less about operating than seeking mergers and making acquisitions. The prices paid in these acquisitions are often so great that the interest payments alone will *force* the reduction of public service. That, along with the fact that the FCC is deregulating, is resulting in a new approach to broadcasting: one based more particularly on profit.

What is needed is an FCC responsible to the consumer instead of being almost solely concerned with deregulation. Deregulation frequently has absolutely no regard for the consumer. Example: the assumption that the consumer is able to identify which of the systems he should buy for stereo AM radio. That's beyond the general consumer's capacity. That's the type of engineering regulation and decision the FCC was inaugurated to make, and they are not making it.

At King, we devote 30% of on-air time to news and public-service programming, and often we don't see much difference between the two. Recently we used prime time to broadcast a three-hour program a couple of weeks ago on the Washington State economy: what export/import means to us, what trade barriers are, what's happening because we're losing timber industry, what could happen if we lose the aluminum industry. It examined all the technological changes that are going to take place, how we can provide better ecology and at the same time get new industry in the area, what will happen if we discourage the total smoke-stack industry, the production industry. We didn't count on a high rating; we did it because the public must be informed. And besides, there is continuing value since the program is now being used by the high schools and colleges. Is that public service or is it news? I think it's a dilemma, but who cares? Such programs meet community needs, and educate and inform, and that's what it should all be about.

Our five happy years in Portland ended in 1970, when I was asked to come to Seattle as Executive Vice President of the company. I returned knowing full well that the organization alignment was doubtful. When I assumed the CEO position, it was very difficult because we had undertaken a massive diversification program. It was the age of diversification. We had to return to our basic business, so we just sold others off or closed them down—not an easy task: for a year I had to take a "food taster" to the coffee shop! We reorganized the company, separated the real estate properties, and I became President and CEO of the broadcasting properties.

I should backtrack and explain that King Broadcasting Company took over the Bullitt Company lock, stock and barrel. When Dorothy bought the radio or television station, the TV call letters were KRSC. To change those call letters, a check was made to the FCC to see what call letters were available and who had them. We found out that K-I-N-G were the call letters of a maritime ship then at sea. When the ship came into port and the captain was asked if he would sell the call letters, he said, "Well, I don't want to give them up because I've got all my stationery printed and everything like that." Mr. Owens said, "Well, how much do you think it would cost to reprint your stationery? The company will

be glad to pay for that." The guy said he thought it would cost $100. Henry, the old fox, said, "I think we can handle that." K-I-N-G are apt call letters because we're in King County.

We've had great good luck in attracting to King very strongly opinionated leaders. Our vice presidents today are *very* opinionated, and they do not always agree with me or each other. If you have only "yes" people around you, your company is headed for destruction. We've always sought strong people for our management team.

When doing editorials, I always think the best response is to be given an argument by anyone in the halls or by the people running the cameras. One time, a cameraman said, "*God*! I've heard everything! How could you come to a conclusion like that?" With that kind of openness and feeling inside the company of 1,035, you can conclude no one is being brainwashed or is afraid of you—and besides, one of them just may be right! All opinions count.

King now has four television stations and six radio stations. We put KINK-FM on the air in Portland in 1968 before I left there. In 1980 we bought KTVB, a television station in Boise, Idaho. We bought KYA-AM and KYA-FM radio in San Francisco. About a year and a half ago, after having bought KSFO, we sold KYA-AM to the Mormon Church but retained KYA-FM in San Francisco; KGW-AM and FM in Portland and KING-AM and FM here in Seattle. KING-AM is the only all-news-and-information station in the Northwest; KING-FM is classical and is the fourth-most-popular classical music station in the nation. We have almost 100,000 units of CATV, mostly on the Pacific

KING TELEVISION

Coast. King Videocable is a wholly-owned subsidiary. We own and operate Northwest Mobile Television, the largest mobile-television company on the Coast. We do a great deal of work for all three of the networks.

We've always had a strong interest in news. King stations want to be known as leaders in news and public service. We're a decisive Number One in television news in three of four markets, but we have always been more concerned with content than ratings.

We were the first of the television stations on the Coast to open a Washington, D.C. bureau, now staffed by five people. We made the decision to open the bureau some years back because, at that time, the Northwest had the most powerful Congressional delegation in the nation. We had the Chairman of the Ways and Means Committee, the Chairman of Senate Appropriations Committee, the Chairman of the House Agricultural Committee, the Chairman of the Budget Committee, the Chairman of the Atomic Energy Committee, the Chairman of the Interior Committee, the Chairman of the Foreign Affairs Committee, all here in the Pacific Northwest. We decided we had to report what these people were doing. It's one thing to talk about agriculture, but, *God*, they've got the power to blow us square to hell. And I wanted them to know that while they had access to our news, we were going to report what they were doing, both good and bad. The bureau there has been very effective.

In the 60's and 70's, NBC has series of highly competent leaders. Julian Goodman was a news-oriented, intelligent leader whose only Achilles' heel was his deep loyalty to those who worked with and for him—not a bad sin. Don Durgin had to be the smoothest, best presenter in the broadcast business. The first time he presented the season's programming, I kept looking around for the "idiot cards," but he used no props or prompters. Amazing! David Adams was one of the smartest men I've ever known; he could always handle the affiliates because he both wrote and spoke good English—a rare commodity in broadcasting. Bob Howard was one of the first network presidents I served with who had managed a station and understood the practical problems of management—and, since he had managed KNBC, even knew the difference in the time zones and that, when it was 9 a.m. in New York, it was not 12 noon on the Coast!

During this period the network generally "explained" to the affiliates what the network was about to do. The relationship was more or less paternalistic. Because of a continually weakened position, that condition changed markedly in the period following 1975; the network and the affiliates developed mutual respect and learned to work well together—out of real necessity.

I became Chairman of the Board of Delegates in 1975, a terrible period for the network. It was running fifth in a field of three. A year before we were all laughing about ABC; we said ABC was so weak there were only two-and-a-half networks. Now ABC was moving up to number one, and NBC began slipping. News was beginning to have trouble, the TODAY show had declined, our programming was missing and had grown old. It's impossible to put a finger on any one reason for the decline, but we all could see the losses and the drifting. Management was defensive and apologetic, but the job was not getting done. During the four years I was Chairman, our progress was consistent—consistently downhill!

NBC had long been very comfortable as number two; with some adjustments, we might have remained in that position, but with the approaching 50th anniversary hard upon the network, the desire to achieve the number one position had become obsessive and resulted in management changes and unfortunate risk-taking. While Chairman, some affiliates suggested we intervene and demand a participating role in programming the network. There was a proposal that affiliates buy RCA stock and put a member on the Board of Directors of RCA, an action which would probably have been devastating—certainly demoralizing to NBC.

We did believe we could help stabilize the relationship between the network, the affiliates, and RCA if we could build a relationship with RCA. David Adams responded to a suggestion of a meeting with the new RCA Chairman, Ed Griffiths. I met with him in his dining room (one of the most expensive diners in the United States), invited him to address the upcoming affiliates' meeting (which he did), and suggested he meet from time to time for informal discussions with the present and past chairmen of the Affiliates Board outside formalities so we could speak openly: after all, we didn't report to him and could give him advice without fear of reprisals. He agreed, and we met several times. This policy has continued with Thornton Bradshaw and Bob Frederick, and I think has proven useful to RCA, NBC, and certainly to the affiliates.

These meetings gave us an opportunity to explain the long-term damage done to the network through the disaffection of stations—NBC's branch offices—as well as the importance of stabilized management and the need for consistent programming. And of great importance was the recognition that broadcasting is a business different from any other. Thornton Bradshaw recognized and appreciated that fact from the very beginning.

Midway in my chairmanship, Ed Griffiths called me early one morning to say he'd hired Fred Silverman as President of NBC and asked how the affiliates would react to that. I said, "We're in deep trouble in programming; you've hired the best programmer that you've got in the country, and I think psychologically this will be a tremendous shot in the arm for the NBC affiliates. I assume that, in your judgment, you have concluded Fred has the ability to manage the company?" And he said, "Well, he has the capacity to learn how. We're going to have to get help for him." I said, "He's got to be the greatest programmer who has come down the line. His record is absolutely great, but it isn't just programming that is causing the trouble back there." He replied, "I know that, but we'll get somebody to help." And that is why he hired Jane Pfeiffer, introducing an amazing management organization in which Mrs. Pfeiffer reported to Silverman, but served on the Board of Directors to which Fred reported. The Harvard Graduate School of Business should pay NBC for the rights to make a case study of that period.

But all was not negative. Fred Silverman brought us "Hill Street Blues," "Real People," and "Diff'rent Strokes," and it was Silverman who hired Brandon Tartikoff. His management style might have left a lot to be desired, but Fred had a genuine love and feel for television, and he never ceased trying.

It was not until Grant Tinker assumed the CEO role that the affiliates knew we were on the road to success. Grant brought to NBC a knowledge of our business, an unparalleled sophistication, and a commitment to excellence. Who could asked for more?

What about the future? Technological changes will affect news. There will be much greater satellite distribution which means that we will be able to use news in more dayparts. I think that's good for us and good for the network. It will strengthen the local stations by enabling them to supply additional information to the public; it will strengthen the network through additional revenue. I think another breakthrough that NBC has made is the Ku-band. They singularly pursued the use of the Ku-band in spite of all the engineering and weather problems. Bob Mulholland and Ray Timothy deserve great credit for that.

My successor, Fred Paxton, was the best possible representative of the network and of the affiliates. He's a very broad-gauged person, and now his successor, Jim Lynagh, is doing a first-rate job.

The NBC management team today is just first class. The leadership has changed so greatly: Tinker is not a product of the network bureaucracy; Ray Timothy and Bob Walsh have served as station managers, and they know both sides of the equation. Bob Butler is an excellent financial man. NBC's devotion to the news is evident; NBC News President Larry Grossman is an intelligent man who is willing to experiment.

Even in the dreariest days, King never seriously considered leaving NBC. First, life is cyclical, and so is business. Secondly, we have a tremendous and major loyalty to NBC. Our association with NBC has always been good. When we were in trouble we expected our long-time associates to stick with us, so we stuck with NBC. A personal relationship develops with all of us; that relationship is very important, and we cherish it.

My birthday wish for NBC's 60th? To continue with the management and programming policies established by Bradshaw and Tinker, always striving for excellence in news, information, and entertainment programming, keeping in mind that communication is the principal ingredient in the cement that holds any society together. Our highest function should be to make men good by choice.

October 21, 1985

A. Louis Read, former President of WDSU-TV, and former Executive Vice President of The Royal Street Corporation of New Orleans, is known among his peers in broadcasting as an exceptionally able executive, as his many industry awards attest. He was Chairman of the NBC Affiliates Board from 1963 to '67.

"In 1948 New Orleans had about 1,700 television homes. I had to take out a loan to buy a Magnavox with a 9-inch screen. Being in the business, I needed a television set. I went to New York to sell WDSU to a number of agencies. One of these was George Castleman, who handled Griffin Shoe Polish for Bermingham, Castleton & Pierce. He asked me, 'How many television homes do you have?' I told him about 1,700, and he told me to come back when we had 2,500 homes."

I was born in New Orleans and, except for a few years, lived here all my life. My roots here go down very deep. After high school, I worked for a year before enrolling at Loyola University. At the end of my third year, I had to go to work again, but I completed my A.B. degree in 1937.

My first job was for my dad in the insurance business. A year later, in 1938, when Loyola decided to hire one of the graduates to work at their radio station, WWL, I was offered the job of Merchandising Manager at $75 a week.

To increase sales for our radio advertisers, I made many calls on store managers asking for a particular product, and, most of the time, I'd be told, "Well, if we get a call for it, we'll stock it." Then I'd get people to call, and, in that way, we sold a *lot* of merchandise and got lots of schedules. At that time, Vince Callahan was the very able manager, who had come down to WWL from WRC, WMAL in Washington. He was a great guy to work for. I'd been with the station a short while when he said, "Louis, if we can expand this sort of promotion throughout our signal area, I think we might develop some new business as well as some good sales ammunition." My job grew to cover Louisiana, Mississippi, and parts of Alabama, because WWL was a 50,000-watt station. I got letters from listeners to WWL, put them in a brochure and sought advertisers. Letters were our main audience measurement at that time.

To check their audience coverage, Procter & Gamble depended every year on the "Ma Perkins Seed Offer" made on the show. One time, I made a call on the research director of Procter & Gamble in Cincinnati and showed him our engineering map of the station. He pulled out a Ma Perkins Seed Offer map which was better than mine. So I said the only thing I could think of, "You take my map and I'll take your map and use it in New York."

I remained as WWL's Commercial Manager until I joined the Navy in 1941. Callahan had by then gone to WBZ in Boston, another NBC affiliate, and Howard Summerville from Atlanta had replaced him. With the help of Harry Butcher, who was Vice President of CBS Washington, and others, I applied for and received a Navy commission and worked as a Public Relations officer for about five years—the last two in the 10th Naval District which covered the Caribbean, with headquarters in San Juan.

After the war, I returned to WWL (although Gene Katz had talked to me about the possibility of going with Katz in New York), and, a year later, I left because of a problem with Summerville. I suddenly found out how many friends I had. John Blair, President of Blair Television, was the first one to call me to say, "If you want to go to work in New York, we would love to have you; if not, I know of a couple of station positions that I'd like to discuss with you."

My wife, Nathalie, and I didn't want to leave New Orleans, so I went to work as Advertising Director for Wembley, Inc., the world's largest manufacturer of neckwear. I was not at all happy out of broadcasting. So, the following year, I took a job for radio station WABB in Mobile. A few months later, friends in New Orleans called to say WDSU had a television grant and was about to go on the air. Mr. and Mrs. Edgar Stern, Sr., realized the potential of television in 1948 and thought it would be a very good thing for Edgar, Jr. The original licensees, Stevens and Weber, sold the operating AM and TV license to Mr. Stern for $500,000. Edgar, Jr., had just returned from the service, and they were seeking someone to work with him in broadcasting. I was recommended to them by New Orleans and Mobile. Bob Swezey was recommended to them by P.X. Page, a communications engineer in Washington.

We both came down to meet with Edgar B. Stern, Jr., and his father. I like to say that Edgar's father, in his wisdom, hired both of us—Bob to be General Manager, and me to be Sales Manager, starting on March 1, 1949.

Edgar is an engineer. He loved the technical and engineering side of broadcasting. About a year later, Bob and I were given a chance to acquire an interest in WDSU-TV at a price we could afford. Edgar was No. 1 man, Bob was No. 2, and I was No. 3, and Lester Kabacoff, Administrative Assistant to Edgar's father, was No. 4. It was the only station I knew that had 100% ownership on duty all day, everyday. We could make any decision we wanted to make. We had a good working relationship; we balanced and complemented each other very well.

Television was brand new. In 1948, we went on air, and the WDSU-TV program schedule in the *Times Picayune* was picked up by *The New Yorker*'s "Brave New World" department: 4 p.m. Sign on; 4:30 To be announced; 5:00 To be announced; 6:00 To be announced, and so on. Every half hour was "to be announced," up to 10 o'clock when it said "Sign-off," followed by, "All programs subject to last minute change because of non-arrival of film."

At that time, New Orleans had about 1,700 television homes. I had to take out a loan to buy a Magnavox with a 9-inch screen. Being in the business, I needed a television set. I went to New York to sell WDSU to a number of agencies. One of these was George Castleman, who handled Griffin Shoe Polish for Bermingham, Castleton & Pierce. He asked me, "How many television homes do you have?" I told him about 1,700, and he told me to come back when we had 2,500 homes.

At that time, WDSU was affiliated with four networks: NBC, ABC, CBS and DuMont, and we were on the air from about noon to about 10 o'clock at night. We did a lot of news. We were the only TV station in New Orleans for about six or seven years. We measured our financial progress by a reduction in losses. At first we didn't make any money, but, luckily, we had the Sterns behind us.

By September 1951, the station was operating very well. We were in the black and could repay the money that Edgar's parents had advanced. I'll never forget, at a dinner party at Antoine's for Mr. and Mrs. Stern, Edgar, Jr., Bob and I gave them a very large check signed by the three of us. When Edgar's mother looked at the check, she said, "You know, this is amazing because when Edgar was a little boy, I thought he'd never learn to write."

We had the field all to ourselves and were the envy of a lot of people. We made a lot of friends when we weren't interconnected; we had plenty of business. We made a lot of friends because we took good care of our clients. This really paid off later on. When the time came to settle on one network affiliation, we decided on NBC. To help us work this out, Edgar's father invited General Sarnoff to a dinner at Antoine's. I'm sure this contact helped us finalize our NBC deal, which we signed with Carleton Smith some months later.

We used to carry Pabst Blue Ribbon on kinescope or film. When we finally were interconnected with NBC, I decided we would take the full NBC schedule, so I had to take off the Pabst fights and other network shows. The Pabst guy in New York was furious and demanded to talk to Edgar Stern, Sr. I told him to go ahead and call Mr. Stern, but I also told him that we would run an ad to explain why we had to do this. The Pabst slogan was "What will you have?" I worked on a full-page newspaper ad listing some of the other network shows we could no longer carry as an NBC affiliate. When I came to Pabst, the copy asked, "Now, what will you have?"

The Sterns didn't have to set standards for our operation. We knew what they wanted, and we knew what they wouldn't want us to do. In my 35-year association with Edgar, Jr., he has never second guessed anything. It was a wonderful relationship. The New Orleans community knew us to be men of integrity. We, more than any station before or since, have been supportive of community efforts in all areas.

When I took over the station, I wanted to expand our news operation. New Orleans was a one-newspaper town, *The Times Picayune-States Item*. WDSU News Director, Bill Monroe, formerly with the *Item*, was one of the first News Directors to do daily editorials. A number of years later, we were definitely the first to put on editorial cartoons. We took a positive position on some important issues, such as racial segregation—this was a terribly turbulent period—and our strong editorial position on that issue commanded attention.

From '58 on we had competition. WWL began in '57 as a CBS affiliate, and ABC was on the UHF, Channel 26, which has since become VHF Channel 8. Television homes increased from 1,700 to maybe 50,000, 60,000, 70,000 homes (now it's about 400,000).

We were solicited, not by CBS, but ABC. ABC threw tremendous pitches at us in the 50's. They would have paid us a lot more money on an hourly basis than NBC. Leonard Goldenson, Chairman of ABC, appointed my friend, Ollie Treyz (head of the Television Bureau of Advertising), President of ABC. Ollie really made us some fantastic offers: a couple of hundred dollars an hour more, no free hours, and everything else. However, I've never felt any regrets about not taking that ABC offer. ABC is certainly more stable now, and with the Capital Cities merger should be even better. Edgar and I had listened to Ollie's pitch many times, but we had too much faith in NBC to switch.

WDSU began TV operations in the Hibernia Bank Building with one studio. If you needed a long shot, you had to back out of the studio door. The cameras had to move all the way back into the ladies' dressing room. On occasions we had many funny experiences down there. One night we were advertising deep freeze Frigidaires by demonstrating one full of frozen foods. A cleaning man had knocked the plug loose the night before, and we had a sodden mess—on camera! At least our viewers were spared the *awful* smell.

WDSU-TV moved from the Hibernia Bank Building to the Brulatour Building on Royal Street in November of 1951. We leased that building for 30 years, and bought the one in back. The problem now is that the property is not big enough, and the Vieux Carré is too crowded. However, the location worked well for us and was a natural for promotion. When I first went to work out of college, New Orleans had a population of about 390,000 people. Today, it's a little over a million.

When WDSU took an editorial position during the period of school desegregation, it was risky. A number of our top advertisers were not happy, but we never lost any business. One time during this period, Martin Agronsky did a news show on school desegregation, and I was quite critical of Agronsky's handling of our Congressman, Eddie Hebert. Martin injected himself gratuitously into the interview. People were critical, and we took a lot of abuse. It was pretty bad, but we knew we were right. However, every now and then I was pleasantly surprised by people's attitudes. One of my dearest friends, a very prominent man, was most supportive. The tough time was when we showed film of racial violence. I took more criticism from my peer group because they didn't understand desegregation and didn't believe it had to happen. In a small way, it was like South Africa today.

We took strong editorial positions on political issues.

I have a book written by our editorial cartoonist illustrating the station's positions in political races. In one campaign, we asked the mayor to appear on a desegregation program. When he didn't, we were quite critical of him. He never forgot. In a race for District Attorney, we invited the two candidates and the incumbent to debate. We felt that New Orleans needed a change and took that editorial position. One candidate didn't show up, so we left his chair vacant. Jim Garrison won that race and gave WDSU full credit for his victory. I don't know whether it was so smart to back him because he gave us a lot of trouble later, especially during the Clay Shaw incident.

Cory Dunham (now head of NBC's Legal Department) came down after NBC had put together a show based on information that Walter Sheridan, an investigative reporter for Bobby Kennedy, had dug up about Clay Shaw's alleged involvement in President Kennedy's assassination. Cory wanted to make sure there were no legal pitfalls. Bill McAndrew, President of NBC News, and David Adams had asked me to come up to New York to view the film to make sure that, in my opinion, it was a true representation of what was going on down here. Garrison was pursuing Clay Shaw, but I never thought Shaw had anything to do with the assassination.

Jack Harris succeeded Walter Damm as head of the Affiliates Board. NBC's affiliates developed an excellent plan of succession. Walter Damm had been the perennial Chairman of the affiliates group until Jack became Chairman. He felt the term should be four years and out. I followed Jack as Chairman for four years, then Hod Grams was Chairman for four years followed by Bob Ferguson, then Ancil Payne. Each, in turn, stayed on the Nominating Committee. We were extremely loyal to NBC—we served on the Affiliates Board during tough times and good times.

It was great that David Adams was very supportive of what the committee did. The very early 60's was a tough period, but we had a very good working relationship with NBC. We had a lot of funny times with Kintner.

I was Chairman of the Affiliates Board of Delegates when I had my first lunch with Bob Kintner and David Adams. Kintner was extremely critical of me. I was so mad I told him at the end of the meeting, "Bob, if you feel the way you do, there's no sense having this Committee." I went back to my hotel, and during a sleepless night, I wrote out everything on my mind. I was back at NBC at 8 o'clock the next morning and was told by David Adams that he'd told Bob he shouldn't have been *that* unpleasant. Thereafter, Bob was very friendly, to the point of calling me one time to ask if I thought it was a good idea from the affiliates' standpoint, for NBC to put out a lot of money for the Baseball Game of the Week.

Kintner was difficult on occasion. In my opinion, he started what I called "tonnage coverage" of all news events. NBC would be on a story first and stay with it longer than the other networks. During some world crisis, Bill McAndrew told me that on one occasion Kintner had stayed in his office all night, and next morning sent McAndrew 11 memorandums. In 1962, Nathalie and I made our first trip to Europe. Bob Kintner called to say, "Louis, I want to make some arrangements for you." He wrote the NBC correspondents at every place we were going, and, as a result, we were treated royally. That's the kind of guy he was. I would say that he certainly has to rank among the best presidents NBC has had. After he left NBC, I went to see him when he was working for Lyndon Johnson at the White House. That was our last visit.

Joe McConnell had a different approach to the presidency. I think you can be a good businessman and a good broadcaster; I don't think they're mutually exclusive, but Joe was primarily a businessman and not a broadcaster. Some people have said the General was basically a businessman, that he didn't understand broadcasting from the stations' point of view. I thought he did; I thought he was wonderful. I'll never forget some of the talks he gave at affiliates' meetings—the one at Princeton was especially memorable.

I didn't know Pat Weaver as well as I would have liked. I thought Pat was brilliant, colorful—an unbelievable man. I can see him now balancing himself on his Bongo board in the middle of his office.

One of my nicest associations was with Walter Scott, who was very, very good for NBC. All the major advertisers liked him; every station man liked him, especially those on the Affiliates Board.

News was always one of my prime interests. I'm very proud of our News Directors. I was on the Affiliates Board when Bob Kintner told me that NBC was going to offer our News Director, Bill Monroe, a job. The lure of going to work for NBC in Washington, the source of most world news, was an irresistible opportunity for Bill. We remain very, very close friends. Another, Ed Planer, is now a Vice President with NBC News; and yet another, John Corporan, now heads WPIX News.

I admired Bill McAndrew. I thought he was marvelous, and wonderful for the station managers to work with. I came to know Julian Goodman when he was Vice President of NBC News. When Julian was named President of NBC after Kintner left, Bob told me that he had wanted Julian to become president of the company because he thought he would be a strong leader, but he added that he didn't expect it to happen that fast! Neither Julian *nor* Kintner expected it.

I didn't know Ed Griffiths very well, but when he first took over as Chairman of RCA, he invited Hod Grams, Jack Harris, Bob Ferguson and Ancil Payne and me to a luncheon. He wanted to learn something about NBC's relationship with its affiliates. He wanted very much to make a good impression on all of us. Talk about a clean desk, *nothing* was on Griffiths' desk. At the luncheon table in his private dining room were little place cards, and my name was spelled *Reed*. Ironic, because he was so intent on making it a perfect occasion. I'd say he was a great businessman but not a broadcaster. He told us that day he was going to hire Jane Cahill Pfeiffer and indicated that he was planning to hire Fred Silverman. Griffiths said, "We're going to put NBC in top position, no doubt about that!" He looked all around the table. "Any places where we don't have the best in the business, we're going to get them."

I was in David Adams' office just after Herb Schlosser learned he was no longer President. David gave him some very good advice—to take the job he'd been offered at RCA. As it turned out, Fred Silverman wasn't the right man for NBC. Although he had done great things at ABC and CBS, he was a disaster at NBC.

Our station properties were prime targets for ABC, but NBC's management and, particularly, Station Relations, understood the stations' needs. We made some progress in getting breaks for the stations, some extra time, co-op fees, the things that really mattered. At the same time, we realized that it was important that NBC enjoy the fruits of its efforts. They were a great part of the industry, and I wanted it to stay that way. I never felt that ABC had the stability. We were never approached by CBS, for which I compliment CBS. They were loyal to WWL. I think some station managers who switch affiliation are unduly motivated to make a quick buck.

Is there creative tension between the affiliates and the network? I'll give you a good illustration of that. When the networks wanted to go from the 15-minute news to the 30-minute news, many of the stations didn't think about that objectively. They had a selfish, self-serving view. There's a lot of movement now to go to an hour network news; it was going on when I was active. The stations will resist because they make so much money with local news, and they can stall it for a while. We cleared all the prime-time programs and news (however, we didn't always clear every daytime show). I think the affiliates owe that to the network which takes the program risks. I felt pretty strongly about that, as did the other committee chairmen.

At the same time that I was active on the Affiliates Board, I was involved with the NAB. That gave me wider exposure to others in the industry. The NAB took a lot of time. There was a big fight about cable when I was Chairman of the NAB Television Committee. On one occasion, I got a phone call in the middle of the night at the St. Regis Hotel in New York. The operator said, "This is the White House calling." It wasn't the White House, it was Clay Whitehead, who headed the White House Office of Telecommunications Policy. He said, "Mr. Read, we're having a meeting down here tomorrow on the cable situation which is fighting for access. Can you come to the meeting? You can bring someone else with you if you wish." (NAB was very much involved in the cable situation.) I asked Jack Harris to go with me.

We had several meetings with Dean Burch, Chairman of the FCC, and all the White House people. It was dif-ficult trying to figure out cable's position vis-a-vis the Must Carry rule. I flew to Washington at least 20 times just for one-day meetings. In addition, we had four or five NAB Board meetings on the subject. Nonetheless, I felt that my experience serving on the NAB Board was very worthwhile. I learned a lot, and I enjoyed it.

I was involved in helping to get the Television Bureau of Advertising (TvB) started. From 1958 to 1962, I served as Director and was Chairman in '61. The stations felt a need for a television sales organization in addition to the NAB, but I thought that television had to have its own sales organization.

TV Stations, Inc., was started by Tom Bostick out on the West Coast as a film buying organization. From 1968 to 1969, I was Chairman.

Another very effective organization, the Television Information Office (TIO), was started by Lou Hausman to counter some of the criticism of television. TIO is a useful industry arm which could not function as efficiently within the NAB. I served on that board for a number of years.

I've made some wonderful friends in the industry. Some of the best people were at NBC. Tom Knode was a great Station Relations Manager. He knew a lot about the business. He was a strange, tough fellow, and he was a dear, loyal friend of mine. He was followed by Don Mercer, whom I admire and enjoyed working with. He too understood our position and worked well with the affiliates.

The NBC News correspondents liked our operation and loved to come to New Orleans for our News Forums. It was a big deal—over a thousand people came to the Forum on Friday night; I'd take the newsmen to the races on Saturday, and to breakfast at Brennan's on Sunday. I used to put them up at the Royal Orleans Hotel, but one time, the Jung Hotel manager said he'd love to give us complimentary accommodations for the correspondents. One particular Sunday morning after they had stayed at the Jung, I asked the group, "Fellows, how are your accommodations at the Jung?" Joe Harsch said, "Louis, do you have any interest in the Jung? If not, I'm going to tell you something. In hotel parlance, there are two kinds of hotels: wooden coat-hanger hotels and wire coat-hanger hotels. The Jung is a wire coat-hanger hotel." Live and learn.

We had the "Today" show here several times. Garroway came the first time with Jack Lescoulie and Frank Blair, and the show was a big success. The second time, we had the "Today" show with Hugh Downs; Al Morgan was the producer. We were all set to do the show on the upper deck of a riverboat when the rains came. Our men had to break the set down and re-set on the deck below, which they did promptly. Morgan wrote me a letter. "Louis, if that had happened in New York, we couldn't have made that switch in two days, and your guys did it in about three hours." We appreciated that compliment.

Ours was one of the first stations to venture into color. We wanted to be the forerunner, regardless of cost.

We demonstrated color shows to the dealers and worked very closely with them. At first, color sets were hard to sell. We bought all the equipment then available, and ran expensive ads to promote color. An early and great public affairs color show for children on Sunday mornings (prepared by the Council of Jewish Women) was "The Magic Tree." The end of an outstanding ad for this program ran, "'The Magic Tree' is not for sale." To show you the power of those ads, many years later when I was in New York, Pete Cash (head of TvB) told some agency friend that I was from WDSU-TV, and he said, "The Magic Tree is not for sale."

I've seen many technological advances. I remember how bad kinescopes were when you were doing a delayed show. Then I remember how excited we got about Ampex, the one-inch tape. And now they're down to ½ inch, ¼ inch. I remember the first two RCA cameras we bought. They were monstrous. Now we have these small studio cameras and minicams that can be put on the shoulder. The unions did not welcome these technological developments. They were scared to death their jobs were in jeopardy with all the technological advances. We promised not to fire anybody, but we also had to go along with the advances.

WDSU-TV always supported worthy causes. Fortunately, we had a very capable staff (particularly my indispensable secretary Irma Stiegler), and this permitted me to give the necessary time to volunteer work. When the Symphony needed to raise $150,000 to avert a strike, we put on a benefit show in the auditorium. Lorne Greene (then the star of "Bonanza") was the Master of Ceremonies, and we had Victor Borge and many other talented people.

You asked of the many agency boards I've served on, which meant most to me. Without doubt it was the United Way. I've worked with this organization for many, many years. I was Campaign Chairman in 1968 and President in 1975. My community service helped WDSU. The station was identified with every prestigious organization. I wish that other stations would do a lot more than they do. Service was part of the Sterns' philosophy, and it was always a part of mine.

In 1972, Edgar and I made a major decision—to sell WDSU. Cosmos and Combined Communications were interested in buying the television property and both made bids. Cosmos was the winner. After we made a deal with Cosmos, someone from Combined called me that night and wanted to offer us more money. I told him he was a day late.

The radio station was sold to Covenant and has since been sold to someone else. We couldn't sell both properties to the same ownership. Both sales were finalized on December 31, 1972, to start the New Year, 1973, under the new ownership. That was a tough Christmas and New Year's Eve for me.

When Cosmos first came in, they made an announcement that there would be no changes. But, as always, changes came. I stayed on as President and as active manager for a while. Charlie Batson, President of Cosmos, thought it might be a good idea to bring somebody from Cosmos headquarters to take over as Manager. Jim Yager was the first to come down, and since then the station has had other managers; each of these men has contributed to the progress of the station.

When I reached 65, my active employment with Cosmos ended, and I entered into a consulting arrangement which continues until I'm 75. I've also continued to serve on the Cosmos Board. I do what I can to help the local manager, but I miss being totally involved.

As I look back on my years of broadcasting, I can truly say if I had had the chance to pick the sort of work I wanted to do, it would have been just what I have been privileged to do. It was great to be involved in television at the beginning. I don't think anyone has as much fun in television today as we did in the early years. The years from 1949 to 1965 were tough, but we had the Sterns behind us.

My wish for NBC for its 60th: continued success. Top-rated news, high prime-time ratings, a weekly news magazine with a big viewing audience. NBC has given great communications service to the nation. The business end will take care of itself now that there is stability on the executive level. I think NBC has a lot to be proud of and a lot to look forward to. A happy future to my favorite network!!!!

September 16, 1985

David C. Adams retired as Vice Chairman of the National Broadcasting Company in 1979 after 32 years of distinguished achievement.

"I remember a momentous meeting in Bob Kintner's office to take up the question of going 'all-color'...I was strongly in favor of going to color...it wouldn't be just a prestige move; it would give NBC a strong competitive edge...."

How did I come to NBC and continue there for 32 years? Well, it was more a matter of chance than choice. I'd been at the FCC from 1941 to 1947, with a couple of years away in the Army. I worked in the Common Carrier Division as a lawyer, specializing in international communications. Because of this background, I was sent to a preparatory five-nation conference held in Moscow in 1946, to organize a series of three world-wide telecommunications conferences scheduled for the following year; and the next year, I was a delegate to those conferences that ran from May to September, 1947, in Atlantic City.

Charles Denny, Chairman of the FCC and Chairman of the conferences, asked me to be his administrative assistant, setting up daily agendas, briefing him on what was going on at the other delegations and doing general follow-up.

Almost as an omen of the future, a meeting of NBC Radio affiliates also took place that summer in Atlantic City. As Chairman of the FCC, Charles addressed the meeting, but the centerpiece was a speech by General Sarnoff, urging the NBC affiliates to seize the new opportunities offered by the emerging industry of television. General Sarnoff was *the* visionary, and in most cases, he was in a position to make his vision come true by his will, his shrewdness, his energy, and the RCA resources. I heard he pointed out with fervor and force that just as this generation of broadcasters had joined NBC when it was formed 20 years before, in 1926, to create a new American enterprise—a radio network system—they now had a second chance to create an even more powerful medium by joining NBC in building a national television network. Such a second opportunity, he said, was seldom given to a single generation, and he called on the stations to seize it, as a service to the country and a source of new and larger profits for themselves. One affiliate, Harold Hough of Fort Worth, left the hall before Sarnoff's speech was over, called his station

engineer, and directed him to order television equipment that day.

After the conferences ended, Denny accepted the position of NBC's Vice President and General Counsel and asked me to be Assistant General Counsel. My first reaction was no—I didn't know very much about broadcasting, and at the FCC we Common Carrier types thought we were engaged in serious stuff, while they were fooling around with glamour. I liked Washington, and didn't relish the idea of living in New York. But, as in many cases when an opportunity like this is offered, you know immediately in the bottom of your stomach that you're going to take it, even as you draw back to mull over the question.

In 1947, when I started with NBC, it was a small organization, almost entirely devoted to radio. Niles Trammell was President, Frank Mullen was Executive Vice President—the only one then—and there were less than a dozen Vice Presidents, compared to the numbers of Executive Vice Presidents and swarms of Vice Presidents the company now has—and needs.

For the next six months, I reported to Charles Denny while we both learned the business of broadcasting. In mid-1948, after an executive upheaval at NBC, I was told that General Sarnoff wanted to promote me to VP and General Counsel of a sister company, RCA Communications, which was engaged in my old field of international communications.

Day by day, the pressure mounted for me to take the new job. The General wanted me to know that *he* wanted me to take the job, and it was hinted that one didn't disregard the General's wishes. It was either take the job or else. I spent the July 4th weekend thinking it over and decided, reluctantly, to take it. I found that I was not only commuting daily to downtown New York, but commuting weekly to Washington for those endless hearings on circuit applications, rate proceedings, FCC inquiries, and other pretty dull stuff, compared with the variety and emergencies at NBC.

Was General Sarnoff an "or else" man? I guess so, but he was a very stimulating man to be with and talk with. Years later, he'd call me up to the office, and we'd talk about NBC and its future in a changing world. He was so immersed in the communications business that he lived it day and night, and it was fascinating to see how lucidly his mind worked.

The only time I heard him stumble on a speech was one I wrote for him. They were not his words and he began to skip pages, lost his place, and couldn't find his thoughts. Later, I told him that his best speeches were the extemporaneous ones, and I'll never forget his answer. He said, "I appreciate your comment. The reason you feel that my extemporaneous speeches are the best is because I've been rehearsing them all my life."

About six months later, in 1949, there was another reorganization at NBC. Charles Denny had been made Executive Vice President and he asked me to come back as his administrative assistant, which I gladly did. Joe McConnell had just replaced Niles Trammell as President, and in that change, you could see the break from the past to a new order in broadcasting. Niles was the epitome of the Southern gentleman of the old school—courtly, polite and a little bewildered at the rapid changes in the industry. His style was to play golf and drink bourbon with his old friends—the heads of ad agencies and sponsor companies—and, in the long course of personal socializing, to sell a time period for 39 weeks of regular programming and 13 weeks of "summer replacements."

But sponsorship of whole time periods, with advertising agencies supplying the programs, was disappearing as costs of television time mounted with increasing television circulation. The unit of sale was changing to the 60-second commercial, giving advertisers flexibility to spread their commercials over various programs and time periods, cutting their risks. And now the programs were supplied by the networks, at the networks' risk. It was not Niles Trammell's orderly world, but it became the fast-moving world of Joe McConnell, a hard-driving boss, who had come from the legal and management ranks of RCA. In moving back to NBC, I saw a symbol of the changes that were taking place, personally and acutely, when I had to draft Joe McConnell's first speech—and Niles Trammell's last speech—for the annual meeting of the NBC affiliates that spring.

Back at NBC, my new responsibilities covered follow-up on almost everything passing through Denny's office, and since most of the company reported to him, that was a handful. But I never had much to do, either then or later, with programming itself. My field, almost from the beginning, was in the staff areas of NBC, and as time went on, more and more of them came under my supervision.

Television grew faster than any other enterprise in industrial America. In 1950 there were 5 million television homes, and five years later, there were 35 million.

The power of the television image is also its weakness so far as information and understanding are concerned. The image occupies the mind of the viewer as if it were reality itself. By the very selection of images for the screen, television must often depart from the messiness and complexity of reality and present it in a simplified and orderly form. So it can become a make-believe medium, not only in entertainment, where this is accepted, but in news coverage, where it is not intended.

After a few years, Joe McConnell resigned to become President of Colgate, and General Sarnoff came downstairs to NBC for one very unhappy summer as President pro-tem. It's one thing to survey the workings of a tumultuous broadcasting operation on the 53rd floor of the RCA building, and it's another thing to sit in the middle of all that turmoil. The General was a man who worked in a quiet office, planned and thought, gave orders, had visions and had a staff to carry them out. He left in the fall with great relief, to go back to the 53rd floor and dream his visionary dreams.

Back to 1947. NBC, with the backing of RCA, pushed very hard for television growth, not only in programming, but in building a network of television affiliates. At NBC's urging, many of its radio affiliates applied early on for television licenses which were there for the asking, so that we soon had the basis of a national television network.

In contrast, CBS dissuaded its affiliates from entering the new field prematurely and pulled back some of its own television license applications. They may have felt that the values of radio ought to be fully milked before launching a new, expensive and competitive medium. In his autobiography, Bill Paley says he was persuaded by top CBS officials that the company was on the verge of a successful color development, and that it made sense to enter television with a full-fledged color system from the outset, instead of starting in black-and-white. In any event, CBS dragged its feet and years later had to buy its way in. ABC was scarcely a factor in television networking; it concentrated on its own television stations, a source of quick profits, which it needed.

In 1948, the FCC put a freeze on granting new television licenses because of technical problems with tropospheric interference. That freeze lasted until 1952, and during those four years, CBS was caught short without a national television network, so from 1948 to 1952 NBC often had nine out of the top ten programs, because it had a national affiliate structure. Toward the end of that period, the FCC actually considered proceeding against NBC for dominating the television field. Well, we dominated the field, not because we used domineering tactics, but because we had a national program distribution system, and our competitor didn't.

The growth of television and the decline of network radio created enormous tensions among network affiliates. To develop an orderly transition that would bridge two media of shifting values, we formed a joint committee of leading radio and television affiliates and NBC executives. Jack Harris of Houston and Charles Denny were co-chairmen, and I handled the paperwork for the meeting, which went on for more than a week at the Westchester Country Club. (One of the affiliates on the committee, Harry Bannister of Detroit, a very urban type, left for New York City every evening and returned every morning because, as he said, "I can't sleep out there with all them damn squirrels stamping their feet all night.")

There was unanimous agreement among the affiliates on the committee on the final document, "A Basic Economic Study," which I drafted. To the surprise of everyone except Jack Harris, I stayed up all night, near the end, to finish the draft. Jack—who had worked equally hard—is a wonderful man, intense and intelligent, astute in the politics of broadcasting, a lover of long, funny stories, which he'd tell while holding your shoulder in an iron grip that prevented escape or motion.

Essentially, the plan provided for a steady escalation in television network station rates—on which affiliate compensation was based—geared to the increase in each station's television audience; a steady reduction in radio station rates geared to the decline in radio circulation, to keep radio a good economic buy; and an overall correction of the radio rate structure, which had become lopsided over time, with some affiliates greatly overpriced and many underpriced.

Our Affiliate Relations Department then fanned across the country to sell the plan to all the stations, and returned with the job done, as the head of that Department reported with some pride. At the general meeting of all affiliates that followed, NBC, for the first time, suffered the indignity of an affiliate revolution. The overpriced radio stations that would be financially hurt by the plan—even minimally and short-term—condemned it without considering its long-term value for the whole system. Jack Harris, whose station would not have benefited, suffered the wrath of some fellow affiliates by strongly defending the plan. The plan was scuttled.

The head of NBC's Affiliate Relations Department was transferred to Washington, and Harry Bannister (who had absented himself from the final meeting, sensing it would fail) became NBC's new Vice President in charge of Affiliate Relations, now reporting to me for the first time.

The catastrophe was preceded by another affiliate meeting in 1953 with a wholly different conclusion. There was some concern among the affiliates over the successive changes in NBC management, so it was decided to bus them all to the David Sarnoff Laboratories in Princeton to show them through the technological wonders being born there, followed by a rally-'round-the-NBC-flag address by General Sarnoff. The affiliates wanted to express their complaints and concerns first, but we held them off until the General had spoken.

He spoke for an hour and a half. It was so hot (pre-air conditioning) that he had to take off his jacket, then his tie. Sweat was running down his face. He really laid it on in powerful fashion. At the end, our Atlanta affiliate, Johnny Outler, stood up and said: "Well, boys, it's all over. Let's piss on the fire, kick out the ashes, go home and stop horsing around here."

Almost from the beginning of television, the affiliates formed an organization to represent them in overall dealings with the Television Network, although each station continued to deal directly with NBC on its own relationship—a parallel to a similar organization that existed in radio. The affiliate organization produced remarkable leaders, gifted with diplomacy, firmness and understanding. Jack Harris of Houston, Louis Read of New Orleans, Harold "Hod" Grams of St. Louis, Ancil Payne of Seattle were successive chairmen of the Board of Delegates, and working with them was one of the real satisfactions of my job because they became friends.

When there's a need for a new direction in any enterprise, it takes a combination of luck and judgment to identify the people who can move it ahead. Pat Weaver was such a person. He almost perfectly fitted the times and the needs—and the times called for new concepts in programming, not television adaptations of radio shows. Pat Weaver in charge of the Television Network, Mort Werner and Dick Pinkham, head of the Program Department, literally invented those new concepts— the magazine formats like "Today," "Home," "Tonight" and "Your Show of Shows"—and set television off on a course that fitted its character and strengths.

Pat had no use for budgets—they got in his way; he had little interest in overall management. As a programmer, his imagination roamed free and wild, which was fine in those early years of television when there were no rules and everything was an experiment. The American public was developing such a love affair with the new medium that you could try everything—but not forever. As time went on, television became a major business, with high costs and risks and ferocious competition. Ultimately, Pat's weakness as a top-management executive outweighed his talents as an innovative programmer.

In the early 50's, there was a period of about eight months when Frank White served as NBC's President. He was a fine man, but he was not made for the presidency of the company, and he soon realized that. During his brief tenure, he decided to appoint me as Vice President of the company. I told him, rather timidly, that I didn't care one way or the other about the title, but that I would like a raise, because I hadn't had one during all the years I worked as Charles Denny's assistant—assistants weren't supposed to get raises. He said, "You silly son of a bitch, why do you think I want to make you a Vice President?" So I got the title *and* the raise, and in the next few years my responsibilities started increasing, until about a half-dozen staff departments reported to me.

To pick up with the chronology, Bob Sarnoff had joined NBC many years before and had worked at a variety of jobs, learning the business as he went along. In 1955, there was the "Pat" and "Bob" management team, with Pat Weaver, the flamboyant member of the duo, writing 27-page stream-of-consciousness memos and charming the press and others with his nerve and verve. But as television matured, and had to be managed as a complex business rather than a gay experiment, Pat's influence and position waned, until he left for adventures elsewhere.

Bob Sarnoff became Chief Executive Officer in 1957 and, shortly after, a new and quite different executive came over from ABC to head the Television Network— Bob Kintner. He became President of NBC in 1958, Bob Sarnoff became Chairman, and the "Pat and Bob" team became the "Bob and Bob" duo.

Bob Kintner was an original. I think he was also one of the best presidents NBC had. He devoted himself to NBC as nobody had before, coming to the office early in the morning and staying until early evening. Then he'd go home and during and after dinner, he'd tune his three sets to the three network channels and keep watching until the small hours of the night. And the next morning, a flood of memos would flow from his office: "Watch what CBS is doing at 9 p.m." "Remember to see ABC's morning lineup." "I want to talk to you about the 10 p.m. show." By his own example he created a spirit of energetic activity throughout the company, and a good deal of grumbling too. We had to win in everything. During a political convention coverage, he phoned the head of NBC News at the control desk to tell him how well we were doing in the ratings. Instead, he reached Shad Northshield, our producer, and said, "We've got an 82 share" (which was stunning). Shad, awed by this presidential call and by the news, mumbled, "Gee, that's wonderful." Kintner snarled, "I want 100," and hung up.

He had great shortcomings. He was idiosyncratic and willful, and he was just as tyrannical when he was wrong as when he was right. But all in all, he gave NBC a spirit of enterprise and devotion that flowed through the company. He also displayed a touching sense of personal humanity, worrying about NBC people who were sick, sending emissaries to the hospital with funny presents. And when one of us had a birthday, there was a great festive lunch in Kintner's dining room, champagne, jokes and Kintner's standard speech that began: "At great trouble and expense, I have found this gift (always a pair of expensive cuff links) to express our fondness for you." At that time, NBC was a place of very hard work, a good deal of abuse, and high spirits—a mixture of opposites.

My personal dealings with Bob were both close and troublesome. I became his right-hand man, which put me at the heart of the company but a little too close for comfort. On most days, I had to sit in his office from mid-morning to late afternoon while meetings followed one after the other. He wanted me there so I'd know everything that was going on and could follow up when necessary. It took quite a toll, because I had my own work to do, and my own departments to supervise, and I had to go back to my office late in the day and stay far into the evening to catch up on my own work. I had to take unfinished work home or come in weekends to complete whatever was at hand, because the next week would bring a new avalanche.

In 1965, NBC had almost the entire prime-time schedule in color, the first network to do so. The conversion to color was a bold and expensive move at a time when NBC was behind CBS in audience position—not a great deal behind, but enough to sting. And in this move, as in others, NBC led the way, while other networks came later and picked up the rewards.

I remember a momentous meeting in Bob Kintner's office to take up the question of going "all-color." Kintner did his usual "go around the room," calling on each executive to give his views and the reasons for them. Most were in favor of going all the way in color. There were some doubters, and a few avoided committing themselves and suffered Kintner's taunts for their fence-sitting position. Kintner himself was troubled about going all-color at that time. He recognized its advantages, and, although he did not flinch from bold decisions, he knew it would take an immediate bite out of profits, and he was very profit-minded.

For the first time ever, I was not called upon, because Kintner knew I was strongly in favor of going to color, and he wanted to keep the matter open for a while. Research had demonstrated that viewers with color sets watched the few color programs much more than

people with black-and-white sets. Going all-color wouldn't be just a prestige move, it would give NBC a strong competitive edge in attracting audience, and that edge would continue for several years until all networks went to color. So without being called upon, I spoke up—a sacrilegious act in Kintner's office—and made my argument, followed by a real dressing-down by Bob for daring to speak when I wasn't called upon.

A few days after the meeting, Kintner concluded that the advantages of going all-color outweighed the cost disadvantages. He and Bob Sarnoff strongly presented that conclusion to the NBC Board, and we were on our way.

In the fall of 1965, Bob Sarnoff went to RCA, where he later became President and Chief Executive Officer, and then Chairman. It was good for NBC to have him in that position. He knew the ins and outs of the broadcasting operation and continued to follow it closely, but his familiarity with NBC did not lead him to interfere with its day-to-day operations, which he left to the NBC management people.

Bob Kintner left at the end of 1965 and was succeeded by Walter Scott as Chairman, and Julian Goodman as President. At the same time, Don Durgin became President of the Television Network. The company changed most of its principal management all at once. Nine years earlier, I had been promoted to Executive Vice President. Most of the staff areas, with the exception of Finance and Personnel, reported to me—about eight departments, each headed by a Vice President. They included the Law Department under Tom Ervin, one of the finest men I've known, who thought deeply and clearly and said what he thought quietly and patiently, whether it was in or out of fashion at the time. If he discovered a problem, he went privately to the person concerned and helped to straighten it out. At about the age of 60, he decided to take early retirement.

The other staff Vice Presidents reporting to me were also exceptional, each in his own way.

Mal Beville, a scholar with hard practical experience, was in charge of Research and Planning, a man of great professional skill and professional honesty. He decided to retire in order to teach and write and was succeeded by Tom Coffin, and then Bill Rubens, a thorough and able research head, who continues to run the department today.

Tom Knode, originally in charge of Affiliate Relations, was instrumental in a very key sense in bringing in the stations to create the Television Network. That was creative, innovative, fun, a lark. But when the network was built and the job became one of maintenance, he lost interest, his personal problems overwhelmed him, and he had to leave. He was succeeded by Don Mercer, who had been at NBC almost from its creation. He was a true expert, knew all the affiliates as friends and was wholly sensitive to the delicate and contradictory nature of the affiliate relationship. He stayed on as head of that department until a few years ago.

NBC's Washington office was first headed in the 30's by "Scoop" Russell, a colorful and canny old-time political operator, a headstrong man, both interesting and difficult for me to manage; and then by Peter Kenney, a quite different type: astute, modest and low-key, who knew everything he had to know, looked and acted like a Congressman himself, and was on friendly and personal terms with all of them, in or out of power. Peter was on the phone with me almost every day, sometimes two or three times a day, including weekends. I always knew that he knew more about the scene than I did, and I almost always followed his good judgment, but when I knew something he didn't, I'd persuade him that what he proposed wasn't right, and we'd quickly agree on a course of action.

Other departments reporting to me were Standards and Practices, the NBC in-house "censor;" Public Relations; Press; Advertising and Publicity. For a few good years, a young man, Larry Grossman, was in charge of Advertising. He was one of the best executives NBC ever had, professionally competent and very good at handling people. He was about the only person I knew who had the skill and grace to turn Kintner around in the middle of a meeting without Kintner knowing it. When Larry decided to leave NBC, he set up his own agency; he invested in a New York station application, and then became President of PBS. More recently, Grant Tinker persuaded him to come back to head up NBC News. I think the two stars that NBC has acquired in recent years are Larry Grossman and Bill Cosby.

The Publicity Department was headed by Bud Rukeyser, extremely competent, versatile, a quick study and the most broad-based practitioner who ever served in that field at NBC. He had at least two distinctions: he was straightforward in a publicity operation where forthrightness can be rare; and he was the youngest Vice President in NBC's history. Now he's one of NBC's Executive Vice Presidents and still a good friend.

How did I handle my workload? I've always been a worrier, with a terrible compulsion about getting things done on time, because tomorrow there would always be more things to handle. At NBC, I felt I had to do everything that came my way, to do it right and right away. I was carrying quite a load, leaving home about 7 a.m. and getting back between 9 and 11 at night. Looking back, I'm very sorry that I devoted so much of my life to my job, with so little time for my close-knit family.

I was elected to the NBC Board in 1958, a position more honorary than functional. The proceedings were not new to me, because I had been preparing the Board reports for some time, but it was a new experience to become part of the process and the discussion. About half of the NBC Board were members of the RCA Board, and the rest were principal executives of NBC, an arrangement that has rightly gone out of style.

Sometime early in 1965, an emissary of General Sarnoff's and Bob Sarnoff's made a pass at me to become President of NBC; and this is the first time that anyone has heard about it, outside of the General, Bob, and their representative. We had a long and soul-searching discussion—more his soul than mine—because it was clear to me that I didn't want to be President for sensible personal reasons. I am a private person, and a necessary part of an NBC President's job is to be a public person, to engage in ceremonials, make speeches, attend public functions, be important. I don't like that and I'm no good at it. Maybe I don't like it *because* I'm no good at it, or maybe vice versa.

And, finally, I was beginning to tire of the work after almost 20 years of running around the same track, and I was beginning to think of early retirement—perhaps at age 55 when NBC retirement benefits vest and would provide me with a modest income. I didn't think it would be honorable to accept the presidency and retire three years later—and to do so might constrain my decision to retire. So I turned off the whole matter and it was never raised again, until very briefly a few years later, when it was quickly defused.

Now back again to NBC, under the top management of Walter Scott and Julian Goodman. The three of us would meet briefly every morning, later joined by Tom Ervin, to review current issues and consider approaches to upcoming problems. An era of peace and goodwill set in. There was a minimum of politicking and everything was friendly and civilized. It was a period I personally enjoyed, with some misgivings. The pressures of the Kintner days were off—the frenzy of incessant high-key activity, some of it unnecessary. But there also seemed to be an absence of energy, and there was more of an air of accepting things as they were, because they were not at all bad. On a couple of occasions, I raised questions on this score in relation to particular pending problems, but they were turned off, and we rolled along.

But the reality was that NBC lived in a highly competitive world, and, generally, the emerging success of an aggressive network meant a declining audience for a less aggressive network—and that's what happened.

In 1970-72, the profits of all three network companies took a dive, the combined result of a steep recession and the sudden withdrawal of cigarette advertising. Then, after 1972, the profits of CBS and ABC started up again and continued to climb steadily, while the NBC profit lagged behind, increasing at a much slower rate.

ABC was beginning to press hard as a competitor, and two FCC actions helped it along. One was the Prime Time Access Rule, cutting network prime time back by a half hour to 8-11 p.m. That created network scarcity, which helped ABC become a full competitor. Equally important was the Family Viewing Hour Rule, requiring programs suitable for young people in the 8-9 p.m. periods. ABC filled that time period with mindless, fad programming for teenagers who had a good deal of control of the set, and followed that time period with hard-action shows at 9 p.m. This commercially brilliant move was an audience success for a number of years, before the fads faded. As a result, ABC came from nowhere to contend for audience leadership at night and was doing very well in the daytime, the source of major revenue. Fred Silverman was in charge of programming at ABC at that time, and these developments helped make his reputation as a programming *Wunderkind*. ABC publicity did a marvelous job in building that reputation to legendary levels—a carefully deliberated effort to attract affiliates to ABC.

CBS, a respectable leader with long-term success in solid entertainment programming, was also modernizing its prime-time schedule by dropping old favorites with good ratings that attracted older audiences and seemed about to decline. The network shifted to new and controversial programs aimed at the 25-49 age group, the darlings of the advertisers. It was a bold and costly move, and it paid off, begetting new hits like "All in the Family," which changed the character of the CBS schedule—and of television entertainment—for the future.

Between these moves of ABC and CBS, audience was siphoned away from NBC, and it began to decline across the board, reflected in the profit trends I mentioned a few minutes ago.

In 1968, I was 55 and eligible for retirement benefits—the first year I could afford to retire. My wife and I agreed that my personal and family life and our marriage—all central values to us—were passing us by, because I was spending all my time and energy at NBC. So we decided that I would take a year off to experiment with retirement and see whether it would work for us. I didn't want to commit myself to return to NBC, and I didn't want the company to commit itself to take me back, because that might form a pressure to return. So we left it open-ended—if NBC wanted me back, they'd let me know at mid-year, and I'd give them an answer in a couple of weeks. If they didn't, I'd certainly understand and go my way.

Early in September of 1968, we had a hilarious goodbye party in Croton for the 30 to 40 people with whom I'd been most closely associated, and the next week my wife and I left for three wonderful months in Europe. It was one of the happiest periods in my life. Within three weeks after our equally happy return for Christmas, my wife was diagnosed as having terminal cancer, with less than a year to live. In July 1969, the mid-year point, Julian Goodman asked me to return to NBC, which I did that fall. My wife died a few months later, and I stumbled around at first without any of the departments reporting to me and later with more and more of them added. In June 1971, I married Ilyana Lanin and started my personal life all over again.

When Walter Scott resigned in January 1972, as Chairman, the title was shifted to me, reporting directly to the Board. My duties remained exactly the same. Julian was President and CEO, and to avoid misunderstandings, I made it clear to all and sundry that I was working for him, that he was in charge of the company and my job was to help him in any way I could.

As time went on, there was growing concern about NBC's competitive position. Something had to be done, but not precipitously. Bob Sarnoff decided that Herb Schlosser, in charge of all program operations on the West Coast, would return to New York and be given a series of management assignments. He started as the Number Two executive at the Television Network and soon was promoted to head the network. He and his staff worked intensely at shoring up the program schedule, but in such effort, results are usually not apparent for at least two or three years. Later Herb was made President and CEO of the company, with Julian as Chairman, and I became Vice Chairman, with exactly the same duties as before.

NBC was now trying to recover momentum, with widespread changes in executive positions throughout the company, and some new people were brought in. All these rapid and sweeping changes in executive structure resulted in some disarray and shocks, and some of the executive changes proved unworkable, but the intense pace of activity continued. Long before this, NBC had dropped to a poor third place among the networks. The efforts of restructuring did not produce any immediate results in audience gain, except for some occasional spurts when NBC, as I remember, surged ahead to first place during one quarter. The problems were amplified by a continuing loss of affiliates, mostly to ABC, which resulted in NBC audience erosion.

In the meantime, RCA had been rocked by two top-management changes in two years. Bob Sarnoff was gone. His successor for less than a year—Andy Conrad—was gone, and Ed Griffiths was in charge. He was determined to bring every operation at RCA to first place in its field, particularly NBC, so much in the public eye. Ed was a bottom-line executive who could pick a single figure out of a complicated financial statement and interrogate the NBC people about it, because he understood more about it than they did. He was also an impatient man, and although in 1977 NBC reached the highest earnings ever in its history—$152 million—that was not good enough, because CBS and ABC had much higher profits.

In January 1978, Griffiths told me he had just met with Herb Schlosser to tell him he was going to replace him with Fred Silverman of ABC. He offered Herb a new position at RCA, in charge of developing programming for the video disk, even though a decision had not yet been made to market the disk. But if that didn't work out, he said, there would be other opportunities for Herb at RCA, because he recognized Schlosser's values. He asked me to try to persuade Herb to move to RCA in his own interest.

Soon after, he took the job, which grew to cover all of RCA's expanding entertainment ventures except NBC, and, as of now, he has spent seven productive years at RCA.

I don't want to prolong my recall of those years by any detailed account of the unbelievable Silverman/Pfeiffer regime, which started normally enough but soon became bizarre before it descended into chaos. I had reached age 65 early in 1978, and raised the question of retiring then, but was strongly persuaded to stay on. I now regretted that I hadn't left before the storms that swept through NBC and almost wrecked it.

ABC wouldn't release Fred Silverman from his contract for five months. During that period Herb Schlosser stayed on as a lame-duck President, working hard and responsibly, making the decisions that couldn't wait and passing up those that could wait for the new CEO to take office. Silverman started at NBC in June like a fireball, junking the expensive fall program schedule that had been planned over the previous months and was already going into production, and trying to build a new one overnight. Jane Pfeiffer began showing up at meetings, with the explanation that she was an RCA consultant, temporarily helping Silverman get started.

Early in October, on a day I was due to leave for Europe, Ed Griffiths called to tell me that in mid-October Jane Pfeiffer would be elected as NBC's Chairman, and he hoped I would give her full support. By the time I returned to my office a few minutes later, she had called to see me, and said she counted on me to call her, anytime and anywhere, on any "goofy" mistake—her term—she might make, because she was not familiar enough with broadcast operations. I followed this requested course on my return from Europe, and it lasted just about three weeks because, by then, she made it clear that she wanted to run by herself.

Some eight months later, she offered me a consultancy with the company, her way of telling me that I was fired, after all her urgings during the preceding year that I continue with NBC. I left in June 1979, happy in my new freedom, but sad for the company and the associates who had become so large a part of my life.

During the next couple of years, NBC was almost destroyed, and it gave me and other old NBC hands the deepest personal grief. Silverman, as CEO, was to be in charge of the program operation while Pfeiffer, as Chairman, was to manage the overall company. Her IBM credentials (she had served in a public relations capacity) were regarded as adequate, but she had had no broadcast management experience, and it showed.

Inevitably, the situation became intolerable, and some months later, Silverman fired his old friend and mentor, Mrs. Pfeiffer. There followed the most unseemly exchange of nasty memos between them, which they released to a delighted press that highlighted the scandal at NBC. Within a year, Ed Griffiths resigned as head of RCA, and Thornton Bradshaw, an RCA Board member and former President of ARCO, succeeded him. In Herb Schlosser's last year at NBC, its profits stood at $152 million. In Silverman's last year they had fallen to about $48 million, while CBS and ABC's profits had risen to the hundreds of millions. Silverman then committed corporate hara-kiri by demanding a public vote of confidence from Bradshaw. The request was declined and Silverman left. Wow!

Bradshaw set about systematically cleaning up RCA, getting rid of the internal politicking that had weakened the company, and concentrating on its central communications enterprises. One early accomplishment was to bring in Grant Tinker as NBC's Chief Executive Officer. They are very much alike—laid-back, thoughtful, orderly, and sane, with long-range timetables for rebuilding their respective companies and no need for parading their egos in public.

At NBC, I hear that Tinker delegates broadly without abdicating. He has a strong program and people sense, but most of all, he has given the company a spirit of endeavor and purpose. He's a modest man—he knew that he could not produce miracles and that the rebuilding process would take a very long time.

It took four years for NBC to rise from a poor third place to a strong competitive position near the top during last season, while ABC has fallen to third place. As we speak, on July 23, 1985, NBC has been first in prime time for 10 successive weeks, with good prospects for the coming season. Its profits stand at all-time highs, and it is reclaiming the position it had in the early days, when it was the most respected and stable network, with economic success that did not sacrifice quality programming.

And so the story, after great travails and confusions, ends happily for the company that enveloped me for more than 30 years. My very last word is my wish for NBC's 60th birthday: May it continue on the course now set, with the flexibility to meet the unpredictable changes in a communications world that is being transformed at a stunning speed.

July 23, 1985

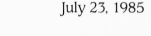

Mal Beville, known as the dean of broadcast research, was one of the most dedicated of NBC's executives for many years. His reputation as the pioneer in audience measurement is unassailable. From 1930 on, his expertise was an important and significant key to NBC's growth and success.

"Bob Sarnoff called me to a meeting and said the 'Tonight' show was about to be cancelled. I said it would be the worst mistake NBC could make. I pointed out how valuable station time was to the network—the *one* thing of value the network had was station time.... If NBC gave back 'Tonight's time to the stations, we'd never get it back...we should keep the program, fix it...but not give up the *time*."

I grew up in Washington, D.C., and completed a B.S. in business administration at Syracuse University in 1930. I had accumulated credits by going to evening school in Washington, which enabled me to graduate in January of my senior year. I decided to graduate early because we had had the stock market crash in September of 1929, and I could see us headed for something of a recession. I didn't realize it was going to be the worst depression in the country's history.

Fortunately, I had an offer from NBC. A friend from Washington, Paul Peter, who had graduated from Syracuse in the Class of 1928, had gone to work in the Station Relations Department of NBC doing statistical work. The company was just three years old. When I began looking for a job, Paul wrote to say he'd like an assistant. He and I had taken the only one-year statistics course Syracuse gave, which apparently qualified us as statisticians. I was interviewed by Glenn Payne, then the head of the Station Relations Department, and given an offer which was very great in those days—$155 a month. The only other offer I'd had was one in the Accounting Department of General Electric for $125 a month. That was an easy decision to make! I accepted on the spot. Paul was Chief Statistician (the only one) and he wanted me to help him form a Statistical Department. Glenn Payne was a former AT&T man, a bright, sharp fellow who was in favor of statistics in the AT&T sense—not in the research sense used today for audience measurement.

When I joined the company, NBC didn't have a widespread reputation—radio was a new, unusual but exciting business. I had the feeling that it was going to be *the* company in the network business. Over the years, it was considered to have a certain amount of class because General Sarnoff was interested in the image presented by such NBC programs as Walter Damrosch's "Music Appreciation Hour" and the NBC Symphony with Toscanini conducting.

Paul and I started making plans for organizing a separate statistical department, to include people in the Promotion Department who did figure work, and those analyzing audience mail. At that time, before ratings, mail was our only feedback mechanism from the public. We weren't doing any research ourselves. In 1932, at 711 Fifth Avenue, the Statistical Department was formed with elements from Station Relations, Promotion, Program Analysis, plus Audience Mail, and the General Library.

My first assignment wasn't really research; we did a whole variety of jobs, one of which was connected to our rapidly growing number of affiliated stations throughout the country. We had to make an analysis of the coverage area, the population, the radio sets in the area and stations to determine the station rate. That was the reason that statistical group was part of Station Relations.

The network rate policy was determined before I came to NBC. Local rates grew like Topsy—the stations just pulled things out of the air, and a pattern developed. But NBC had a more systematic system unrelated to local rates. Our minimum rate was $120 an hour for all the smaller stations, a set rate for many years. Eventually, it dropped to $100 an hour for a smaller market. We had two networks—the Red and the Blue.

The Blue carried more public service and quality programming than the Red, but that was only accidental because the Red Network was older, larger and more sold out. The original network was an AT&T network. When NBC was formed, RCA bought the New York flagship, WEAF (the call letters stand for Wind, Earth, Air and Fire), from AT&T for $1 million. The Red Network went out as far as Omaha.

The Blue Network had been a Westinghouse network of five or six stations taken over by NBC in January, 1927. It was always smaller because there weren't more high-power, clear-channel stations available at that time. It was hard to find other stations to fill in the interstices, and it grew rather slowly.

NBC quickly developed two networks on the West Coast into geographical groups. WHAS, Louisville, was in the South Central group, WSB, Atlanta, the Southeast group, WFAA, WBAP, Fort Worth-Dallas in the Southwest group. These groups were shifted from Red to Blue Basic connections based on client orders. The ultimate goal was an entire national network for the Red and the Blue so NBC would have two completely separate national radio networks.

Station Relations was the cover title for many diverse functions. I had nothing to do with Station Relations *per se*. In those days, there were no Station Relations

Department contact people other than Glenn Payne and Fred Weber, who handled clearances for commercial orders. Contact with NBC depended on the station managers coming to New York, or by Niles Trammell, NBC's Chicago Vice President, or Don Gilman on the Coast. Most of it was handled by telephone. Direct contact developed later.

After we moved from 711 Fifth to Radio City, Henry Norton, NBC Vice President and Treasurer, was moved up to RCA in the same capacity and took Paul Peter with him. I became Manager of Research in 1936.

We had about two dozen people then. We had installed an IBM card-counting sorter system to analyze the audience mail and establish station coverage. A card was punched for every piece of mail. We attempted to have all the mail addressed to the stations, although a few sponsors wouldn't allow it. Stations got sack loads of mail each day, and they would then send NBC mail on to us. Every day we got stacks and stacks of mail. In 1930, we received two million letters. The mail room clerks segregated the audience mail by state and sorted it by postmark—in those days, a big round thing with the name of the town and the date. We had racks for every post office in the United States, listed alphabetically by state and county.

Clerks coded the letters by county, state and radio station and an IBM card was punched for them. Cards were tabulated to give a basis for calculating the coverage of our stations.

That was the raw material for developing our station area maps. It was more scientific than the previous guesswork. We had used some field-strength measurement. To measure the stations' signals, they would section the signals at different points and develop contour maps that showed where a half-million volt signal went. This was usually done when a station wanted to go to the FCC to increase its power, or when somebody needed this kind of information for promo-

tion. Otherwise it wasn't available, although crude estimates were often made.

The 1930 census was the first census to ask whether you owned a radio. With the published results, in 1932, we knew how many radio sets there were in each county. We could calculate the mail return per thousand for radio sets for each station and develop county audience maps for each affiliate. In the mid-thirties, David Rosenblum, one of the owners of an outside consulting firm, Trade Ways, and a friend of General Sarnoff's, sold him on the idea of using the firm to develop a new NBC rate and compensation plan. (Sarnoff later brought Rosenblum to NBC as Vice President and Treasurer. He became my boss.)

Unlike CBS, which had executives with an advertising background, NBC people came out of AT&T and were operational or business-oriented. We had salesmen with some background in the media who contacted the advertising agencies, but we didn't have any people with sophisticated knowledge of the advertising and marketing world. The whole marketing concept of broadcast advertising was unknown. However, one man in the company who had any understanding of it was E.P.H. James, the head of the Advertising and Promotion Department.

The first President of NBC, Merlin H. (Deac) Aylesworth, testified before the Senate Interstate Commerce Committee in 1930 and said, "I doubt that radio will ever make any money, and, of course, I hope that NBC might, but I doubt it." NBC's function was to entice people to buy radio sets and thus enrich RCA. That was a mindset that lasted for a long time, unfortunately. I tried to change it in the late 1930's, but it wasn't until I got involved in a policy-making way, after Niles Trammell became president.

I talked to Trammell about our rates because I was convinced that radio was undervalued and worth a hell of a lot more than we were getting for it. He was the one who had to be convinced.

I thought NBC ought to be more aggressive about rate increases, but he preferred to keep the rate lower to keep out the competition. He didn't want NBC to charge too much because that would discourage the competition and keep us out of trouble with the government. His reputation was built as a salesman, and a salesman never wants high rates.

This was Trammell's only flaw. I think he was one of the best presidents we ever had. He had the most all-around experience: he was good at station relations, he was great at sales, he worked well with program people, and he knew how to handle Washington, with Scoop Russell's expert help. His grasp of figures was weak; it finally caused his demise as president.

My involvement with rates and station compensation, which was tied to advertiser rates, became known gradually to our affiliates. Before long, managers—Stanley Hubbard, Sr., Harold Hough, Johnny Gillen, Harry Bannister, Walter Damm and Dick Shafto—called on me to plead their case or challenge my numbers. Later, the highly respected television station managers, Clair McCullough, Buddy Sugg, Jack Harris, Ray Welpott, Louis Read, Bob Ferguson, Bill Schroeder and Wilson Wearn, were in touch with me. In time, I came to know every NBC affiliate manager!

In establishing the television rate curve, I was determined to learn from radio's mistakes. We priced the medium at three to five times radio circulation, with greatly accelerated rates for top audience stations. This steeper curve produced very high (relative to radio) rates for O&O stations. Network television would lose money for years; we knew it had to be subsidized by station profits. However, the curve worked to produce many affiliate station millionaires, most of whom hardly knew how it happened. One precedent in our O&O rates was to price local minute spots at 20% of the hour rate, not radio's 10%.

I was continually involved as a witness with Washington hearings. Facts and documentation were needed for NBC witnesses in such matters as the chain broadcasting regulations, the Barrow Report recommendations, affiliate exclusivity and "must buy" rules, network spot representation, network program practices, sex and violence. I worked closely with the Legal Department.

In 1941, before the Senate Interstate and Foreign Commerce Committee, NBC challenged the FCC's chain broadcasting regulations which would force NBC to give up one of its networks. Those of us involved moved into a floor of the Mayflower Hotel for ten days to prepare Niles Trammell's testimony. NBC lost its case in the Supreme Court, and the Blue Network became ABC under a new owner, Ed Noble, with Mark Woods, former NBC Treasurer, as President and Ed Kobak (later Mutual President) as Executive Vice President.

Before McConnell became President, the General had a big Booz, Allen & Hamilton study made at an important, critical period in the company's history. (The study went all out for television.) Radio and television were to have duplicate operating departments, including Station Relations. A few departments, the Press Department and some service department, were called Integrated Services, headed by Bill Hedges. Charlie Denny was in charge of radio, and Pat Weaver was in charge of television. Niles Trammell was eased out as President, and McConnell came in.

Booz, Allen decided that the Research Department was a marketing tool for the Sales Department, and they split the department into Radio and TV groups. Before Niles had left, McConnell gave me the study to read, and when I brought it back, I said, "As far as research is concerned, it's no good. It doesn't recognize what research contributes to company management." He said, "You've convinced me. I'll make one exception. We'll follow this report right down the line but create a third research unit, Management Research, which you will head. Tell me what you want, how many people, and work up a budget." He approved my proposal, and I had about a half dozen people dealing with rates and covering some broad research and management issues. The plan was carried out by each unit, but later the wisdom of reuniting radio and television research units was realized, and we regrouped.

McConnell and White followed Trammell, and then the General took over as President of NBC for a relatively short period. At a staff meeting, the General said, "NBC has never turned over any of its profits to RCA in all these years." That was a stunning revelation to me. I don't think any of the other people knew what he was talking about. We had never been privy to the financial reports so we never knew what the profits were. I assumed RCA was raking in the money from NBC, but it had never gotten a dime. The profits were being poured back into the company, into expansion and television. I realized immediately that management had not been sufficiently profit-oriented. The General had appointed Joe McConnell President of NBC because, as Financial Vice President of RCA, Joe quickly realized that NBC could make a lot more money. RCA needed cash because it was expanding product lines and introducing television.

When World War II came along, I went in as a reserve officer and was assigned to General Bradley's Planning Group in London for the Normandy invasion and remained in Europe until V-E Day. By August 17, 1945, I was in the Philippines planning for the invasion of Japan which, fortunately, never happened. My years in the service meant a great deal to me for I felt I made a contribution, learned a lot about organization and staff work.

In the early thirties and forties, there was an inauguration of syndicated audience rating services. I was personally involved with several, including the Hooper Service. Hooper launched his measurement of radio audiences largely with support from the networks. Later, Hooper had the idea that by putting together two or three months of data from this National Service, he could produce a local radio report in major markets. I told him that NBC would be interested in subscribing in markets like New York and Chicago, where we had stations. In 1940, he decided to go to the NAB Convention in San Francisco, and I steered NBC affiliates to his suite to see what he had to offer. Frank Stanton, then Research Director of CBS, likewise encouraged CBS stations to subscribe.

When television came along, I attempted to get Hooper involved in a television survey by giving him a mailing list of set owners that NBC had gotten from mail requests for WNBT's schedules, and from RCA distributors' warranty cards. He didn't believe in television. I knew Hooper was a great baseball fan so after I showed him a Yankee game on the first commercial 10-inch television set in our engineering department, he became convinced.

Eventually, Hooper sold his service to Nielsen. However, two of Hooper's enterprising young men, Bob Rogers and Ted Hynes, formed Trendex. It was a struggle until we convinced them to start a regular syndicated network service—the first coincidental overnight TV surveys—on a regular basis. They had a good business for ten years. I was involved in a new service with Jim Seiler of the NBC station in Washington. In the mid-40's, he came to me with several excellent ideas. He had no budget so I funded the studies for him. He began in Washington with viewers recording the programs they watched in diaries, and then extended it to Baltimore and Philadelphia. He got support quickly from the other stations. I tried to get him to come to New York to head our Television Research Department, but he decided to start his own business, American Research Bureau. ARB, Arbitron, is today a major service.

T.V.Q., a qualitative rating service, had its genesis in radio days. George Gallup interviewed people to find out their favorite movie stars on a five-point scale, and he developed what he called an E.Q. Index of the results. It occurred to me it might be a good thing to try for radio. I had George do two studies for radio which seemed interesting and valuable, but a little expensive.

I decided it was such a simple thing that we could get somebody else to do it for a lot less money. About 1955, I suggested to Henry Brenner, head of a research company in Port Washington, N.Y., that he set up a service to include not just personalities but programs as well. Television was coming in very quickly, and it would be important to find out about new stars, new people, and to learn how Bob Hope and radio stars came over on TV. Henry was keen about the idea and started T.V.Q., and it is the only successful qualitative rating service.

When I was overseas, my assistant, Barry Rumple, got little management support and resigned. I kept getting reports that the Research Department was falling apart, and I wrote Niles a long letter about this problem. I told him that they did not have to hold my job for me. If I did come back to NBC, I might want to try something other than research. I got a nice reply from Niles saying you know you've got a job here and don't forget us.

In June, 1945, when I was in New York on the way to the Pacific, Niles told me about the report done by Sheldon Koons, a consultant for RCA. He wanted me to read the many recommendations. It laid out elaborate proposals for greater scope for the Research

Department, including planning and top management reporting. Over the years, I had always reported to someone who was either the sales head or the financial head. This report put the department into top management. I was impressed; it seemed heady stuff. Niles said if I wanted to take this job, he was sure he could get me out of the service. Niles told me NBC needed me to represent them at the FCC Clear Channel hearing going on in Washington. I told him I was interested in returning to NBC and considered this job a great challenge. We settled on a salary, but when Niles tried to arrange my discharge from the army, he could not do it, and I went to the Pacific.

After V-J Day and the Japanese surrender, I called Niles as soon as I got back to the States. My wife was disgusted with me—I came home one day in uniform, took it off and went out the next morning to NBC. I began implementation of the Koons blueprint and, at the same time, geared up for the important Clear Channel hearing. I hired dozens of temporary employees to do jackass calculating of population counts within engineering contours where loss of radio service would occur under the proposal being studied. It would change all IA channels to IB status, thus reducing coverage of stations like WMAQ, KFI and WSM and making room for new full-time duplicate stations on clear channels. NBC and key affiliates resisted this move. However, both Trammell and Frank Mullen, Executive Vice President, opted out as NBC witnesses. They and John Cahill of Cahill, Gordon picked me. FCC Chairman Charles Denny presided. I took the greatest heat from Louis Caldwell, famed attorney for Regional Broadcasters. The Clear Channel docket was finally closed several years ago. By and large, we succeeded in a long rearguard action.

In 1952, I was named Director of Research and Planning, and in 1956, Vice President of Planning and Development. I was about to leave the company in 1958 when I was reporting to Ken Bilby, head of Public Relations. I thought this was completely inappropriate, and had said so to Sarnoff when he made the arrangement. Bilby knew absolutely nothing about what I was doing. I was the Secretary of the Program Board. I was Chairman of the Rates Committee. Bilby knew nothing about any of these. I had a very tempting offer from an advertising agency, and I went to Bob Sarnoff about it, and he

began ringing bells.

From 1948 to 1953, the FCC put a freeze on the granting of television licenses. During that period we knew we wanted a national network. We had, way back in the McConnell days, worked out a 200-station network. I made a speech and talked about a 200-station network to opponents of commercial TV. They said, "You're crazy. How can Fargo, North Dakota, support a television station?" They were talking about Pay TV and all kinds of crazy things. We had the blueprints for the television network long before 1953, and, of course, many of our radio affiliates were getting into television as a result of General Sarnoff's urging.

One day in my office, an affiliate took a license for a television station out of his pocket, threw it on my desk and said, "What the hell am I going to do with that thing?" He was from Johnstown, Pennsylvania. His station became a golden goose because Pittsburgh was a one-station market, and Johnstown's signal covered about two thirds of Pittsburgh.

After the war, when I talked to Niles about a research program for television, we decided we needed three things. First, we had to have a circulation figure to know how many television sets were served by each station. Second, we had to have a rating service, and third, we had to have a sales-effectiveness measurement that showed that television was really more than just advertising, it was a selling medium. I applied all of these requirements, and we became *the* head outfit which supplied the television numbers to the industry. *All* of the television circulation numbers came out of NBC. Black-and-white and color. We started the first rating service in television—Hooper. We carried out a series of sales-effectiveness studies in the late 40's and 50's which documented the sales results possible with TV. The first Hofstra study, conducted by Tom Coffin, head of the psychology department, created a sensation and put TV on the advertising map.

When RCA came in with color, I advocated a premium charge for color programming. Pat Weaver would have none of that. He wanted to get as many color programs on the air as possible and not make any extra charges for color. John Royal, Vice President for Television, and I, as members of the Rate Committee, determined long before that we were not going to give away studios in television. In radio, the advertiser paid the time rate for the network, and he got our studios for nothing, including Studio 8-H or audience studios in Hollywood. In television, we decided to charge for facilities. Pat said, "They're going to have to pay extra for the color studios." I knew the color medium was worth a hell of a lot more than the advertising in black-and-white. Magazines charge 40% to 50% more. I could never sell the color premium rate to Pat. I was back on square one, as I had been with Niles earlier on radio and its rates.

In 1961, David Levy, Vice President of TV Programming, came in with a 20th Century-Fox film package proposing that NBC present movies on Saturday nights. We were having trouble competing with CBS's strong lineup of Saturday night shows, "Have Gun, Will Travel," "Gunsmoke," a bunch of westerns. Bob Sarnoff and Bob Kintner didn't like the idea because Kintner tried motion pictures on Sunday nights when he was with ABC, and they hadn't done very well. Sarnoff didn't understand why our Program Department couldn't produce original programs. In addition, his father had always castigated the merchants of motion pictures and was totally opposed to putting motion pictures on television. So Bob was quite reluctant to agree to this. When Levy made his presentation to the management, they turned it down. Then Walter Scott, who was head of the television network, made a presentation, and management turned that down. Walter told me he thought we might put it over if I did the presentation.

Sarnoff was really the guy who had to be persuaded. I gave the third presentation to a small management group, Walter Scott, Levy, Don Durgin, who was in sales, and a financial guy. It carried because we just didn't give up. That was a beginning of a new era as far as network programming was concerned. It wasn't too long before NBC added a second movie night, and the other networks followed suit.

How much influence did the General have? Joe McConnell said one day, after a meeting with the General on a five-year budget forecast, "The trouble with the people at NBC is they don't understand General Sarnoff." Joe felt he was primarily interested in profits, and someone who understands how to make the company profitable would not have any problems with him at all. It's only when things aren't profitable that you'll hear from him. I think Joe was absolutely right. That goes back to what I said about Trammell, and certainly it was true of Weaver.

Pat had absolutely no interest in budgets. He was a very, very creative person whom I had known at Young & Rubicam and the American Tobacco Company before he came to NBC. He was the right man at the right place when he took over the television network at NBC, because he did more to create new forms in television than anybody else. Consider "Your Show of Shows," the specials, "Today," "Tonight," and "Home" programs. Pat was not particularly interested in money. When anybody came to him with proposals for station rate increases, he'd moan and groan. He'd usually go along with them but he thought putting money into *programming* was important, *not* giving it to the stations. I was not then privy to the financial figures; I'm sure that the bottom line on Pat's budget was probably red most of the time. He was constantly fighting with McConnell, who didn't have any particular understanding of programming and wasn't always sympathetic with Pat's ideas, although he fully appreciated Pat's creativity.

There wasn't any way to control Pat because he was the head of the television network. If anybody could have controlled him, it would have been Bob Sarnoff. When Pat became President of NBC, the General made Bob Executive Vice President so he could curb Pat's spendthrift activities. I don't think anybody could do that because Pat had an enormous number of ideas all the time. He'd get two or three people working on them, and they'd start spending money. His kind of creativity cost money, but it produced results, not necessarily financial results in all cases. However, "Today" and "Tonight" have been major, major money sources for the company.

I had something to do with keeping both of them on the air. When Weaver left, Bob Sarnoff looked at everything Pat had created with a view to cutting costs. I worked out a formula for keeping the "Today" show on the air by getting the stations to give up the compensation we had been paying and go on a time-trade basis. Management accepted this, and then at management's request, I persuaded the Affiliates' Committee to accept it. That decision kept the "Today" show on the air after the financial people recommended that it be cancelled. The cost of these lines were charged to the program, *but* they didn't realize that if they gave up the program, they'd still have to pay for the lines. When they figured that expense, that changed their decision. This kind of thing went on all the time!

During that same time, Bob Sarnoff called me to a meeting and said the "Tonight" show was about to be cancelled. I said it would be the worst mistake NBC could make. I pointed out how valuable station time was to the network—the *one* thing of value that the network had was station time. And "Tonight" had station clearances. If NBC gave "Tonight's" time back to the stations, we'd never get it back. Regardless of what it cost at the moment, we should keep the program, fix it, replace it— but not give up the *time*.

By 1964, I was involved in all the management areas—color programming, video tape, network schedules, station relations, station affiliations, advertiser rates, satellite transmission, cable system ownership, and scheduling of theatrical motion pictures. These were things we started as a result of my recommendations and the studies we had made.

NBC presidents I have known? The first president was Aylesworth—1926 until 1936—with the improbable name of Merlin. He was called "Deac." I didn't know him well. For the latter half of his term, Aylesworth was most involved with RKO, which he also headed. Executive Vice President, Colonel Richard C. Patterson, Jr., actually ran the company for five or six years.

I knew the second president, Major Lenox Riley Lohr. This is probably an apocryphal story, but it was said that when General Sarnoff was looking for a new NBC president, he was, at the same time, looking for a Chairman of the 1939 World's Fair in Flushing Meadows. He asked General Dawes, then on the Board of RCA, about an engineer named Lohr. Dawes, under the impression that the General was talking about the Fair, recommended

him highly. Sarnoff hired Lohr, who was much more interested in the technical side of NBC. While he was president, he spent most of his time writing a book about television.

The General replaced him in four years with Niles Trammell. He was a great guy. He inaugurated an ad hoc affiliates advisory group during WWII which became a permanent organization after the war. I participated in the first annual meeting, which coincided with the NAB in Atlantic City in 1947. At my last, at the Waldorf in 1968, I gave a two-hour presentation entitled, "Television in the Seventies," based on a planning project initiated by Julian Goodman.

Trammell had been spotted by D.S. (the corporate designation for David Sarnoff before he became a Brigadier General in WWII) when he was an Army Lieutenant at the Presidio in San Francisco. Niles, with his Georgia accent and Sewanee background, possessed great charm and powers of persuasion. When he became president in 1940, after Lohr's welcome departure, company morale went up, just as it has with Grant Tinker's appointment.

I've described Joe McConnell, who came in 1949. His management wasn't very popular, and CBS, at that time, had pulled up in the ratings despite Pat Weaver's great programming genius. At meeting after meeting, Joe McConnell would say to Pat Weaver, "You've got to get some of those situation comedies, some of that half-hour stuff CBS is knocking us out with." Pat was not interested in that kind of program. Pat didn't have a real grasp of mass audience appeal. He really was trying to reach a somewhat elite audience, and, at first, that's what the television audience was. As penetration of lower-class homes gained, the audience taste changed.

Frank White was McConnell's successor for a brief time, and then the General took over the presidency. He found all the detail and headaches of the position burdensome and brought in John West from the Coast to be his deputy. He also had all these cats scrambling for the top job: Weaver, Jack Herbert and Charlie Denny. Weaver got the presidency.

After Pat, Bob Sarnoff took over. He was a reasonably good man, but he had trouble making up his mind. The old man knew that Bob by himself wasn't enough, and Bob Kintner, formerly President of ABC, was brought in as head of Color Television and subsequently was put in charge of TV Programs and Sales replacing Tom McAvity. I had known Kintner at ABC, and I got along well with him. He was much more aggressive than Bob Sarnoff, hard-working and dedicated. Kintner, along with Trammell and Weaver, was one of our more effective presidents. He sought everyone's advice and opinion, and discussions were frank. Bob Sarnoff, David Adams, Walter Scott, Tom Ervin (Legal), Don Durgin (TV Sales), and David Levy (Program) or Aaron Rubin (Finance) and I attended many a meeting. Adams was usually delegated to draft the position paper, letter, or other written document reflecting the action to be taken.

I had known Walter Scott from the time he was a salesman. He had clout with the advertising agency people, yet he seemed to be a modest personality. People respected him and wanted to help him. The business in those days was not really the number business of today, and his sympathetic relationships with many people enabled him to get things done. Julian Goodman came in as president just about the time I went out. He was good—more articulate and more forceful than Walter. The two of them worked together closely and were a fine combination.

I met David Adams when he first came into the company and spent time educating him in the business. He was a workhorse, and his advice was sought on most issues, with the exception of programming. He was a facile writer and had a vital effect on policies. He became my boss for several years, and we had a cordial and mutually sympathetic working relationship—the best I ever had at NBC. I'd known Herb Schlosser when he joined the Legal Department. I was not there when he was president. I remember Grant Tinker in the meetings of our Program Board, of which I was secretary for many years. Grant was a real pro and has demonstrated it by turning the company around and putting NBC ahead in prime-time ratings.

General Sarnoff was a visionary. My admiration for him built over the years. At first, he was just a name upstairs, a kind of ogre when something went wrong. Over the years, I got to know him. One of the most critical meetings was with the affiliates in the spring of 1953 at Princeton for a demonstration of color when we had a serious station-relations problem. The General was persuaded to take part in a very effective presentation to show what NBC was doing in color programming. Pat Weaver swept back a curtain, and color television sets came on, which wowed the affiliates. It was a performance as impressive as the General's at Atlantic City in 1947. He was there at two very critical times.

I admired Bill Hedges in Stations Relations for his common sense and compassion for people. People like Bill shaped the character of NBC. Don Mercer was somebody I admired greatly.

Bob Kintner once remarked that NBC is a far different company when you get into it. From the outside it looks well-managed, no problems, no politics, just a great organization. When you get in and see what's going on, you wonder how in the world this industry was started and created. I was proud to be associated with the company, and delighted as my role became more significant. I felt I had accomplished much and made a difference in what was going on at NBC. Tom Knode, Vice President of Station Relations, once said to me, "There are two guys in this company who make it run, one is David Adams, and the other is you. I don't know what NBC would do without you."

When it slipped into third place in the seventies, I was heartsick. After Walter Scott and Julian Goodman left, there was one problem, one new regime after the other. Tinker has turned NBC around. He's getting good press, and morale has risen phenomenally.

We're seeing now what I have predicted for several years in speeches and articles: cable has slowed down. Most predictions were off because growth is measured by a curve, never a straight line. Cable is a good business, but it is relying on rerunning old network programs and feature films and has not lived up to its initial promises for creative programming. Few still appreciate the gains and important role that VCR's will play in electronic media of the future. By 1990, VCR homes will exceed cable subscribers.

The challenges are great and events will change old network relationships and the relationship of broadcasting to other home entertainment. Running a network anytime is exciting and interesting, because it is a dynamic field made up of show business, electronics, journalism, sports and advertising. The challenges will be solved depending on how creative leadership will be. I believe the network/affiliate relationship will endure and continue to be the industry bedrock.

I wish the company best wishes for another 60 years of success and glory.

August 28, 1985

Robert J. Butler began his career installing television antennas on Manhattan apartment house roofs in 1947. His career moves since then have touched almost all areas of NBC Operations and Engineering. He is today Chief Engineer, Satellite Network.

Robert J. Butler

"In 1956, Tom Phelan, head of the Maintenance Operations area, had assigned four of us to do the Eisenhower Inauguration. Ampex had just introduced, in 1955 perhaps, their black-and-white videotape machines. We did a temporary installation in the Wardman Park Hotel to pick up the Inauguration…to relay back to New York for network distribution. We were on the air for five hours that day, and we were able to replay some of the Inauguration on Ampex tape. A *wonderful* invention!"

T here are actually three Robert Butlers at NBC right now, but I spent my career, probably 30 years of it, as the only one here. When Robert C. Butler (*my* initial is "J") came to the company as a financial guy in top management, probably in '79 or '78, I began to get vouchers to approve that my signing authority just wouldn't cover.

I was born in New York City, in Queens, where I was raised. A part of my education included studying Electrical Engineering at NYU for a time. But my real introduction to electronics was in the Navy, which I joined in 1944 when I was 17. I hadn't been a really good student, so what the Navy did for me was to put me in

school. The difference was I liked the Navy school. It was all electronic, radar, sonar, things like that, which led me into a career in something I had always wanted to do.

After several years in the Navy, I joined RCA in March 1947. My career began with hanging television antennas in Manhattan. The record books say that in 1947 there were only six television stations operating in the U.S., at the outset at least, and there were only 14,000 to 16,000 sets in the entire country. But by the end of 1948, there were 47 stations in operation and a million sets.

You could say I caught the brass ring in terms of activity back in 1947. We worked out of a branch of the RCA Service Company on Stillman Avenue in Long Island City. We worked in the city because those were the people who were buying the sets at the time. I put many a television antenna on top of apartment houses on the West Side of New York, and some of them were very interesting. Manhattan has never been an area for good reception because of reflections. Luckily, at that time, there were very few stations operating so we didn't have to contend with all of them.

My transfer over to NBC came about in a curious way. Fortunately, I got transferred out to the RCA Springfield

Gardens branch in Long Island. A very nice, older gentleman ran a radio shop down the block, and he often asked for my help. I learned that his son, Walter Miller, worked at NBC as a projectionist. One day, he walked into the shop and said, "Let's go to lunch." I had three quarters of an hour for lunch, so we got in his car and started to drive. Forty minutes later, I asked him where we were going. He said he knew a little restaurant very close to NBC. I said, "I only have 45 minutes for lunch!" He said, "Well, don't worry about it, you're not going back."

I was interviewed by Ferdinand Wankel that particular day, and he passed me on to one of the nicest people I ever knew, Whitney Baston, who was then interviewing new applicants for Operations and Engineering. Two weeks later, I was offered a job.

So, in 1952, I transferred to NBC. In the interview I had with Whitney Baston he told me that my experience would allow me to be hired directly, or I could go through a training course. It was a real option he offered me; I chose to take the training course—for which I was never sorry. That course lasted three months. There were about 15 people in the class, which was held across the street in the building that then housed the Center Theatre. At the end of the three months, I elected to go to Maintenance, Technical Maintenance, and that's where I went, working for Noah Sprecher and later for Rudy Gebhart.

In 1953, RCA's (NBC's) compatible color was approved by the FCC. That was a tremendously important date in the company's history. I wasn't affected by it that early, although some of the people in NBC Engineering were. I should differentiate between the Engineering Department, the Technical Operations area and Technical Maintenance. Engineering didn't do the day-to-day operational maintenance. That was an operational function and they were charged with the work in Studio 3-H, which was then NBC's area for development and demonstration of the color system.

The first color shows came out of 3-H. I don't know how many people saw them in color, but they were available to the whole audience because they could be seen in black-and-white, too. The one absolutely fantastic thing RCA did, probably at the direction of the General, was to make a compatible system which allowed the color programs to be viewed by people who owned black-and-white sets. If that hadn't been done, I think color would have been delayed ten years. Much credit goes to RCA for this all-electronic system. It was an uphill struggle for them to get that accomplished because the FCC had earlier authorized the non-compatible system using color wheels developed by CBS. I hate to think what the diameter of that spinning color wheel would be today with our new 25-inch sets.

Beginning in 1953 and on into '54 and '55, color really began to move. I remember that in 1954, the NBC Brooklyn Studios opened, after we took them over and converted them to television use. They were, of course, staffed by Technical Maintenance, but I was not assigned to the Brooklyn Studios until quite a bit later, possibly around 1955, about the time "Matinee Theatre" started as a show totally in color.

In 1958, I made a significant career move when I became an Audio-Video Facilities Engineer. The entire plant was changing and expanding, a lot of the equipment was being upgraded, and a number of studios were being converted to color. There weren't enough skilled people at that time, nor was there hardware being manufactured; everything was designed and contracted here, because we didn't have the Tectronics or the Grass Valleys or the Quantels that now exist as suppliers. Everything was designed and specified by the Engineering Department.

The Milton Berle studio, which was 6-B in '55 or '56, was going to be upgraded with new cameras. It was to be a black-and-white change, but the Engineering Department borrowed me from Technical Maintenance to be the construction supervisor on that particular project. At the same time, I think Brooklyn Studio 2 was being constructed. So these things were happening when they invited me back to be a Facilities Engineer in 1958.

Getting back to the Berle studio and that black-and-white change. We were using, in the early fifties, the originally designed black-and-white field cameras, even in studio operations. There was no differentiation between a studio camera and a field camera at that time, and 6-B had the earliest of cameras, even though the Berle show, originating there, was a tremendous success. Berle moved across the street to the Center Theatre, and new black-and-white studio cameras were installed in

6-B. Shortly thereafter, every single one of the studios was converted step-by-step to studio color cameras, which were much larger, heavier, much more complex. But they worked. That was the important thing. The Operations people became very skilled, as did the directors and producers, in making them do what they had to do. They did a very good job with the tools that they had, even though a number of things would seem make-do by today's standards.

In the Engineering Department at NBC the work is done by union contract people. With my move to Engineering in the late fifties I was still in the union, and I progressed up the ladder from Group 3 to a Group 6. I was appointed a Supervising Engineer in 1966, so that's when I moved to the management side of the company. The same tasks, conversion of studios and so forth, had to be done, except that my responsibilities shifted to estimating, projecting, planning, rather than the actual implementation of the drawings and supervising of the testing and proving out. I should mention that my duties all along the way took me to wherever we were originating regular programs. Even while I was in the union, I was assigned on occasion to the Burbank Studios out on the Coast.

About three years after I had moved to the management side, I was given charge of the Development Engineers upon the retirement of Don Castle. He was Director of the Technical Laboratory, which was associated with Engineering. Castle's group had responsibility to provide certain very important missing pieces to Engineering. In our work, if you plan to do a job, you try your best to buy off-the-shelf hardware that's been proven and works, but you will always find yourself in a position where there is one piece of equipment that you can't buy. A typical case: you want to improve the facilities by one increment—maybe it's a new camera, maybe it's a new camera control—and you find yourself in a position where you can't buy something. You have to therefore specify and deal with a sub-contractor and have it built to your specifications. Don Castle's small group supported Engineering in specifying "black boxes" that would support the projects that Engineering was working on.

Castle's group had been reduced since the development of color because RCA/NBC adopted a policy that all design and development work would be shifted to either the RCA Broadcast Group or the RCA Princeton Laboratories. In retrospect, that may not have been as good an idea as it seemed at the time because we then had to depend more and more on outside vendors other than RCA and the Princeton Group. There were people building products at the time who met our needs, whereas RCA had many masters to serve, and we were just one of them.

As an aside, I recall an earlier time when we were a little more on our own and when Ampex tape hadn't been on the market for very long. In 1956, Tom Phelan, head of the Maintenance Operations area, assigned four of us to do the Eisenhower Inauguration. Ampex had just introduced, in 1955 perhaps, their black-and-white videotape machines. We went down and did a temporary installation in the Wardman Park Hotel to pick up the Inauguration activities and to relay back to New York for network distribution. I can remember we were on the air in that location for five hours that day, and we were able to replay some of the Inauguration on Ampex tape. A *wonderful* invention!

The technical development and those "black boxes" we worked on call for an explanation. In a studio, you take the video or audio signals and you put them into some piece of equipment, a piece of equipment that does something for you, and then you get the signal out. The kinds and variations of the processing that go on are myriad, so you usually term something like that a "black box" because you don't yet have a name for it. It may turn out to be an audio processor; it may turn out to be a video effects amplifier, it may turn out to be chroma-key or something like that, but while you're working on it, you just generally call it a "black box." Something goes in, and something comes out. Here we can differentiate between a systems engineer and a black-box engineer. A systems engineer takes already existing black boxes and hooks them up; a development engineer *makes* the black box if it isn't already available. It probably sounds more arcane than it really is.

In Technical Development, obviously, we got into areas to include studio design; in fact, we got into many, many other areas of development. I was fortunate to have two of the best NABET engineers in technical development, both very creative people, John Donahoe

and Tom Alfieri. They still work here. To give you an example of the kinds of things that were done, Ampex had developed the two-inch videotape machine back in '55. As things progressed, Ampex had converted the black-and-white tape machine to a color tape machine. To do this, special "black boxes" were involved because the stability of the tape machine has a lot to do with making color work on tape. As a consequence, there were quite a few "black boxes" that had to be designed, checked out, implemented. I was involved with that activity.

One of the most far-reaching achievements was when Sony came in with an early version of the 3/4-inch tape machine. One of our News people came back to us and complained bitterly that when you rewound the tape you couldn't see the picture. He indicated that it would be absolutely fantastic if it could work much more like a moviola machine, where, if you wanted to rewind the film, you could see the film going backwards or forwards at any speed and stop it wherever you wanted. The 3/4-inch Sony machine, because it was a segmented field recorder, was technically capable of doing this. However, Sony had not built the machine that way, and this was a problem.

I should explain that, unlike a segmented field machine, the original Ampex tape machine recorded 16 lines of television picture at a time, and if you stopped the tape all you would see is 16 lines which wouldn't make a picture. But the way the helical machines worked, they recorded a complete television field in one pass, so if you stopped the tape, you could really see that picture over and over again. Now the problem was that when Sony designed the machine, a helical type, they did a very good job, but one thing they didn't do; if you wanted to rewind the Sony or make it go forward fast, it would actually extract itself from the reading head, and you couldn't see a picture while it was rewinding. So I charged John Donahoe: "Here's a machine, do what you can. This is what News would like to have."

I think in approximately four to six weeks he had modified the machine, and in a very exotic way, and now we could push the buttons on the machine and watch the tape while it was going backwards or while it was going forward. The fascinating part about this was that I had shown it to the then General Sales

Manager for Sony, Dave MacDonald. He insisted that he bring Sony engineers over and show it to them. A troop of ten Japanese engineers came in, and while I couldn't understand what they were saying, the bottom line in English was: "You probably will destroy the tape if you do this." Our answer was that after the news story is on, the News Department doesn't really care whether the tape is destroyed. This is a functional thing that they need, it works, and until the tape breaks we're not going to worry about it. Well, it wasn't very long, I would say within a year, that there wasn't a Sony machine put out that didn't have that capability. There was later a patent issue on the subject, and it was John Donahoe's work that supported Sony in their claim that they had that particular capability. There isn't a machine today, even a home recorder, that doesn't have the freeze capability, and the fast forward and the fast reverse. That development was achieved right upstairs on our seventh floor, by John Donahoe, a NABET engineer.

That was the kind of work that we did. We solved problems in putting things together that weren't available in hardware off-the-shelf. I think our group did a very good job. I enjoyed it. I was proud of being Director of Technical Development. In 11 years, I had been around the world twice; I had purchased and introduced hardware in New York, in Burbank, at the Olympics site in Moscow, all of it state-of-the-art. Now I'm asked, wasn't it a long jump from that activity to take on the job of Chief Engineer of NBC's Satellite Network? I guess it was, but I didn't make the jump; I really was bumped.

I should mention that my job changed in 1981 to Director of Engineering Planning for Broadcast Operations. It was later, in 1984, that I became Chief Engineer, Satellite Network. And I've enjoyed every minute of my work with Jack Weir, Vice President, Technical Operations, and Don Kivell, Director of Broadcast Communications, both of whom had been studying satellite transmission possibilities a good while before I came along to offer some help in their studies and review. I suppose you could call it a fortunate mistake that I wound up with them.

Our program ratings were sliding downhill, and when Fred Silverman and Jane Pfeiffer took over the top slots at NBC, things really started to come apart.

And it wasn't just the cancellation of the Moscow Olympics. A lot of really good people at NBC were swept out by some of the new brooms, and oftentimes, some less competent people were put in their place. Eventually, my boss at the time, Frank Fleming, who was a fine executive, was let go as Vice President of Engineering after 11 years and replaced by an RCA engineer from the Princeton Laboratories. I worked under the new man for two years.

Finally, the Board of Directors of RCA made a very wise move and put Thornton Bradshaw in, and Bradshaw did what had to be done; he made changes, he turned the activities of RCA and the activities of NBC around. One of the most important was to appoint Grant Tinker, who does his job in a low-key way, and the results tell you how well he's done.

Eventually, the fellow who had come down from heaven (RCA) to be Vice President of Engineering left us. But I got caught in the grinder while he was still around and found myself out of the department as part of this wholesale clean sweep of the place. So I didn't jump into satellites; I happened to wind up, probably because I had many years in the company, being assigned to Jack Weir in Technical Operations. I joined not because they asked for me, it was just that I had to go someplace. Jack was then working with Don Kivell reviewing the potential advantages of satellite transmission, as compared to terrestrial transmission, because they had anticipated the difficulties that would occur when AT&T was divested. It was under Jack and with Don's guidance that I was able to aid their effort, having a technical background and an understanding of what was being offered by the world in the way of satellite transmission systems. I was another piece in the puzzle that Jack and Don were working on.

It was Kivell who took me on a whirlwind tour around the country to visit every vendor that possibly had anything to offer at all, so that I might evaluate and report on what the vendor really said. It fell right in line with my past experience. That's how I got into satellite, although I had done some satellite work in anticipation of the 1980 Olympics because the programming from Moscow would have come back via satellite.

Credit Grant Tinker, Ray Timothy and Mike Sherlock for some good top management decisions about satellites. They gave a clear direction to Jack Weir and his group that there was to be a real exploration, and that if there was anything to be gained by NBC in going into satellites, they would support the activity, and they did. The project was handled in what was, to me, a very unique way. Top management was fully involved; they set up a task force of knowledgeable, concerned people to investigate all avenues, such as legal, purchasing, engineering, operations, sales, affiliate relations. A dedicated group of about 12 people really did the logistical and technical studies.

To set up a network-wide distribution system, you set up one affiliate at a time. The first station was in El Paso, Texas, the second was in Quincy, Illinois. That was in late 1983. From there, we proceeded to set up 20 more stations, moved along, and now we're up to 169 stations. If you want to describe a "good" engineering project, the job is never really complete; it's 95% complete, under budget, and it works. That's where we are. The system continues to grow, and functionally, it is being given greater use by the people now operating it.

There is a close analogy between satellite operation and the microwaves we had been using through the 50's and 60's. Microwaves use basically the same range of frequencies, and we have been using parabolic dishes to transport microwave signals from point to point, maybe 30 miles in a typical case. Because of the curvature of the earth and because the microwave signal travels in a straight line, as you move away from a given point you are in a sense moving downhill, and so the range is limited. All that a satellite system is is a microwave relay.

The key technical achievement that was accomplished in the sixties was to be able to raise a satellite to an orbit where its rotational speed around the earth was equal to the speed of the rotation of the earth. In effect, it then stood still over the equator, so that an antenna could be pointed at one spot and hit the relay point.

Prior to that, satellites, working in lower orbits, had been rotating at speeds different from the earth, which meant constant moving of the antennas. The real breakthrough was when they achieved geo-stationary orbit. At 23,000 miles, this allowed the satellite to hold a fixed position so the parabolic dishes could be pointed at one spot. We microwave now in a straight line, through the atmosphere, which is only about 14 kilometers deep, then we're in free space, shooting in a straight line, right up to the satellite. The satellite turns the signal around and shoots it back down. That development makes television distribution, even telephone distribution, from satellites possible. To continue the analogy, think of having a 20-watt light bulb up there 23,000 miles high, and how bright the light signal might be when it reaches the earth—that's the reason why you need large dishes to collect enough of the signal so that you can recover it fully.

Some folks still ask why NBC's system operates on Ku-band and not C-band. Keep in mind that satellite transmission utilizes basically the same frequencies as microwave. The C-band is a frequency band which runs from four to six gigahertz or four to six billion cycles per second. Previous users of those frequencies already were in existence, licensed for terrestrial microwaves. This meant the C-band, which was the first to go into operation commercially, had one very significant problem. If you didn't locate the receiving antenna in a very secluded spot, then it might well be interfered with by the already existent terrestrial users of the same frequency. That danger of interference would be the reason for locating the antennas great distances from cities, away from microwaves, putting them out in the boondocks.

With conspicuously good judgment, the FCC decided that a new band would be assigned for satellite transmission, the Ku-band, which operates from 12 to

14 billion cycles per second. There had been few if any previous users of that band, and the Commission limited the use of those frequencies to satellites only, to ensure that there would be no terrestrial causes of interference. That meant that we could locate our antennas, hopefully if the physical room was there, on the studio sites of our affiliates. This was very fortunate technically, because if you want to deliver more than one signal, and had to locate the antennas *off* premise, then you'd be forced to microwave them back to the studios. That could have involved lots more money, or another potential operator in the system, which we didn't want.

Of the 169 stations that we now have in operation, only three are not co-located. There was one particular concern we had to consider in looking at the Ku-band. You're aware that as the frequency of a signal gets higher and higher, it begins to behave more and more like light. If you get up to the light frequencies, and a cloud comes by, you're going to have a shadow. At the Ku-band, 12 to 14 gigahertz, normally clouds don't bother you too much. But if liquid water forms in the air, then those radio signals get absorbed by the liquid raindrops, and in very heavy rain the signal will be attenuated. That was the negative feature about Ku-band, all other features being positive. These technical reviews that we went through all over the country put in perspective the balance between the co-location and the attenuation problem due to rain. Eventually, we decided that, if we built the system correctly, we could tolerate the attenuation from rain, and the benefits to be gained by using those frequencies so far outweighed the choice of C-band that it was no contest. It wasn't C-band or Ku-band; it was Ku-band or nothing.

In my 38 years as a member of the RCA family, 33 with NBC, the best engineering job I've ever been involved in, barring none, is the satellite project. It hasn't always been fun. There is absolutely no question that the scope, the magnitude, the importance of the individual decisions, the conduct of the job, the people I worked with, made it the best job.

There have been a lot of funny happenings along the way. One in particular I remember. As part of my job in Engineering, we had designed mobile units which had been sent out to cover the first Super Bowl game in California. Perhaps you remember how unusual that coverage was: *two* networks carried the game, CBS and NBC. CBS supplied the cameras, and they had their own mobile truck just as we had our mobile truck, and we took a bridge off their camera feed.

I was sitting at home that Sunday, and I got a call from Bob Galvin, also in New York. He said, "Bob, we've got trouble in California." I asked how I could help. He said, "Here's a telephone number, call Warren Phillips, the technical supervisor at the Super Bowl game, and find out what you can do for him." So I called Warren, who said, "*Nothing* works." I said, "Nothing works! What time is air?" He said, "Twenty minutes." I said, "When did it stop?" He said, "About 40 minutes ago." I said, "Was it working this morning? Was it working yesterday?" He said, "Yes, but nothing works now." And I said, "Let me speak to your maintenance man." He put the maintenance man on the phone. I said, "Tell me, what were you doing 40 minutes ago? Give it to me step by step." He gave it to me step by step. I said, "Now I'm going to give *you* step one, and I'm going to tell you what to do. You do it, and then you come back to the phone and I'll give you step two."

So I told him what to do, he handed the phone to Warren, and Warren asked, "What did you tell him to do?" I said, "I told him to do step one." After a short delay, Warren said, "*Everything* is working." I said, "Thank God, I didn't know what step two was." Then Warren, being the polished operator that he was, said, "Okay Bob, hang on to the phone." I said, "Wait a minute! This is a long distance call from my home to California." He replied, "I don't care. You don't think that I'm going to sit out here *alone*." I sat there in my bathrobe watching the first Super Bowl game with a phone in my hand.

In addition to some good laughs now and then, I've met some very good people, both union people and management people. Most of the people who work for NBC earn their money. In addition to mentors like Whitney Baston, there was Noah Sprecher, many, many other good people including Steve Paganuzzi, Dick Edmondson, Jack Kennedy, Reggie Thomas, Bill Trevarthen and Frank Fleming. In recent years, I think the person who has impressed me the most is Ray Timothy because, in the satellite project, he was, from the beginning, the top man under Tinker to get the job done. Never having had much direct contact with top management, I was surprised to find out how bright and intelligent they were.

With NBC celebrating its 60th anniversary in 1986, I wish everyone who works here well.

November 12, 1985

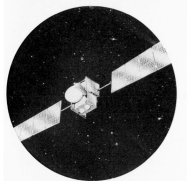

Don Durgin began his NBC career in National Spot Sales and rose to be President of the Television Network in 1966. He is widely admired as the peerless, superb presenter in the business, blessed with the wonderful gift of mimicry.

Don Durgin

"The Standard Brands people were our guests in Bob Sarnoff's dining room.... As dessert was being served, Gus, the phlegmatic Danish butler, as he came through the door, said simply, 'The President has been shot.' Julian Goodman said, 'Gus, what did you say?'..., 'Mr. Goodman... we heard on the radio....' Julian turned on the TV set...a newsman was announcing the report. Julian shot out of the room. Chet Huntley sat there stunned.... That weekend, Kintner, watching with his news obsession...said, 'When they transfer Oswald...I want us to be there.' NBC was the only network to catch Ruby shooting Oswald."

I was born in Chicago in 1924 and was sent to school in the East. While I was at Princeton, World War II erupted; I left college to become a B-17 bombardier in the 8th Air Force. I returned to Princeton. Although I was to get an A.B. in history (*summa cum laude*), what was to be invaluable were my extra-curricular activities: cast lead in the Triangle Club touring musical show, Editorial Editor of the *Daily Princetonian*, and active on the college radio station, WPRU. I realized then that I wanted to be in communications or show business. Everybody else wanted to work for a bank or for *Time* magazine.

I went to work in the mailroom of Foote, Cone & Belding. (Another mailroom trainee was Carl Lindemann, later to be President of NBC Sports.) I graduated to junior account executive on Pall Mall—"famous cigarettes, outstanding, and, they are mild." And "The Big Story." One day, the agency lost the American Tobacco business, and all the trainees and junior juniors were fired. I knew exactly where I wanted to go—NBC—because I had loved the weekly commercial rehearsals for "The Big Story" in the NBC radio studios at 30 Rockefeller Plaza. Doris Ann (then in Personnel and later head of NBC's religious programs) told me, "You're *just* the kind of young man that we are looking for, but we don't have any openings right now. If we do, I will send you a postcard." In other words, "Don't call us, we'll call you."

Three weeks later I got a postcard. Jacob Evans, Manager of National Spot Sales, Advertising and Sales Presentations, said he would like to hire me, but he had noted that I was seeking employment at $3,900 a year—$75 a week, more than I made at Foote, Cone. This was 1949. I wanted to work for NBC even if it meant a big salary cut, which I could ill afford. Would it be all right, said Jake Evans, if I got paid $4,500 instead of $3,900, because the lowest labor grade for this job paid the minimum salary of $4,500? I knew from that moment that I *loved* NBC.

National Spot Sales, part of the Owned Stations Division, was then managed by a legendary man who had much to do with setting all of NBC's rate cards and station break policy, James V. McConnell (no relation to Joe McConnell, President of NBC in the 50's). I wrote presentations to interest advertisers in buying spots on NBC's O&O stations. Before the FCC forbade it, NBC Spot Sales also represented stations that we did not own, to wit, General Electric's WGY and WRGB.

Two years later, in 1951, being young, unmarried and unafraid, I quit NBC in a pique to go to ABC. Jake Evans was promoted to Network Advertising Manager, and I didn't get his job. Jim Gaines, head of O&O Spot Sales, told me that I was too young and too inexperienced. A man from Macy's department store was hired to lure retailers into television. He didn't know *anything* about television.

The first week at ABC, we were told that our paychecks would be held over until the following week because Leonard Goldenson and United Paramount Theatres had just announced their intention to buy ABC, owned by Edward J. Noble, head of Lifesavers. ABC had just started to go into television. (Noble had bought the Blue Network personally for $8 million from NBC in 1943. ABC was recently sold for $3 billion to Capital Cities.) In any event, Mr. Noble had to take out a $1 million personal note for our salaries over the next several months because ABC could not borrow money during the negotiations.

I stayed at ABC for five years. I wasn't sure that broadcasting was for me, and I had done well in college, and I missed the intellectual stimulus. I applied to Yale, Harvard, Columbia, and NYU law schools and was accepted every place, but NYU was the only school with night classes, so I went there. I barely graduated. However, having those law books on my office bookshelf was worth the effort. Those books said, "This guy is not some sales guy up from stickball, he's a *lawyer*." I never took the bar exam because I wanted to stay in broadcasting, but more to the point, I would have flunked it.

Early in my ABC days, we were about to lose to NBC the renewal of one of network TV's earliest programs, the "Hollywood Ironite Theatre," sponsored by the Ironite Company in Michigan. The presentation got the renewal and brought me to the attention of the President of ABC, Robert E. Kintner, later to become President of NBC. Kintner was like a father to me (I'd lost my own father at age 14). He taught me everything I knew about the business, and his knowledge was considerable. He taught me how to sell television, how to reach particular people, what those people reacted to, and what they were like. He and I went around the country presenting ABC programs to advertisers and their agencies. On the Twentieth-Century Limited. On every kind of propeller-driven airplane. We visited every advertiser's office of any size, because most of the programs were advertiser-controlled then. For a young man to meet the chairmen of the biggest companies in America week after week was a heady experience.

The climax for me was the day Kintner said, "Look, Charlie Ayers (a laconic man who was a super radio salesman), is leaving us to become the head of the NBC Radio Network. I would like you to take his job. I don't want to hurry you, but I need your answer in an hour and a half because I want to announce it to the press so that we'll have an image of moving quickly. What do you know about a balance sheet?" At 32, Vice President in charge of the ABC Radio Network! I said, "Mr. Kintner, all I've ever done is *spend* the company's money on presentations and research, nothing on the income side." He said he'd assign a budget officer to the division. I wasn't married, and I certainly didn't have to ask my mother. I said, "Fine."

Bob Kintner was, by most people's account, although tragically flawed, the most brilliant broadcaster of his time. His greatest strength was in adversity: when the ratings were low, the resources scant, the possibilities slight, he could overcome incredible obstacles to make a sale or get a valuable program. If you worked for him, he demanded all of your time. It was not unusual to stay up all night writing a presentation, shaving, and giving the presentation the next morning. It wasn't that he expected that. All he expected was that the presentation be perfect, and for me it took that effort.

People were afraid of him, but I never was and always told him exactly what I thought. Many fudged, and he had an unerring sense when somebody was bluffing. He was amused when he found out that I imitated him before other associates. When there was acrimony or we were vamping in a meeting, he would turn to my associates and say, "Do me." Not easy! When the General (Sarnoff) asked Kintner to be President of the NBC Television Network, he was delighted, because Leonard Goldenson had just fired him. Leonard wanted to be a hands-on broadcasting executive, and he knew that Kintner wouldn't relinquish

power. A year later, Kintner asked if I would like to come over to NBC as Vice President in charge of TV Sales Planning. I jumped at the chance—it didn't take much brains to know television's potential.

When I came back to NBC in 1957 at Kintner's invitation, Pat Weaver, the graceful, witty, handsome, attractive visionary, had departed. Weaver's people regarded him as a Messiah, a brilliant creative person, confident of what the present and the future of television might be—the window of the world. An ugly man with a tough, brusque manner replaced him. It was a culture shock for the company. Kintner was a demanding businessman, used to operating with reduced budgets, limited resources, not afraid to cost-cut, not afraid to fire executives. He many times was as wrong as he was right—but never in doubt.

What Kintner realized was that CBS was the clear leader. NBC was always second, but CBS and NBC had a hegemony. ABC was so far down that, as Brinkley and others joked, if you wanted to end the Vietnam war, put it on ABC and it would be over in 13 weeks. Kintner decided to build up NBC News, specifically the nightly news. News grew to a thousand people, the "largest news-gathering service in the free world." Huntley-Brinkley in the late fifties made it Number One.

After rejoining NBC, I was in the presentation job for about a year and a half, reporting to Walter Scott. Walter came to have a more profound influence professionally on my life, my personal values, than Mr. (I always called him Mr.) Kintner had. Walter Scott was totally different, detached, quiet, almost so reserved that many couldn't believe that he was head of sales, until they realized his superb grasp of that field. Bob Kintner realized that and quickly promoted Walter to Vice President of Sales. Walter then appointed me, after about a year, Vice President and National Sales Manager, even though I had never been a salesman or a sales manager. A year later, in '59, nicely timed to when I got married at the ripe old age of 35, I became Vice President of Sales and was that until '65. In '66 I became President of the Television Network.

In those days advertisers needed the medium more than the medium needed them. Walter would get orders for a weekly half hour, or an every-other-week half hour (two minutes one week, one minute the next week) full sponsorship from the blue-chip 500 companies of America. He'd say to Joe Iaricci, head of sales administration and me, "Reject this and thank them for the letter." It was like the Chanel perfume manager saying to Saks, give them only 50% of their Christmas order. He knew the leading agencies and the leading advertisers; what they wanted and what they would accept as reasonable, and whom he could move.

Kintner dared to move time periods around. Kintner had no regard for any of the written or unwritten rules, so Walter and I had to execute unbelievable moves. Loyal sponsors felt that they owned their time period—it was called a "customer position," which had no legal force of an option. Never again would there be a period like this. The industry was dominated by powerful, colorful advertising agency television heads and by advertisers. It was a people business, and Walter was absolutely without parallel in handling those people. He was the opposite of the back-slapping, walk-through-brick-walls, extroverted salesman; he seemed more like a banker.

Example: Ed Cole, head of the Chevrolet division, liked to watch action-adventure programs, particularly Westerns. He saw a new program called "Bonanza" on Saturday night, 7:30 to 8:30. He called up Tom Adams of the Campbell Ewald agency and said, "We've stayed with Dinah Shore long enough, maybe we can get her for specials; you work out whatever she wants, but I want 'Bonanza,' and we'll take all of it, Sunday, 9 to 10." So Tom Adams calls, "Are we set for 'Bonanza?' Walter says, "Well, Tom, it might be a little difficult because we have sold 'Bonanza' to American Tobacco and RCA." Kintner immediately saw the program strength of Mr. Cole's demand. Other people thought he was just craven and would do anything General Motors said. But Kintner knew that if we had a hit show on Saturday night with no one watching it, all we had to do was to move it to Sunday nights, and we'd kill 'em. It was a 10

stroke. He told Walter to stay calm. Fortunately, RCA was one of the sponsors of "Bonanza." We went up to the 53rd floor, lay on the rug, and, with a straight face, told RCA it was good for the corporation to relinquish the program.

Walter and I walked into the board room of American Tobacco to face Paul Hahn, President of American Tobacco, a smart lawyer, his company officials and agency people—our former friends. They resembled a firing squad. They kept battering away, and Walter kept saying, "Paul, I recognize the difficulty in this situation for you as well as for us. It is quite true that you have a customer position. As I have told you, and I mean this sincerely, I convey this from Bob Kintner, who respects you greatly, we are going to make this up to you in terms of whatnot. But you do not have an option." And, boy, General Motors never tired of reminding us, some $38 million later, of *their* time period! Paul didn't want to lose "Bonanza." Walter kept saying the same thing about nine different ways, and always perfectly. And so we accomplished these incredible moves. Within three weeks, "Bonanza" was the Number One show in America. Kintner was a hero, Ed Cole was a hero. (He became President of General Motors.) It made our whole Sunday night impregnable.

Walter is a very organized, very positive, very disciplined man, and he knows the difference between right and wrong. He's so smart! An undervalued man. Many of us who worked at NBC were buoyed by the headiness of the business, and by the tremendous deference that agency people and advertisers showed us. When I was first promoted, Walter said, "Don, remember in your own interest, as well as in the company's, that you only wear the NBC uniform. Without the NBC uniform, these agency guys and others wouldn't pay much attention to you." Walter was one of the reasons that NBC was thought of as a first-class operation. RCA, to the General's great credit and to Bob Sarnoff's, wasn't looking to be Number One in the ratings at the sacrifice of quality.

In December, 1965, Bob Sarnoff called David Adams, Julian Goodman, Walter Scott and me into his office and said, "We're going to have a reorganization. Bob Kintner has resigned from the company, and Walter, you're going to be Chairman and Chief Executive; Julian, you're going to be President. David will continue as Executive Vice President. Don, you're going to be President of the Television Network." Overnight, I was going to be President of the Television Network!

Cigarette ads were a very important part of the schedule. The Tobacco Council brought up questions about the Surgeon General's warning that had to be shown in the advertising. Finally, Phillip Morris took the bold position to drop television advertising provided no other tobacco company could be on television, because they could save so much money, and warnings would be less visible in other media. Liggett & Myers and the others wanted television. When the ban on cigarette advertising on TV came down, it was about 9% of our overall schedule, but in prime time it was more like 17%! The cigarette companies bought time first because there was product protection of at least 10 minutes, and spot adjacencies had to respect the network. Hard to believe this with competitors virtually back-to-back in commercials today.

With the tobacco companies, we'd start a stampede much the way networks start a stampede for the limited product categories today in the Olympics. They'd fall all over themselves to pay the top dollar to get the show they wanted. In terms of profitability, tobacco was more like 21% in prime time. We thought the ban was devastating. CBS panicked. CBS's head of sales, a nut, persuaded his management, at the very time all of us were mortally struck with the defection of cigarettes, to lower the basis of sale from 60-second units to 30-second units. That nut's stroke of genius unlocked smaller advertisers we didn't know existed who could now afford network TV. The debacle ultimately turned into a bonanza.

CBS always set their new season's schedule first, and then NBC and ABC would counter-program. NBC's network group—Mort Werner as Program Head; Grant Tinker as the VP, Programs; Paul Klein and Bill Rubens (research); Jack Otter (sales); Herb Schlosser (program

negotiator); Bob Stone, the General Manager of the Television Network (business affairs, operations and engineering)—all of us would thrash and thrash around the program-schedule magnetic board. Once arrived at a schedule, we'd bring in Station Relations—Don Mercer, Ray O'Connell and others—to see if the schedule would fly with the affiliates.

One of the time-honored concepts of broadcasting was: never take talent to a presentation. I personally spent three weeks pumping up Richard Boone—who was not only a man of a thousand faces, but the man of a thousand drinks—to describe his new show in no more than 10 minutes to the Reynolds Metals brothers and the Reynolds board in Richmond, Virginia. (We were *somewhat* suspect because years earlier NBC, with the William Morris Agency, brought a Mickey Rooney situation comedy to the Reynolds brothers. The whole joke turned on Mickey being 4'11" and sort of a midget. The Reynolds brothers didn't laugh once, since not one of the brothers stood much over 5 feet!) Before the Reynolds board on that fateful day, Boone described the concept of the show eloquently (in less than eight minutes!). David Reynolds said, "Before you leave here, we're going to work out a way for Reynolds Metals to sponsor all of 'The Richard Boone Show'—one hour every week, even though my brothers and Joe McConnell (former President of NBC and then general counsel of Reynolds Metals) don't want anything from NBC."

I went to Walter Scott, keeper of the rate card and conscience: "Walter, if we do something about daytime for Reynolds Wrap, we can get the *full* hour. Walter said, "Don, I know you will find a way to work it out." That was code for saying, "I don't want to know about it." We got the order.

One of the most colorful scheduling crises we had was when Mr. Kintner sold R.J. Reynolds 9:30 to 10 p.m. on Tuesday. "The Kaiser Aluminum Hour" had long been the occupant of 9:30 to 10:30 p.m. on Tuesdays, and we had to tell Young & Rubicam (Kaiser's agency) that their hour had to move to 10 to 11 p.m. Y&R was rightfully afraid of losing Kaiser. Walter was calm throughout, but Kintner was going crazy.

About 4 p.m. one afternoon, Mort Werner and I were called up to Bob Sarnoff's office. Bob said, "Mort, Don, I want you to go out to Hawaii tonight (no jet planes then) and do a presentation to Henry Kaiser for the 10 to 11 p.m. period." "Tonight? Y&R has already turned us down and they'll hand us our heads." Sarnoff said, "Mort knows Kaiser, and you'll find a way of telling him." Mort said, "It's only a television show." Bob exploded: "We've got to do something; we're third in the time period and CBS is announcing their schedule.…"

In Hawaii, Mort said, "Mr. Kaiser will meet us at the airport, put a lei over our necks, and take us to his home." He did just that. Next morning, as I was about to make the presentation to the old man (in his Hawaiian shirt, barely able to sit behind his desk with his enormous belly), the old man said, "Young man, I know they wouldn't have sent you out all this distance unless what you have in there is very persuasive, and, after all, you know this business cold, and I don't, and I'm *prepared* to accept what's in that case. Before you open it, I just want to ask you one question. You want us to move to 10 to 11 p.m. on Tuesdays; we're in 9:30 to 10:30 p.m. Let me make it simple, I believe you wouldn't be here unless 10 to 11 is better for us, and I'm sure you believe so. Because you know more about it, and you strike me as an honest fellow, and I've known Mort for years, and the integrity of NBC, I just want to ask you, do I have a choice?"

I said, "Mr. Kaiser, I wish you wouldn't put it that way." He said, "I *know* you wish I wouldn't put it that way, because I *don't* have a choice, and you're going to tell me that I have to take10 to 11. I will see to it that Kintner will rue the day! Forgive me, I shouldn't take this out on you; you're in an impossible position, but I ask you once again." I said, "Mr. Kaiser, let me put it this way, you have a *lot* of choices."

About halfway through the presentation in Mr. Kaiser's office at his newly completed Hawaiian Village Hotel, of which he was immensely proud, it started to rain outside. Leaks developed in the ceiling. Drops started bouncing off Kaiser's bald pate; Mr. Kaiser didn't move; the sycophants around the table looked as if nothing was happening; Mort looked inscrutable; and I seemed to be the only person noticing the water. Some secretaries rushed in to place waste baskets under the leaks, and Kaiser just sat there. The green line on my chart melded with the blue and the red lines.

I thought I was hallucinating as the water poured down, until Mort said, "You know, Henry, I can now understand why so many of those Liberty ships that you built during World War II broke apart in the sea." I thought, Mort has gone crazy! We'd better head for the hills. Suddenly the large belly began to shake like Sidney Greenstreet's, and Kaiser began roaring with laughter. As we left, he said, "No respectable boss would send a fine young man like you out on a goddamn imbecile mission like this; that is unconscionable, dishonest!" He was so mad that he told Y&R he wanted to get even with Kintner by sponsoring something opposite NBC. Something so strong that it would bring Kintner down and make him rue the day. He liked Jim Garner in "Maverick," even though it was far different from the hour of fine drama he had been sponsoring, and he bought it. "Maverick" became Number One—on ABC.

In its day, "I Spy" with Bob Culp and Bill Cosby was a breakthrough, teaming a black and a white man in an action-adventure series. However, the real breakthrough, and we got credit for it, was "Julia," which Mort had recommended. Here was a black, single parent trying to raise a child and hold a responsible job. Diahann Carroll, a sexy singer, played "Julia." When she came to the affiliates' meeting, Mort told the William Morris guys, Lou Weiss and Sammy Weisbord, "Goddamn it! Bring her out in a pleated skirt with white gloves and a purse and a hat (genteel and lady-like)!" Boy, she was peaches and cream. General Foods thought it was the greatest thing we ever did. In retrospect, it was a whitey-type black show, but sincerely done.

A very important change happened in the 60's: the implacable dominance of film over live; it took the birthright of television, which had been predominantly live, from the creative control of the broadcaster to the control of the film maker. Film was a different culture. Story telling on film was, by definition, formula, emotional, shortcuts, and emphasis in quality of production, but not necessarily in quality of content. TV became slicker and slicker with the production techniques of film. The three-camera sitcoms permitted the cutting and editing to get laughs in a different way. The short form gave way to the long form—from half hour to one hour to one-and-a-half hours, and then two-hour made-for-television movies. Movie nights became fixtures on all three network schedules. Increasingly, the so-called "World Premiere" television movies scored impressive ratings.

We thought Lew Wasserman, head of Universal (MCA), was trying to con us with made-for-TV movies instead of offering us good theatrical releases. Little did we imagine that the "made-for-television movie" would outrate the bigger movies that we paid a lot of money for. Lew Wasserman was a street fighter. He had a big advantage. We had to go back for big, big commitments on movies to our management, whereas Wasserman would sit there with nothing in his pocket except a white handkerchief and make decisions. He was a superb tactician, he controlled his company, and he would reveal or represent only what he had to disclose legally. I'd never seen brilliance like his. If you had the upper hand (and he deduced that long before you did) he would be charming to the point of obsequiousness; but if he had the upper hand, he would act arrogantly, brutally. Lew never talked in terms of shows, but rather hours of production. The shows were like salami to him. If you didn't like this, try that.

Walter Scott was an absolute enigma to the Hollywood producers because they couldn't believe that this controlled, nice man was chairman of NBC. Incidentally, Lew would alert Universal when Walter or any network biggie was coming out to "dress the party"—shorthand for gorgeous starlets and their handsome "dates," all under contract. Walter, Julian and I made two deals in about eight months' time: we gave Lew Wasserman $100 million for the privilege of running his pictures on the network and then handing them back, and we paid Arthur Krim and Bob Benjamin (then United Artists) $110 million for the same privilege. We found out, as we did with Walt Disney Prodctions, that we could have bought United Artists for less money than we gave them to rent their features. Julian wanted us to negotiate to buy Disney, but the anti-trust lawyers said no.

One day, Bob Sarnoff said to Walter, "Charles Bluhdorn has just taken over Paramount Pictures. (Bluhdorn, chief executive of Gulf & Western, had, at age 27, cornered for a brief period the world coffee market.) I'd like Durgin to talk to Bluhdorn and Marty Davis of Paramount." Mr. Bluhdorn invited me to lunch. Widely separated front teeth, hair parted in the middle, a wild look and accent. It was *not* the NBC dining room. A man in a soiled white coat served salami sandwiches on Bluhdorn's desk. Bluhdorn said, "Now let me tell you

something, Mr. Don Durgin, that you can tell Mr. Walter Scott: you're not going to get any locomotives without a lot of box cars, if you get my meaning." Don't try to get a blockbuster without taking "Myrtle Went to War" and a lot of other films. He ranted and raved, using unbelievable language. No wonder the guys in the movie business have male secretaries.

Walter was so intelligent he thought losing one's temper was a waste of time. But about every six months or so, Walter would, in his quiet, meticulous way, say, "Herb, Grant, Don, I want you to go over and tell these *goddamn sons of bitches...*" That had impact. We'd bolt out of the room as if we'd been shot from cannons. He was no fool. We always pleaded, "Walter, these studio guys are *thieves.* If we give them this money...." He'd answer, "In the end, we will pay twice as much." He really was like a chess player; he plotted the moves. He was trusted by everybody because they knew that if Walter told them something, it was absolutely true without any spin on the ball.

Scott had more mental courage than I've ever seen. When Kintner or Bobby sent him on those missions where the time had already been sold twice, or a relationship that had gone on for years had to be abrogated overnight, Walter would unflinchingly walk into the board rooms, lay the cards on the table and outline the problem, but always maintain the NBC position like a military field commander. His was a great example to me—to realize that honesty and intelligence could overcome chicanery, and all the other trickery of the business. And triumph. His adversaries often said they wished he was on their side. Walter never underestimated the essential power and strength of the simple letters "NBC," and he represented us in a way that did the whole place proud.

David Adams was a very powerful, modest, albeit disingenuous figure because he had bridged so many administrations, was close to the Sarnoffs, and seemingly had no personal ambitions. A brilliant man, he would listen to an hour's ramblings on different issues in a meeting and then quietly say: "I think these are the points that have been developed, and while I should be the last to express any opinion, I think the issues are these, and I really think that among the four alternatives, there are probably only these two that are really actionable. I don't mean to short-circuit the process that we've all gone through; however, of the two, each has clear advantages and disadvantages, but on balance it would seem to me that alternative 'a' is the one that may expose us to the least trouble and risk, and the one from which we can really expect the most gain."

The Friday JFK was assassinated in 1963, the Standard Brands people were our guests in Bob Sarnoff's executive dining room, along with Chet Huntley and several executives from the J. Walter Thompson advertising agency. Attending for NBC were Tom McAvity, Julian Goodman, then NBC News Executive Vice President, and me, then head of Sales. Planter's Peanuts (Standard Brands) was an advertiser on the "Huntley-Brinkley Report," which they were about to renew. As dessert was being served, Gus, the phlegmatic Danish butler, as he came through the swinging door, said simply, "The President has been shot," to no one in particular. Julian Goodman said, "Gus, what did you say?" Gus said, "Mr. Goodman, the President has been shot. We heard on the radio in the kitchen." Julian turned on the TV set in the dining room and there was a newsman announcing the initial AP report. Julian shot out of the room. Chet sat there stunned until an NBC page came for him within minutes. Over that weekend, Kintner, watching with his news obsession, much to McAndrew's and Goodman's annoyance, said, "When they transfer Oswald to the Dallas prison, I want us to be there." NBC was the only network to catch the Ruby shooting of Lee Harvey Oswald.

In the 70's, President Nixon met with the heads of the networks. When it was NBC's turn, Julian Goodman, Walter Scott, David Adams, Tom Ervin (our general counsel), Reuven Frank, and me, President of NBC-TV, went to the White House Oval Office. The infamous Chuck Colson was to my right and Ron Ziegler, Nixon's press secretary, was to my left. The President said, "Well, Julian, it's nice to see you down here. Is there anything that is particularly troublesome to you in the government process that you would care to talk about because, you know, sometimes we never know all the things that are going on, and broadcasting is such a vital enterprise in the United States."

Julian immediately put the ball in play, saying "Well, Mr. President, we're generally able to get along all right. But we are quite concerned about the Federal Trade

Commission inquiry into the pricing practices of the networks and requiring documentation of all our contracts, all our pricing." With that, the President turned to Chuck Colson, "Chuck, under what House or Senate bill did this inquiry arise?" Colson said, "Mr. President, this is not a matter from Congress at all, it was initiated by the FTC." Nixon went on at length and ended with the statement that the FTC was more supportive of business than it was anti-business. Nixon added, "Now, of course, I'm accused often of being too pro-business—for you in this room, the fact is that I am. There's a point at which government asks for too much. It is a free marketplace, and it doesn't worry me. I think these advertisers are big enough boys to take care of themselves. And you fellows are pretty fair. I think the FTC is a little excessive. I'm glad you mentioned it, Julian. Chuck, make a note of this, and we'll take care of it."

I couldn't believe what I heard—after the carloads of documents we had to supply, the heavy-handed hearings. "Okay, Chuck, we'll take care of it." And I thought, this is the way it's really done. On our way from the Oval Office to the President's office in the Old Senate Building, we couldn't say anything, but like trusties in prison who speak without moving their lips, I said to Ervin, "What's this with the FTC? 'Okay Chuck, we'll take care of it.'" Tom, in his wonderful way, said, "Don, you didn't buy any of that did you? You graduated from that night law school didn't you? The FTC is an administrative agency, the President can't stop it. What you heard was all baloney."

Many other things were discussed, and then Mr. Nixon said, "By the way, Julian, you don't let Spiro Agnew's speeches against the networks bother you too much?" Julian looked at Nixon and said, "No, it doesn't bother us too much, Mr. President. We don't like it, but it won't curtail our activities. I realize Mr. Agnew is making the speeches, but, on the other hand, Mr. President, you do nothing to gainsay him." A great moment to see. It came quickly, it passed quickly, but a nerve was struck there. Nixon's face and ears became very red.

Nixon went on to talk about the liberal slant of newsmen. The clear implication was that NBC wasn't addressing the balance. Before that, Clay Whitehead, his telecommunications man, had come in to NBC to complain about the smaller number of originals and repeats the networks were putting on, and pointedly referred to the vulnerability of station licenses.

Nixon then asked how much lead time NBC would need to cover a very important foreign trip. Reuven Frank explained, and then the President asked Colson if there had been any problem with leaks by network newsmen. Ziegler said no. *Now* we're interested, and Julian and Reuven asked for appropriate information, which Nixon said he couldn't give us for a matter of weeks. It turned out to be the historic China trip.

One of the most harrowing and amusing aspects of heading the network was resolving disputes with major talent. The sessions with Bob Hope were always memorable. He would open the door at his suite in the Waldorf Towers with golf tees spilling out of his pocket as he stooped to pick up the morning paper on the rug. He had a disarming way of reopening terms of the contract he had just signed. When I would tell him that Chrysler wouldn't renew if he held to the outrageous price increases on his specials, he would say, "You're probably right, but I've never failed to get the increase I wanted in the past despite the same kind of advice and prediction you are giving me now." Of course, Chrysler renewed, and at Bob's price.

Johnny Carson was a formidable negotiator, because he had a formidable weapon: he'd walk off the show. He resented censorship of any kind and his writers were always trying to put one or two over every night on NBC Broadcast Standards, who kept saying NBC is a *family* medium. Johnny was so wrought up over the continuing hassles that he

suggested that the renewal contract specify that in case of unresolvable differences, the final decision be left to me. This seemed to be a victory, but Johnny was shrewd enough to know that by establishing a "summit" procedure he would probably get more calls his way from me than he would from the professionals who had to do battle with him every day.

One of the fun aspects of the Carson relationship was the annual Christmas luncheon in the NBC executive dining room, where we would present him with a previously negotiated "gift." He would accept the box of James Robinson silverware as if he had no idea of what was inside.

Walt Disney was a wonderful man. Very smart and very determined. I had the thankless task of flying out to see him one day to try to make him understand why we couldn't run a Disney feature because Merlin the Monkey, who was the star, hypnotized a few people in some of the comic sequences. It seems that the National Association of Broadcasters Code proscribed hypnotism of any sort in programs because of the possible harmful effect on children who might become hypnotized themselves or, worse, try to hypnotize other kids. To Walt Disney this was all nonsense. He put his arm on my shoulder and said: "You have one of the toughest jobs in America. You know that Merlin is harmless. I would be able to produce more psychologists and expert witnesses than you could any day, but really, someone in New York should have more sense than this. Why don't you go back and run the picture anyway and trust your own intelligence. And thank you for your courtesy in coming out to see me. Good luck." Back in New York, after thinking about the NBC/Disney relationship for a few hours, we decided to trust our intelligence and let Merlin hypnotize as many Nielsen homes as he possibly could.

In the early 70's, RCA was reasonably happy with NBC's performance, but ABC had become much more of a force, as they had gotten more affiliates and achieved parity or near-parity with flamboyance and program savvy. We were losing affiliates; our programming was not as strong as it should be, and ABC was getting very big numbers in the cities. Wall Street was beginning to do invidious comparisons on network performance. RCA was having problems of its own, and it was decided that NBC's profit contribution (always the biggest of any RCA subsidiary) should be X plus a lot more than it was.

In the midst of NBC's declining fortunes came bigger trouble at the top in RCA. Bob Sarnoff resigned as CEO to be replaced by Andy Conrad and then by Ed Griffiths. Griffiths saw his mission as getting a top programmer to head NBC. Enter Fred Silverman.

Under Walter Scott and Julian Goodman we created a climate: people were proud of their company, they liked to come to work and weren't afraid of being fired. That same climate has been created anew by Grant Tinker, as it was by Thornton Bradshaw at RCA. What Grant did was to say to everybody, let's go back to work.

As rewarding as any of the sales or talent relationships in my years at NBC were the deep friendships established with affiliates and their families. Especially the affiliates we got to know the best who served on the affiliate advisory boards. The chairmen of these boards during my tenure have become lifelong friends: Jack Harris, Louis Read, Hod Grams, Bob Ferguson. And Fred Paxton, Ancil Payne, Wilson Wearn. They are great broadcasters and leaders in their communities. Equally important: they like to play golf!

After leaving NBC in 1975 to become President of McCaffrey & McCall advertising agency for two years, I moved to Dun & Bradstreet as a Group Executive Vice President with responsibility for three D&B companies. One was Corinthian Broadcasting, which owned five CBS affiliates and one ABC affiliate—since sold to A.H. Belo. Now Vice President, Marketing Services, I've been at The Dun & Bradstreet Corporation for 10 happy years. The fun of 20 years at NBC is still vivid in memory, and the NBC people still as interesting, vibrant and engaging as ever.

My birthday wish to NBC is never to allow the pressures of marketplace, competition, technology, or changing patterns of the industry to overwhelm the goal of providing the balanced program and public service that has characterized NBC's operation from the beginning, and for each decade throughout its proud history. Maintenance of this NBC tradition not only assures NBC's continuing leadership, but also that of the nation's broadcasting service, which remains the envy of the world.

October 31, 1985

Robert J. Galvin joined NBC in 1946 as a Studio/Field Engineer and rose to the rank of Vice President, Production Operations Planning, Operations and Technical Services, in 1983.

"I was interviewed by Doris Ann in Personnel in October 1946. At that time, no one understood television...Radio was king, and all the experimenters, the neophytes, were assigned to television so they wouldn't hurt the company product."

I grew up in Hempstead, Long Island, New York, and I took engineering courses at the University of Dayton for a year before joining the Navy Officer Candidate Program, a V-12 program. They laughingly gave you a choice and asked where you would like to go to school. I said Columbia, so I ended up at the University of Illinois, which turned out to be great for me. I got my B.S. in Electrical Engineering there and went to Midshipman school at Notre Dame. After another year and a half in the Navy, I was mustered out.

I had a job in the Navy research and development facility at Port Washington for a couple of months, and a school friend's father, Jack Flynn, Chief Engineer of NBC's Port Washington transmitter, arranged an interview at NBC with Doris Ann in Personnel in October 1946. At that time, no one understood television; radio was the big field. Doris Ann told me, "You've got your degree, and you're highly recommended, but you don't have much experience, so I don't think we can put you in radio. We'll put you in television." Radio was king, and all the experimenters, the neophytes, were assigned to television so they wouldn't hurt the company product.

There was a small cadre in television engineering then. My first job was in a mobile TV field group, "Group One," as an apprentice engineer, the lowest of the low, but probably the only guy in the group with a degree. I was assigned to the mobile unit field garage in Long Island City. Even though I had good technical knowledge, I couldn't just jump in. I pulled cables and lugged equipment in the setup for football and baseball in the stadiums. I did a lot of grunt work and, as low man on the totem pole, I drove the truck back after events.

At that time there was only one television studio, Studio 3-K. We would do a fight at St. Nick's Arena on Friday night, break down the equipment, go to Radio City and set it up in a radio studio, either old 6-B or 6-A, to do a program that Saturday, a quiz, or a show like Winchell and Mahoney. Then we hauled equipment down to the loading dock in Radio City and put it back in the mobile unit. It was great experience because I learned how to do every job: technical directing, camera, audio, and setting up microwave.

In 1951, five years after I started with NBC, I was made a Technical Director. I directed three, four, and sometimes five cameras. I started on local operations doing shows like the John Cameron Swayze News, "Rooti Kazootie," "Alma Kitchell's Kitchen," and Gabby Hayes, and then rotated through everything, working uptown at the NBC 106th Street studios on weekends.

The first big show I did was the Kate Smith afternoon show at the Hudson Theatre. Carl Lindemann, later to become Vice President, Sports, for NBC, was production manager, and Barry Wood, the championship swimmer from Yale, was the producer. That's where I met Greg Garrison; we worked together a lot over the years and became very close. Greg Garrison was the principal director with whom I worked until we went on to bigger and better things. It was fashionable to be a director in those days. Some of them were socialites, but all of them were knowledgeable. I've worked with all kinds of directors. Larry Schwab was fun, a little wild but crazy about us. I worked with Alan Newmann and with Herb Susann, who later directed the Coca-Cola show. "Coke Time" was a 15-minute show starring Eddie Fisher and rotating guest stars.

In 1955 I became a Technical Supervisor, and worked on "Wide, Wide World" with Barry Wood for two years. You may remember that this was a pet project of Pat Weaver's, and it got a lot of attention from the press. We went all over the United States getting live programming, and using NBC's affiliated stations wherever we could. There were three or four units, and I traveled with them for three weeks at a time, and then I'd be at home base for a week. The show ran for 90 minutes on Sunday afternoons, and it was a tremendous challenge because we did innovative things with, by today's standards, rudimentary equipment. We had to fight for facilities at undeveloped areas of origination.

I set up plans with the local chief engineer and met a lot of affiliates that way. "Wide, Wide World" encompassed a variety of pickups, including steamboat races on the Mississippi River, ice fishing up in Saginaw, Michigan—that kind of thing, and *all* of it live. One of the most interesting pickups was out of Havana, the first time live television came out of Havana. The Cubans put a high-gain receiver in an old DC-3 transport, used a low-power channel 13 transmitter, parked in an airborne figure eight off the Florida coast, and picked up the United States television transmissions of the World Series. They retransmitted the signal to Havana where the Cubans popped in their own commercials. I thought if it goes one way, it can go the other way. This was a year before Castro, and the Cuban television people and Goar Mestre laid out the red carpet for us. I spent weeks there, going up in the plane, doing the figure eight, testing the system. We set up a microwave link through Homestead, Florida, where we picked up the signal receiver. We also had a backup system on the roof of the Fontainebleau Hotel in Miami from which we received a signal to transmit back to New York. We originated a good, ten-minute segment. It was a television "first."

By 1957 I was Manager of Studio/Field Personnel, which meant I had to analyze a show's technical requirements and schedule the people to carry them out. About 300 engineers were scheduled through my office.

In 1959 I became Manager of Film Operations. NBC had a heavy film load at that time, and I got involved in the telecine operation and the quality control area. I was a neophyte coming from live television, but Bob Stone assigned Don Carswell and me the onerous task of cleaning up the Telecine Management Group, which Stone thought was overstaffed and inefficient. He was right! It was like the sorcerer's apprentice: after moving people around and streamlining that bureaucracy, I was put in charge of it. But I learned about film operations, which I had understood only technically before.

I was also involved with kinescope recording, which was always an adventure. Herb DeGroot was in charge of it. The process used a camera which shot right off a kinescope tube. Everybody thought it was the cat's meow, but it produced a passable picture, not a decent image, and it was fraught with technical problems. The main problem was the quality, my responsibility. It was used for the network delay. We had a processing room for kines and for film negatives we occasionally developed for the News Division.

One experience I remember with film for the news people was when Reuven Frank shipped some footage of the Queen of England getting off an airplane, and it sank in the processing vat. I *hated* to call and say "Reuven, we've lost the Queen at the bottom of the vat." Those were precarious operations compared to the present day.

In 1961 I became Manager of Videotape, Film and Kinescope Recording Operations. Tape was on the scene then, and it made sense for these operations to be organized in one department. Tape was going to grow and the kine recording and film business would, eventually, fall off. Videotape was a marvel for its time. Editing was crude and time-consuming, not electronic. To watch a guy edit a show by cutting it with a razor blade was incredible.

I've seen many innovations. When I was a Technical Director, we didn't have any way to dissolve one picture to another, we just cut. Depending on who your switcher was, you couldn't do certain supers. I remember with Garrison, who was wild, we were able to do three-way supers because some of the relays would hang up. I was okay until the maintenance man cleaned the relays, which effectively wiped out the supers and then I was out of business. Our problem was to create the technique for whatever the programmer felt he ought to have. And sometimes he asked for too much.

We tried to be innovative. Garrison and I used an electro zoom, with a square or rectangular opening. I'd take a picture. I would effectively super both cameras, and we'd put a black card in the supered picture, one half on one zoom and the other half on the other one, and then we'd pan the cameras so you'd have the split screen. To wipe out of that, one guy would pan and the other would pull the card out. We did this in the Berle show and other big productions.

By 1964 I was Manager of Studio/Field Operations, and then became Director of Studio/Field Operations in 1968. We tried to involve the affiliates as much as we could. We always got wonderful help from Cincinnati when we televised baseball and the World Series. We did pickups from KSD, St. Louis, and we also went to KPRC, Houston. Of course, if the local affiliate had problems, we tried to help them.

NBC had a close relationship with RCA in those days because the whole industry was developing quickly. We coordinated technology, exchanged information about engineering problems and used their cameras. Fred Himelfarb, our camera expert today, was active then. RCA was on the move and aggressive. They had a turn-key approach to a station, and would set up the whole thing, from the cameras to the transmitter. They really were running with the ball.

In 1972 I became Vice President of Television Network Operations, and that broadened my duties because I became involved with more departments. Communications, Telephone Services and Film Coordination were added responsibilities. The scope of my job changed, and although it was basically New York, I was involved with the West Coast on mutual problems.

I worked my first political convention in 1948. That year, I was in Philadelphia as a junior audio man, when radio was king, and I was told to put a TV mike on the podium. I thought the radio engineers were going to kill me. Tom Phelan, a senior management radio engineer and a highly respected guy, said, "What are you *doing*? This is radio, and *we'll* give you a feed. Take this stuff away, kid!"

Conventions were a challenge; in technical developments, RCA's mini-camera revolutionized field work and was first used at the conventions in the 60's, as I remember. When NBC went from black-and-white to color, the color equipment presented a special challenge in technical complexity. It took a while to train video operators. Black-and-white cameras were simpler to set up and smaller than the first color cameras used in the field, those enormous TK-41's. Nowadays, cameras are miniaturized and have automatic control function. A guy still has to know what he is doing, but it's a lot more straightforward to set up the cameras quickly.

I would have had an operational role in the 1980 Moscow Olympics if they had taken place. Jack Kennedy, my boss at the time, was deeply involved and went there many times to do some surveys. We were all set to handle the games. Millions of dollars of equipment was in place in Moscow.

When I joined the company, the big boss of engineering was O.B. Hanson, a legendary figure. I was in awe of the guy. When I was brand new, I went to a function where the troops set me up and arranged for him to say to me,

"Hey, you're doing a *great* job." That was one of their standard jokes. Ferdinand Wankel was involved then, plus Ray Guy and Bob Shelby, names the old timers might know.

My present post, Vice President of Production Operations Planning in the Operations and Technical Services grouping, gives me responsibility for planning major news, sports and entertainment productions, including the massive technical effort required during the 1984 presidential year. When I finished the conventions and the elections, I was supposed to do the inauguration, but Mike Sherlock said there were serious problems in Brooklyn with the Bill Cosby show. He decided to reorganize, assign one person "with stature," as he put it, to be in charge of that facility and report to him. I went to Brooklyn after the elections in November and met with the production group. I found them to be demanding perfectionists. They realized I was there to do a job; they trusted me and we started turning the place around. It required complete renovation, major construction of technical offices and writers' offices, and the installation of new tape machines, new cameras and a new audio console. We had to finish it before the first air tape in August. "The Cosby Show" is the number one show, and that's the way I treat all the people involved with the program.

We are also responsible for "Another World," which has been on for 19 years. There is a possibility that I will be involved in organizational planning for the 1988 Olympics in Seoul, Korea. The Olympics will present us with tougher logistics than any of the major events in the past.

When you asked me about memorable characters, I remembered Greg Garrison with affection. He is a character, a very bright guy. We worked together a lot and had a close, trusting relationship. I respect him as a creative director whose credits started with the Berle show, and then went on to "The Show of Shows" and other big productions.

I did work on "The Colgate Comedy Hour." By the time spectaculars like "Peter Pan" and "Annie Get Your Gun" came along, I was a managing supervisor. Greg Garrison and I worked in Brooklyn on an Esther Williams live spectacular with a swimming pool. That was a first! All the parts were shipped from London, and we had a bag of bolts to put it together. At the start, everything seemed to go wrong. When we put a camera on an arm that went around the pool circumference, the problems disappeared. Just about everything in those days was live, and doing commercials live was painstaking and quirky, especially when the camera showed products which did not work as advertised.

From the booth, I got to know a few talented people pretty well. Kate Smith was charming, really, she was great. Pat Kennedy, later Pat Lawford, was a Program Assistant when I did the Kate Smith show. Eddie Fisher was Eddie Fisher, but he was all right. Berle was Berle, and he and I had mutual respect for each other. Working with him was no slap-on-the-back routine because he was a demanding businessman, and he knew he was good. Martha Raye was terrific. After the show, she usually joined the crew for a couple of drinks. Some performers and choreographers I've known have become directors.

It was fun doing live television. I worked with directors who went bananas and practically collapsed, but they had to keep the show on the air. In a live band number, when a guy would get out of sequence, you'd cut to the trumpet player, who wouldn't be with it, then you'd go to the next guy and then *he'd* stop his instrument, and it would *all* go downhill. We had to keep our cool and ride out the storm.

I've had great experiences at NBC, and I enjoy the medium, the medium's great. I've never lost my enthusiasm for it. I feel the same way I did when I started. It's always satisfying to get the job done, to be innovative. People like Grant Tinker are sensational. I've known him a long time, a guy who remembers your name from the first time he meets you. I think we're on the move, we've got the right people. A top company.

I wish NBC well on its 60th Anniversary.

September 11, 1985

Julian Goodman joined NBC News at WRC in Washington in 1945. In 1966, he became the youngest President in the history of the National Broadcasting Company. As Chairman of the Board, he took early retirement in 1979.

Julian Goodman

"In 1955, I was responsible for the first broadcast of a Congressional Committee Hearing—the Greek-Turkish Aid Grants with Dean Acheson testifying. I rode up and down an elevator in the House of Representatives and confronted the Chairman of the House Foreign Affairs Committee, an elderly white-haired gentleman, named Charles 'Doc' Eaton, every time he got on. I think he thought I was an elevator boy. Eventually, he gave in, and we did the broadcast. The problem now is not getting them on; it's keeping them off."

I was born on May 1, 1922, in Glasgow in Barren County, Kentucky, so called because Indians cut down the trees to make grazing pastures for their buffalo. It's a big burley tobacco country, and I still own a farm there.

Before I went into the Army in 1943, I almost finished my four years in English and journalism at Western Kentucky State Teachers College. When I came out of the service, I wanted to transfer credits earned at George Washington University in Washington, D.C., to Western for graduation, but Western wouldn't accept credits from a night school, which irritated me considerably, and I had to start all over again at George Washington University and earned an A.B. in economics. (In the 1970's, my cousin, Dero Downing, President of Western Kentucky University, was embarrassed by this and granted me an official degree.)

From my earliest school days, I intended to work in the news business, to be a reporter or a writer. At 15, 16, 17 I worked for $3 a week on the *Glasgow Daily News*, which was too poor to afford a wire service, so we listened to WHAS radio station, jotted down the ball scores and put them in the paper. I remember putting in a little story as a bulletin "box" gleaned from radio on Jean Harlow's death. Later, with NBC in Washington, when I took stories out of newspapers and put them on WRC radio, it occurred to me there was somebody out there listening to the radio and putting those stories in the small newspapers—a never-ending cycle of news.

When I got out of the Army, I worked for 18 months as office manager for the Combined Production and Resources Board in Washington, one man in a gaggle of 21 women, writing précis of cables and reports. It was there that I met my wife, Betty Davis. She was from Dawson Springs, Kentucky, and we married after I had started to work for NBC.

William Vaughan, a Glasgow friend and then assistant to Senate majority leader Alben Barkley, sent me to William R. McAndrew, head of NBC News. Bill McAndrew and I hit it off from the start and remained good friends until his death about 15 years ago. I still miss him. Bill was an excellent broadcaster and a consummate newsman who devoted himself to NBC and to his family. His contribution to broadcast news is an undervalued part of the history of broadcasting. He had an important asset vital to any leader: people wanted to do their best for him.

Bill is remembered for his friendly face, his cheerful manner, and easy conversation. He was cherubic, smoked a lot, sparkled, twinkled and always had a wise remark about whatever was going on. He was primarily interested in the news. One of my fondest memories of him is when, as President of NBC News, he was being interviewed by a lady reporter from *The Christian Science Monitor* and tried, in his double-breasted blue suit, to be a model executive. Hurley's bar, a treasured, traditional bar for newsmen at 6th Avenue and 49th Street, caught on fire. Bill really wanted to go down and follow the fire, but he had to stay and be an executive. His conflicting desires were amusing.

NBC News was a relatively small operation when I came to work between V-E Day and V-J Day in 1945. I got a job there because David Brinkley wanted to leave the night news desk and work in the daytime. Had I not replaced him, he might still be there and the world would have lost a great correspondent. David was my first supervisor, and I still have the personnel form on which he rated me pretty well, but not perfect. In spite of that, he and I remain friends.

CBS, with Ed Murrow, had achieved broadcast news dominance during the war, and NBC was trying to build up a staff equivalent to CBS. It hired Morgan Beatty from the Associated Press, and H.V. Kaltenborn signed on as a commentator. In Washington, we had Beatty, one of the first of the big commentators, Earl Godwin, Richard Harkness, Leif Eid, and the late Robert McCormick, another outstanding correspondent. It was a small group but a good one.

NBC News was not profitable for many years. We were a loss leader. One of our able executives, the late Frank McCall, always made the point that, at any station, the newsroom was located near the men's room. We all knew that stations did news as a public service and paid for it, but it was not profitable as it is, or can be, today.

My first promotion was to become Washington Editor of the Morgan Beatty "News of the World," the big radio program sponsored by Alka Seltzer. About 1950, I was made Manager of News for NBC Radio in Washington. Radio and TV news were still separate. TV news was just getting off the ground; there was hardly any until 1948.

Between 1945 and 1950, there were the closing events of World War II, the dropping of the atomic bombs on Hiroshima and Nagasaki. The White House was two blocks from where we worked at 14th and New York Avenue in Washington, and running back and forth to the White House was a regular occurrence. It was much easier to get in and out in those days during Harry Truman's Presidency. The big steel strike, the post-war events, the Marshall Plan were in the news; 1948 was memorable for me. I was in radio then and went to both the Republican and Democratic Conventions. I can still remember how hot Philadelphia's Convention Hall was—no air-conditioning.

I was sent to the conventions to edit audio tapes for radio because I had experience working on Morgan Beatty's "News of the World." I would, for instance record what President Truman said, lift a sentence or two out of it and play it on the air. It was a modest technique, but I was the only one to do it, so I was rated the expert at excerpting.

NBC Television News was poorly equipped to handle television at the time because its executives didn't realize the promise of it and had not devoted resources, energy and skill to it. Radio was dominant and had all the attention and top people. Pat Weaver, the head of NBC then, had a theory that big media companies could help us by lending their resources. So NBC made an agreement with *Time* magazine. I remember Andy Heiskell of *Time* pacing the convention floor, getting people on the air to be interviewed. But our television coverage in 1948 and 1952 was not very good.

In 1955, I was responsible for the first broadcast of a Congressional Committee Hearing—the Greek-Turkish Aid Grants with Dean Acheson testifying. I rode up and down an elevator in the House of Representatives and confronted the Chairman of the House Foreign Affairs Committee, an elderly white-haired gentleman, named Charles "Doc" Eaton, from New Jersey, every time he got on. I think he thought I was an elevator boy. Eventually, he gave in, and we did the broadcast. It started what has become a landslide of Congressional broadcasting. The problem now is not getting them on; it's keeping them off. It was a great thing; it would have come eventually, but I'm pleased that I was the first to bring it off.

CBS dominated the 1952 political conventions in Chicago. NBC had Bill Henry, a marvelous man as anchorman, but it did not have the necessary resources to do a first rate job. The years between 1952 and 1956 were a critical time for NBC in planning coverage of the 1956 conventions. What happened in 1956 formed the basis for what was to come later.

We thought about little else except how to beat CBS during the 1956 conventions. Davidson Taylor, Vice President of News and Public Affairs, was a fine man but totally unsuited for the job. He was trained in the Southern Baptist Theological Seminary in Louisville, Kentucky. He'd been with CBS in programming jobs, including supervision of the now legendary Orson Welles' "War of the Worlds." He was an intellectual man of great gentleness, put in charge of a brawling bunch of reporters. He did the best he could.

I remember being asked at a meeting in New York to model a jacket NBC reporters were supposed to wear, like the ones ABC Sports people now wear. We all laughed because it would have been so inappropriate to cover the news in flamboyant red jackets. I was instrumental in throwing it out.

We searched for people to combat CBS, not only for the conventions, but for their special programs with Walter Cronkite on the news and Murrow on the special events. We thought of everyone possible to combat Murrow. We talked to John Hersey, the writer, and we considered Stewart Alsop, brother of Joseph Alsop, and I, at least, thought about Jimmy Stewart, the actor. I thought of him because Jimmy Stewart had come out of the war with good credentials, a General, a patriot. He had made plenty of money and achieved honors in Hollywood, and might be looking for something new. I mentioned this to Jimmy Stewart at a dinner one night in Hollywood years afterward, and he, characteristically, said, "That might have been very interesting." I'll never know.

Taylor hired Chet Huntley from the West Coast, where Chet built a reputation as a commentator, and it was then decided to have a two-man team for the 1956 conventions. When the decision about the other man was made, I was told his name. I thought it was the wrong decision and recommended strongly that David Brinkley be teamed with Huntley for the convention coverage. I worked with him every day in Washington and knew how good he was. He was the obvious choice to me. I urged them as strongly as I could to take him, and finally they did.

I wasn't thinking of the balance between the two men. I didn't know Huntley at the time and I had not seen him on the air much. The contrast of personalities developed the first time Brinkley went on. It was not a planned match in that sense. I was thinking of Brinkley's ability as the best writer and the best mind on television at that time. I think he still is.

Huntley and Brinkley set a new style in television the very first day of the 1956 conventions. Pomposity was never the same again. The public took to the team immediately, and Jack Gould wrote a rave review about Brinkley that gave the whole concept the approval of *The New York Times*. It was the beginning of a fortunate partnership for both that dominated television news for many years.

Reuven Frank was the producer who made it all work. He was a part of the process of choosing the two men as co-anchors for the conventions, and later the producer of "The Huntley-Brinkley Report," which replaced John Cameron Swayze. Reuven thought up the closing line, "Good Night, David...Good Night, Chet." I objected at first because I felt every night club comedian in the United States would soon be using the line, but Reuven knew what he was doing. It was a self-generating promotion and a stroke of genius.

Reuven was with the "Huntley-Brinkley Report" when I came to NBC in New York. He is a brilliant writer and thinker who liked to make things happen with television images. Reuven set the style for NBC News. He forced himself to become an administrator when Bill McAndrew's early death made him President of NBC News. For too many years, Reuven was the only producer NBC had, the reed we leaned on too much. With his knowledge and consent, I hired Lou Hazam, Ted Yates, Stuart Schulberg and others for

our production staff when I first came to New York.

A little later, we hired one key news executive from the outer world, and it was a happy choice. I brought in Dick Wald with some unconscious prescience because, just two months later, Bill McAndrew died unexpectedly, and Reuven Frank was put in charge of NBC News. We needed some administrative strength and news experience and got it from Dick. I had long been impressed with him as one of the finest executives in the news business. He was Managing Editor at the *New York Herald Tribune* at 36 and had been Jock Whitney's associate at the *Paris Herald*. He's doing well now at ABC.

Back to earlier days. Washington was a heady place for a young newsman. With easy access to the White House down the street, I could watch Harry Truman literally grow every day in office, from a Vice President who said he felt as though a load of hay had fallen on him when Roosevelt died, to a firm, decisive, popular President with a solid place in history.

I remember the Eisenhower years fondly, perhaps because of my admiration for and friendship with his press secretary, James Hagerty, the best press secretary ever. Jim was a good man, a solid newsman, who did much to help the country. I played a prominent part in persuading Jim Hagerty to televise a Presidential press conference for the first time. The first television press conference was for film cameras only. I agreed reluctantly when Hagerty insisted that we develop the film and wait until he released it, because he was afraid the President might make an error. At that first one, the President did say Indonesia when he meant Indochina. That press conference was so popular with the public and with politicians that when Kennedy came in, live television became an instrument in frequent use.

My decision to move to New York in 1959 as Director of News was a tough one to make. I knew a lot about the Washington scene, and I liked it. I was not anxious to fling myself into the maelstrom of New York life and company politics, certainly the politics. Bill McAndrew had advised me not to accept previous offers, and I had refused them. Then, Bob Kintner, President of NBC, wanted to strengthen the News Department, and he wanted Bill under him, and Bill wanted me.

It was a period of great growth for the News Department. Kintner was the best thing that ever happened to NBC News, and all the stations' news operations. He gave broadcast news encouragement and money, and he gave newsmen the self-respect they had long sought and been denied.

All of us at NBC felt the most important thing was to do a good professional job, with integrity, and then look for the ratings. The ratings and the material success did come afterwards, but our first intent was to do the best professional job we could.

The Great Debates between Kennedy and Nixon in 1960 were a very interesting part of my life. The candidates agreed to four debates, and we drew by lot when the three networks would do them. CBS drew the first, and NBC the second. I was named producer for the second debate, and Kintner sent me a telegram pinning the full responsibility on me. I went to Chicago to see how the first debate was handled. Before the first debate, Nixon hurt his knee on the car door before he went in; he was badly made up, and, on the air, he appeared to have a day's growth of beard and was sweating all through the debate. When it was over, it was obvious that it was a big hit, and our turn was next. The candidates had selected Cleveland as the site.

I surveyed 19 places in Cleveland for the NBC debate and found no place where we could do it. Bill McAndrew persuaded the candidates to move the site to Washington. I was editorially denounced in Cleveland, and I haven't been back much since. In Washington, we had a station as big as Chicago's WBBM, where the first broadcast originated. It was a harrowing experience, but a successful one. I picked Frank McGee to be the moderator, and the candidates picked the reporters who would ask the questions on the air. A lot of colorful and interesting things went on.

It took us four days to set the lighting properly, and then the candidates came to look at it. Kennedy objected to his lighting because he thought it was set in a way that would glare in his eyes and not in Nixon's. I looked at both lighting setups and said, "No sir, they're both the same, and we're going to leave it the way it is." I remember saying to Frank McGee just before he went on the air, "Frank, be calm, take it easy. And remember, at no time will you be talking to more than 100 million people."

From those debates, I thought Kennedy would win the election. Television images are in a voter's mind when he goes into the booth. I think a lot of people who intended to vote for Thomas E. Dewey had two images of the men in the minds, but pulled the lever for Truman. Many may have done the same thing in the Kennedy/Nixon voting. I believe Kennedy would not have had a chance if the debates had not taken place. Now, an aspiring Presidential candidate can't afford to say no to a debate.

In its first 50 years, four people shaped the destiny of NBC: General David Sarnoff, Robert Sarnoff, Pat Weaver, and Bob Kintner. We would not have existed without the vision of the General. But he was more than a visionary; he loved broadcasting even when it disappointed him, and he backed his people up. Bob Sarnoff deserves more credit than he is given. He was a smart man who understood broadcasting and used his executives well. His father was a hard act to follow, but for all their vanities, both of them made invaluable contributions to NBC for many years.

But the one who had the strongest influence during my time was the man I succeeded, Robert Edmonds Kintner. He had written a column with Joe Alsop for the *New York Herald Tribune*; he had been President of ABC, where he put Walt Disney on television, and when I first knew him he was President of NBC. Kintner was a strong force, but it was not difficult for me to work with him. I really loved the man. I think he was a fine, fine man with personality flaws which many found difficult. I respected Kintner's ability. He wanted to do the same thing I wanted to do: make NBC News the best organization in the world.

Because Kintner worked so hard and was so competitive, he lifted the morale of the entire company. He was feared by people who didn't work well for him, but he was not a cruel man who would fire people for no cause, and he was quick to commend and reward those who did well.

Great credit is due Bob Sarnoff for his management of the company in the way he used its executives. Bob was always a participant, but he was never an operational man. I give him credit for getting the most out of Kintner. I think Bob Sarnoff sat in on everything Kintner did. He would walk into his office, unsolicited, unannounced, which Kintner hated, and take part in everything. Bob Sarnoff should be given credit for letting Kintner do things which must have been offensive to Bob many times.

If you did a survey of people on the street today and asked who's the President of NBC, I think a surprising number would say, "Pat Weaver." I think he was a remarkable man; his creative concepts were brilliant. However, he couldn't carry out a lot of them. He once spent $500,000 on "Richard the Third" and played it on a Sunday afternoon because he couldn't sell it to anybody. The General called him on the carpet for it, and he said, "Well, General, that's show business." That's one of my favorite stories.

In addition to creating "Today," he created the concept of "Home," a good morning service program which should have endured. But he overdid it. Everybody was in a white jacket. He was great at thinking but not too good at doing. His budgets could have been contained. I think the reason Pat left was very simply the fact that he overshadowed Bob, and the General didn't want him to. Pat was a brilliant contributor to television's development, and I have great respect for him today.

Pat left NBC many legacies. Pat's favorite program executive, Mort Werner, supervised "Today" in its early days, and when Mort came back to NBC for a second tour of duty, Grant Tinker was Mort's strong number-two man in the Program Department. You might say that, in spite of occasional aberrations like "My Mother the Car," which everyone remembers, there's been a strain of quality in NBC programming from Weaver to Werner to Tinker—with just a little bit, please forgive me, left to chance. Mort Werner was really something.

Mort's crowning achievement may have been his selection of Johnny Carson for the "Tonight" show. Mort made a presentation to Kintner and Sarnoff which is now part of television folklore, but it actually happened this way: Without mentioning his name until the end, in true show-business style, Mort went through a long litany of programs based on his opening sentence. He said, "The man I'm going to suggest has been a failure in everything he has ever done." He pointed to Johnny's skill at ad-libbing and his radio experience on the CBS and ABC daytime shows. They accepted Johnny, who owes more to Mort than to anyone else in his life.

After 1960, we pioneered in program techniques for radio and television. Instant news was one. It was any newsman's natural instinct to go on the air whenever something happened, but Kintner made it possible and automatic by giving us the time. We started that without commercial intent—we wanted to establish a habit of having people look automatically at NBC when a news event happened. We started breaking into every show whenever an important event happened and staying on as long as we could. Kintner said, "Interrupt the network," and we did.

The Gulf Oil "Instant Specials" began in an interesting way. NBC and Young & Rubicam made a presentation to William Whiteford, Chairman of the Board of the Gulf Oil Company, to sponsor a big entertainment series. NBC had a checkered history with Gulf because NBC had dropped "Life of Riley," which annoyed Gulf. The agency developed an elaborate entertainment package, and, as a backup plan, also proposed that a commercial go on whenever we interrupted the network for a news story. I worked on the instant-news part of the presentation which Young & Rubicam made. After a long delay, Mr. Whiteford walked into a room full of people, talked about the history and relationship of the companies, and said, "I'm open-minded about this. I'm ready to see whatever you have to offer, but I don't want anything in entertainment." Bud Barry, head of programs for Young & Rubicam, quick on his feet as he always was, said, "That's good, because we don't plan to show you entertainment," as though he had only planned to present the news proposal. Whiteford said, "That sounds like a great idea." And it was.

We worked out an informal contract based on good faith. We would put the program on the air, Gulf would put the commercial on and trust us to do it right. We did many special programs for them, and, at the end of a 10-year relationship with them, Gulf gave me a replica of the Liberty Bell as a symbol of good faith, which I still treasure. While I was Chairman of NBC, Gulf asked me to be a director, but I couldn't accept because of the news conflict. When that conflict no longer existed, I became a member of its board.

Throughout all my years at NBC, I made a point of listening to what our affiliates had to say. The affiliates wouldn't be doing their jobs if they didn't take pot shots at NBC, but they were generally strong in support of what we did, even during the difficult years when there was a concerted and orchestrated attack on television news programs and the people who did them. There were some who disagreed with what we did. This was at its height during the Nixon-Agnew years, with the growth of pressure groups like the amusingly named "Accuracy in Media," which is not about accuracy at all, but should be called "Do It My Way Or Else."

The day begins on NBC and all the other networks with a blank screen, just as a newspaper begins with a blank piece of paper. All through the day there are people pulling at it, wanting to get on it to serve their own purposes, and it's the responsibility of a good reporter to sift that out and print the truth, and that's what we did. The truth hurts a lot of people, and they object to it.

Kintner was fired in 1965. He had achieved everything that he'd ever wanted in life, the chairmanship, the presidency, the chief executive of NBC. There was a psychological explanation for this self-destructive path, but I don't know the reason. Bob Sarnoff fired him personally during a six-minute confrontation. It was a tragedy because he was such an able man.

Bob Sarnoff told his father he was going to pull an Eisenhower and reach down into the ranks, pick somebody and lift him above those who were senior to him, and, at the age of 43, I became president, the first person chosen from the news area.

I called to give my father the news. My father was born and lived all of his life in Kentucky. He lost his money during the Depression, refused to take refuge in the bankruptcy law and eventually paid all the money back. He was a good Baptist with a strong moral character, and was proud of his three sons. On this occasion, I called him and said, "Pop, the board of directors of the National Broadcasting Company has seen fit to elect me as its president, and since I hardly could have done it without you, I wanted you to be the first one to know about it." And he said, "That's great, that really is fine. I'm very proud of you, and I hope you won't think that I'm being short with you, but I have to hang up because I have to go to the mule sale in town. They only have a mule sale once every three weeks, and a man can always use another mule." Later he told somebody, "I didn't really need another mule, but I didn't want Julian to feel uppity." "Uppity" is a good Kentucky word.

When Val Adams wrote a *New York Times* column about my being elected President of NBC, he said a man who had never asked for a raise was elected president of the company. That's true; people gave me one when I did my work well. Things have always come fairly easily for me. During my career at NBC, CBS tried to hire me a couple of times, and I never told my bosses at NBC, but I told CBS that NBC had enabled me to learn the skills which made me worth a lot of money to them, and I preferred to pay NBC back. I think I did that and more. Also, I liked what I was doing and I liked the people. Kintner had intimated that he would have made me head of the television network some day, and he was sorry that I didn't have the opportunity to get that kind of training before heading the company.

Walter Scott was Chairman when I was President. He was remarkably well ordered, a highly respected man of his word, and I learned a lot from him. He had influence among corporate sponsors and advertising agencies because he was a good salesman and a good person. He was interested in people, easy to get along with, but knowledgeable and firm about the business. Walter didn't like publicity, and, as a result, he never got much of it—which is one of the reasons he is, like Bill McAndrew, an underrated part of NBC's history. He and I formed a good working partnership with complementary talents. Walter's reputation came through his integrity. The sales business changed as much as anything in television, except technology. There was an earlier time when Walter would go to Chicago, have lunch with the head of Kraft, and Wednesday night

9 o'clock would be locked up for 52 weeks. Then he would go to the Bell Telephone people and make a similar sale. Walter was there at the time of the one sponsor, and when the change to magazine concept came, he was flexible enough to go with fractionalization.

When I was thrust quickly into the top operations job in 1965, I felt I knew news. There were many ready to educate me about programs. Jennings Lang of MCA-Universal sent me a real straightjacket, and I often felt I or my callers needed it. My first program purchase was from the inimitable Sir Lew Grade, head of the British television company ITV. For $300,000 we got a program on art in the British Royal homes, narrated by royalty, but wound up with an art professor with bad teeth.

My next callers, the Network Television Program Department, told me we should pay Danny Thomas $600,000 *not* to do a 13-week program called "My Six Blocks." It took them two days to convince me that if we paid the $600,000, we would save a couple of million not to put on a poor series. My Scotch blood still tells me that this is a lousy way to run a business.

I encouraged George Heinemann to put on good children's programming. We put "Watch My Child" at 1:30 to 2 in the afternoon on our own stations, but the affiliates rejected it, and we lost a couple of million dollars on it. I was dissatisfied that an attempt to do something good on television had not worked. I tried other children's programs, and, in addition, experimental programs in the theatre to develop young talent for the business.

I think my instincts in the entertainment business are good, and I wish I had spent more time on programming. I deferred to the judgment of people in the program business. I was disconsolate when Grant Tinker's MTM Enterprises brought "The Mary Tyler Moore Show" to NBC first, and the television network thought it was a women's show and would not succeed. Presumably they had research to back up their decision, which had to be made quickly (we had 24 hours to think about it), but it's etched in my memory that the head of sales at the time said, "I'd like to program against her," and he sure as hell got the opportunity. My instinct was that it was a fine program, but there were occasions like that when I trusted other's instincts because they'd had more experience, whereas in news, I trusted nobody's more than I did my own.

My own was far from perfect. I saw the "Flip Wilson Show" the day before it was to go on the air and woke up Don Durgin, head of the Television Network, and Mort Werner, head of Programs, in California, and said, "We can't put that on the air—Flip Wilson dressed as Geraldine. We'll be destroyed from coast to coast." They persuaded me I was wrong, and the show was a big hit. The public thought Flip Wilson in drag was very funny. I still think I was right.

The late 1960's and early 1970's were difficult for anyone in network television news. Everybody wanted a piece of its hide, just because it was there, just because it was showing us some terrible things we didn't want to see, and 1968 may have been the toughest year; Martin Luther King, Jr. was killed, Bobby Kennedy was killed, the Vietnam war raged on, Nixon won the Presidency and promised to bring us all together and proceeded to tear us apart. It wasn't just the Republicans; Democrats had it in for us too. At the convention in Chicago, Mayor Daley's cops beat the demonstrators, then blamed television for not showing the provocations that caused it, when his restrictions on camera movements kept us from showing almost anything. And Walter Cronkite put him on the air for half an hour to justify himself—unchallenged. It was a dark time for TV news; people turned on us as never before.

And the Nixon hatchet men didn't miss any opportunities to try to turn the screws. Charles Colson, Nixon's point man, was sent to New York to talk to the three networks. His real mission was to intimidate us. This was before Watergate when the Nixon Administration was strong. We were so prominent that people wanted to influence what we did, but if somebody tried to pressure us, I resisted as best I could when the position was unfair. When somebody came to us with an honest proposition and we had done something wrong, I tried to right it. I tried to deal fairly. But dealing fairly was not enough for the Nixon men; if you weren't for them, you were against them. Other politicians were not much different.

For some reason, I was the only broadcasting member on the original list of Nixon's 200 enemies made by John Dean. I never have figured this out, but I have a theory. I believe Frank Stanton and Leonard Goldenson gave contributions to both parties, and the computer automatically spat out contributors' names.

I made no financial contribution to either party. I felt I shouldn't, mainly because I didn't have the money. Thus, the computer had no reason to keep me off the list. I was not disposed to be anti-Nixon. I had known Nixon since he and I wore size 36 jackets (which I remember for some reason), and he helped us get our cameras and recorders into the House Un-American Activities Committee hearings because he recognized the value of the publicity that would come from NBC's coverage. I got along well with his staff. I did nothing that justified my being placed on the enemies list except my effort to be fair in allocating time on the air.

Colson, when he came to my office, said, "We have made a compilation of people who appeared on the air in the last few months, and this many have been pro-Administration, and this anti-Administration. I think you have to deal with imbalance. You need more people who favor us." I said it wasn't a fair assessment, that we saw no imbalance that needed redressing, and that we would continue to treat both sides fairly without his help, and according to our news judgment. His salesman's report to Bob Haldeman was a little different in tone. He indicated that he had scared the hell out of us.

It was an unpleasant experience. I admired Frank Stanton and resented it when Colson said to him that same week, "I will bring you to your knees in the marketplace." This was bitter, hardball politics, and Colson deserved to go to jail for that, if for nothing else.

That was a tense time for broadcasting. The Agnew confrontation ("nattering nabobs of negativism") speech was written by Pat Buchanan, and Nixon pretended to stay above it. Agnew really didn't care what he was doing. I met Agnew several times after that. He asked Arnold Palmer (the champion golfer and pro who had a business association with NBC) to arrange golf games with me—Palmer played too. He tried to get at us by persuasion when public denunciation failed. Agnew was a second-rate politician who didn't belong in politics in the first place.

I never resented him as much as I did the people who put him up to it like Buchanan, and Nixon who *did* condone the whole thing.

About a year later, Nixon invited each of the networks to the White House and, on the occasion of NBC's visit, told me he had not known anything about what Agnew tried to do. I said, "But you did nothing to gainsay him, and the Government is not operated by memos; it's operated by a set of hand signals. Your signal said to attack the broadcasters." That was all part of the territory, and freedom has to be defended if it's going to be kept.

That became a major theme for my speeches. I care about it deeply, but it's a theme that has to be repeated over and over. I think our freedom is in as much danger today as it was then. There are pressure forces still working against broadcasting, and the broadcasting companies must defend themselves against them, and stand up for their people on the firing line.

NBC is only as good as its affiliates, and I think the relationship between NBC and its affiliates when I was there was enlightened self-interest and interdependency. There may have been a few complaints about news, but I think the big, important affiliates, Harold Grams of St. Louis and Jack Harris of Houston, Louis Read of New Orleans, Ralph Jackson of Louisville, Bob Ferguson of Wheeling, Ancil Payne of Seattle, and Fred Paxton of Paducah, supported and understood what we were doing in news and urged us to do more.

I think the world is going to change and the relationship between the network and its affiliates may not be as vital as transmission through satellite becomes cheaper and easier to do. There will be a vast supermarket of suppliers for the stations, and they will have many choices for their programming. We will see a network in which things are not on the same time every night in every city. That will be prodded by the time, which I believe is rapidly approaching, when sports gravitate toward pay television, if they can find a graceful way to do it. Then the *raison d'etre* for a network will be less. As suppliers compete to sell to stations, stations will be more important than networks.

I hope networks will choose the right people to plan creatively for this, but I'm not sure they are doing that. Radio broadcasters did not perceive the fractionalization and fragmenting of radio, and so its networking is an impotent force today.

Grant Tinker can prepare the way for technological changes but he can't do it alone. He has good programs; I think he has calmed the panic at NBC and made it a good place to work, a place where people enjoy their work. It shows in the performance of the company, which has an opportunity to be Number One this season, and I hope it is. But this is such a competitive business, nobody can ever be sure. One sure thing is that ABC is going to fight back. CBS is aging in its programming and its philosophies, and it is ripe to be taken. Grant can't be there forever, and it's as important for him to establish a succession line of bright, young executives at NBC as it is for him to pick good programs.

Nobody likes to walk through the sand without leaving any footprints, and I am comfortable with mine. I came through my NBC career with my integrity intact. I played a part in building one of the world's great news organizations, and made NBC a place where people liked their work and were treated fairly. The advancement of women to key roles played an important part in our thinking, long before we knew it was progressive: Pauline Frederick, Nancy Dickerson, Lucy Jarvis, Aline Saarinen. We tried experimental program techniques, encouraged young people, met our responsibility to serve the public and made a good profit.

I kept Johnny Carson working for us when many thought he wouldn't, for a mere $1 million a year. I kept baseball at NBC, and one of my favorite recollections is the part I played in the pro football on screen today.

We lost television rights in 1964 to NCAA football games in a bidding contest with ABC, which was carrying a ragtag and bobtail professional league, the American Football League. I suggested to Kintner, who readily agreed, that we try a long-term deal with the AFL and pay more than it was worth during the first years so the teams could pay good players and, in the last years, we could get our money back.

I wanted ten years and we settled for five. Carl Lindemann, an outstanding sports executive, signed a five year deal with Joe Foss, then the league commissioner, and hounded the teams to do better. Some just pocketed the money ($800,000 per game versus the $150,000 ABC had paid). But some, like the great Sonny Werblin, used the money the way we intended it, to pay players like Joe Namath, and brought the quality of league play to a standard that literally forced the National Football League to merge with it. And when the Jets beat the Baltimore Colts in the Super Bowl in 1969 by a score of 16-7, it was surely the Number One sports event of all time for the late Carl Lindemann, bless his soul, and for me, and everybody who had a part in it.

But, like everything else in the past, all that's not as important as the future. As it approaches its 60th birthday, NBC is a company in pretty good shape, once again. It gives high priority to news; its prime-time success has been achieved with programs that have positive social values—the "proud but popular" type of schedule that was always our goal, but not always achieved. NBC recognizes the importance of sports in American life and continues to build its sports presence. It recognizes its true partnership with its affiliates, and deservedly gets good marks from them.

These are all the things that occupied my attention, too, during my 34 years with NBC, and while Grant Tinker does it much better, I do like to think I laid some of the bricks in the foundation. I wish you all a happy birthday.

September 10, 1985

Peter Kenney held the sensitive post of Vice President, Washington, during some hostile and challenging administrations, until his retirement in 1983.

"It was not a friendly Congress during my 22 years. The Members feared and distrusted broadcasters. In general, they regarded broadcasters—particularly networks—as too big, too rich, and too powerful. I recall one typical report which referred to us as arrogant and unresponsive."

Hartford, Connecticut, was my birthplace, and also that of my wife, Gerry. After three years at Princeton my education was interrupted by World War II. I was sent to the European Theater of Operations with the Signal Corps. When I left the Army in 1946, I joined the Radio Department of the Julian Gross Advertising Agency in Hartford as a copywriter/account executive. I was more intrigued with radio, which had become a strong local and regional advertising tool. So, I joined the sales department of a one-kilowatt daytime station in New Britain, Connecticut.

In the 1940's, a non-network, daytime station was not the easiest advertising vehicle to sell. "Drive time" was not yet a sales tool, and, as the leaves fell, so did our advertisers. WKNB-AM branched out into FM and UHF television. During the 50's, I acquired a financial interest in the company and became an Executive Vice President and General Manager.

WKNB-TV, Channel 30, went on the air in February, 1953. It was one of the first 10 or 15 UHF stations. The period following the FCC 6th Report and Order was a tremendous challenge for all of us who entered the television field by way of UHF. The headaches and frustrations for the operators and viewers were almost beyond description. Transmitter and antenna equipment was still in the experimental stage. Equally serious was the "chicken-and-egg" situation with sales and programs. The advertisers, the networks, and the programmers were waiting for UHF to develop an audience before they came on board; the audience was waiting for good programs and a better signal before they would convert or buy UHF. Happily, the daytime radio station was doing well and carried part of the TV overhead.

Then the FCC began to pressure the networks and the major broadcast groups to move into UHF and provide more economic, engineering and industry support. The Connecticut Valley market looked attractive to Charles Denny at NBC, and an offer was made to purchase our properties. As a corporate purchase, NBC acquired not only our UHF station, but also the radio station, which it held for about two years. The market, of course, was the Greater Hartford area, and the station later became a Hartford/New Britain outlet.

The change from being part owner of a TV station to that of an NBC employee occurred while I was attending the NBC 30th Anniversary Affiliates' Meeting at the Americana Hotel in Miami as an affiliate. The sale of Channel 30 had been pending before the FCC, and one afternoon, while I was with other affiliates at the pool, Tom Ervin, head of the NBC Law Department, and his wife, Norma, arrived at the pool to announce the FCC approval of the sale. Norma prefaced her announcement by putting her hand on my shoulder and saying, "Look what we bought today." That was my introduction to NBC as an employee.

Although the TV station was making a small profit, it quickly fell victim to network union scales and to division-allocated administrative charges, which no UHF station could absorb. It was clear that a UHF station could not be profitable under network ownership, and it was sold. I made every possible effort to purchase the station. The price for a UHF was around $1 million. I borrowed heavily and thought I had a firm deal. We went to New York to close but found that George Matson, NBC Treasurer, had changed the price. P.A. (Buddy) Sugg, President of the O&O Radio Stations, continued to offer the property to other buyers. Finally, short by about $50,000 on the new asking price, I had to bow out.

In 1959, while I was waiting for a new assignment in the NBC Owned Stations Division, Al Stern, head of the International Division, asked if I would go to Buenos Aires to explore the prospects for an NBC investment in a TV station on Channel 9. The market reportedly had close to a million viewers for the single government-owned station. The International Division under Stern was active in construction and management contracts in a number of locations around the world. I believe the Argentina project was the first big ownership interest outside the United States for NBC.

The trip to Buenos Aires took 33 hours on a DC-7! Based largely on the political risks, business practices, taxes and exchange problems, I returned to New

York and filed a negative report. However, Stern was already deeply committed to the project, and many people in New York, including Bob Sarnoff, were optimistic about the chance for success. I returned to Argentina, accompanied by an engineer, and put the station on the air. Little did I dream the headaches that were ahead.

Hundreds of thousands of dollars worth of urgently needed operating equipment (transmitter and studio) remained in dockside warehouses until I discovered a quaint local practice. It was quietly suggested to me that I should hire an "expediter." So, I found and hired Señor Brun, an expediter. For weeks we would go to the waterfront at 7 a.m. Along the endless corridors of warehouses, we would stop at the offices of dock officials. After an 8 a.m. coffee and brandy, Señor Brun and I moved on to the next office, leaving a little envelope on the desk. Our equipment soon started to roll! The station finally got on the air, but it was a most difficult project. I returned to New York after air date, and Dick Hollands took over in Buenos Aires to furnish NBC with management supervision for the company's 40% interest. Eventually, the operation was not profitable and it was sold.

NBC assigned me to Channel 4 in Washington in 1960. WRC-TV in Washington was then in the midst of a proposed transfer involving Philadelphia, Boston, Washington, San Francisco—a four-way station-ownership change. I had already been designated Vice President and General Manager of WNAC-TV Boston as of the date the ownership change took place. NBC, under the agreement, was to deliver operating management to RKO. Buddy Sugg expected me to sharpen the operation and make necessary personnel changes, not an assignment in which one wins popularity polls. However, I liked Washington and had a ringside seat for the Great Debates and the sparkling Kennedy Inaugural. Camelot was fascinating to watch from that position; I was to see the other, less attractive side, within a year.

Tom Ervin designated me as the company witness in the hearings on violence in television because I managed the Washington station, and the testimony could be offered on a local basis (also, Tom knew that I had earlier contact with Senator Dodd, the Chairman, when I was in Connecticut). It was my first appearance as a witness and, thanks to Howard Monderer, NBC's Washington attorney, I survived. It was the first of a long series of company appearances before Senator Dodd and the Subcommittee on Juvenile Delinquency.

In 1960, Bob Kintner asked me to be the corporate representative in Washington and report to David Adams, whom I greatly admired and respected. Tom Ervin, familiar with my earliest activities in Washington at the FCC and the Congress, recommended me to Kintner. Scoop Russell had held this post for many years. He was a gruff, colorful man who had come to Washington with the Hoover Administration and had fine contacts in Washington, and he had been effective for NBC.

After talking with Scoop and numerous other Washington "experts," and after weeks of mental debate, I accepted the offer. In January of 1962, I opened an office at 1725 K Street with a small staff of secretarial and research personnel. Howard Monderer moved his office from Nebraska Avenue to join my group downtown. Howard is still working at the present K Street office, and those of us who have worked with him over the years are convinced that he is one of the most able communications lawyers in the city. Bud Rukeyser worked out of that office for the Press Department for a brief period. By 1983, the office would have a legal and government relations staff of about 15 people.

During the years that followed, David Adams was an ideal boss. He did not attempt to limit our activities and permitted great flexibility in operating policy. We made decisions and moved ahead while our colleagues at CBS and ABC were trying to obtain authority from New York.

Very few people within the company are fully aware of all the activities handled at K Street. I believe we could narrow the definition down to three principal areas:

First, it serves in the role of an embassy. It is a listening post, reporting and interpreting what is currently taking place and what is expected to happen; it conveys company policy and information to those in need of specific data. It is NBC's visible point of contact for official Washington in that sensitive and critical area.

Secondly, the office presents industry and company positions in the legislative and regulatory arenas. The arguments for or against pending matters are presented to the House, Senate, FCC, White House, and many other government offices.

Thirdly, the office handles industry-relations activity. The staff works with other network representatives, the NAB and other trade associations such as MST, AAAA, ANA, AAF, and numerous other groups, including the broadcast and advertising trade press.

Although the three network offices are generally similar in structure, there has been a difference in selection of personnel. Both ABC and NBC selected heads of office on a career or long-term basis. CBS seems to use the Washington office as a "staging area" for incoming or outgoing executives.

When Bob Kintner cautioned me that it would take time to become effective in this role, he must have been drawing on wisdom gained in his days as a Washington columnist. It takes time to build the kind of relationship that causes a Member of Congress to grant appointments on a regular basis. As some lobbyists in Washington say: "The true test of having made it with a Member is when he or she calls you for information or advice."

A single phone call from "inside" can head off disaster. One evening, for example, I received a call at home from a committee member regarding a very important piece of broadcast legislation. The bill was scheduled for markup the following day, and industry people believed it was safely on its way to the floor. My informant told me an amendment would be offered the next morning that would eliminate all benefits for broadcasters and would create new problems. The amendment appeared innocuous and would probably be adopted. We were on the Hill at 7 a.m. the next morning working the cafeteria and the offices of committee members. The amendment was defeated, and our bill remained intact. There were many such incidents.

The frequent lack of a "horse" has been, and still is, a major hurdle for the broadcast industry. A "horse" is a Member who is sufficiently committed to an industry position that he will present industry legislation and carry the fight to the floor. An equally serious problem is the absence of a broadcast industry spokesman in the House or Senate who will support and argue for an industry position on a regular basis. At no time that I can recall has broadcasting ever had a spokesperson in Congress.

It was not a friendly Congress during my 22 years. The Members feared and distrusted broadcasters. In general, they regarded broadcasters—particularly networks—as too big, too rich, and too powerful. I recall one typical report which referred to us as arrogant and unresponsive. Many government officials had this strange love/hate attitude toward broadcasting; they desperately wanted to be on the air and take advantage of the publicity benefits. But, at the same time, they were afraid of the medium and how it might hurt them as politicians, candidates, or public figures. Fortunately, the industry has been able to present some very articulate and effective witnesses in broadcast proceedings.

Frank Stanton of CBS was superb. I think most Washington observers believe that he was the recognized industry spokesman over a 25-year period. Julian Goodman was a close second, and I believe he would easily have earned the recognition given Stanton had he been on the scene a few years earlier. Julian was always a very poised and knowledgeable witness.

Industry witnesses spent countless days before Senator Pastore on a variety of issues ranging from sex and violence to Section 315, Fairness and Equal Time. The Rhode Island Senator chaired the Senate Subcommittee on Communications when I arrived in Washington and continued until he retired in 1976. More than any other Member during that time he focused on broadcast issues and held ongoing hearings regarding broadcast matters. Pastore was given almost complete authority in this field by the chairman of the full committee, and he was close to being a television czar. The industry was fortunate to have him in this critical position for such a long period. He was an outstanding senator, and he had a tremendous impact on our business. He was a short, fiery and mercurial man who could be tough and demanding but was always fair. A very religious family man, he found it extremely difficult to accept what he saw as a growing pattern of sexual permissiveness and excessive violence in action programs. Once, Julian was reprimanded by Senator Pastore, who was outraged over the appearance of Faye Emerson on a "Tonight" show. He stridently pointed out that if Miss Emerson had leaned over another inch, "they" would have popped out. Responding to lectures of this type required great skill.

Pastore heard countless days of testimony looking toward repeal of equal time provisions of the

Communications Act in order to permit a continuation of the 1960 Great Debates. On one occasion, the Senate was ready to pass an exemption for debates, but Lyndon Johnson called the Senate leaders and told them to "knock it off." He had no intention of debating the Republican candidate. From that day on, we all knew that repeal would never take place unless it was politically acceptable to the party in power.

Cory Dunham became a very fine witness, and I believe he continues in this role for the company today. He is careful in his approach to committees, accurate in his statements and is always well prepared. He has established credibility in Washington, which is all-important for a witness.

Bob Kintner was not a particularly good witness, but he was always under such heavy pressure, as with the Dodd Committee, it was not a fair test.

Walter Scott had some very difficult days with the Dodd Committee and was always distressed and uncomfortable when he had to appear. Walter is a refined and gentle man who was horrified at the crude and sometimes vicious demeanor of members and staff of the committees. He was not alone in that reaction. There were two or three occasions when it was necessary for me to appear as a witness, and it is a very unnerving experience. I recall one comical incident when I was appearing before Congressman Rogers' Communications Subcommittee. The subject was excessive commercial content in television, and a Member, I believe Dan Rostenkowski, suddenly asked what we were doing about loudness. This was something I was not prepared for, and, in trying to explain the equipment in control rooms that cuts off highs, I made the memorable comment: "It is not loud, Congressman, it just sounds loud."

Oren Harris was Chairman of the full Committee on Commerce when I arrived in Washington. He was the last of the "strong" chairmen. During his term, the committee was completely controlled by the Chairman. This was a plus and a minus for a lobbyist. On the plus side, only the Chairman had to be seen and convinced of the merits of an argument. On the minus side, if the Chairman was against you, there was nothing you could do about it.

Today, because of changes in the Congress, it is necessary to visit about 40 Members on an issue instead of a single chairman. As the nation's political viewpoint changed with the Vietnam war, younger, more active and liberal Members insisted on a greater voice in committee affairs, and the old, all-powerful committee structure collapsed. I do not mean to say that later chairmen were not strong individuals; they simply could no longer wield the authority and power that was possible in the days of an Oren Harris.

The present Chairman of the full Committee is John Dingell, a tough, hard-nosed member from Michigan with lots of House experience. John finds lots of fault with our industry, but he is basically a fair man who is willing to listen. Unlike Harris of earlier years, Dingell frequently has to make deals with his committee members in order to retain control, but he is a skilled politician and knows how to survive.

Torbert Macdonald, who replaced Walter Rogers as Chairman of the Subcommittee, was another strong personality. Unfortunately, Torbie always had a chip on his shoulder for most of the world, and broadcasters in particular. At one broadcast meeting, he told the group not to ever try to see him, that they were all liars and phonies, and that he listened only to Wasilewski (NAB) and Kenney.

The sex-and-violence issue was the subject of several years of hearings before Senator Tom Dodd, Chairman of the Juvenile Delinquency Subcommittee. These were rough-and-tumble hearings that became more brutal and vicious as they progressed. At times it was like a CIA activity, with records disappearing, indications of bugging and tapping of phones, and witnesses being moved to different hotels in the middle of the night.

The Committee staff was intent on discrediting the network witnesses and proving that network executives ordered Hollywood producers to add violence to programs.

This was the hearing in which Committee staff spliced dozens of clips from action shows and then presented, out of context, a long tape of violent scenes to show the Members (and press) what was running on television. Kintner was pressed hard in their effort to build a perjury case but they did not succeed. These hearings may have played a part in the subsequent departures of ABC's Ollie Treyz and CBS's Jim Aubrey from their networks. Both had spent many difficult days testifying.

With the arrival of the Kennedy Administration and "The New Frontier," a new trend developed in the attitude of government agencies and personnel toward broadcasting. The Administration was not friendly toward broadcasters. It pioneered new and creative uses of TV and radio to suit its needs and purposes. The licensees had to live with implied threats of government actions. Newton Minow sounded the bugle call for the Administration with his "Vast Wasteland" speech. Small but active special interest groups following the New Frontier challenged broadcast policies, content, and structure. Restructuring became a buzz word, and all kinds of groups gathered under that banner to influence or dismantle the system. Their activities peaked when Congressman Van Deerlin, much later in the 70's, attempted to rewrite the Communications Act. Van was a likeable man and easy to get along with, but as he approached retirement, he wanted to leave some lasting monument to his efforts. With the urging of his staff, headed by Chip Shooshan, he launched a horrendous proposal that included huge fees from broadcasters, limitations on ownership, specific program activities and controls, and other "restructuring" devices. Eventually the plan died, but it took many months of lobbying by the Washington corps and individual stations.

The Johnson Administration was much easier to work with than Kennedy's. The open antagonism from staff people was no longer present. The NBC office had very good cooperation from the Executive Staff at the White House. When Nick Johnson was appointed to the FCC,

Walter Jenkins, the President's right-hand man, called to inform me. He said Nick had alienated just about everyone at the Maritime Commission but, in a seven-man Commission, he certainly could not do any harm at the FCC. As we know, it was a most unfortunate choice! While Nick soon became known as a gadfly, our problems were serious ones. He did not wish to see or talk with broadcasters and reached decisions in his own strange way.

The Nixon years gave all of us a bunker mentality. The Agnew speeches and the Clay Whitehead attacks provided some insight into Administration thinking. The questionable approach of Charles Colson in his visits to network heads seeking better understanding and more support was really intimidating. At one time or another, it seemed that every office and every agency was programmed to undermine the broadcast system. Dean Burch, as Chairman of the FCC, appeared to offer more resistance to protect the integrity of his office. Not that Dean was not loyal to Nixon; he was. On many occasions when he was expected to perform some act of sabotage through his agency, he declined.

It is interesting to note that broadcasters have been equally unpopular with both political parties. The usual Democratic theme is that broadcasters are wealthy "fat cats" who should be under stronger controls and have their operations broken up and redistributed. The usual Republican cry is that most broadcasters are too liberal or radical and in need of more controls.

The Ford White House was easy to work with. President Ford was always extremely pleasant and cooperative. After the open-door policies of Ford, we found the Carter Administration hopeless. There was just no way to establish working contact with the Executive Offices. We had to use outside sources to obtain information or supply input.

The Reagan Administration was helpful and cooperative while I was there. The deregulatory policies were most welcome and a pleasant change from earlier trends. Of course, the loss of the Financial Interest project (programs and syndication) was a major blow to the network offices. The opposition, using such Hollywood people as Charlton Heston or Clint Eastwood, was more successful in influencing the President than we were. The campaign to change the Financial Interest rule gave the network Washington offices an unusual opportunity. As we have talked, you must have noticed that most of our actions are of a defensive nature. For one brief moment, we had an opportunity to charge—and we lost.

Section 315—Equal Time and Fairness—is perhaps the longest-running broadcast show in Washington. The 1960 debates between Nixon and Kennedy focused attention on this issue, and it has been with us ever since. It has taken enormous amounts of time and effort to present the arguments in this case, and, strangely, many broadcasters do not feel that strongly about repeal. Equal time has not been a problem at the local level, we are told, and in some cases it is a blessing (or a crutch). Fairness has been a "sacred cow" in Congress and, apparently, many broadcasters are happy to live with it instead of a new Congressional effort to balance things out.

The most frustrating loss in Congress on any issue has to be the cigarette advertising ban. Actually, the industry did not lose this battle; the tobacco industry won. John Banzhaf, a lawyer with a cause, filed a petition with the FCC that brought the tobacco advertising matter under the Fairness Doctrine. The cigarette issue wound down to a final determination in 1970.

In the final year, NBC offered a plan to reduce the levels of tar and nicotine (it became known as the Kenney Plan, although Tom Ervin was the author). The plan would amend the code so that each year, over a four-year period, no advertiser's product would be accepted unless the tar and nicotine had been reduced to a predetermined level. The staff of the Senate and the Surgeon General's office liked the plan, but the tobacco people had already made their deal; it was too late.

The manufacturers were buying television to sell brands, not product. They decided since they were not increasing volume of sales, they could eliminate the huge TV cost, save money, and eliminate the anti-smoking ads then required on TV. The manufacturers made an advantageous deal with Senator Ted Moss and the Committee: Congress would preempt State legislation on labeling, and the tobacco companies would get protection on labeling and warnings in other media by offering this voluntary package. In order to keep all manufacturers in line, they told the Senate it was necessary to put this plan in statute form.

The Federal Communications Commission has widened its turf over the years, as happens with all government bureaucracies. However, the FCC, unlike many other agencies, has an open-door policy that is a major plus for broadcasters. It is not difficult for any broadcaster to visit with staff or Commissioners.

The program activities of the News Division frequently created great problems for us in the Washington office. The Division was nearly autonomous and well protected, as it should be. In Washington, nothing angered an official more than a newscast or news program that he felt did not treat him fairly or, in his opinion, did not accurately state the facts. I was constantly called to the Hill or to some government office to hear the outraged roars of anger that resulted from some news story.

Cable and pay-TV has been, and still is, a source of bitter argument and frequent confrontation. The history of this battle is strewn with contradictions. At the outset, cable was welcomed as a means of extending the broadcaster's service area. At that time, cable would have settled for broad controls if it could have a few extras, such as two-week non-duplication. The NAB Board was not about to give an inch to a system that could become competitive. What was once a strong broadcaster position has crumbled as cable gained in public acceptance and Congressional support. This was probably a case of broadcasters wanting too much and, as a result, losing a great deal.

Children's programming, in both program content and advertising, has been a complex issue for years. The best efforts of networks and stations do not satisfy those who feel there should be much more programming designed exclusively for children in key time periods, and who wish to protect young people from "harmful" advertising. The problems of creating programs young people will watch and then scheduling them are well known. The question of which ads are "harmful" is a tough one. Certainly the government agencies—or Congress—should not be dictating content, format, frequency and time periods. But, they will continue to try to do just that, and the industry will have to stay ahead of the regulators.

Congress feels that early election projections disrupt normal voting patterns on the West Coast. It appears the logical answer is a fixed closing time for polls in all states—at least the contiguous states—and that action requires legislation. When the polls are closed in all states, there is no harm in using key precinct and exit polls to predict state and national winners. It seems the ball is in Congress's court on this one.

As I look back over my years in the industry, from 1946 to 1983, I feel very fortunate. It was a period of explosive development and dramatic change in direction and technology. We saw a parade of fascinating people and a continuing series of momentous events.

And, for the company, I can only wish a continuation of all the successes it is enjoying this fall of 1985 under the superb leadership of Grant Tinker. Good luck to everyone at NBC and to all our fine affiliates. It must seem good to be back on top.

September 25, 1985

Donald J. Mercer, having spent his entire career at NBC, retired in 1981 as Senior Vice President of Affiliate Relations. NBC was a very young company when he became a Page and a Guide, so his observations span colorful years.

Donald J Mercer

"I think all of us in Station Relations at that time would agree that the early 1950's were the most exciting years in our careers. We were building the NBC Television Network! By mid-1953, our reception room had more daily traffic than that of a credit dentist."

I joined the NBC Guest Relations Department as a Page and a Guide in the early 30's. At that time, it was the entry level access for bright, ambitious young men who wanted to become part of the new glamorous world of radio broadcasting. There are many distinguished alumni—management and talent at NBC and elsewhere—who began their careers as NBC Pages. Within the National Broadcasting Company, its alumni/alumnae are almost as proud of having been on the Page and Guide Staff as those Americans who proudly claim to be descendents of the "Mayflower" settlers. Incidentally, a couple of years ago NBC had a wonderful party for 600-plus former Pages and Guides in Studio 8-H which was, by consensus, a memorable evening.

I got out of high school in 1933, which was not one of the banner economic years in our land, and I knew that I wasn't going to be able to go away to college. A neighbor, a great name in broadcasting and at NBC and RCA, O.B. Hanson, talked about plans to move NBC to newly built Radio City.

O.B. Hanson was a legend. He was originally English, a Renaissance man—a Fellow of the Royal Architects who became a very gifted electronics engineer. We owe a great deal to him. He designed the studios that are still used at 30 Rockefeller Plaza.

O.B. mentioned that NBC in its new location would need young men to serve on the Page Staff. I jumped at that, of course, because it was everybody's ambition in my high school era to become a radio announcer and do the late night dance bands. When I applied, one of many, it didn't hurt that O.B. Hanson had introduced me to the Personnel people as someone with some promise and potential.

We all loved it. It was just a great experience. Pages and Guides came from all parts of the country and from all elements of our society. The staff was made up of men only, and it included sons of the great and near great in the arts and commerce. Reinold Warrenrath, Jr., Efrem Zimbalist, Jr., and numerous other bearers of well-known names wore the blue uniform of the Guest Relations staff. At that time, there was no management training program at NBC. This was really the access to promotion within. You had to make a name for yourself in the uniform and, at the same time, look around to see if you wanted to advance in program areas, in commercial areas or in engineering.

A great many of us took the announcers' test, and I'm happy to tell you that I passed it. Many of us attended the classes supervised by NBC's chief announcer, Pat Kelly. In addition to mike technique, I remember the stress and emphasis given to musical terms and the proper pronunciation of composers' and artists' names of all nationalities. I decided that announcing really was not for me—I didn't have the special gift that would lift me above the average in the field.

As a Page, I started at the princely salary of $65 a month. That was the going wage in that era, but if you studied hard and learned the tour routine and could handle it well, you immediately got bumped to $80 or $85 a month. Most of the fellows had to live at home. I did. Fortunately, NBC furnished the uniform, and our white shirts and black ties were also supplied by the company. It was a formal time—the night crew wore wing collars and bow ties. As a matter of fact, announcers, after 6 o'clock, wore tuxedos. Not only in Radio City, but also at many affiliated stations up and down the land.

One interesting aspect of the early days on the Page Staff was that you worked both sides of the building. The studio section on some shifts and the office area on others. If assigned to a studio floor you reported to an attractive, personable (sometimes even pretty) lady who was the "hostess" on that floor. She would receive the calls and visitors for the producers, writers, directors, actors and musicians who were in rehearsal or on the air, and we would run the messages or escort the visitors into the studio or rehearsal room.

If you were working in the office section (the east end of the RCA Building) you ran the mail and memos and announced the visitors to the managers and executives located there. It was a great way to learn who was who and something about the structure and organization of the broadcasting building.

That was the Golden Age of Radio—the 30's and 40's. Most of the actors and creative people spent a great deal of their spare time in the NBC studios because that's where much of the casting was done, and they wanted to be on the spot when an important program was put together. In no time at all, most of us felt we knew all the great and the near great of radio. Another great plus was the ability to get broadcast tickets on our off hours. A super way to impress a lady friend. A nod of recognition from one of the stars and our dates were certainly impressed by what appeared to be an important position we had.

Most of the big network shows in those days originated in New York, and it took years before the time zone problem was solved. Repeats to the West Coast via recordings were not permitted. In those days recordings were considered not up to broadcast quality, and so the cast came back to the studio and repeated the show three hours later for the Western time zones. I think this rule was first broken at NBC when the exciting account of the Hindenburg disaster, recorded by a WLS Chicago engineer who was at the scene, was fed to the network.

I was in Guest Relations until 1936, and then I moved to the Promotion Department. That came about because I was taking some courses at New York University. One English course was taught by Bill Parsons, a key member of our Sales Promotion Department. (He's still a good friend.) When NBC's tenth anniversary came up in '36, he tapped me to work with him on a very special anniversary dinner—50 years ago this coming year. Following that, I went in as a copy cub and keeper of the mailing lists in the Network Sales Promotion Department.

When Bill Parsons left Promotion to handle sales and promotion operations for the Transcription Department, which offered transcribed radio programs to stations all over the world, he took me with him. By this time, broadcast quality had been achieved in the recording

art—16″ vinyl discs with about a quarter hour of program material on each side. We had a music library of these discs—everything from Bach to boogie-woogie. We also had drama, fashion features, a sound effects library and a whole variety of transcribed program series that we sold in all the lengths—full hours, 30 minutes, 15 minutes, some as small as 5-minute segments. During WW II, I got a big kick going into Radio Luxembourg's studios and seeing our library there. It was a commercial station and a very valued subscriber to our service.

I took military leave of NBC a month after Pearl Harbor, having been well along in the draft process since the previous summer. I returned near the end of 1945 with the rank of Captain in the Field Artillery. I had served with an infantry division in the European Theatre. When I came back alive, and healthy, I returned to NBC and was happy to be accepted back in the Radio Recording operation. In 1948, I was named Director of the NBC Recording Division.

Because of the changing world of radio and the increasing demands on management made by the new excitement at NBC—television—the prospects of growth for the Recording Division were not very promising. Our problems were soon solved when we were absorbed by the RCA Victor Division and moved into new space near their recording studios downtown. I stayed there for about a year showing the RCA people where the handles were on the music library service we continued to market. They did a nice job with it until the art changed and the itinerant disc jockey with his own personal record collection and his own way of structuring a program became a way of life in radio in the late 40's.

My goal was to return to NBC, preferably in Station Relations. I felt I could continue to use and expand my knowledge of stations and markets gained through the transcription sales experience. Furthermore, I enjoyed working with the stations' ownerships and managements. In 1950, I won a berth in Station Relations (now Affiliate Relations) as a Contact Representative (now Regional Director).

In the summer of 1947 NBC held its first affiliates convention in Atlantic City. It was timed to be contiguous to the first post-World War II National Convention of the NAB (which was also held in Atlantic City). There the radio affiliates and a handful of pioneer television affiliates heard a rousing exhortation from General Sarnoff to hurry home and apply for a television channel and join with NBC in the development of a most exciting new era in broadcasting.

During the war years, government restrictions on travel ruled out national conventions, but an affiliate-appointed Stations Planning and Advisory Committee (SPAC) met with NBC management representatives to discuss problems of mutual concern. Since 1947, annual affiliate conventions have been held almost without lapse, and the successor affiliate panels have met regularly with NBC's top people between national gatherings.

Walter Damm, who headed the stations of the Milwaukee Journal for many years, was the first SPAC chairman I knew. (In fact, he may well have been the very first.) Mr. Damm very clearly and effectively voiced the affiliate views, their wants and their needs for a number of years to a succession of NBC presidents, beginning with Niles Trammell.

The 1947 Atlantic City meeting set the scene for General Sarnoff to raise the banner and promise the affiliates that NBC would take them to great heights in television. His message was, "Get into it *now*!" Many station owners heeded it. Others, for whatever reasons, decided to wait, and that delay was costly for many of them—and for NBC, for in 1948 the FCC placed a freeze on additional TV station licenses while they reworked the channel allocation plan. The freeze was to last four years, and so network growth was also frozen.

In 1950, when I joined Station Relations, Carleton Smith was head of the department. I was assigned to radio stations in the central part of the country. I came to know and love the Dakotas, Nebraska, Iowa, Minnesota and Wisconsin.

Some people at NBC Radio realized that television was really going to knock it off its pins, but there also was a lot of whistling in the dark. There were a great many people who thought that it would be a *long* time before television inroads would be a major force in the diminution of radio, and, in one sense, they were right. The rapid growth of television certainly changed the fate of networking in radio. It didn't reduce the number of stations because what evolved was stratified radio where all the different audiences would have their needs and wants met by specific stations in each market area.

Television showed promising early growth to '48 when the FCC instituted the freeze because they had discovered that, to their embarrassment, the Allocations Plan didn't really give full multi-channel service to a number of important markets in the country, and some projected growth centers would soon become more important than they had been pre-war. The FCC research fellows took four years to redesign the Channel Allocation Plan. In 1952 the freeze was lifted, but it wasn't until 1953 that we began to see new television stations blossoming.

In 1951 (or early '52) Joe McConnell recruited Harry Bannister from the Detroit News stations to head up Station Relations when Carleton Smith moved on to manage our owned station in Washington. A large and imposing figure, Harry managed WWJ Radio very successfully for the Evening News Association and led them into television back in 1946 and 1947. Because WWJ-TV was one of the small select group of NBC's pre-freeze TV affiliates, Bannister had a high profile throughout the industry. Like Walter Damm's, his views on broadcasting issues were widely sought and quoted across the country.

Harry was a "character" in every sense of the word—though Brooklyn-born his style, manner and dress were anything but New York. With one exception: his speech had overtones of the borough of his birth. (Some of us were certain that he took occasional refresher courses to keep the accent intact.)

Harry's platform ability was extraordinary. Not only did *he* write all of his many speeches—he was widely sought on the banquet circuit—he memorized them for delivery. Harry's followers among the affiliates grew despite the fact that he had joined the network.

In preparation for the lifting of the freeze and the "gold rush" for television licenses, Bannister fused the department. When he joined us there was a team of Radio Contact Reps and a smaller group assigned to television. It was important that we all work as one team in that era to share information on the status of our affiliates with TV aspirations.

I think that all of us in Station Relations at that time would agree that the early 1950's were the most exciting years in our careers. We were building the NBC Television Network! By mid-1953 our reception room had more daily traffic than that of a credit dentist!

Harry Bannister had appointed Tom Knode as his second in command, and we all reported to Tom. Our mission then was to implement as nearly as possible the national television coverage plan developed by Mal Beville and Barry Rumple and their associates in the Research Department. We wanted to provide television service for *all* America and ensure our advertisers of an effective, efficient media buy.

I believe that all of us who worked on that TV affiliate recruitment task force, among them Ray O'Connell, Bill Kelley, Paul Rittenhouse, Paul Hancock and Joe Berhalter have reason to share pride in the results. Tony Cervini joined us "in progress," but he learned quickly and is amply qualified for the bigger and more complicated responsibility he handles as today's Vice President for Affiliate Relations.

About this time Pat Weaver, who had joined us in 1949 as Vice President in charge of television, was named President succeeding Joe McConnell. Early on, Pat became recognized as one of the great creative names in the development of the medium. He was a worthy successor to NBC's John Royal, who was regarded as radio's outstanding programming genius. I knew Mr. Royal, but only after he was officially retired. He was still active, however. He kept an office on the 6th (Executive) floor at 30 Rock, and, for many years, a flow of memos issued forth from his corner with program and talent suggestions and critiques of programs he heard

or watched. Perhaps his finest hour during his senior years was to calm the affiliate body, who were understandably restless when CBS succeeded in luring Jack Benny and a few other major talent properties away from us with capital gains deals. His impassioned speech before a full affiliate gathering won the day.

In the spring of 1953, at the NAB convention in Los Angeles, the rumor spread like wildfire that CBS was about to steal a handful of NBC's major television affiliates. Within a couple of days, confirmation of the defection of WTAR-TV, Norfolk, and WBEN-TV, Buffalo, became public. During a hurried war council in Harry Bannister's suite, a list of the most susceptible stations was agreed on, and Tom Knode and Bannister decided that the situation called for an appearance by General Sarnoff. John West, RCA's well known and widely admired West Coast Vice President, handled the details. An affiliate meeting was called at the earliest possible date following the NAB convention. It was held at the RCA Laboratories in Princeton to a full affiliate turnout. The location not only gave them an opportunity to hear the General, but to see first hand some of the exciting electronic wizardry RCA had in development which would shortly become part of their business.

The General's performance was magnificent. He spoke without a note for something close to 50 minutes. He reminded his audience of the distance they had traveled thus far in bringing broadcast service to their audiences and advertisers. And in the midst of the laboratory wonders, he expanded on the tremendous excitement ahead. At one point, he even "second guessed" himself, saying something to the effect that he just couldn't believe that a comedian could be more important than the time and technology the network and its affiliates contributed to his popularity. With a twinkle, he admitted that he had since learned differently.

Of course we had to do more than trot out the General. Among the advantages that CBS had at the time was an early jump on Monday night, when their schedule was filled with new and quickly popular half-hour shows designed for television, including "Arthur Godfrey's Talent Scouts," followed by "I Love Lucy," while NBC was turning cameras on one of its most respected radio programs to lead off the night: "The Voice of Firestone." A fine show and very popular for a number of years, but essentially a radio program. We had to reprogram for a television audience. And we did.

In the early post-freeze years television stations were popping up across the country faster than AT&T could extend its coaxial cable and microwave links, and so stretches of the network were available only through allocation of an existing line. Steve Flynn represented NBC in regular meetings held by AT&T with the four networks. (DuMont was still in the picture.) He did a great job in getting us at least a fair share.

Many of the vast distances in the Mountain and Pacific time zones were linked by privately-built microwave lash-ups that involved difficult surveys and courageous construction men. It also required some ingenious financial arrangements in the affiliate contract, because many of the cities most difficult to reach did not command a rate high enough to offset the cost of bringing network service to them.

Joe Berhalter patiently worked out the financial plans which enabled us to fill out NBC network coverage in some pretty remote areas of the country. My hunch is that most, if not all, of those special links are now superseded by satellite receiving dishes at the transmitter sites.

In the mid 50's, when RCA's compatible color system was approved and the CBS whirling disc abandoned, we enjoyed an advantage over our chief rivals in affiliation pitches. Ours was the network that started to program color in ever increasing volume. People who bought color sets wanted to watch programs in color. Affiliation prospects responded to that point.

In 1956 or 1957, Tom Knode was named Vice President of the department, still reporting to Harry Bannister, and I was named Director. Through those years all of us handled affiliate relations for both the radio and the television networks. Because we assisted so many of our radio affiliate ownerships into the television network, a great percentage of them remained with us in both. Our department didn't relinquish the radio responsibility until the mid-70's, when the changing world of radio saw the introduction of new NBC radio network forms and programming that demanded full attention from an affiliate relations group.

When Tom Knode left in 1967, I was named his successor and was delighted to have a man with the knowledge, skills and experience of Ray O'Connell move along with me as the next in command. The decade ahead, we'd soon learn, would tax all of the resources in the department.

Through the years our primary mission was to keep management informed on the probable affiliate reaction to plans and projects in discussion but not yet released from 30 Rock. This became more difficult as the medium developed and new commercial forms and lengths became a fact of our business. Added to those areas of affiliate challenge was an ever-growing list of products which Walter Damm thought would never be accepted on TV. In fact, a number of them weren't even on the market during his era.

Perhaps even more difficult for us and the affiliates was the growing demand of the creative community for a more liberal and relaxed code in our Standards and Practices Department. From my years on the NAB Board I know that this was an industry-wide movement.

In the mid-70's, our program fortunes slumped, and we experienced too many successive third place positions in a three-network ranking. It didn't matter if our rating was only a tenth of a point from the second network; we were third. The trade papers headlined this news regularly and soon the consumer press took up the ratings sweepstakes as a regular feature.

For years I have harbored the theory that the overnight ratings capability of the major audience measurement services killed a number of programs that could have been successful. In television's early days, it seems to me, a series might have been halfway into the 13-week commitment before the researchers had a real fix on its prospects. And by that time the creative group involved had an opportunity to doctor the areas that needed strengthening.

The mid-70's were a trying time for our department. For years ABC's "war" chest full of attractive compensation plans was used to woo affiliates away from CBS and us. They tried, but with relatively little success. In the mid-1970's, however, they added a new and important page to their pitch: program successes, a schedule that vied with CBS for first place.

An added dimension to the problem from NBC's standpoint was the fact that many of the old-line affiliates, family-owned since the early days of radio, had been bought by larger corporate organizations, frequently publicly held and almost invariably managed by bright young business school graduates. The days of the "old boy" network were fast vanishing.

Through the years following Walter Damm, NBC has been most fortunate in the affiliate choices for Chairman of their Board of Delegates (now Board of Directors) and the board members who meet at regular intervals with NBC's top management to discuss problems of mutual concern. Jack Harris of Houston, Louis Read of New Orleans, and Harold (Hod) Grams of St. Louis were all TV pioneers in their markets. They succeeded Mr. Damm in that order. They were followed by Bob Ferguson of Wheeling, Ancil Payne of Seattle and Fred Paxton of Paducah. These men were dedicated to harmonious and mutually profitable network-affiliate relations. They certainly helped our department considerably.

Who were my heroes? Who set the standards for NBC? Of course there is only one answer: General Sarnoff. The source. He had the dream and invested the time, energy and drive to make it come true. Pat Weaver left an indelible impression on me, as he did on television. He sparkled and crackled with creativity.

In my view, he, more than any other person or persons, freed television from the shackles and patterns of radio, both in terms of program concepts and commercial form. His "Wide, Wide World" was on the air about 25 years before the technology it really needed was available!

Julian Goodman was NBC's President during most of my years as head of Affiliate Relations. A fine, thoughtful, articulate man, he was universally admired and respected by the affiliates. Of all the NBC leaders I knew over the years, Julian is the one I worked with most closely, knew best, and admired greatly for his decency, fairness and readiness to pitch in and help when called upon.

Harry Bannister is not only on my list of unforgettable characters, but I daresay also on the lists of a great many affiliate owners and managers. The reason? The baseball cap he wore at his desk all day. He started this shortly after his arrival at NBC. His explanation was that the air conditioning gave him a headache and that capping his bald dome relieved it. It got to be Harry's trademark, and it wasn't long before affiliates all over the country sent him a great collection of caps. A few months before Harry retired, he paid his dentist a visit. The dentist checked Harry's bite and found some malocclusion. He told Harry that malocclusion had been known to cause headaches as he filed down the offending tooth. No more headaches and no more caps for Harry Bannister!

What's given me the most satisfaction in my years at NBC? The most satisfying years were the early '50s when I was part of the task force signing up television stations to join the new NBC-TV Network. The sense of participation in fleshing out the network was exhilarating for me, and I think for all the others in our department.

My wish for NBC on its 60th Anniversay is for many more years of leadership in *all* the important areas of broadcasting, including program popularity.

July 22, 1985

Bob Mounty, Executive Vice President, Radio, came to NBC Radio in 1974 after a very successful career in radio at Metromedia's WIP in Philadelphia and WNEW in New York City.

"I compare our business with a big corporate Iowa corn farm where brilliant young scientists test, then enrich the soil to grow more and better ears of corn per acre. Our goal in radio is to grow more and better audience ears per quarter hour."

The Golden Age of Radio began on November 15, 1926, with a four-hour broadcast on NBC's 25 affiliated radio stations. A dream of General Sarnoff's became a reality that evening. This was the birth of a network which grew in the thirties and matured in the forties. The fifties were difficult for network radio. Television exploded after World War II.

My brother worked for an advertising agency. He talked about the radio salesmen who called on him. The field sounded kind of glamorous and interesting, so I decided to try it. Before that, I had sold paint to retailers. Getting a media job was difficult. I thought they'd want anybody who looked as if he'd work hard, hit the boondocks, and bang on enough doors to get the business. Because television got all the attention, radio was hurting and radio stations couldn't even pay a modest base salary to help support my wife and family.

I was finally offered a small "draw against commission" from WIP, a station owned by the Gimbel's Department Store. I decided to take a chance. That first year, I made 20% less than I had the year before as a paint salesman, which wasn't very much of a salary.

At the time I started, the radio industry was faced with change. All the wonderful things radio had boasted of in the so-called Golden Age had moved to television. The glamour left it when Bob Hope and Jack Benny and other stars went to television. Radio was left with none of its birthright programs and services. Rather than a radio station being like a theatre, as a television station is now, radio had to learn to program differently because its lineup of variety shows, serials and dramas had all crossed over to television. Radio stations began to specialize and program for a particular segment of the community.

In 1957, WIP, Philadelphia, was an independent station programming music and news, with "chatty" disc jockeys—the antithesis of its former image. Radio started to take off again around the mid-fifties, when people like Todd

Storrs and Gordon McLendon created Top Forty radio. Rock'n'roll radio was just beginning to happen. The format was geared for younger listeners. We called it "Top 40" because we actually played the 40 top records over and over again. *Very* quickly, stations were getting ratings measured by Hooper, Pulse, and Nielsen, and we sold on those numbers.

Many radio stations tried to remain omnibus stations, and they usually weakened. They soon had to specialize (not necessarily in strict, rigid format) because they realized that they could no longer reach all the subcells of the broad, demographic spectrum. They catered to adult tastes and found large audiences too.

Many of the radio stations had always been independent because they couldn't get a network affiliation with ABC, CBS, NBC or Mutual. NBC was *the* innovative network in radio. They not only started networking, they maintained creative leadership with exclusive programs like "Monitor."

In 1957, when I went to work at the radio station, it never occurred to me it might be a toe-in to television. I just wanted to get a job in the business, and I liked radio so much that, before very long, I was making a good buck and *enjoying* it. Three or four years later, I was in management.

I became General Sales Manager in 1960 and stayed at WIP for five more years. A wonderful General Manager, Harvey Glascock, one of John Kluge's chief lieutenants at Metromedia, let me do everything I wanted to do. He watched me, let me train myself and just made sure I didn't ruin the radio station—and I really learned the business under his tutelage.

When he moved to WNEW in New York City, the most wonderful independent radio station in the world, he brought me with him. In 1965, I became General Sales Manager of America's Number 1 music and news station. I'd always wanted to be in radio in New York City, and here I was. Wow!

In 1968 I was promoted to Vice President and General Manager of WNEW. Airlines were probably the number one advertiser group in New York radio, and cigarettes may well have been the second largest advertising revenue souce. All that went out the window in the early seventies.

The ban on tobacco ads was a big blow, but radio had by that time become an important medium for the national advertiser. If it had to happen, it was a good time, because it was an up time in the economy.

Then, in 1972, I became Executive Vice President of Metromedia, the marketing chief for the radio division. I was expected to show everyone at Metromedia how to do it as well as we had done it at WNEW. I was not happy with the job because I wasn't in the middle of the real action.

Late in 1974, I was *delighted* to be hired by Jack Thayer, President of NBC Radio. He started the ball rolling at NBC to make us an important radio company again. To Herb Schlosser's credit, as NBC President, he wanted to rebuild radio. Radio had been allowed to wither as television absorbed the attention and energy of the company. That happened at CBS for about ten years, but CBS got "back" into radio by going all-news on the various stations in the mid-to late sixties. NBC was a few years behind. I had known Jack Thayer at Metromedia. He is a natural leader and was the highly visible type of person NBC needed, a very dynamic guy who has done everything there is to do in broadcasting. He came up with the News and Information Service, knows as NIS, which was regarded as one of the most creative and innovative efforts radio has ever seen. We delivered news and feature material to local stations 24 hours a day. Stations could use up to 50 minutes of programming each hour. This endeavor was prompted by the success of a number of all-news stations around the country.

I came to NBC specifically to build NIS. We had a superior product, beautifully developed to make it economically possible to have an all-news station in almost any market.

We began the project in January of 1975, and we were on the air by June. We really moved. We enjoyed critical acclaim throughout the industry, but we never achieved the proper number of affiliations to make it pay. Painfully, we were forced to shut down in 1977. There were a number of reasons for it. When we put it on the air, the economy was soft. It looked like a good opportunity for stations to get into an exclusive format at a reduced cost. Then the economy turned around very sharply in 1975 and a lot of stations which were marginal in 1974 were suddenly making a profit. The desire or the willingness to make a drastic change like that dropped significantly from the level our research people had predicted. Radio is a local medium, and many broadcasters have an aversion to giving up the control and autonomy this format would have required. We underestimated that emotion.

Today, Randall Bongarten, President, NBC Radio, has developed many exciting alternative programs under the aegis of our new NBC Radio Entertainment Division. In addition to our three established networks, Talknet, Source and the NBC Radio Network, we now have relationships with over a thousand radio stations in the U.S.

Local advertising sales, the mainstay of radio, are very rapidly becoming the mainstay for television stations. The growth of local expenditures is far outpacing the growth of national spot dollars in radio, and the balance is changing in television as well. Most advertisers use a media mix, and radio really augments television very effectively. So most of the major advertisers use both, and, in some cases, newspapers and magazines as well. No single medium is perfect for every kind of marketing job or objective.

You have to find the people that your medium fits and show that advertiser how to use your product best. That's the way it was when we sold a single radio station. NBC's multiple networks now relate to the younger adult as well as to the mature demographics. We sell them professionally. To be a successful salesperson, you have to have empathy. Put yourself in the advertiser's position, look at his needs.

To manage and run a company, you must motivate people by explaining your purpose, evaluating your assets, and reach those targets by bringing people on board who believe in those goals.

Jack Thayer left during the Silverman years, in 1979. The Radio Division became three divisions—an AM group, an FM group, a network group, all reporting to Vice Chairman Irwin Segelstein. NBC was the last of the big three to separate AM and FM. There had been a rationale for that earlier when FM was a new medium. We broadcasters like to think we're so smart and so forward-thinking. We're really rather conservative. If the government hadn't legislated that you can't simulcast your AM on FM, we would still be duplicating programming.

The industry was convinced that you had to be rich and old to afford FM radio. Station operators were convinced that only classical music would work on FM. Thank goodness I wasn't quite old enough to be that stuffy. Some station group heads decided to give some bright, young kids their FM stations and let them do something with them. They wanted the FM's out of their hair because all the money was rolling in from our AM stations. Those young kids didn't believe that only old people would listen to FM, so they put good old rock'n'roll on the air and showed us how to program FM successfully with very few commercials. We couldn't sell them in the early days. We didn't realize how many people turned to FM to get away from commercials, and we kept putting our heavy commercial loads on our AM and just chasing the audience over to the FM. We were brilliant! Just brilliant!

FM is now the dominant medium. As late as ten years ago, only one third of the audience was FM, two thirds was AM. Now it's two-thirds FM and one-third AM. Suddenly, everybody is saying, "What do we do with our AM? Let's get some young, bright fellows in to program those AM stations." Now we're taking risks on AM, and new, exciting things are starting to happen in AM radio. We at NBC are the leaders, and I think the most notable example of an outstanding radio station is WNBC. Several years ago, I said, "We're going to make WNBC the 'Saturday Night Live' of radio." AM radio has the wonderful opportunity to be the medium you turn on if you want to hear interesting people and not just music. The music business has changed a lot; it's not as exciting as it used to be. We all listen to rock'n'roll nowadays, even if you don't call it that.

The other key element is news. For years, FM said, it's AM for information and FM for music. And the FM operators were willing to concede morning radio, which is service-oriented, to AM. But they're not doing that anymore. In market after market, FM audiences are dominant all day long because FM is doing news and

service as well as music. Total radio revenues are about one quarter of television's gross income. Nearly 9,000 radio stations do one-third less business than 1,000 television stations.

Networks are still dominant, and, for the foreseeable future, the television network is going to be the dominant program service and the most dynamic advertising medium. It's glamorous and affords the greatest opportunity for innovative creativity.

However, from an advertiser's standpoint, most television people have always felt that radio was a good supplement, a good way to add to TV's reach. A lot of television stations buy radio time to advertise their programs, and radio stations buy television time to advertise theirs, so they really go hand in hand. Television is much more research-oriented. A lot of television people envy us in radio because we can market creatively. None of the industry's pros think of radio as a stepsister.

The television industry began to look at radio for its success in demographic targeting, and NBC today is a very desirable television network because we reach a more desirable viewer than our competitors. We see television beginning to be fragmented a bit by cable movie channels, advertiser-supported cable and videocassettes, the latest craze.

Radio has remained very stable for more than two decades. Radio was supposed to go away when television came; radio is still here. AM was going to disappear when FM arrived; AM is hanging in and coming back. AM and FM were going to die when eight-track was developed; they are very much alive. Radio was going to be undermined when CB became popular; again, radio survived. Radio has withstood all these threats and has become the more stable of the electronic media because we've learned how to live in the fragmented media world. Some call it "narrowcasting," but it's not "narrowcasting" at all, it's target broadcasting.

We sold our Washington AM station and bought an FM station in Boston in 1983. In New York, our AM station has become the prototype of an exciting AM radio station. We have "Imus in the Morning"—he's one of the most outrageous disc jockeys and most sophisticated radio humorists in America. We took Soupy Sales out of night clubs and early television to do a midday show;

and we broadcast over 250 sporting events each year. Stations all over the country try to emulate what we do. There is, however, a dearth of talent; you don't find exciting talent standing on street corners.

Our New York FM station is basically an adult, contemporary music station and we are making it crisper with foreground personalities. We have developed a service-oriented morning show which gives more news and traffic reports than FM normally does.

In Chicago, WMAQ-AM is the second-largest country music station in America. It went country in 1975 and peaked with the urban cowboy craze in the late 70's but, right now, country music (as an art form) is suffering. Fortunately for us, we broadcast the Chicago White Sox and the Bulls, a total of nearly 300 sporting events.

WMAQ, like WNBC, is a 50,000-watt clear-channel station, which means there's nobody east of the Rockies broadcasting on that channel. It is heard over the largest land mass of any radio station in North America. At night, we run a show programmed for truckers. Those knights of the road love country music, and we give them all the detour and traffic information in 38 states. We have a wonderful FM station, WKQX, one of the top contemporary music stations in the Chicago market, with a very strong personality in the morning, Robert Murphy. In San Francisco we have a super FM station, KYUU, positioned along the lines of our Chicago station. KNBR is our 50,000-watt AM station hosted by unique personalities.

Market conditions are constant challenges, but each of our stations is quite healthy or right on track in a development plan. We don't have any stepchildren in that radio group anymore—that was not the case when Jack Thayer came here in 1974. FM was duplicating AM or just playing tapes. Our technical facilities were very, very run-down, and between the Schlosser and Silverman eras, we rebuilt them all. They're all state-of-the-art operations. WKYS in Washington is the number one urban contemporary and frequently the number one station overall in the market. Our most recent acquisition, in December 1983, WJIB, is an important station in Boston. Its format is "Easy Listening."

My responsibilities have sometimes been network, sometimes station, sometimes both. Currently, my primary responsibility is the eight radio stations. They're making progress because we've got some darn good people working very hard. It is a very competitive business, very competitive.

By and large, major broadcast companies operate stations in the top 20 or 30 markets. Our competition includes outfits like CBS, Group W, Metromedia and CapCities/ABC, all big leaguers. We meet that competition, stand toe-to-toe with them.

Twice a day something comes across my desk which reminds me that we have become leaders in the radio business. We may not have the most stations and may not be doing the most business, but I think people in the industry today look to NBC as pros and *the* innovators.

That goes for the radio network business too. In 1976, we added our second network, The Source, designed for the young adult, and that was a smashing success. Three years ago, we added Talknet, which is two-way talk programming. We do six hours of live programming nightly, Monday through Sunday.

For the first three hours, Bruce Williams gives personal finance advice. He is not a Wall Street authority in finance or stocks, but more like the uncle in the family who might have done a little better than the rest of the gang, and before you bought your first house or before you bought a car, you asked Uncle Charlie what he thought of the deal. He's Uncle Bruce—for families are not as close as they used to be; so we give them an Uncle Bruce.

In your neighborhood, there was probably a friend who, over the back fence or at the coffee klatch, gave personal advice. We have our own Sally Jessy Raphael who does that from 10 p.m. to 1 a.m., Monday through Friday. She's not a radio "shrink," but a woman who gives practical advice about human relationships. She's become so popular on Talknet that Multimedia, Inc., now syndicates a half-hour TV show in about 80 markets. We're very proud of our "Dear Abby."

The Source is a news service targeted for contemporary music stations. We develop the news stories and the positioning of the stories to appeal to 18 to 34-year-old adults.

Finding talented people is the biggest frustration in the radio industry today. We are just coming out of a long period that began with format radio, when the disc jockey with a fake name was important. A generation and a half of on-air people were not allowed to talk or even think. Now we are looking for interesting people. It's disheartening to develop talent only to lose them to television or film or even the theatre. Some people do not perceive radio as show business. Radio's big stars are very well paid, frequently comparable to TV.

Hundreds of applications come over the transom. Some of them are from young kids who will eventually be trained, but we need some who are developed right now. I think the way radio is changing, there's going to be a generation of these talented people in five, six, seven or eight years. I'm proud that radio, particularly NBC, has many outstanding leaders. I think the success of women in all areas of the radio business is very gratifying. Parenthetically, when the FCC told us to separate FM from AM in my days at WNEW, I had the brilliant idea of making our FM station staff all female. Because there were so few trained, it didn't work. An idea about six or seven years ahead of its time. Today, women in radio and television have proven to be excellent account executives, wonderful sales executives and sales managers, and even general managers.

I tell young applicants to take any job they can get. The first two jobs are the toughest. It's the one business where, even if you have a Master's degree, you have to start at entry level, and they have to accept the fact that some of their fellow graduates will make more money initially. When they get that first promotion, that means they've proved themselves, and the second job will be the one to showcase their talents, whether its sales, programming, promotion, whatever. If they're good, they'll never have to look for a job again in this business. By the third one, they'll be making more money than their contemporaries and having more fun. That's the kind of business it is! Everybody wants to be in it.

I want the people who work with me to have a sense of priority and know that everything is not reducible to a numerical equation, even finance or research. I want them to develop their own skills and, in turn, to motivate people, to train people who will take some chances. I always urge young people to take their jobs seriously but not themselves. That will make them better at their work, and they'll have fun doing it. We're the most "people" business in the world because our very product is people, always people.

There are many countries throughout the world where radio is still the primary medium, and next to human one-to-one, mouth-to-ear, ear-to-mouth, the number one communications form. Radio will be a viable medium and a good business for at least the rest of this century. Radio networking is not a huge industry, but it is a very important service for the radio stations of the United States and their audiences. It should be enhanced by getting our best creative talent and attention. I think network radio's growth will accelerate.

My wish for NBC's 60th birthday (and for me) is to see NBC as a company embark on a new search for excellence to maintain the leadership that we have recently rediscovered. I would like to see us be the innovators.

July 23, 1985

Richard A.R. Pinkham came to NBC during the very early years of television. From 1951 to 1957, the legendary Pat Weaver years, he was, with Mort Werner, in large part responsible for the production of "Today," "Tonight" and the "Home" shows.

Richard A.R. Pinkham

"I really learned the broadcasting business right from the top from the man who, I still think, is the outstanding broadcaster of our time."

I was an English composition major at Yale, a writer. I hoped to write the great American novel. We all did. In 1936, after college, I headed for that haven for Yalies, TIME, Inc. It had been founded by two Yale alumni, Briton Hadden and Henry Luce, and had attracted many brilliant young writers. (It still does.) I was hired as a college boy/office boy at $25 a week. The very first day I was there, somebody gave me a document addressed to Archibald MacLeish. I had no idea one of my literary heroes was at *Time*.

I moved from *Time* to *Fortune* as Assistant Promotion Manager and discovered I could make more money as a copywriter. Then, in 1939, at the age of 25, I moved from there to become Advertising Director of James McCreery, which, like DePinna's and B. Altman's, was a very staid department store. I couldn't wait to get out of that job.

In 1941, I moved to Lord & Thomas, which was a great advertising agency. I got the account executive's job on Half-and-Half Smoking Tobacco because the advertising director of American Tobacco Company—Lucky Strike cigarettes—was my friend, Pat Weaver.

When World War II erupted, I was an Ensign in the Naval Reserve assigned to Naval Intelligence, and then to a subchaser in the Mediterranean, and after that to the subchaser school in Miami as a teacher. My final assignment (by then I was a Lieutenant Commander) was Executive Officer of the destroyer "Dent."

When the war ended, I returned to New York to decide what I was going to do with the rest of my life. You know what I did? I put a display ad on the inside cover of *The New York Times* and *New York Herald Tribune*. I said I was a naval officer interested in going into the newspaper business. I got about 40 different replies from insurance agents and answers from the *Trib* and the *Times*. Both offered me similar jobs. On November 5, 1945, my Navy leave terminated, and I had no money. It was decision time. I accepted Helen Reid's (owner/publisher of the *Herald Tribune*) offer to be Director of Circulation. I tried to build up the circulation, but it just couldn't be done. I stayed from '45 to '51. By then, I had become a member of the Board of Directors.

Had I found I had a natural bent for business? Not really. I wish I had. I can't even look at a balance sheet now and understand it. I knew what made things hap-

pen if you did things the right way—a basic marketing approach. I was always able to translate ideas into facts and action.

In 1951, I decided the *Tribune* would be in real trouble in three or four years. Television was beginning to grow, and Pat Weaver had become head of the NBC Television Network. I called on him at 7 p.m.—the only time he could see me because he was so busy—and asked him if he'd hire me for $20,000 a year, in spite of the fact that I had no television experience. He said, "You're on! You're my assistant." He hired me right then. I'll forever be his slave. Bobby Sarnoff and I worked for him as assistants for one year, and during that entire year, I sat in on almost every conference Pat had with anyone of any importance in the company, with the exception of General Sarnoff.

I really learned that business right from the top from the man who, I still think, is the outstanding broadcaster of our time. I've worked with many, many people in this business, but Pat is, undoubtedly, the most creative man who ever ran a network. The only person who even comes close to him is Grant Tinker. The same kind of a solid, sensible approach to problems as well as good taste. Fabulous.

In those early days, 1951 to 1956, Pat was convinced that television should be more than just a toy in the living room. It had to do something important and raise the taste of the American public. Pat felt very, very strongly (as did I) that it should not turn out inferior programs. That's what he talked about. He was great fun to work for and with. He's almost impossible to quote. I used to work on his speeches, but he wouldn't let me do anything with them. They're almost too visionary.

He wrote all those memoranda which I, a college graduate, didn't understand! He scares people because his ideas are so big. His idea of how unimportant money is seems to put people off. Ken Bilby, who is doing a book on RCA, quotes Paley as saying that the only good president NBC ever had was Niles Trammell. Ken asked about Pat Weaver, and Paley said, "Well, he is a brilliant, creative man, but no businessman." That's what many people say about him, but look at the figures. In the days when he ran that network, it was very profitable.

Basically, we had to change the whole nature of television commercials. Largely because of Pat Weaver, we did it with the "Show of Shows" by introducing the magazine concept, which he invented. NBC never realized until Weaver that the magazine concept was the only valid approach for that and the present time. Instead of having to buy an hour or half hour, an advertiser could buy minutes.

When I started under Pat, Mort Werner was producing Jerry Lester's late-night comic show with that deep-cleavage blonde, Dagmar. Pat came up with the idea of putting the "Today" show on, and, because I was a newspaper man, I was the logical person to be put in charge of it. He moved Mort over so he and I worked on "Today" together.

I replaced Abe Schechter, who was an old WOR newsman, as Executive Producer on January 10, 1952. Abe Schechter was originally a P.R. man and then the first to head NBC News, such as it was in those first years.

"Today" faced many difficulties. It was hard to get *anybody* up at 7 o'clock in the morning, including every Senator and every Cabinet member. Now they're on their knees begging to get on, because it's one of the few programs everybody in Washington sees. Pat Weaver had the revolutionary concept that television was going to be so powerful and such an important part of our lives, that it probably was going to replace most of the newspapers. Now, 1985, there are only five or six good newspapers left—most of them are junk. His idea was to turn out a television show that would be like *The New York Times* or the *New York Herald Tribune* every morning from 7 to 9, and repeat from 9 to 10 for the West Coast. Something habit-forming.

The basic idea for that program was to report on everything that was happening: all the news, the latest books, the latest plays, the latest movies, the latest weather, and the latest baseball scores—all in the first five or six minutes. Somebody waking up would realize that we were not at war; the Giants or Yankees had won, and we would have all the latest

news. The rest of the program would be a combination of features about individual people involved. It was not to be an entertainment program, but it has become more and more that. Pat Weaver and Mort Werner chose Dave Garroway to be the host because the NBC people in Chicago knew him from his charming, low-key show, "Garroway at Large."

The hours were hellish. We'd start commercials along around 5:30 a.m., and then we'd start rehearsing around 6 right up to 7. It was just great for me because Mort Werner was a man who liked to get up early. He never slept. As the producer, he was there on schedule every morning. And I would spell him one day a week. After that one day, I was exhausted, because I showed up at 5 or 5:30 and go through the 9-to-10 third hour. There would be a break for about an hour from 10 to about 11, followed by our editorial conference from 11 to noon. At that point, most people went home and went to bed. But the people who were producing and writing the show had to stay on until about 4 or 5 o'clock in the afternoon. That was a *long* day.

The show built slowly. Almost all of the reviews were bad. I think essentially the newspapers (which were very hostile to television anyway) felt that we were infringing on their territory. That show is certainly one of my proudest accomplishments. I remember so well how horrible the reviews were. I remember that terrible man with the *New York Journal-American* saying it's a mishmash; it's *nothing*.

"Today" appeared to be a disaster; the ratings were abysmal. Nobody really cared about it. All the network salesmen who'd be out selling "The Perry Como Show" or some other popular show would, as they'd go out the door of an advertising agency, mention "Today," but nobody paid any attention to it. We were told that we had to get the ratings up to a certain point or the show would be cancelled. It had a pretty high budget —$2 million a year. I think Dave Garroway was getting about $100,000 a year—quite a small salary. Halfway through that second year, when I was Executive Producer, the show really was going down the drain.

One day, a fellow named Len Safir came in my office in the RKO building and said, "Come out. I want to show you something." He took me next door to the NBC casting office, and there were two NBC pages with a little baby chimpanzee. I said to Safir, "Grab him and put him on tomorrow." And bless Len Safir, who suggested that we put him on every morning because he reasoned that the kids would check around to see if anything was on, see the monkey, and stay tuned to NBC. Their parents would then start watching the show. And that's exactly what happened. That wretched little J. Fred Muggs made approximately $100 million for the National Broadcasting Company. And that damn little monkey got bigger and stronger all the time. Garroway had a hilarious sense of humor, except when he was in a bad mood, and then he was awful. Dave *hated* J. Fred Muggs—whenever there was a commercial break, he'd give him a hefty swipe.

When the ratings on "Today" were rising very nicely, J. Fred Muggs was suddenly a celebrity. Marlin Perkins, who ran the Lincoln Park Zoo in Chicago, had a television program on NBC for years. He agreed to a publicity scheme to send J. Fred to chat with his chimpanzees. It grew into a big operation. While three or four limos were waiting in front of 30 Rockefeller Plaza to take the entourage to the airport, Marlin Perkins called me and said, "Have you checked to see if J. Fred has any tape worms?" He added that I could check that out myself. With Marlin on the phone from Chicago, I put that terrible beast face down on my desk with people holding him by the arms and legs. When Marlin told me what the next step was, I just said I couldn't do it. So off J. Fred went in the limo to the airport with all the publicity people, worms and all.

Pat decided that the "Today" studio should be on the ground floor of the U.S. Rubber building. That was a wonderful site because passersby would stop to watch the live show through the windows on their way to work. One day, there was President Harry S. Truman out front taking his morning walk. Estelle Parsons did the weather—drawn on a blackboard! Eventually, to our great disappointment, RCA wanted the space back.

Producing "Today" was hard work but really fun—we were riding the crest. We had all the guests, including all the Senators and Congressmen, we wanted.

While I still was working on "Today," they gave me the "Tonight" show. Here I was, a newspaper man; I didn't know anything about show business *at all*. We first went with Steve Allen, who'd been doing a local show with Eydie Gorme and Steve Lawrence. We needed another boy and girl to sing because it was a two-hour show. I personally chose Mickey Malo, a real sex boat, and I thought she was absolutely marvelous. She was a wonderful singer, but she was a complete disaster. And 30 boys auditioned, all looking exactly like Frank Sinatra, except for one man. He came out with a cigarette in his right hand and sang. Andy Williams.

The "Tonight" show built very quickly. In addition to producing it, I had to sell it. To sell it, I'd go around to various advertisers and talk about the show with a copy of *TV Guide* and I'd read the description of all the old movies, circa 1935, that would be on at 11:30 at night. I'd say that people would not sit still and watch them for very long before they would look for something fresh and new or turn the set off. I'd never sold before, and I got damn mad at people who didn't deliver promptly, when they didn't do what I wanted them to do. It was difficult because late-night commercials were a totally new idea. We got the money for the "Tonight" show.

When Pat was in radio at Young & Rubicam, the agencies produced all the radio shows, such as the Fred Allen and the Jack Benny shows. When he got over into television, he realized that in order to make it profitable, to make it the way he wanted to do it, the network had to produce their own programs. And so he did—successfully. While I was Executive Producer of "Today" and "Tonight" we were having sponsor problems, and Jack Herbert, head of sales, brought in Joe Culligan from Hearst magazines. I found out he played golf at my golf club, and I went to the caddy master and asked if he knew a fellow named Joe Culligan and would he describe him, and, in addition, if there was anything distinctive about him so I could check him out. The caddy master said no, that he had dark hair, was nice looking, a good golfer. And, as I walked away, he said suddenly, "Wait a minute, he has a patch on one eye." Joe came to NBC, and we harnessed our own sales

people (some of them now top people at other networks). He gave them a bonus, lifted their morale, and, all of a sudden, advertising started coming in because of Joe's efforts. He was one of the best sales managers I ever knew.

One of the things that Pat used to say was that General Sarnoff was a visionary; he was *never* a broadcaster and never should have been. For example, Pat went to him in the early days and said that Jackie Gleason, who became one of the great comedy stars of television, was on DuMont and all NBC had to do to get him was to pay him $235,000 a year. And Sarnoff said, "That's more than I make, and I'm not going to pay any comedian more than I make."

I had the "Tonight" show as well as the "Today" show when along came the "Home" show. We had a press conference to announce the show. I took a model of the circular set out of a glorified hatbox and said, "Everyone is in a do-it-yourself mood these days. It's tough to do on television. The material, such as interior decorating, is inanimate. Wallpaper doesn't sing and dance. Our idea is, if the stuff is inanimate, to make the set animate." The set cost $200,000, a theatre-in-the-round, completely mobile with cameras in the air, around the outside, in the middle. I went on, "Even a soufflé will be exciting. The camera will be right on top of it. Oven doors will be glass, and we can show cakes rising."

We had a very hard time finding the right host for it. I can remember Ted Mills brought in people like Eric Sevareid, who was such a serious newsman—no sense of humor at all. The next person he brought in was Victor Borge, and finally, Arlene Francis, a bright and able woman, was selected by all of us. She was absolutely marvelous. She and Hugh Downs made it a great show. When it first went on it was reviewed as a mishmash. Someone sent me a dog license. Ratings were low for the first six months, and then it got moving. It did pretty well. It was *very* expensive so, after two years, it folded. They moved it from 11 to 10 a.m., but that didn't save it. It was decided to put on a less expensive game show. It is still regarded as a fine, experimental daytime show, and we were proud of it. Again, Pat Weaver's idea. The "Home" show was to be a televised *Good Housekeeping*: children, sewing, cooking. With color, it would now be marvelous.

During the past terrible years, NBC, under the worst possible executives, one after the other, at least had the shows that made the money—"Today," "Tonight" and, for a while, "Home"; the spectaculars *and* the magazine concept for sponsors. All Pat's.

In those days, the morale was great. Before the "Home" show went on, as I've said, Joe Culligan and I went out and sold it. We got $2 million of advance billing before the show even went on the air. We went from agency to agency because, at that time, I had to describe what the show was all about— I was Mr. Show Biz—and then Joe would come on and give them all the details in dollars and cents. Joe had enormous self-confidence; he was a brilliant salesman.

Some time later, Steve Allen thought he was doing so well that he should go on in prime time, so we moved him to Sunday night. We had the terrible problem of replacing him on "Tonight." I've forgotten who followed Allen, but he didn't work. Jack Paar called me up almost in tears and said he had just been bounced by CBS and that he had to find some work and could he do the nighttime show. I told him I knew all about him and would talk to some people about him. I told Dick Linkroum about Jack Paar, and he said yes, he's the man for that job. We hired Paar, and I can only tell you, after his ratings started to go up six months later and he was in like Flynn, he called to say he didn't want Dick Linkroum in his studio ever again. Paar was impossible!

By that time, I had moved on up to be Vice President of Participating Programs—a new title in the company. Bob Bendix, a marvelous producer who was doing the "Today" show, was assigned to "Tonight;" I moved Dick Linkroum to head up the "Home" show, and Mort at that time was producing the "Tonight" show. Had I developed executive skills by then? Yes, which surprised me somewhat, having wanted to be a writer. Actually, what I did was to surround myself with the best people I could find and to delegate. Most of the people I brought were all first-rate people. I looked for brains and judgment.

Six months later, I became Vice President, Network Television Programs, which came as an absolute and distinct shock to me. My first reaction when Bobby Sarnoff told me about this was that I had still much to learn. All I knew was "Today" and "Tonight"; I didn't know about prime time, and so forth. (When Bobby Sarnoff and I were Pat's assistants, Bobby was very conscious of clothes. He used to look to see what shoes, suit and tie I was wearing each morning when we reported to Pat. I felt then and for a long time that if he had not been his father's son, he could have been something. He had brains, had some drive, but his father really put the kibash on him. He moved him up much too fast.)

As Program VP, my responsibilities, believe it or not, were to handle not only all the prime time, weekend and daytime, but also the news part of programming. News was not a separate department then. The Vice President in charge of News reported to me. Pat had already turned out a marvelous prime-time schedule which was doing wonderfully well. I was told to direct my energies to daytime, which was a disaster, and the 7 o'clock news, because Ed Murrow on CBS was killing us.

Our newscaster was John Cameron Swayze, an excellent reader, but we wanted a broadcast journalist. To replace him, I thought of my old friend and classmate, John Hersey, a top reporter for *Time*, with great taste and a wonderful, distinguished personality. When I called him (I knew he didn't have a television set), I asked him to go at 9 o'clock that night to some friend's house and watch TV. He said, "What's this about?" I said I would tell him in the morning. And that was the night that Ed Murrow destroyed Senator McCarthy. I called him up the next morning and asked, "What did you think of that?" And he said he thought it was journalism at its best. It would make William Randolph Hearst revolve in his grave and was the most important thing Murrow could have done. I told him I had a contract on my desk for him to be another Ed Murrow. He called me when he got back from vacation to say, "I can't change in the middle of my life; I'm a novelist and that's what I want to be. Thanks very much, but no thanks."

At that point, I came up with the next brilliant idea. Jack Kennedy had just defeated Henry Cabot Lodge for the senatorship in Massachusetts. Cabot Lodge used to work for the *Herald Tribune*. He had a marvelous face, like an American aristocrat. Pat Weaver, Bobby Sarnoff, Davidson Taylor (then head of News) and I sat down with Henry Cabot Lodge—known as Cabot—for two and one-half hours. When it was over, we talked among ourselves and agreed 100% that he wasn't the right man.

Davidson and I then went to California, talked to Chet Huntley, and signed him. I remember on the plane trip home that Dave said it would be just wonderful to have someone like Chet in New York and that young Brinkley in Washington. I said I thought Brinkley was too callow, not strong enough for a 15-minute network news show, and, further, to have two different people on a news show was absurd. I said no to the idea of putting them together, and shortly thereafter, I left the company, and Huntley-Brinkley were great successes. At that time, our biggest competitor was CBS. ABC was such a weak third that it was really nowhere. Two and a half networks.

I didn't do a hell of a lot about daytime. We had a few things going. I brought in as head of daytime a bright young man, Gerard Chester, Phi Beta Kappa—top I.Q. I took him from some intern's job, and he's now at Goodson-Todman and a multimillionaire. (He has exactly the same personality as Goodson, goes to the same tailor.) One day, he brought in Mark Goodson who put on a show, "The Price is Right," in my little office (the most beautiful little office you ever saw in your life, overlooking the ice-skating rink at 30 Rockefeller Plaza). Goodson made us the panelists. In came various beautiful girls dressed in bikinis and fur coats with the merchandise, and it was hilarious to hear what our bidding was. We repeated the whole show for my boss, Tom McAvity, Vice President in charge of the Television Network. We put it on the air, and it's still on today, 30 years later! A wonderful concept.

McAvity was a marvelous man, one of the best men I ever met in my life. Very sweet and kind. He was too nice. I was fortunate; making decisions wasn't hard for me. The group that operated the programming department in those days was, *without doubt*, the finest bunch of people you could possibly have. Mike Dann was very bright. Fred Wile was a brilliant, impossible person who worked 24 hours a day. Sam Fuller was in charge of all the nighttime programs. Gerry Chester was in charge of daytime. And Mort Werner was doing all that stuff on the side—an extraordinary bunch of people.

I'd like to describe Mort, whom I know very, very well. He's a workaholic. Before he came to NBC he ran a radio station in Ventura, California. He loved to play the piano; he was marvelous with people; he was marvelously decisive. For example, if we had some terrible problems with eight things at once, he'd spread his hand on the table and say, "That's it! This is what we do." People had a lot of faith in his judgment—an honest, decent person. When he moved up to programming, he did a very good job there, too. He had a sketchy educational background, so he made it on his own. When I went over and joined him on the "Today" show, about which I knew nothing, the very first thing I did was to move his desk right into my office so we'd be side by side. I'm a great admirer of his. That goes back a long way.

Pat Weaver wasn't afraid of losing his job; he was a free spirit. He was never in thrall to the General. He refused to kowtow to him. A man of absolute courage and integrity. They'd have terrible battles, and he'd lose on issues important to him. Weaver wanted to spend more money and do more things for the network programming, and the General wanted to save the money for the RCA products and research. I used to urge Pat to take it easy, respect him a little more so that he'd feel at ease with him, and that way he could get the General to agree to what he wanted. Pat never would.

Programming is a very tough job and not many people last for long. When I was head of programming, I'd work until about 7:30 p.m., come home dead tired, barely say hello to the children, have dinner and then have to watch television so you could talk about it the next day. With all the tension, I developed the General Sarnoff ulcer. Tremendous tension all the time. Most of the endless phone calls would be about a disaster—rarely good news. And endless trips to California after writers, and production shifted to California.

When I first went to work for Pat, he made me liaison between NBC and a fascinating genius named Norman Bel Geddes. He'd won Pulitzer Prizes for various shows and was one of the country's top architects. White kitchens, the first car with air flow. Pat commissioned him to design a television city on the site of the present Time-Life building. The first 20 floors were to be NBC; the top 20 Time-Life. Of NBC's 20, the top 13 floors would be offices; the bottom 7 would be a television production factory. We became great pals, but Norman had one problem, he embellished everything. You just could not believe him.

He made a marvelous model of the building. The bottom floor had aircraft elevators from the street to the 7th floor, and all the sets would be moved to the 7th floor and moved down as rehearsals took place on successive days. The 2nd floor was dress rehearsal and the dimension of the 1st floor rivaled the Radio City Music Hall with no pillars. None of the engineers at NBC believed that would work at all. Norman finally invited all the NBC engineers and me down to Bermuda for a weekend, and by the time we came back, they were all in our corner. We next were invited to meet with Rockefeller Center Corporation in an enormous board room. Norman, a small touseled-haired man, had next to him a little man with pince-nez glasses. Opposite Norman sat the formidable Wallace K. Harrison, architect for Rockefeller Center. Harrison said, looking at the model, that it wouldn't work—a 40-story building could not be put on top of a 400-foot unsupported arch.

Norman lost his cool and called on the little man next to him, who turned out to be a famous Italian architect who said he agreed with Mr. Bel Geddes. When challenged by Harrison, he pulled out a picture of a building he'd built just like the model. We won. Rockefeller Center agreed to build the building. Pat took Bel Geddes up to Sarnoff's office, and after Norman's vivid pitch, the General said, "We're not going to do it. Gentlemen, television is going to be a film medium, not live." And that was that.

30 Rockefeller Plaza was never built to house a television network. NBC should leave the sales and account executives in New York and move everyone and everything else to California.

In 1957, I was given another job: I was in Europe when I got a cable from Gerry Chester: "Do you have any idea of what's going on back here?" I called to find out Pat and the General had had a terrible battle, and Pat had walked out. Pat quit after telling the General he didn't know anything about the broadcasting business. The General really thought he knew it all, and, because of that, he and Pat had many confrontations. Like an idiot, he quit instead of being fired, so he lost all that settlement money. I, to this day, think Pat was the *best*—there was no one like him.

I came back to find Jack Herbert President of the Television Network, and Fred Wile and many of the guys in the program department had been fired. I got word that I was to stay. My friend, Ken Bilby, was moved down from RCA to build Bobby Sarnoff up and had been made Vice President in charge of Public Affairs. To make me feel at ease, somebody came up with the idea of making me Vice President of Promotion, Advertising, Exploitation, Publicity and Guided Tours. I said no way, so I became Vice President in charge of Advertising. Meanwhile, I was approached by various advertising agencies and decided to move on to Ted Bates, which was heavily into television advertising.

By the time I moved to Bates I was a businessman/broadcaster. I was a generalist. That sums up the difference in point of view of people who've done both sides of the fence, as Tom McAvity, Mort Werner and I did. There was a profile in *The New Yorker* about David Susskind, who said he knew a lot of people in the advertising business like Dick Pinkham, who go to the opera and go to concerts but never put that stuff on television. What that says was that if you do feel that way, and you run a network, you *can* do those things if you have the right guy on top, but if you're on the other side, you're buying for clients, which is very specific: cost per thousands. You don't pay any attention to what the network really is.

Bates hired me as Vice President in charge of radio and television. Ready for a good one? The first daytime show I put on the air became number one in *all* television in nine weeks: "Dotto." It went so well we put it on at 9 o'clock at night on CBS, and it died. I called in our public relations guy and told him I wanted him to put the show on every front page of every newspaper in America. About three weeks later, he put *The New York Post* on my desk with a 72-point headline: DOTTO RIGGED.

I put on the soap "The Doctors" for 20 years, and that made a lot of money. As I moved up in Ted Bates (I retired as Vice Chairman of the agency), the media—radio, television and print—were merged.

When I went over to Bates, it was said I didn't like NBC any more, but I couldn't even talk over the dinner table with the idiot salesmen they sent from NBC. Dumbbells! Ollie Treyz was President of ABC at the time. ABC came to us, asked us to put some of our clients together, pick the program, and they'd put it on any night we wanted. The magazine concept at a 50% discount. We put "77 Sunset Strip" with Efrem Zimbalist, Jr., on ABC. The show went right to the moon. We did the same thing with "Surfside Six," and "Hawaii Five-O."

After I retired from Bates, the reason I went to work as a volunteer for Public Broadcasting was because the networks have to produce programs for the mass audience. When people talk about the Golden Age of Television, if they look down those lists, they'd find only about three or four good ones per year. It is not a personal reflection of the taste of the men and women who run the networks. Not a bit. I think the networks will probably continue to side with mass audience for advertising. But it will never do what Pat Weaver wanted it to do in the first place.

What is now being considered in Europe in order to do the really good things is to use the Direct Broadcast Satellite System. Right now, the continent of Europe is divided up into three different companies. One will have Iceland, Scandinavia, UK; one will have France, the low countries and Germany, and the other will have the Mediterranean. Mostly American and English programming, and for about $200 for a window, you can receive the programs.

Any young person with ability as a writer, director or actor should get into that. The money will be unbelievable. Look at the baseball players who average $230,000 a year; it's going to be three times that much. Eventually, with pay television, by satellite, you'll get $1 million for one program.

I don't think Pat Weaver could have pulled it off the way he envisioned. I think only one man could have—a man who is largely responsible for what's happened to television—Bill Paley.

Leonard Goldenson and David Sarnoff had a small percentage of ABC and RCA, but Paley really owned CBS. He could have made the difference because he had judgment and all that money. It never occurred to him! He went the other way—for the mass audience—and hired all the best stars and let Jim Aubrey do all the terrible shows.

In an odd way, Ed Sullivan did it. He put on entertainment programs, but he had the ballet, Itzhak Perlman at age ten along with vaudeville acts. Mixed the two together. Only creative people should be in charge. I think Grant Tinker comes closest to Pat; he has judgment and cares about quality, as evident in what came out of MTM.

"Today" and "Tonight" have not changed too drastically. "Today" has a few more features than it had. Stars of Hollywood, less news-oriented. I think they're fine.

I've belonged to a number of professional organizations. I headed IRTS and liked that immensely. I was a member of the Academy of Television Arts and Sciences, which isn't all that prestigious. I went on the board of Public Broadcasting to make up, as I told my friends, for all the sordid things I put on network television. I care a lot about that. There I was on the Channel 13 board with names like John D. Rockefeller, Jr., Brooke Astor, and many other important people, and I was the only person on that board with any broadcasting experience at all. They never used *any* of my broadcasting experience.

My time at NBC was exciting because those were pioneer days. I was so fortunate to be with the company then. I know it wouldn't be as much fun today.

My 60th birthday wish for NBC is that it come back to the top—to be Number One—the way it was when we were there!

August 6, 1985

One of the most respected and skilled sales executives in broadcasting, Walter Scott assumed the Chairmanship of NBC in 1966. He is now living an active life in retirement in Carmel, California.

Walter D. Scott

"When I started to work for Moe (Maurice M.) Boyd in the Sales Department, the President of NBC, who had been hired by the General, was Lenox Riley Lohr, a fascinating man, virtually unknown. I'll never forget the Fourth of July picnic he and his assistant, Martha McGrew, had at his place in Tarrytown, New York, for many of the NBC employees in 1938. After a lunch of, as I recall, rabbit stew, Lohr, attired as an English country squire, with a shotgun under his arm, led the employees single file around the grounds. He was an *unusual* man."

149

I was born in Kansas City, Missouri, and after my early education there, I went to Washington University in St. Louis, and then transferred to the University of Missouri to go to their journalism school. I'd been interested in journalism in high school, and I thought I wanted to pursue a career in it. When I graduated at the age of 20, during the Depression of the 1930's, I could not find a job as a journalist, so I took a job as an advertising salesman on *The Daily Oklahoman & Times*. My salary was $25 a week, but, in 1936, it was not hard to support yourself on that.

In 1937, I went to New York to work in the advertising department of Hearst Radio, the result of an interview I had had as a student at the university. My job was selling spot radio, dealing with the agencies' principal time buyers. Hearst had a number of stations; a couple were affiliated with NBC. Linnea Nelson, chief buyer for the J. Walter Thompson Company, asked me if I could be interested in a job at NBC. She said Moe Boyd, then the sales manager at NBC, was looking for someone, and she'd be glad to recommend me. So, at the age of 22, I went to work for NBC.

When I started to work for Moe Boyd in the Sales Department, the President of NBC, who had been hired by the General, was Lenox Riley Lohr, a fascinating man, virtually unknown. I'll never forget the Fourth of July picnic he and his assistant, Martha McGrew, had at his place in Tarrytown, New York, for many of the NBC employees in 1938. After a lunch of, as I recall, rabbit stew, Lohr, attired as an English country squire, with a shotgun under his arm, led the employees single file around the grounds. He was an *unusual* man.

Radio was a glamorous medium, the focus of more interest than print advertising, although there was not a great deal of knowledge as to how to use it best. We had to experiment.

All kinds of advertisers bought our time: Scott paper towels, Kraft food products, Dodge automobiles, Lifebuoy soap. Spot radio was different from selling an entire program to a large sponsor for national distribution through the network. NBC had its own owned-and-operated radio stations and also managed and operated the radio stations owned by General Electric and Westinghouse. The spot sales department sold advertising for those stations; program sponsorship of 15 minutes or more, participations in household programs or musical clock programs, and the station break announcements on the G.E. and Westinghouse stations. NBC's owned stations did not sell station break announcements other than the brief Bulova time signals, until a little later. We competed with all other radio stations in the markets where our stations operated.

I thought NBC was *the* company to go with, the clear leader in the field, the innovator, the strongest force by far. It was overshadowed by David Sarnoff. The public thought of NBC as David Sarnoff's company, and they were surprised to learn that he was not its principal owner. He was, nevertheless, a giant presence.

I moved to network sales a couple of years later. Chick Showerman was the Eastern Sales Manager. Roy Witmer, Vice President in charge of Sales, set the tone and standards for the department. Ed Hitz, his assistant, was in charge of policies. There was a policy book clearly defining which products were acceptable and which were not, and the manner in which the business should be conducted. At that time, the whole field of personal products was off limits. Now, of course, the world has changed.

There were a few women in the sales department then; one was Caroline Herbert, a wonderful person in charge of the Esso news reports. In the program area, Bertha Brainard was a delightful, very capable figure, in the 1930's and 1940's. There was the well-known story of her dancing with George Washington Hill, President of American Tobacco, in the NBC Board Room during rehearsals of "Your Lucky Strike Hit Parade," on radio.

During that period, I became acquainted with John Royal. He was a perfectly wonderful man, a good showman, and a delightful person. He had been on the old Keith Orpheum vaudeville circuit, I believe. His first association with NBC was as manager of the Cleveland radio station, WTAM. He established a close relationship with David Sarnoff in the early years. Royal was vigorous indeed! Perhaps he could be compared to P.T. Barnum, but a Barnum with great taste and integrity. He was responsible for all the early programming on NBC.

In those days, we were still called salesmen, not account executives. After making the sale, we were each individually responsible for arranging studio time for rehearsal and broadcast. Also, seeing that the scripts were submitted on time and acting as liaison if there were any questions on commercial copy or advertising claims. All network originations were live repeats for the West Coast, and we usually attended the broadcasts in order to greet the sponsors in the client's booth. It wasn't until the late 1940's that pre-recorded programs were accepted for network origination. It was Pier Mapes' father, Pierson, at the Hutchins Agency for Philco, who broke down the barrier with a Bing Crosby program pre-recorded on the new high-fidelity Ampex system and scheduled by ABC on a clock-hour basis for the different time zones.

The transcontinental coaxial cable was opened in the early 1950's, and General Sarnoff sent John West to California as Vice President in charge, and to supervise the building of the new color studios at Burbank, replacing the old facilities built for radio at Hollywood and Vine Streets.

In 1949, I became Eastern Sales Manager. That was my first experience in management. What makes a successful salesman? I think that long-term, big-ticket selling is primarily a matter of building relationships of mutual trust and confidence. When they exist, selling becomes relatively easy. A salesperson must identify the prospective customer's needs, meet them, deliver, and follow through. I worked very hard, but most of us then were wrapped up in what we considered an interesting business, and we willingly worked our heads off. We were convinced that the American system was serving consumers well, that businesses were being built because they manufactured good products and priced them fairly, and that we had an important role in that process. Broadcast advertising was an efficient means toward building mass consumption. Broadcasting is the most effective marketing tool available.

Television was coming along in 1949 when I started the radio job. Radio and television were split as a result of the first NBC Booz, Allen and Hamilton study. The company went through a period of being torn apart, put back together, then torn apart again. I was disappointed at the time not to go with the new medium. On the other hand, radio did offer the opportunity for a promotion, and a step into management. At that time simulcasts were relatively common, and we had some success in our strenuous efforts to induce advertisers to use the two forms of broadcast in complementary fashion. The first radio/television split lasted for a couple of years and then they were combined again.

Those were troubled times. The whole field of broadcasting was in flux. Literally, *no one* knew what direction it was going to take. Those who were solely radio-minded, particularly the affiliates, demanded that full attention be paid to radio, that it not be treated as a declining or different medium. These demands and the explosive growth of television presented difficult management questions, and, unfortunately, for three or four years, the company couldn't decide what direction it wanted to take.

I became National Sales Manager in the early 50's, and a Vice President in 1955. By then, many who had been carried away in 1947 by General Sarnoff's famous speech to affiliates about getting into television right away were in operation. I think the General was a real genius, with the normal complement of faults that go along with outstanding ability. There's no question that he was a marvelous, charismatic leader. I have always thought that NBC was well-served by having a father figure like General Sarnoff upstairs. I always felt that he was a supporter of the company, and of me personally.

You ask if I had any role models for a salesman. I tried to learn, as anyone does. I liked Niles Trammell immensely, everyone did. He was a delightful companion, but his style was entirely different from mine. Niles was highly extroverted; I'm not. I have never regarded myself as having the characteristics of a super salesman.

I was successful because we served our clients well, and they believed in us. I like people, and I was lucky.

I was in television continuously from the mid 1950's. Jack Herbert ran both radio and televison for a while. He was controversial, not a terribly popular man, but interesting in many ways, and I always had a perfectly wonderful relationship with him. George Frey was there for a number of years before Herbert and, then, at the same time. When he became Sales Manager of the radio network in 1946, I took over all of his principal accounts: Jack Benny, "The Hit Parade," Edgar Bergen and Charlie McCarthy, Kraft and many others. Working under Herbert and Frey in the Sales Department was challenging because the business was going through *such* changes in those days We were confident that broadcasting was growing, so we treated it like an adolescent with growing pains, which one day it would outgrow.

I like Pat Weaver and respect him enormously. Except for Fred Wile, Pat seemed to me to be somewhat suspicious of people and their motives. He did *not* feel that he could give them his trust and confidence and turn them loose to do the work they were hired to do. Brilliant, brilliant man, but, in my opinion, he should not have been the Chief Executive Officer.

I was very much excited about the programs Weaver put on—"Today," "Tonight," "Home." The "Today" show had a terrible time getting advertiser support in the beginning, and on at least two or three occasions it was a close call as to whether it would continue or not. Pat Weaver and Jack Herbert were at each other's throats, but, fortunately, Jack believed in the program and had a great deal to do with keeping it alive. J. Fred Muggs did, too!

Weaver developed the famous magazine concept of advertising. We in the sales area didn't necessarily think it was a wonderful solution for television; it was one more experiment in a growing medium. It was clear that the sponsorship patterns were going to change. Whole program sponsorships would always be around, but in declining numbers. Participating programs or programs on a magazine basis would be some of the different sponsorship forms, unquestionably entailing smaller and smaller units.

Incidentally, I have a clear recollection of a very interesting young man who came to work for the company's Radio Program Department in the early 1950's. His name was Grant Tinker. I was then Eastern Sales Manager for Radio, and it quickly became evident that, after 5 o'clock when everybody else had gone home, if you needed an answer from someone in the program area, Grant Tinker was there to give it to you, or he knew where to go to find it. It was clear that Grant would have a very good career somewhere, somehow.

When Bob Sarnoff became President, and Pat Weaver moved up to Chairman, I became a Vice President. Bob was anxious to establish his own identity. I think his relationship with his father was very complex, with strong emotional pulls and tugs both ways. Bob and I have always gotten along well, and I often thought that Bob might have been better off if he had worked for a company other than NBC or RCA. It's never easy to step into the shoes of a founder or a pioneer and even more difficult when the pioneer is your father. A good friend of mine, chief executive officer of one of America's largest companies, invited Bob to go on his board at least 15 years ago. He later told me, "Bob Sarnoff does a great job for us as a Director. He does all his homework; he's very valuable."

In 1956, the sales and programming departments were united under Tom McAvity, a wonderful man, lovely man, but terribly disorganized. Poor guy, he should never have been put in that job. This often happens. He was marvelous at programming. Later, he went to J. Walter Thompson. When I ran the television network, Mort Werner said to me, "Why don't we get Tom McAvity back? He'd be great as head of Specials." He came back, and it was splendid to have him in the right slot. He was wonderful fun, a delightful companion.

Sales and programming were combined and then separated so often that it's hard to follow. When I was Vice President of Television Network Sales, Kintner was President. He was not easy to work for. He made excessive demands, had excessive expectations, and he had excessive personal habits that interfered with his work, but he was one of the most brilliant guys in the world. In many ways, morale was very high when he was here. I got along just fine with Kintner. We really had no problems, but I established a ground rule with him—I could not work effectively for him if he called me late at night or on weekends just to talk about things when there was no emergency or crisis. So he didn't, but he hounded others. I think Bob respected people who stood up to him. He was not unreasonable if you had something reasonable to say to him. I read a pile of memos from him every day, put *most* of them in the wastebasket and did not respond to them. I'm sure Kintner sent them to create a record, not necessarily to call for action.

When I became Executive Vice President in charge of the NBC Television Network in 1959, it was, in NBC's structure, a corporate position. The other networks called the job President of the Division, but it was essentially the same. Later, it was called President of the Network. I wasn't terribly interested in taking it, but Kintner insisted. I was *very* happy as Vice President in charge of Sales and would have been content to stay there so I could retire from broadcasting at age 55. After World War II, I thought seriously about my life and decided I wanted to live it in phases, and that was a satisfactory working phase.

Actually, I didn't have any choice when, in December of 1965, Bob Sarnoff said, "I want you to be Chief Executive Officer." Aside from luck and being in the right place at the right time, I had created a climate in running a sales department and a television network where people could work and use their intelligence, where they knew what goals were expected. Also, I hope I let them grow. The Television Network, in the early 1960's, was really a splendid organization, with Mort Werner and Grant Tinker running programs, Don Durgin running sales. Kintner had brought Durgin from ABC in 1957 to do presentations and sales planning.

When I moved from the sales job into the network job, Don was my choice to succeed me, and, when I became the Chief Executive Officer, Don was my choice to succeed me as President of the Television Network. I believe in him. I think he's an outstanding broadcasting executive. Mort, and Grant, who was on the West Coast, were a great team in the Program Department. They and Don got along very well together. Bob Stone ran the Back

of the House; business affairs, engineering, etc. A lot of people thought he was tough, cantankerous and unpopular, but he had an unpopular job, and he performed a vital service for the network.

Mort was so disarming! When Jack Paar took a walk from the "Tonight" show in early 1962, Mort was new in his job as Vice President in charge of Programs, and one of the first things he had to do was find a replacement for Paar. He put together an easel presentation of every failure Johnny Carson ever had, and he wound up with a conclusion: Carson had failed in each of these things, and, therefore, had learned what *not* to do. He would be successful with the show because he knew what not to do, and he was basically a communicator from mid-America. As they say, the rest is history.

The three corporate staff people to whom I went most frequently for advice, help and counsel from the 1940's onward were David Adams, Tom Ervin, and Mal Beville. Those three, to me, represented more combined wisdom, judgment, and knowledge than could be found anywhere. David Adams is one of a kind, so unique, so wonderful. He is brilliant. He worked incredibly hard.

Ervin's legal advice was always sound, thoughtful and perceptive. The company couldn't have operated nearly as well without him. He didn't just keep us out of trouble but was creative in finding ways to help accomplish our goals.

I found Mal and his research department to be an enormously dependable and valuable resource. He was frustrated many times because others in the company didn't realize that if they would only consult him and pay attention to his figures, they might come to totally different conclusions.

After the Weaver period, things calmed down to some extent, but not for a while because there was a terrible, just dreadful time for a couple of years, until Kintner came in.

One of the hardest things for me to do was to fire someone, and I had to fire quite a few people over the years. I hoped to do it with an explanation which would help them learn, but I was really never good at it. I hated it. The worst management mistakes in any business organization are to promote people beyond their level of capability or put them in jobs where they don't belong.

My appointment as Chief Executive Officer was a complete surprise, although I obviously knew that something had to happen. It was announced in the summer of 1965 that Bob Sarnoff was going to RCA. He wasn't spending any time at NBC; he was trying to learn what was going on up at RCA. That fall, with David Adams as moral support, Sarnoff said, "I cannot turn the company over to Bob Kintner." Then he said to me, "I want you to be Chief Executive Officer, and Julian Goodman to be Chief Operating Officer."

Julian was clearly a get-it-done, love-to-run things person, an in-charge guy. He and I always got along beautifully as far back as the time when I was in sales and he and Bill McAndrew were in news. Sometimes our interests collided, but we respected each other, and worked well together. We complemented each other. Kintner, even though he wasn't coming to the office, insisted upon retaining the Chairman's title until April, perhaps because of his contract. So, from December 1965 until April 1966, I was Chief Executive Officer and President, and Julian was Executive Vice President and Chief Operating Officer. In April, I became Chairman and Chief Executive Officer, and Julian became President and Chief Operating Officer.

One day over lunch, I had a discussion with Sol Taishoff, Editor and Publisher of *Broadcasting* magazine, about whether or not Kintner could have been saved if he had gone to a rehabilitation clinic, and Sol didn't think so. He thought Kintner's personal behavior excesses were so ingrained that he never could have been cured as long as he was in that job. I think much of it was stress.

You do what you have to do. I didn't want the job; I didn't seek it, but I thought that it would work out all right. By then, I think I had an eye for picking out good people. Julian did the operations, and I served as a front man and was responsible for setting policy. Prior to going into the job, I did not have any clear ideas of what I would like to accomplish.

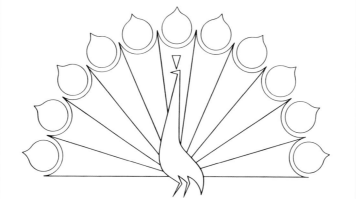

My main objective was trying to create a climate in the company where people were motivated by self confidence in their ability, not fear.

I think that the affiliates probably felt, in fact several of them have told me, that Julian and I were both "good broadcasters." One of my earlier impressions was of Walter Damm taking over an affiliates' meeting with his demands for a middle-station break in "Howdy Doody." I like and respect Jack Harris; one of many reasons for my regard is the enormous amount of work he put in on the Basic Economic Study. Louis Read, his successor, was one of the most delightful affiliates that we ever had. Hod Grams, a different kind of man, a more serious person, was so easy to work with and very competent. Hod was followed by Bob Ferguson, with whom I had less to do with than his predecessors. NBC's relationships with our affiliates, with Don Mercer and Ray O'Connell and others at NBC, were, during those years, really outstanding.

I remember Joe McConnell called them outlets. Jack Herbert called them partners and they didn't want to be partners. Herbert was promoting some new sales forms, such as one called Market Basket, in which the affiliates would be asked to perform merchandising chores for advertisers, much as the merchandising departments of magazines do. Needless to say, the affiliates had no interest in being partners in such an operation.

It was my decision to go "all-color" in 1965. I had to clear it with Kintner and Sarnoff, but I took the risk, and they made it very clear that I was the one who wasn't going to meet the numbers because of the costs involved, and that the Television Network was going to suffer, and that when the MIC was passed out, the people in the Television Network and I would feel it. On the other hand, I've always thought that at the end of 1965, when RCA decided to choose the next Chief Executive Officer of NBC, that decision of mine influenced them.

Programs had been presented in color on an

occasional or special basis since the early 1950's. By the late 1950's, some of the series programs, such as "Bonanza," were being filmed in color, and because of their wide popularity, the number of color receivers in the homes grew. By 1964, NBC, always the leader in the color field, was presenting nearly 50% of its nighttime schedule in color; CBS very much less and ABC very little at all.

The colorizing process went on at several levels. The studios had to have color equipment—cameras and film which are more expensive than black-and-white. Shooting a live show in color adds to the production time. The old chicken and egg puzzle was evident. There weren't enough color sets out there to justify the additional cost of colorizing a program. Mainly young, affluent, upwardly mobile people had them. By the time we made the decision to go all-color, only 6% of the television homes in the U.S. were color-equipped, but they were very valuable homes because they were identified as having more viewers per set who spent more hours watching television. The problem was to create a critical mass where enough homes had color sets to justify the cost of programming.

Someone had to move first, and I wanted NBC to be the one. We were neck and neck with CBS in programming ratings at night. I was convinced that going all-color might furnish an edge to push us clearly into first. It almost did. It was the right thing to do, and the prestige of it was wonderful. It was a well calculated risk, and I am proud of it.

Kintner and Sarnoff were of two minds when I told them we wanted to go to color. I said the Television Network would take the responsibility, but they were concerned because they knew that not just the Television Network, but the company would fail to meet its RCA budget requirements for the year. There were many reasons for RCA to say okay, that this is a good long-term investment for the company, and it will pay off in the future. Before making the decision, I was awake nights developing it, but once it was made, I felt very comfortable with the decision.

In 1970, when I was 55, I told Julian that it was time for him to take over the Chief Executive Officer's duties. I had every confidence that Julian could handle the job. I think that he would have handled it successfully if Bob Sarnoff hadn't called signals. Until 1970, Bob left us very much alone. Julian and I met with him once a week; otherwise we were almost completely on our own. In the early 1970's Bob started to be interested in the minutiae of NBC's operation. He may have wanted to go back to familiar territory after taking a big loss in the computer business. I don't know what it was, but Bob started telling Julian what he thought ought to happen down at NBC, and, I think, that became a big problem.

I stayed as Chairman for two more years, then I retired. I left the NBC Board in 1974, two years later. When I decided to take early retirement, I was following my timetable, and I had no second thoughts. There was a good replacement. I didn't worry about that. Arline and I choose to live rather simply, so I was free to retire, and I wanted to do different things. I have considerable free time now, and enough to occupy me to the extent that I want to be occupied, which is not all that much.

I was saddened by the turmoil NBC went through in the 70's. I would have hoped that Grant Tinker might have returned to the company earlier, much sooner.

My 60th birthday wish for NBC? That it stays on the right track. NBC appears to me to be in the best shape it's been in in an awfully long time—maybe the best shape ever.

October 16, 1985

Marion Stephenson's trailblazing career included many firsts which made it easier for women in the industry to reach the executive level. Her peers learned to respect *her* as well as her financial acumen during her 37-year career at NBC. She retired in 1981.

"Good things have happened while I've been on vacations. In 1962, I returned from Greece and was summoned to Bob Kintner's office…Bob told me that I had been appointed Vice President. The first woman Vice President in the history of NBC and RCA! It probably was my 'sweetest' first. Syd Eiges, Vice President of Public Information, came in with a few others, and we celebrated with champagne. I felt that it was my responsibility to be successful so that other women would have a chance."

I was born in Green Bay, Wisconsin. Just before the Depression, my father, an architect, decided he wanted to have the experience of working in New York City for a few years. We moved to Mt. Vernon, New York, where I went to local schools. We never returned to Wisconsin. My father thought it would be a good thing if I worked my way through college. I went to Antioch College in Yellow Springs, Ohio, because of its innovative curriculum of a work/study program.

In writing the "Life Aims" and "Vocational Aims" papers required of second year students, I realized that I should change my major from math to business administration because the only choices open to women with math majors in 1939 were to teach or be lab scientists. (In 1963, I was cleaning out files at home and found my yellowed "Life Aims" and "Vocational Aims" papers. When I read the vocational paper, I discovered I had written that some day I would be controller of a company. Six months earlier I had been made Vice President of Business Administration for NBC Radio.)

My first job as an accountant was with Esso during the war years. At one point we had worked 13 nights out of 14 handling the imports of oil from Venezuela and Aruba. I saw no future in the accounting area and decided to search for a job involving writing. In September 1944, I applied for a job at *Fortune* as a researcher/writer. That was a very short interview!

As I had taken a vacation day for the interview, I decided to find an Antioch friend at NBC who just happened to be in Personnel. NBC had never entered my mind as a place to work, but I realize that I'm a semi-fatalist—things often happen because they're meant to happen. Betty Beale persuaded me to fill out an application. I decided to request an unlikely combination of advertising and business. After being interviewed by Ruth Hurd, I went home.

Three weeks later, I received a telegram from Ruth Hurd. When I called, she said a budget clerk job had just been approved for the Advertising and Promotion Department. It was exactly the combination I had asked for. Jim Gaines, Director of Advertising and Promotion, hired me, and I started the day before Election Day in 1944 (Roosevelt was running for his fourth term) at $160 a month.

In the Advertising Department were Charlie Hammond, Hartley Samuels, Charlotte Stern, Jim Gaines, Jim Nelson, Dick Blake, Roy Porteous, Charlie Vaill, Ethel Gilchrist and Hank Shepard, great people, but *characters*. I thought I'd made a huge mistake, because I'd been with a bunch of business people at Esso. As months passed, the job grew and I assumed more responsibility. I decided that it was time to get more education and move on.

I went to New York University at night and received an MBA in 1948. I wanted to major in marketing, but the marketing professor was so inadequate that I decided to major in banking and finance under Dr. Marcus Nadler. Doc Nadler was an international authority, a sage for Wall Street, and a marvelous human being. In fact, when I got my degree, I received the first Marcus Nadler Gold Key for "excellence in finance." I'd gone to little Antioch, and when I went to NYU with students who worked on Wall Street, I found I was competitive. That boosted my self-confidence, because I realized my Antioch education had been a good one.

I was promoted to Business Manager of the Advertising and Promotion Department in 1948. When I had to say "no" to those creative people, our mutual respect for each other made the job easier and the decisions more palatable. I learned something in that job that I've used throughout my career. The advertising folk didn't understand financial language. To be successful in the job I had to speak "their" language. I never asked non-financial management to speak my language. I believe that's one reason I became Vice President. In all my budget presentations to top management, including Bob Sarnoff and Bob Kintner, I always used non-financial English.

With the birth and growth of television, the 1950's were a difficult period for radio. Radio became TV's financial support. I was appointed General Ledger Accountant and Budget Supervisor in the Radio Network's Controller Department. Henry Sjogren was Controller, and he enlarged his staff and areas of control by transferring all people with any budget or accounting responsibilities to his office. That included me. Having left an area where I had respect and varied and changing functions, I was unhappy to be with "bookkeepers" and limited to accounting chores. Life was drab by comparison, so I started to look for another job.

However, I kept getting promoted every six months, so I stopped looking for a job outside the company. When I became Senior Operations Analyst, I joined others who were charged with the financial analysis of any areas that warranted examination. This great group provided future leaders for NBC, among them Don Carswell, Art Watson, Bill Schmitt, Nick Gilles, and Ken Gorman—who has done so well at Viacom.

I was assigned what proved to be a lengthy analysis of the News Department, with particular emphasis on the financial activities of the overseas offices, their fee structures and travel arrangements. In 1959, I completed a big study on the Radio Network. The game shows and soaps that were its mainstay had successfully transferred to TV, and combined with the new lack of advertiser support, it was obvious that radio could not survive as it had existed before.

That was the time of the first major strike by NABET. It had the mixed support of other unions, including AFTRA, and it lasted six weeks. Some of the talent, Jack Paar for one, did not show up. His announcer, Hugh Downs, did. I learned more about the business up in the control room of Studio 6-B from 9 a.m. to midnight—doing two game shows and the "Tonight" show those few weeks—than I had in all my earlier years. I certainly learned how little work some people did.

Those of us who pinch-hit during the strike were given the magnificent sum of $200, plus a week's vacation. That gave me four weeks' vacation, and with an additional two weeks' leave, I went around the world, emphasizing the Orient. I went directly back to work from the airport and was told to see John MacDonald, VP of Finance. He told me they had kept a job open for me—Business Manager of the Radio Network, a job formerly held by Teddy Zaer. Having done the radio study, I quickly told him I didn't want it. He suggested I sleep on it, and when I came back the next morning, I accepted the job.

Effective communication between the business and operational areas had been minimal, so I concentrated on getting back to my basic English and communicating in their language. I had a variety of bosses, from Joe Culligan, to Bill Fineshriber, to Bill McDaniel, a lovable Irishman who let me make the budget presentations to management. That's how Sarnoff and Kintner got to know me.

Daytime radio programming, as it had been, disappeared. News-on-the-hour had started haltingly in the late 50's. It became a sales concept about 1960. In addition, we developed an assortment of three-to-five-minute strips that were scheduled each hour. Affiliates could tape them and integrate them in their local programming. "Monitor" was an excellent program started by Pat Weaver because weekends were wastelands, the ghetto of radio. NBC could get "Monitor" clearances from Saturday morning to Sunday midnight. The stations were grateful to have good, live programming.

Television by now was a big, financially successful medium. Radio was a loser—of millions. I never seriously considered transferring over to TV because I knew that as a woman I couldn't get a crack at similar jobs in television. At that time, NBC and its peer companies were very macho. I had learned an important lesson which enabled me to do my various jobs. As I progressed through the financial area, I earned the respect of my peers, and from that point on, I didn't have to prove myself to *anyone*. I was accepted. McDaniel was followed by Steve Labunski, who was a breath of fresh air, a radio station manager who knew radio—but not networking.

Good things have happened while I've been on vacations. In 1962, I returned from Greece and was summoned to Bob Kintner's office with Bill McDaniel. Bob told me that I had been appointed Vice President. The first woman Vice President in the history of NBC *and* RCA! It probably was my "sweetest" first. Syd Eiges, Vice President of Public Information, came in with a few others, and we celebrated with champagne. I felt that it was my responsibility to be successful so that other women would have a chance.

What was my impression of Bob Kintner? It changed a lot. I found him brusque. As an outsider, I was in awe of the man, but when I saw him almost monthly, I had the feeling that he was fair. I could be honest in my comments to Kintner, and he replied in kind. The events that necessitated his departure from NBC were tragic.

Being the only woman at a company meeting or convention was a ball, but on a day-to-day basis, I wasn't asked to join a male group going to lunch. When I was Vice President and was required to attend various functions, all relationships were fine. I was a part of it.

I doubt if these informal relationships have changed very much with the passage of time and the entry of more women into management councils. It probably will take several generations for it to change, if ever, because the male world of relationships in business is too deeply ingrained. It's the rare man who's not concerned about and aware of a competitive woman.

In the mid 60's Syd Eiges suggested that it would be appropriate for me to join AWRT (American Women in Radio and Television). Until then I had avoided women's organizations. I always felt that women in women's organizations hide their light under a bushel. Women should belong to the same industry organizations that men do—such as state broadcaster associations, advertising, sales or PR groups. I was the first woman to serve on the NYSBA Board, and the first woman network officer to serve as the representative on the NAB Board. These are a few of my favorite "firsts."

In 1968, AWRT was in serious financial straits, and the newly-elected President, Mary Dorr, asked me to head a committee to provide financial stability. Our small group of four recommended a series of necessary changes, which were approved and are in effect to this day. It was an important contribution which gave the organization a new basis for future operations. It was a wonderful, uniquely motivated committee, and we're still good friends.

The New York City Chapter of American Women in Radio and Television gave me the Woman of the Year award in 1978, and the mid-Eastern area of AWRT gave me the Woman of Achievement award that same year, undoubtedly related to these earlier activities and my NBC career advancement.

Radio had become a stepchild by the time the Radio Network became the Radio Division in 1966, more of a stepchild than at CBS or ABC. ABC expanded its networks to four, using news each hour as its basic format, playing it at :00, :15, :30 and :55, and maximizing the use of its AT&T line. They played rock on their owned stations, were highly rated in their markets, and solidly in the black. CBS went to all-news, supported by the network news, and with their radio network functioning very well, they always had excellent clearances and audiences in the major markets for advertisers.

When Jack Thayer became head of NBC Radio in 1974, he established the News and Information Service, but it was too late, and it created all kinds of feed problems for the "old" radio network. We didn't have satellites, just the land lines, which limited network feeds. Jack spent millions of dollars to create a "Cadillac" service that never paid off. It had to be cancelled. But it was an excellent product, and marvelous for keeping the business traveler informed when on the road. It gave smaller communities a continuing news service that they could never do on their own.

Once television appeared on the scene and radio left the living room, radio fanned out all over the house, yard, beach, in cars, everywhere. But radio audience measurements became less frequent and less accurate. Television measurements could be made with an attachment to a stationary set in living rooms, so TV measurements were a constant. As we got into the micro-miniaturization of radios, and they became smaller and more portable, there was no way we could attach a measuring device to 1,500 radios. Radio research became so costly that it was done only once or twice a year.

Affiliate compensation rates frequently were based

on local-market audience measurements. The intricacies of these arrangements were fascinating, and affiliations could be saved with an "understudies" comp table—which I frequently handled myself. Perhaps this was a misuse of my weekends, but we did keep our biggest, most important affiliates with our very carefully tailored compensation tables. For whatever reasons, network-affiliate relationships have changed in recent years, and many of our longtime affiliations have gone by the wayside.

As head of the network at the time of the Bicentennial and NBC's 50th anniversary year, another highlight I remember was the radio affiliates convention. Jack Thayer decided that we would have two podiums—one for each of us—so we could banter back and forth with good fun and 50-year highlights. Jack had been with NBC for only two years—and the affiliates had known me as an NBC radio presence since 1962. Jack had put me in charge of the network shortly after his arrival in 1974. The repartee that was developed at these presentations made me a much better speaker and presenter. I owe Jack a great debt.

Jack was a very good salesman and merchandiser/marketer. He dreamed up and drew on many clever sales tricks and angles that he had used successfully throughout his career. I learned marketing and merchandising skills from a master. He and I both loved to collect quotations, essays and aphorisms, and I've saved many valuable ones he gave me. He used them in writing "Thayer's Weekly Letter" to NBC radio department heads. They were zesty and read with relish. Jack always was the salesperson, and I tended to cover the other areas.

Today some 70% of the radio audience listens to FM. We always paid handsomely for the big hitters of the AMs—the WSB's, the WJR's, the WOAJ's—but I was always willing to get an FM in a market if it were a station whose format complemented hourly news and some of our features.

In the 70's, companies gave away FM stations to public radio or universities because they saw FM as a lost cause. There weren't enough FM radio sets at the time. The FCC permitted AM/FM programming duplication so there was little incentive to invest in the medium. That *would* change!

In retrospect, a banner night for me was at the radio affiliates meeting in New Orleans in 1979. I was upset about some company problem and for the first time was not involved in running the convention. I do recall that at the dinner the NBC brass present were lavishly applauded. Several years ago I wrote to an NBC friend that on retiring I received no clock, no luncheon, no memento. He wrote back and said he didn't know why I wanted some material thing as a token of the regard in which I was held after receiving the tribute of the audience that night at the dinner in New Orleans. He went on to say he would treasure that night the rest of his life if it ever happened to *him*.

Heroes? I'm not sure I have any. But, there's no question that Niles Trammell was outstanding. He also was charming. When I first started, he and Frank Mullen would walk through the halls, go into every office and greet each employee. There was a "phone alert" system from the first office visited so we could clean up the bulletin boards and desks. I certainly respected him because he cared.

I certainly respected General Sarnoff. I have a framed note from him on the cover of the first speech I made to be included in NBC's daily press bundle. It was thoughtful. Pauline Frederick introduced me to him at an industry luncheon, and I met him again at other industry dinners. He always knew me and was most friendly. At the NBC 50th anniversary dinner in the Grand Ballroom of the Waldorf, I was very pleased when Van Cliburn, speaking alongside a huge grand piano on stage, made a special point of remembering the General and all he had done for him.

He was the only one on that huge dais to do so.

I respected Ted Cott, who was Vice President of WNBC Radio in the early 50's. He had a reputation of being a tough operator, but I always felt that he respected me and the job I did. A perfectionist. He was feared perhaps, but he ran a good operation.

I respected Kintner after I had the opportunity to work closely with him. It was unfortunate that his leadership was lost to the industry. David Adams always seemed to be the "constant" through all the changes dating back to the 40's. So often meetings would last for hours and at their conclusion David would give a two-minute synopsis of what had been said. And always with a "zing" in it.

My major battles over the years were with people I felt didn't have the best interests of the network and NBC at heart. In the main, however, most of the people I dealt with at NBC had high ethical standards and worked as a team.

I'm not a feminist per se, but some kind of concerted action has to be taken by women to open up opportunities. I think militant strategies are counterproductive and basically have proven so. For many women, women's organizations play an important role as a training ground to learn management skills. I feel that in the business world, as elsewhere, you must earn the respect of your peers to succeed. If you don't you aren't going to make it. Even today, it is difficult for a woman to earn this respect from men.

In 1981 it seemed best to take early retirement, because I had worked hard for so many years. It's one of the best decisions I ever made. I'm one of the happiest people in Winter Haven, Florida, where I built a house on a lovely lake. I'm comfortably out-of-doors winter and summer. My tractor and I tame the rapidly growing grass; I at last have the time to read *The New York Times* thoroughly and to enjoy my friends. I do what I want to do.

I have two birthday wishes for NBC's 60th.

May radio continue to rise Phoenix-like from each crisis of discontent as it has over the past 60-plus years. And may our industry seek and once again believe in the attributes that gave it its finest golden hours—over the airways and in the halls of governance.

February 10, 1986

Ray Timothy, now Group Executive Vice President of NBC, began as a page and guide on the Guest Relations staff in 1954. He was responsible for Affiliate Relations during a difficult period.

"I like to think of myself as a creative problem-solver. I could not write a script or book or paint a picture, but I can apply creative approaches and solutions to business problems."

I am one of the few people who can claim to be a native New Yorker, because I was born and grew up here in New York City. I was always busy. I worked part-time after school and summers. I was interested in sports, played all kinds of sports, none of them well. I majored in political science at Queens College, a good major for any business career. I read my Machiavelli!

In 1954, after college, I was interested in the new business of television, and I started at NBC as a tour guide on the Guest Relations staff. It was the only one of the three networks with an entry-level position. I was 1-A in the Draft, but NBC took a chance and hired me. Perhaps they did so because they had a rule: if you didn't move up in the company in 18 months, you were asked to move out. The Guest Relations Department was a training ground for NBC and for the whole industry.

We pages guided tourists who were as interested in the new medium as we were, so it was a good job. The pay wasn't much, about $162 a month, but it included uniforms, and more importantly, the opportunity to get a toehold in this new, evolving business. When we weren't busy, we "hung out" in the locker room, where calls came asking anybody with floor-directing experience to be associate director of a show. Of course, everyone said he'd had experience, because we all wanted to get into production. In the years before I came to NBC, this happened more frequently than it did in my day. But for us there was still at least an occasional chance to get in on the ground floor of television.

I had a vague notion that I would like to be in the business end of television, and to prepare for that, I went to law school at night. I was drafted after the Korean war, and served in the Military Police at Fort Lewis, Washington. I learned a lot about the great Pacific Northwest, where it rains *all* the time (Ancil Payne to the contrary!). After my service, I finished my law degree at Brooklyn College in 1961.

My motivation in going to law school was fear the rainbow would disappear if I didn't go after it. People of high caliber, people who had been officers in the military service, people from the finest schools in the country took jobs on the Guest Relations staff. I said to myself, if a guy from Queens is going to get anywhere against that competition, he'd better have more education.

By the time I got through law school, I had moved up to Assistant Guide Supervisor, which meant half the time I sold tickets for the tours, and the other half I had a minor supervisory role, but the title sounded important.

Next, I became a billings clerk in the Controller's Office, a chance to know and understand the real business for the first time. As an interruptions clerk, I figured out the worth of preemptions and interruptions to us and to affiliated television and radio stations, which gave me a sense of the complexity and the scope of the business.

In 1957, there was an opening for a clerk in Staging Services at the building on 18th Street, where we manufactured sets and scenes for television programs. It was an opportunity to use whatever skills I had learned and to get a peek at a different aspect of the business, so I took it. The union members earned more than I, but I did become a Production Coordinator. After several small jumps along the way, I took a big step up to my first job in Sales Service at 30 Rockefeller Plaza, the place which in some respects is the heart of NBC. I worked there for Steve Flynn, getting affiliate program clearances for the television network.

I've had about 30 jobs and as many titles in my years at NBC. I was never in one place long enough for anyone to find out about me. That was my master plan!

My really big break came in 1964 when I went to the Spot Sales Division to sell time for the five O&O stations. By then, I had learned that I liked managing, and dealing with people. I never envisioned myself as a salesman, but selling in this business was easier than selling in a lot of others. I didn't knock on doors and make phone calls. In television, a professional time buyer with an advertising agency (who is marked on the efficiency with which buys are made), calls the competing television stations and asks them to submit competitive bids. It's not a cold sale, but a rationale as to what I have to offer versus my competitor, CBS or ABC. I took to it, enjoyed it, and was successful at it.

In 1966, I went to WKYC-TV, our station in Cleveland, as local Sales Manager. Ray Welpott was head of O&O. He was terrific to work with, stern and opinionated, but fair, and you always knew where you stood with him. He and Ted Walworth, Welpott's successor as head of NBC TV Stations, were models for me. I thought if I could go as far as Ted in running a station, that would be a good career.

Ray and Ted had absolute integrity. It would be difficult to work with someone who didn't. I sold time for three years, and often the schedule I sold was placed, scheduled, revised, and aired before any papers were signed by the buyer and the seller. Never once was there a real or imagined misunderstanding about what was to be bought or sold. In broadcasting, the oral agreement works. I don't know another business with the same dollar volume and number of transactions where it does.

Companies have individual characters, or at least personalities. I regard NBC as one with high standards. I never attended a company meeting where anybody countenanced shortcuts. For instance, our strong tradition in the news area is to stand for First Amendment rights and accuracy. I've been proud to say that I worked for NBC. I lived in Washington, where it's chic to "beat up" on the media, and I think a lot of it is unfair. I'm not being defensive; it's based on my experience with the good people I've met in this business. Incidentally, 21 years ago, I married an NBC girl. She was George Hooper's secretary, and I stole her away from her job.

My next promotion came when I was moved to WRC-TV Washington, as General Sales Manager in charge of local and national sales. I was there during the upheavals and riots of the 1960's, but my job was so time-consuming and active that I was actually removed from those events. We sold 30-second and 60-second announcements to general advertisers. There were no big sales, but our hands-on, day-to-day operation was responsible for about 98% of the station's revenue.

The old school plan—dinner with the sponsor, which led to a year's sponsorship—was not the case when I was in Washington. With 30-second sales, selling was different, both fast moving and volatile. With computers, buyers were able to analyze what they got instantaneously, so a lot of changes were being made constantly. More and more dollars were involved,

and more and more attention was being paid to what was produced.

At that time, our station was intent on complying with the Equal Opportunity Employment Act by actively seeking out and hiring minorities. Women also came forward with a list of demands about the same time, and since I was responsible for a fair number of people (about 25), we made improvements in our hiring of women and minorities. I did not specifically use my law school training in this, but in everything I've done, I found it was a great mental discipline to have had it.

In 1970, after three good years in Washington, I went back to WKYC-TV in Cleveland as the Station Manager, second job from the top, responsible for the ratings and programming, as well as sales. Cleveland is different from the East Coast. Solidity, a slower pace, old-fashioned values are more evident there, although Cleveland is not really the Midwest. Cleveland is Cleveland is Cleveland! It is hard to describe, but you can't talk about it long without talking about its atrocious weather.

In 1973, I was made Vice President and General Manager for KNBC in Los Angeles, a wonderfully successful station. When someone would ask me how I liked it in California, my explanation—"I just got in from Cleveland"—usually sufficed.

California is an ideal place to live. Working there is interesting because of the time difference, three hours from New York. I reported to Ted Walworth in New York; he was halfway through his day when I got to work, and by our afternoon, New York was closed. Bob Howard, the previous General Manager, had the news, ratings, local programs, and sales working well. Bob had gone to New York as President, NBC Television Network. I kept the station on course for two years. Then I went to New York as Vice President and General Manager of WNBC-TV.

I never felt there was one particular person, some one of the "old boy" system, responsible for my promotions. I was recognized as hardworking and knowledgeable about my job, and, when opportunities for advancement came, I was considered. It was not an unbroken path of successes because I didn't get everything I asked for.

I don't like to dominate or intimidate the people working for me, but I enjoy getting them to work together. I don't have problems making decisions, never lose any sleep over them. I get all the evidence, make the decision, and hope and pray it is the right one. If it's wrong, I change it quickly.

I like to think of myself as a creative problem-solver. I could not write a script or book, or paint a picture. But I can apply creative approaches and solutions to business problems. I think many notions about what abilities are required to do various jobs are not accurate. Some of the creative people with whom I have dealt are very good businessmen. Some of the best salesmen I know are not flamboyant but relatively shy in some situations. Many of them are better organized than accountants.

During the many corporate changes in the mid-seventies, a difficult time for NBC, I was running WNBC-TV, which was doing well, so I was apart from the maelstrom. Then I was asked to be involved in Affiliate Relations, on the theory that somebody who had worked in a television station could bring some insight to it. It didn't take long to discover that we weren't delivering ratings to our affiliated stations. But without immediate solutions to the ratings problem, we shored up the Affiliate Relations effort with manpower and resources, to hold the line until the network program ratings improved.

Competition was from ABC, which came out of nowhere with successes across the board in entertainment programming, in prime time, in daytime. Their news began to be respected, their sports captured everyone's imagination with "Wide World of Sports." They lacked quality television stations, but they had the money and ratings to get better affiliates when they tried to. CBS was doing well, in fact, too well. We were not, so the stations picked on us. I was asked to slow that down or stop it. All I was able to do was slow it down.

I learned about Affiliate Relations at the knee of Don Mercer and Ray O'Connell, who had been at NBC a combined total of 80 years, knew everybody and were respected by our affiliates. Unfortunately, a lot of the ownerships were selling out to corporations, so those relationships didn't mean as much as they had.

Ancil Payne, then Chairman of the Affiliate Board, followed in the loyal tradition Jack Harris, Hod Grams and Louis Read had established. The Board members weren't shy about citing the company's deficiencies, and, I might add, if we had listened to them earlier, we'd have been out of the woods a lot faster. Ancil Payne came to broadcasting a bit later in life and moved quickly in the King Broadcasting Company right up to the top management spot. He is not politically motivated, but he has fine political instincts. Ancil is a thoroughly good man, engaging, articulate, and clear about where he stands. He knew how NBC could succeed. He served both the network and the affiliates well, a tough job in those demanding times.

Fred Paxton, who followed Ancil, came from a family-owned station combined with a family-owned newspaper in Paducah, Kentucky, and had a different style, but, again, the perfect man for the time. Fred was unflappable, a solid, good businessman with a low profile, and a strong, steadying influence when ABC was raiding us for affiliates.

Jim Lynagh, now Affiliate Board Chairman, started in the business when he was 16 or 17, has lived in 15 cities and worked for that many television stations. He had earlier and more varied broadcast experience than Ancil or Fred. Jim's background is just right for current mergers, the new syndicate properties, and the escalating changes in technology. Now, he's President of Multimedia Broadcasting.

Each of these chairmen was good at this job managing a television station or properties, and a respected broadcaster. Each represented his constituency forcefully, honestly, and well.

Network fortunes ebb and flow, but affiliates have to take the long view. They don't look for instant solutions or stampede in a short period of bad times. They wanted the network to recognize its problems and plan to solve them, and they wanted evidence of improvement. Competition for the advertiser's dollar creates tension and conflict. The affiliates feel that unlimited selling of network advertising will leave no money for local ads. That's largely true. They're jealous of the time they use to get our programs into their community. They don't want to give us any more time than they think we should have. By FCC charter, they can preempt us any time, and we're upset if we feel they're abusing that right, leaving us without access to the homes of the community. We, affiliates and network, see eye-to-eye on broad issues, but there's a lot of friction on the smaller issues.

I became Executive Vice President in the Silverman/Pfeiffer period, and I got along well with both of them. Fred Silverman is a creative broadcast programmer without the interest or ability to run a large company. Jane Pfeiffer, with her experience in organization and administration at IBM, was thought to be a good counterpoint to Fred. The theory didn't work, for a lot of reasons. In those days, I was responsible for Affiliate Relations and Network Sales—thankfully, there were very good people running both: Don Mercer, Ray O'Connell and Pier Mapes on the affiliate side, and Bob Blackmore on the Network Sales side. My focus was to keep the revenue coming in and hang on to the affiliates. We were effective enough in those areas, so management left us alone to do our thing. Lucky for me, and luck is a large part of this business. People in it work very hard. To be on the air nationwide, 14 hours a day, 7 days a week, and to sell a commodity as fragile as time, requires work and attention. I leave my house at 6:30 in the morning and come home between 6 and 9 in the evening. That's a long day.

Grant Tinker is the right man at the right time. There's no question about that. Having worked for the company, he respects its traditions and knows what they mean to NBC people. He has worked in advertising agencies, and he started his own successful production company, MTM. He didn't make radical changes but calmly and firmly directed the way out of the wilderness by insisting on quality in programming, quality in writers, producers and directors. Grant really means it when he says get the best people and let them do their own thing.

RCA assured Grant that he was going to be given the time to accomplish a turnaround. If it hadn't worked, if NBC stayed a poor third, we would have lost still more of our affiliates.

Looking ahead, I think satellite capability is going to make news-gathering easier with instant access to any part of the country, and eventually, the world. The ad hoc network is a trend that is going to continue, especially since the Commission relaxed the rules about restricting the number of television stations. At one time, you only had 5 and 2, that is, 5 VHF's, 2 UHF's; now, you may have a total of 12, with some restrictions in coverage. This is deregulation, and since I'm more for a free marketplace than against one, I think it's going to be good overall. But I am for some regulation. Deregulation will increase the trend toward ad hoc, which is not good for the networks.

These things shake out. Either the public is served what it wants or not, and it is quick to decide. The network is a business invention; it risks the money to provide stations with programs bigger than they could afford individually, and they sell adjacencies to it. If the programs appeal to the public, the stations benefit with little risk. Our potential to reach every home in the United States, instantaneously, is enormously attractive to advertisers. The ad hoc network doesn't have the mechanisms to beat our affiliate-network relationship.

If you don't sell time today for tomorrow's program, it's gone by tomorrow, and you're on to the next one. We don't project ten years ahead, but we're studying to determine our best position five years hence. We think it will be much the same, the structure will be the same, and, although there will be competition from many small, emerging media to fragment our audience, no one of them will be a viable network alternative.

The audience is growing every year. There are more television sets, turned on more often, so it's a bigger viewing pie for the networks to share, but the network audience is not growing at the pace it would if there were not competing media.

I like the interesting variety of my job at the moment. In November, 1982, I was given responsibility for the Entertainment Division and the Television Network. Once again I was fortunate to have terrific people heading up each of those divisions: Brandon Tartikoff and Pier Mapes.

In March, 1984, my duties were expanded to include Business Affairs and NBC Productions, most ably headed up by John Agoglia, Senior Vice President of Business Affairs. My previous experience was in sales and with affiliates; there was some responsibility for programming and for presenting the news. This is my first introduction to show business, but I'm not star-struck. I'm more interested in the business aspect of it.

I'm proud of NBC now. Consider the amount of time we're on the air. Watch us tonight, and you'll see programs better than a theatrical movie or a Broadway play for which you'd have to buy tickets. It's uneven, but we put on 22 hours of prime time every week. No other business does that.

My 60th birthday wish for NBC is 60 more, 60 more!

September 26, 1985

Grant Tinker became Chairman and Chief Executive Officer of NBC in 1981. His leadership of the company has helped make it Number One in four short, but arduous, years.

"I'll tell you something which may not speak too well for my RCA Director status: I don't think much about the shareholders... I *do* think about NBC. (I don't want to say 'family,' although we use that word around here. It sounds corny.) I do think of it as a collection of people who come here and to our other locations every day as part of their lives... I'd like to see NBC healthy so they have a good place to come every day. Myself included. If that's the case, we will do good work...."

I was born and grew up in Stamford, Connecticut. Two or three days after I graduated from high school in June of 1943, I went to Dartmouth College in an accelerated class. I had already enlisted in the Air Corps and was called to serve in January of '44. After two years in the service, I returned to Dartmouth in January of '46, majored in English and graduated in February of '49.

When I got out of college, I didn't know what the hell to do. I only came to New York because that was what you were supposed to do. I knew I didn't want to go into my dad's lumber business. The only reason I heard about the NBC training program was that the man in charge of placement at Dartmouth was irritated, because I did not want to work for any of the companies which came to interview and recruit on campus. He called me after I had graduated to tell me about the program, just because, I'm sure, he wanted to draw a line through my name on his list.

I had wanted to be in publishing, so when I first came to New York, I schlepped around where I could get in the door for interviews; but nobody wanted me, nor should they have. I didn't bring anything with me. That's when I heard about the new NBC training program.

I presented myself to the Personnel Department. At the reception desk sat Bob Aaron (he later became the head of daytime programming), who sent me in to see Doris Ann, who worked for Ted Thompson, the Personnel Manager at the time. For about three weeks I didn't hear anything, then they called and said, "Okay, you're accepted."

I became the first of about 60 or 80 in the program over the next few years. I think there were about six or eight of us then: Rick Kelly, Jack Kiermaier, now at CBS, Don Hyatt, who has had an illustrious career. We were paid *handsomely*, $250 a month. They didn't know what to do with us, so they bicycled us around to different departments. Somebody, perhaps Doris Ann, told the head of sound effects or music rights or operations, whatever, "I'm going to send a young man, one of our trainees, who'll be with you for the next two weeks. Please try to teach him what you do. Maybe you'll find something he can do that will make his time worthwhile." It was very haphazard. A nice guy who didn't mind having you around could make it informing and educational, but when you met resistance, it was two boring weeks.

After nine or ten months, I'd *had* it! It was driving me crazy. I was about to get married and I thought I should have a real job. So I went to Doris Ann or Ted and said, "Either I get a real job now or I have to look somewhere else." I got one in the radio area where I had spent most of my time anyway. Once they ran out of places to send me in the training program, I wound up working nights for Bob Wogan in Radio Operations, and he was extremely helpful to me. At that time, in 1949, radio was still the principal thing around here, and I really began to have some idea of how the network worked.

My first real job had a rather grand title: Operations Manager of the Radio Network. Bud Barry, who came from ABC, was in charge right here on the 4th floor. Les Harris, Mitch Benson, Arch Robb were still around, and Bob Wogan was down on the 2nd floor doing what he did. I had the job for the next two and a half years. By then I'd forgotten all about publishing. (I had had no idea what I wanted to do in it. I liked words, and I liked to read. I appreciated people who could write, but I wanted to be in the business end, not be a writer.)

Broadcasting was all radio and I enjoyed it a lot. Pat Weaver, Fred Wile and some other people were in the back room doing stuff we didn't really pay much attention to. I didn't anyway. We were trying to keep radio alive as we had known it. The last hurrah was "The Big Show" with Tallulah Bankhead and Meredith Willson that Dee Engelbach did. (Goodie Ace and Selma Diamond and others were writers.) When that failed, at great expense, I think everybody knew the handwriting was on the wall for radio, and people like Weaver and Wile were ready to enter and take center stage with television.

I was asked to join Radio Free Europe for a very brief time. After that, I went to work for John Moses, a talent agent and manager.

(His son, Harry, produces some of the pieces on "60 Minutes" today.) I had known John when he brought Bob and Ray down from Boston, and he was looking for a young guy to do the leg work. My job was not talent management but programming, packaging and producing shows.

We did some local things, but the only one I'm proud of was based on a one-line idea. I recruited Allen Ludden, from WTIC in Hartford, who had had a show called "Mind Your Manners" on NBC Radio Network. We, largely Allen, invented a program called "College Quiz Bowl," which we did on NBC radio. It was rather successful and later became the television show after I was no longer involved.

In 1954 McCann-Erickson asked me to join their radio/television department as Director of Program Development. Those were the Marion Harper days, and McCann was a big successful agency, growing bigger and more active in broadcast, although not as active in it as some of the others like Young & Rubicam and Benton & Bowles. I did that job for almost four years, and learned a lot about television, particularly the advertising side. I then worked briefly for an agency called Warwick & Legler, which hired me specifically to handle Revlon television, which had been tarnished by the quiz scandal. In trying to clean up their act, they looked for a squeaky-clean guy like myself. I only stayed 18 months because Charles Revson was so difficult. Then, luckily, Benton & Bowles asked me to join them. Bob Lutz, President, recruited me. Tommy McDermott, who ran their television department, went to run Four Star in California, and Bob convinced me I should do it.

As I look back, I think of myself as having spent the bulk of the fifties in the agencies, but always in the television areas. At Benton & Bowles I was *really* in it because they had General Foods, Procter & Gamble, Johnson's Wax—people who bought shows, and even commissioned shows. I met Mary Tyler Moore, my future wife, when I went West to be involved with a Dick Van Dyke show pilot for Procter & Gamble. I spent a lot of time on the West Coast because, at this point, my marriage was over, and in one year between marriages, I spent more time in California than I did in New York, even though I lived here and my office was here.

At B&B, I dealt mainly with evening television shows, prime-time shows. Procter & Gamble had a lot of daytime shows, and some agency people were "soap experts." Irwin Segelstein was one, and I did not get into them, because I simply didn't know anything about them at all.

I guess I must have liked what I was doing because I kept doing it well enough so that nobody fired me. The agency business was volatile at that time, but I stayed ahead. I was quitting and going somewhere else before they caught up with me, probably! The job at Benton & Bowles led to my coming back to NBC because, in the course of it, I met Mort Werner who was at Y&R in a class above me as the head of broadcast there. We shared accounts like General Foods and Procter & Gamble, and I would see him coming in and out of offices or with clients. We had a nodding acquaintance until one Saturday night at a party given by a General Foods executive, where neither one of us particularly wanted to be, we got to talking in the back yard. He had just accepted an offer to come back to NBC himself, and asked me whether I would be interested in coming back also. I said I guessed I would. He followed up, we got together, and I did come back. That was in '61.

They gave me the title of Vice President and General Program Executive, but I think Mort, as my boss, knew then what he wanted me to do in California, although he didn't share it with me. I had only been here for a couple of months when he said, "How would you like to go out to Burbank?" He knew that Mary and I were going to get married, and, since she worked in California, it was just terrific, very convenient. I went there and became West Coast head of programs. Mort was great to work for, a good guy who let you do your job. He did not over-supervise anybody, but encouraged people to be independent.

My programming tastes were formed by then. At least, as they say, I knew when I saw it or heard it if I liked it. Not that I didn't make a lot of mistakes. In our business, you're wrong more often than you're right. We did business with people like Sheldon Leonard, Norman Felton, and David Dortort. They were the people who were the 60's counterparts of the Bochcos, Paltrows and Gary Goldbergs of today. To me, the emphasis should be on the creative person; not the idea, but who is going to execute the idea.

In the 60's Mort and I bought the first Cosby show, "I Spy," produced by Sheldon Leonard. Sheldon was responsible for pairing Culp and Cosby. All we did was approve. As you think of it now, it doesn't seem like a breakthrough, but it was at the time. And, of course, Bill was totally unknown except as a stand-up comic.

In "I Spy," the only risk which concerned us was the expense of traveling the show to those exotic places. At the end of the first year Sheldon, a very good, responsible executive, came to my office in Burbank and made a big pitch for $400,000 of overages that he had incurred, which today is a split. We gave him the $400,000, as well we should have, because he did some awfully good work. I doubt that he was ever in the black. The show didn't last that long. I honestly don't know whether "I Spy" ever made money in syndication. I would guess not because there were too few episodes. But it was a breakthrough show of sorts. Mort and I had to explain the expense to the head of the television network, but that wasn't too bad. The principal players back in New York then were Mort, Bob Stone, Bob Kintner, Walter Scott. Don Durgin was the head of Sales.

As I look back, even though it was only 20 years ago, it was so simple. There were fewer bodies then. I kid Brandon Tartikoff about that now that there are people falling all over each other, but they all have legitimate jobs because the medium has become so much more complicated, and everybody is a specialist of one kind or another. I was lucky to be a generalist when there were just a few of us, and I think that was more fun.

"Get Smart" is the comedy I remember, and I will happily take a lot of credit for it because Dick Dorso, the agent, brought it in and said quite honestly that it had been turned down at ABC. It was late in the season; we had already committed all our development, but I read it. I called Mort and said, "We've got to do *one* more pilot. This is so funny." He said, "If you feel that strongly about it, let's do it." We did, and it went

on to be a very successful top-ten comedy show. That's the most fun—when you take one away from another network. We repeated that recently with Cosby, who also was at ABC first and wound up on NBC.

I came back East when all of that chair-changing took place and Bob Kintner left. Don Durgin was promoted, and he brought me back. Mort was promoted to some super program job, and they put me in what had been his job as Vice President in Charge of Programs, which I thought I would do for the rest of my life, the end-all in television. I did it for about a year, and became disenchanted with things that were going on. I decided to pack it in.

I went back to California and got a job at Universal Studios, doing television from the other side, putting together and selling the shows. They were so busy they needed more manpower, and Jennings Lang, who called on us a lot at NBC, said if you're available, come join us. In short order, I was back in my old office in Burbank selling to Herb Schlosser, among others, who was sitting at my old NBC desk. This was 1967, 1968, and all the movie studios were heavily into television. My first assignment was to sell "It Takes a Thief" with Bob Wagner to ABC. I sold it to Elton Rule, who by that time had come East to be President of ABC. I really enjoyed that. I don't really know why I left Universal. I only stayed for a couple of years.

I went to Fox because Bill Self, head of television at Fox, persuaded me to do so. I was at Fox when Mary was given a series commitment by CBS. They wanted her because she had done the Dick Van Dyke show, and then a special with Dick which was awfully good. That was my excuse for leaving Fox. I told Bill I was going to help Mary make a television show. I didn't have a company in mind as much as trying to make a successful show.

I recruited the creative people and started MTM with the single show, with Mary and Arthur Price, Mary's manager/agent, whom we knew well. He's a good man, and he's president of MTM now. I hired two guys, Jim Brooks and Allan Burns, to write and produce the show which was their creation. It went on, and it was good. Not immediately successful but it soon became successful. It was never offered to NBC because CBS had made a series commitment to Mary. When it became successful, we did "The Bob Newhart Show," and we were in business. I was proud of most of the shows, but not all of them. Happily, the company was small enough so we could do only what we wanted to. I don't think I really appreciated that independence until I left to come back to NBC.

You asked me about selling to the networks. They do have their differences. They change occasionally because people change, but we at MTM did most of our work for CBS at that time, probably because we started there, did "Mary" there, did "Bob" there, then we spun off things like "Lou Grant." We had successfully performed for them, so they were easier to sell. We got a great reception when we went there. Selling to NBC was harder, and it was not until later when we began "Hill Street Blues" that we got our big breakthrough there.

MTM usually had four or five shows on the air. We weren't a very big company; the permanent party was very small. During the production season, each show could take 60 or 80 people to make, so we would swell by that number times the number of shows. The management was small, ten people, involved all the time. That was the fun of it. At MTM I was not the creative guy but the recruiter of creative people, and the man who kept them happy. Arthur handled the business affairs, made the deals with the agents, with the networks, a very important responsibility. I had the fun part, but he thought *his* was the fun part. You do what you think you're good at, and we were a good team.

We never starved, but in a production company you're always dealing in futures. Your big income is in syndication, so you don't begin to make money until shows come off the network and go into syndication. I'd always made a living, so I've never really thought much about money. I like it. It's nice, it's better to have it than not have it, but if it meant a lot to me I never would have left MTM. In leaving, I gave it all up. And gave up the future. MTM was and is today such a going, vibrant, powerful, independent production company

that it has the ability to get into anything it wants beyond television.

I don't have the option to go back to MTM. Coming to work at NBC was such a potential conflict of interest that the only way I could do it was to sell my interest, principally to Arthur and Mary. It took about a year to work that out. In the interim, my interest was put into a blind trust, because my sitting here as a potential customer could influence what went on in MTM. You have to slam the door irrevocably and completely, so that's what happened.

Thornton Bradshaw didn't come to me with a proposal to be Chairman of NBC. We really just sat down to chat about television. He had taken on the RCA job and had NBC, among other things, to be concerned about, and was already, I think, aware that he was going to have to make a change at NBC. He was out in California to consult with people in the business, pick their brains, and familiarize himself with a world he didn't know a hell of a lot about. I have no idea whether he offered the job to someone else, but I'm sure he would have told me so if he had. I'm not sure he intended to offer it to me when we met. I certainly didn't have it in mind and was surprised when he asked me to take it at our second meeting two or three weeks later. I was just full of beans and told him a lot of things about how NBC should work. He called my bluff and said, "Well, why don't you come do it?"

I think there was no reason that NBC should have fallen to the level it had, and stopped being competitive. In talking to Bradshaw (and I'm sure I didn't talk differently from the way I might have talked in my office to Arthur Price about it), I said that NBC kept doing so many dumb things, making so many bad choices, and network watchers (I wasn't the only one) all around town in the production business were probably saying the same thing. It's an easy game people on the outside play—looking inside and second-guessing what the people there are doing. I'm sure I did that with Bradshaw. Whether others could have prevented it or whether it was inexorable that NBC would drift down to third place through the 70's, I don't know. I certainly don't know why they had to. If you had to put something at the top of the list, programs would be it. At times like that, the affiliate-switching becomes an unravelling. But success breeds success, even when there are changes at the top. Look at the history of CBS; it has almost always been strong. You have to go back to the time when Paley stole all the talent from General Sarnoff, to find a cataclysmic change. CBS has stayed right up there in television, with a lot of stability and consistency of performance because they've done their jobs well.

I don't know that NBC can blame RCA for executive changes. Obviously some bad choices were made at some point, and then the people who were chosen had a terrible run of bad luck. That's really all it is. People give me a certain amount of credit for what's happened in the last four years, and, in truth, I don't deserve it. I'm willing to take some of it, but all the senior management people here do the work. I've given them a lot of encouragement but I'm not doing their jobs for them.

Why did I come back? This is where I had my first job in the very late 40's, and I was back at NBC in the 60's for a very enjoyable period, and I just felt that I would like to come back. I took the challenge because I do have an affection for NBC. If people knew what I left on the table at MTM, they would say this man should be locked up. He's certifiable. I guess serious money doesn't mean that much to me. As I think of it now, I'm sure I did have a feeling of having mastered the job at MTM, as it were, and maybe it was time for new challenges. And, Thornton Bradshaw's a very nice man, the kind of man to whom you respond. NBC needed help, and when he asked at that second lunch we had together if I would help, right on the spot I said, "Sure, I'd like to try." It was almost as simple as that—a collection of things that came together.

Bradshaw came to me at the right time. I had had some success, and I could leave MTM, and no one could ever take that away from me. I could have built MTM into something—that would have been fun, too. But I think it has nothing to do with MTM, it has to do only

with NBC, the mountain that was there, that had to be climbed. I soon discovered that there was more of a job to be done than I had realized from the outside looking in. By the end of the first year, I was surprised at the extent of the job, the depth of the hole the company was in, and, from then until now, I have always felt thoroughly challenged.

I tried to turn the job down when I said that I didn't ever want to move back to New York. And Bradshaw said, "You can live wherever you want, or move the company to Burbank." He said to handle it anyway I wanted to. I came back to work in New York and set up a little apartment here, but I maintained my residence in California, and so I commute.

When I'm out in my Burbank office, I relate to the program business because that's my training and my interest. I use that somewhat as an excuse. Brandon Tartikoff doesn't need any help from me, but I *pretend* that he does, so that I can drop by there on Fridays.

My first year back we bought "Taxi," not so much for the show, but for the people who made it; who were the very best in programming. The "Cheers" people are graduates of the "Taxi" creative group. I don't want to take the rap or the credit for programming because I haven't done it since I've been back. It's always been Brandon Tartikoff's job. I think it was true that we were the third network creative people came to, because they had the least chance of success. If you got a show on NBC, it probably wouldn't succeed because it wasn't behind a successful show. That made it very difficult to get the network started from standing still to moving slowly, to moving faster, and finally running, as we are now. Brandon is now more likely to see things first, because we do have those building blocks. We did have, courtesy of prior management, a number of commitments that we had to eat our way through, either by using them or by buying out of them. And we did take a significant write-down the first year I was here, mostly on programming that we didn't want to use the second time. We'd rather choke on it than air it. Then slowly but surely, we've worked our way through the other commitments till we are really quite clean.

"The Cosby Show" has been an incredible help, but it only helps Thursday nights. It doesn't have any effect on the other nights. We would be in pretty good shape even without Bill, but we are in much better shape with him. ABC could have had the show but they turned it down, and, in fact, it is produced by Tom Werner and Marcy Carsey, who worked at ABC.

You ask what would happen now if NBC were still number three. I would probably still be trying; I don't think I would have wanted to leave, having failed to help restore the place. Maybe I'm stubborn, or maybe Bradshaw or somebody would have said, "This guy isn't doing the job, let's get somebody else."

Perhaps I have calmed this company down, but I followed a very excited act, a frenzied failure, particularly toward the end of Fred's tenure, for reasons that I wasn't here to witness, and can't even tell you about. You could get so desperate about all of NBC's bad luck that you could go bananas. When I arrived, just to sit and talk as you and I are talking now was unusual. People were running around like chickens without heads here. To act in a normal fashion *seemed* calm, but it was just normal.

I guess I handle stress by keeping it inside, the way most of us do. I do play some tennis, but that isn't much of an outlet. I spend a lot of time gnashing my teeth about things, but I guess it isn't particularly overt or noticeable to others.

I chose a non-news person to head NBC News on another little theory of mine which I did not invent: hire the man and not the résumé. Larry Grossman's résumé had no news experience *per se*, but I did know the man. I knew him somewhat here in the 60's. When I was in Burbank, he was the head of advertising and promotion here, and I watched him from a distance over the years, particularly as the head of PBS. When I realized that we should be doing something in the News Division, I thought he would be a magnificent choice, and I sought him out. Bud Rukeyser was the only guy I asked about it, and he said, "I think he's ideal." When I asked Larry, his comment was, "That's the only job I would leave PBS to take." The rest, as they say, is history, or it is going to

be history. I think the whole world does not yet know what Larry Grossman is, but the world will discover. That's what they will put on my tombstone, that I hired Larry Grossman. I wish all the things I have done turned out that well. He is candid, accepts his mistakes and learns from them. Larry didn't move into the job that easily, because he was coming into a rather strange new world, but he assimilated quickly, and he's a wonderful executive.

I chose to have three Group Executive Vice Presidents under me, but I didn't do that right away. As Chairman, I made my own mistakes for a while and also learned from them. I had delivered mail on this floor (6th) in my first NBC job, and, in the second, I came up to the 6th floor as a programmer, from the 4th floor or from Burbank. I hadn't *lived* here and seen it from this perspective. It took me a little while to understand how the company should work. My mistakes were in the deployment of people, not the people themselves. Finally, in a second rearrangement, I figured out that threesome. There's no magic to three, it could have been two or four. Among them, they whack up the company, and all areas report to them except for the two which report to me: Bud Rukeyser and Larry Grossman. Timothy, Walsh and Butler have the responsibility for all of the pieces of the company, so I, in dealing with those five, cover the whole thing easily, quickly and comfortably.

If I jumped out that window today, nobody would know I was gone except there would be a breeze blowing in the open window. Those guys run their respective areas so well that they don't need any help from me. They were already here; I only chose them in the sense that I decided their specific areas of responsibility. You make judgments about people, and my judgments of those people were that they were damn good. That's something you sense. I knew, after having spent a little time with them, after a year and a half of getting to know them, that we could structure the company as it is now. My two recruitments were Bud, whom I knew from my earlier days and asked to come back to NBC, and Larry, also a returnee.

I like to be left alone by my boss, and I hope I would behave the same way toward those I supervise. I like to give them a feeling that the whole company is working together. We have a way of demonstrating that once a week in the Chairman's Council, which I created, more for my own benefit and sense of belonging than anything else. It's a group of nine people including myself, which gets together for a couple of hours every week, usually on a Tuesday afternoon, so that we all know the same things. In addition to the five, Irwin Segelstein, the Vice Chairman, is a roving outfielder; there is nothing that he can't address or be asked to become involved in. He's probably the most knowledgeable in the most ways. He never forgets anything he's soaked up from an awful lot of experience. Then there's Cory Dunham, Executive Vice President and General Counsel, and Gene McGuire, Executive Vice President, Personnel and Labor Relations. The whole company is represented in that room for those two hours while we deal decisively with a pressing matter, or we just talk philosophically, but I leave with the feeling that I know everything current and important, and I hope they all feel the same way.

I don't have trouble making decisions. Some of them are the 51/49 kind. Very seldom do you decide one that is clear-cut, they all fall between the 40-yard lines. I'm a guy who is beginning to feel finally that he's getting older. These days as I sit in rooms and meetings, even up at RCA, and look around, I realize that most of the people are younger than I am, and sometimes all of them are younger. That always comes as a surprise. I don't feel older. That may partly be because I started in this building, left it, and came back. I've been out of NBC more than I've been in it, but I feel that I've been here a lot, a good measure of time.

I was ambitious enough to want to be Vice President of Programming, but I never tried to figure out how to get there. I usually made a move because I had a growing family and mouths to feed, and somebody offered me more money. Except for the Radio Free Europe position, which was outside the commercial area and off the beaten path, the rest of my moves, while they were relatively frequent, were sensible and defensible at the times I made them. I think maybe I had a low threshold of boredom; once I'd done a job, I couldn't see myself doing it forever.

Programs come and go, nights of the week are up and down, but companies can be consistent. NBC always was until the 70's. I'll tell you something which may not speak too well for my RCA Director status: I don't think much about the shareholders, and that we are doing something for them. I *do* think about NBC. (I don't want to say "family," although we use that word around here. It sounds corny.) I do think of it as a collection of people who come here and to our other locations every day as part of their lives. From my NBC experiences, working for it or calling on it, I think of it as just a bunch of people, most of them nice people, and friends of mine, and I'd like to see it healthy so they have a good place to come every day. Myself included. If that's the case, we'll all do good work, and everything else will take care of itself.

The affiliates are people too, and mostly nice people, like Jim Lynagh, Fred Paxton, all the others. There again it's a business relationship, but when you get beyond that, assuming you're mutually doing your business well, it's just a people matter. Without them, we are nothing.

What's my wish for the company's 60th birthday? I would like to see NBC lock in on some of the success we're now enjoying, which is not across the board. We have jobs yet undone. I'd like to see NBC get into the habit of succeeding and never forget how again. And that's a modest wish. I don't think there is anything undoable about that.

October 30, 1985

Art Watson became President of NBC Sports in July 1979, charged with the responsibility of the 1980 Olympics. President Carter's decision to withdraw was a traumatic one for NBC, for Watson, and the NBC affiliate family.

"NBC Sports and management started to prepare for the negotiations for both Calgary and Seoul three years ago. We wanted to be aggressive, but responsible as well....We came up with the concept of 'risk sharing' for the 1988 Olympics....We arrived at our figure of $300 to $500 million by estimating how many hours would be meaningful for the network and for our audiences.... Many people think of Seoul as the other side of the world in time. But the Far East is a mirror image of the United States: when it is 11 a.m. in Seoul, it is 9 p.m. the preceding day here in New York."

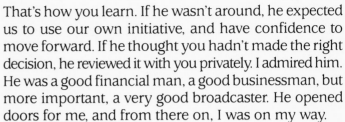

I was born and raised in Brooklyn, New York. At Fordham University, I majored in accounting. I did not go on to graduate work, but I did receive an honorary degree from St. John's University in 1979, which really pleased me.

I started with NBC in 1956 as a financial analyst in the staff area. I got the job by accident, like so many other things in life. I was working for Montgomery Ward in Albany, and they were going to transfer me to Chicago, but my wife and I decided we wanted to come back to New York where we both grew up. That very day, a man at NBC in New York called me to ask if I would be interested in a job. I was interviewed one morning and the next day I was hired.

I stayed on the financial staff from 1956 to some time in 1959 when Ray Welpott, Vice President and General Manager of WRCV Radio and Television in Philadelphia, an NBC-owned station, hired me as Business Manager. I became the Station Manager in 1961, and General Manager and Vice President in 1964. Then, when the FCC decreed that NBC and Westinghouse had to swap the stations that were traded nine years before, I moved to Cleveland when NBC assumed ownership of that station. That was a very disappointing switch for me. I remember the phone call so well saying, out of the blue, that the FCC had made the decree, and it was a shock because Cleveland was a smaller market than Philadelphia. Westinghouse had appealed to the government and said that the terms of the original trade were not fair to them. When the FCC reviewed it and decided to cancel it, NBC became the Cleveland owner and changed the call letters of the radio and television station to WKYC.

Ray Welpott was my mentor. I was about 30 when I started to work at the station in Philadelphia, young to assume that kind of responsibility. Ray taught me a great deal. He had faith in me and gave me the opportunity to find out what it took to get the job done. He gave me freedom to make mistakes.

That's how you learn. If he wasn't around, he expected us to use our own initiative, and have confidence to move forward. If he thought you hadn't made the right decision, he reviewed it with you privately. I admired him. He was a good financial man, a good businessman, but more important, a very good broadcaster. He opened doors for me, and from there on, I was on my way.

When Ray became Executive Vice President in charge of the NBC O&O's, and I was going to become the General Manager, Bob Kintner expressed concern about my age and my limited experience. I remember he said to me, "You're too young for this. But Ray has great faith in you; now we'll see whether you can do it." And he passed on me. I remember my first weekend in Cleveland. We went there on a Friday to assume ownership at 6:30 a.m. Saturday morning. We did all the necessary things, and at 11 o'clock on Saturday night, Bob Kintner called me at home to ask if I was prepared for Monday morning. He wanted to be sure I was aware of certain things the network was doing. He was more involved with Cleveland and with me than the other O&O's.

I learned how to manage a station in Philadelphia, but I always considered it Ray's station. When I came to Cleveland, my first station, I had my own goals and objectives to make it the number one station there. To be a successful broadcaster, particularly in a place like Cleveland, you had to integrate yourself into the community, which we did. My family and I spent four and a half years there. We loved it.

In 1969, I was asked to come back to New York as President of NBC Radio for a couple of years. It was a very responsible position within the company, and I saw it as a challenge, an opportunity to establish my own mark. Radio was going through a transition. "Monitor," a major staple of NBC network radio programming, had outlived its time, and had to be moved or replaced with more modern programming in shorter form.

I was very satisfied with my position in radio, but I always wanted to return to television, my first love. Julian Goodman, President then, knew that, and I was appointed, about two years later, Executive Vice President and General Manager of WNBC, Channel 4, in New York. By then, Ted Walworth had succeeded Ray Welpott as President of the O&O's. I remember starting the two-hour early evening news. Lee Hanna, Earl Ubell and

I put that format on the air for the first time in New York. It took a year to mount it. It had been done only in Los Angeles before that, but we recognized its success out on the Coast.

A network-owned station must, in my opinion, be sensitive to community concerns, problems, community needs, programming needs, and aware of the number of competing independents. We originated and controlled the news programming, which made a good deal of sense to me, since I saw it as a service to our audience. Julian and the whole company gave us the financial and moral support to try the two-hour format because it fit the company's needs at that time. News was very important on the network, and it was important to build that image in our stations around the country. We knew it would be a slow process—it was two and a half years before it really started to build, but everybody had a great deal of patience.

In 1979, I became Executive Vice President of the Television Network, a position created to oversee the administration of the 1980 Olympics in Moscow. The production side stayed inside Sports at that time. I also had other responsibilities in network sales and so forth, but my main responsibility was to supervise and organize the Olympics. A mammoth job of logistics. It involved sports, my avocation, so I was delighted to do it. About a year later, I was made President of NBC Sports, the fulfillment of a dream, a perfect fit for me. Fred Silverman, President, and Jane Pfeiffer, Chairman, wanted a change in sports, and they selected me to replace Chet Simmons, who had succeeded Carl Lindemann.

Fred and Jane were new in the company, and I can only surmise that Chet and they were not on the same wavelength, in spite of the fact that NBC Sports was doing very well at the time. I inherited a healthy operation, but I felt sorry that Chet was let go, because he and I were good personal friends.

We all got the shock of our lives that day in late December 1979, when President Carter proposed to boycott the Olympics. I tell you, it wasn't a very happy day, but we had to realize that it was beyond our control. I was disappointed in Carter's decision but I understood why he did it. Later, I had strong doubts about whether he was right.

We had to be optimistic and continue our preparations so if the decision was reversed, we would be ready to go. We went through the proper channels and learned that the decision applied to us and to the American athletes. We were determined to support the government, and if the American athletes didn't go, we wouldn't go. We explained to our government officials that we had to send a small contingent to record the games for our insurance purposes. We sent very few, about 40 people, under Geoff Mason's direction. They covered the Olympics by using the international feed, recording it and sending it back to the United States daily via satellite. We kept those tapes to prove that we had the capacity to put the games on the air, thereby we collected the insurance from Lloyd's of London. This was the first time an Olympics was ever insured. Some questioned that as precedent-setting and expensive, but it was cheap in the end. The total loss to the company was about $30 million, which included services, but it would have been $100 million without the insurance!

I guess it would be reasonable to estimate that we sent over $20 million worth of equipment. I assure you that every nut and bolt we took over came back. Everybody thinks that we left some there or that some was confiscated. It was not so. The Soviets had a financial investment which they wanted to collect. A major portion of any Olympic rights are paid after the games. We owed them around $25 million, so they were cooperative and businesslike and gave our people the necessary amenities while they were there. We moved all our equipment out and used it in various areas of the country, primarily on the West Coast.

Sports may be the smallest division in the company, with roughly 160 people in management, administration, finance and production (engineers come from another pool). That small staff does some 500 hours of programming a year. Our production staff is constantly on the road. I'm a "hands-on" individual. I do not sit in this office all the time; I probably travel half the time because most of the sports programming takes place outside New York City. Though I have to go to many events, I don't always stay for the full event, but I have to show, and I like to be involved with the promoters, the people holding the event, and my production people. *And* I like sports. If I don't see it live, I watch it and critique it at home.

I don't like carelessness and lack of attention to detail. Sports requires detail, requires people to do their homework, whether they are the talent, the production people, or the staff supporting them. If everybody does his job, things go smoothly. If somebody is careless, it's like a domino falling, causing a chain reaction; everybody is unhappy. Occasionally there is some sloppy production or the wrong graphics go up, but that's very rare. NBC Sports people are professional, they take pride in what they do.

NBC has a proud tradition of sports broadcasting—the first Rose Bowl game in 1927, the first World Series, all the bowl games in color in 1965. I'm not sure I watched all of them that long ago, but we have now three bowl games on New Year's Day, and I guarantee I watch all of them. It was exciting when color came to sports, particularly those outdoors. You get the feeling that you're there, right on the spot. You become critical if the camera is too dark or not focused, because you want that picture to be the perfect picture. Color adds that dimension. Today we just accept it. Now, if you see something in black-and-white, you are in total shock and disbelief!

For 1986, we probably have the "dream schedule." We have the Super Bowl, World Cup Soccer in June, and the World Series in October. We have the French Open, the Rose Bowl, the Orange Bowl, Wimbledon, Breeders' Cup and more.

Five or six years ago, ABC was the dominant sports network because they had the affiliation with the

Olympics, and they were involved in most of the major events. Their anthology, "Wide World of Sports," was the most successful sports program, and they had the reputation of being the best. Today, I would say there is no question that we have become the Number One sports network. ABC has suffered a significant and major decline.

The baseball strike was an issue between major league baseball and the players' association, and during it, I was concerned that the continuity of the game would be interrupted. Compromises had to be made by both the owners and the players. Baseball is also a business, and I hoped that the agents and the players would recognize that there is not a bottomless pit of money, that the owners are limited. It was common knowledge that many of the clubs were operating at a deficit or close to a questionable margin, and that both sides would have to compromise in order to come to an agreement. Neither could survive if players' salaries continued to escalate at the rate they had—quadrupling in less than ten years. It was obvious to me as an outsider with a fair knowledge of the owners' income sources that the owners couldn't afford it. I think the lid is the marketplace, but we're seeing changes today, particularly in the NFL, also in baseball, where owners are announcing, "I can't afford this," and passing on certain players. There's a new hard line being taken.

We came up with the concept of risk-sharing for the 1988 Olympics in Seoul. NBC Sports and management people started to prepare for the negotiations for both Calgary and Seoul approximately three years ago. We wanted to be aggressive, but responsible as well. We took time to understand the people in both countries as well as the International Olympic Committee and its President, Juan Antonio Samaranch, who was very much involved. The partnership is comprised of the originating city or country (Calgary or the Repulic of Korea), the International Olympic Committee, and the American network involved. We were well prepared going into both negotiations. We arrived at our figure of $300 to $500 million by estimating how many hours would be meaningful for the network and for our audiences. Many people think of Seoul as the other side of the world in time. But the Far East is a mirror image of the United States: when it's 11 a.m. in Seoul, it is 9 p.m. the preceding day here in New York. The morning events become prime-time events and can be done live, which we intend to do with our 80 hours of prime-time programming. When they're doing their nighttime events at 9, 10 o'clock at night, it's 7 or 8 o'clock in the morning here. From Europe, there are very few hours you can do live because the time differential puts you on at awkward hours for the United States.

We bid very aggressively for Calgary. CBS dropped out early, and it became an auction between ABC and NBC, which didn't please either of us. We bid $304 million. They bid $309 million, and we didn't want to top that, so we walked away. Advertisers' commitment to spend for all network sports changed dramatically shortly after that. So ABC will find it difficult to make this a profitable venture in 1988 unless things change again.

Sports advertising became soft across all networks, across-the-board, because certain advertisers who had always paid a premium for the huge sports audiences switched to entertainment programs, action-adventure programs. That created a supply-over-demand situation and softened the price levels. We did our homework on the number of hours of programming for the Seoul games, and it became obvious to us that Seoul would go for approximately the same level as Calgary even though it had twice as much programming. The Summer Olympics has substantially more events to it, events of greater interest to Americans—track and field, gymnastics, basketball, boxing, etc.—so that the Seoul Olympics at that point became a much more attractive package to us.

We have to forecast what sporting events advertisers are going to be interested in. We know the advertisers involved today, and, of course, some of those will leave, but hopefully new ones will come on the scene. We have sounded out some major advertisers to be sure they are interested in Olympic programming. It's the premier sporting showcase every four years, and those

involved in the past have found it successful. Naturally, they're interested in the price, but they have a feel for what it is. We have to make these projections—that's part of the business. With the facts, you establish a price level you think the inventory is worth, and you bid for that level.

I wasn't disappointed that we did not get Calgary. At those stakes, when you reach your maximum price, you have to have the courage to walk away if the risk is too great. I strongly believe that the 1988 summer games will be the first Olympic confrontation in 12 years between the Western powers, the Soviets and their Eastern bloc countries. We did not go in 1980, and they did not go in 1984. If it happens again, it could be the collapse of the Olympics.

People in many areas of NBC will put in a staggering number of hours on the Olympics between now and 1988. It will cost over $100 million to produce, with the major outlay in the final year, to send people there, pay their lodging, transportation and time.

We're using the Moscow plan as an outline. In 1984 in Los Angeles, ABC was the host broadcaster, and provided the international signal for the entire world. When it's in another country, you, the American broadcaster, only augment and supplement their signal, and you can concentrate on American athletes or other world athletes who interest the American audience. It's of a lesser production magnitude, but it still must be geared to your 180 hours of broadcasting, a monumental project. We'll have a plan for Korea in six months; most of it is in people's heads right now, but it will be put on paper so that everyone is aware of what must be done in order to have a successful Olympics.

Before we went into negotiations for Seoul, we had meetings with the NBC Affiliates Sports Committee, headed by Pep Cooney, and soon thereafter the Executive Board of the Affiliates designated an Olympic Committee comprised of Fred Paxton, Pep Cooney, Jim Lynagh, and Jim Sefert. We outlined our strategy for them, so there were no surprises. They endorsed our plan and we will have additional meetings with them once our contract is signed. We'll program from 7 a.m. to 10 a.m. in the morning, and 7.30 p.m. to midnight, and 12:30 a.m. to the 2:30 a.m. conclusion each night, plus weekends. The network and the local stations each have their own share of this inventory of spots and inserts. Because we are sensitive to our stations' needs, we have promised at least one news window within our prime-time program block. We will be specific about scheduling when we lay out each day's broadcast. This is part of our partnership.

Over the many years I've been with NBC, I've built friendships at all levels of the company. That's satisfying and gratifying to me. I spend a very large amount of my waking hours here at the office doing business, but the friendships continue on weekends, and when people move to other responsibilities, or retire. Of course, Teddy Walworth was one, and of those still here, I've worked in various capacities with Ray Timothy, Bob Walsh, Gene McGuire. There have been many others!

There's no question that I learned the most from Ray Welpott. After that, I was pretty well settled and spent five years on my own 700 miles from headquarters, learning to be independent and responsibile. The O&O's are probably the best training ground, because there you operate a business and are responsible for all elements: programming, sales, engineering, the whole spectrum of broadcasting. With that experience, you can easily come back and take a position in a specific area of a company where you're more exposed, under the microscope a lot.

In the late seventies, when NBC had its dark moments and ran into its share of mine fields, I firmly believed it would turn around if we continued to work at it. Nobody stays at the top in this business. It's all cyclical, and you have to have perseverance. In the long, long view, your day in the sun will come again.

My wish for NBC's 60th birthday is that the next 60 are just as fine as the first 60.

October 29, 1985

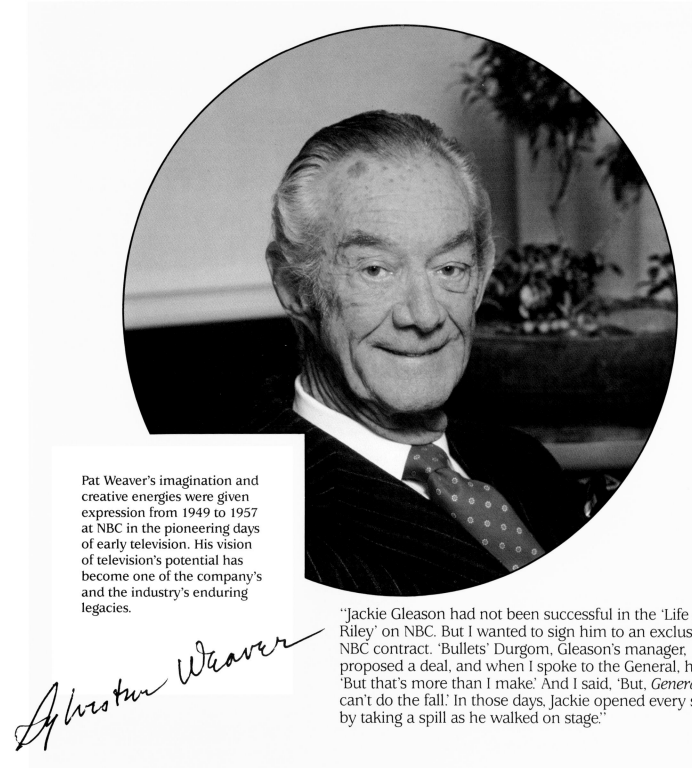

Pat Weaver's imagination and creative energies were given expression from 1949 to 1957 at NBC in the pioneering days of early television. His vision of television's potential has become one of the company's and the industry's enduring legacies.

Sylvester Weaver

"Jackie Gleason had not been successful in the 'Life of Riley' on NBC. But I wanted to sign him to an exclusive NBC contract. 'Bullets' Durgom, Gleason's manager, proposed a deal, and when I spoke to the General, he said, 'But that's more than I make.' And I said, 'But, *General*, you can't do the fall.' In those days, Jackie opened every show by taking a spill as he walked on stage."

I was born in Los Angeles, and I came East to Dartmouth College where I majored in philosophy. My secondary major was classical civilization. While in school during the summers, I worked for my father, but I told him that I did not want to run the family business, a roofing manufacturing company. He, a wise man, sold it in July of 1929, the year before I graduated from Dartmouth.

I was slated to go on to Harvard Business School, but I didn't come back from Europe; I stayed abroad for another six months trying to be a writer. Then I returned to New York. I wanted to be a writer like the writers on *The Saturday Evening Post* who earned all that money and traveled all over the world with their portable typewriters. *The March of Time* was starting up, and *Time* had me on standby as a possible writer, but I got sick and had to go back to California.

In 1932, I was editor of the *Blue Pencil*, the Los Angeles advertising club magazine, when the CBS radio station KHJ offered me a job as a comedy writer, and I grabbed it. I started as a writer but became the primary salesman. Shortly thereafter, I was sent to San Francisco to run the CBS station for $150 a week. I was the head of Program Sales, Program Production, News; I was in charge of practically everything. Parenthetically, it was a great city for a bachelor. Prohibition had been repealed, and life was fun!

I was tempted, as a Californian, to stay in God's country, but I was offered a job by CBS in Honolulu. Ed Fitzgerald, a former AP correspondent and our radio newsman, decided to move to New York with his wife Pegeen, and I did the news while I was trying to find a new newsman. In 1935, CBS asked me to do the news in Honolulu for more money than I was getting running the station in San Francisco. I was so overcome that I resigned and took the boat to New York instead so I wouldn't end up as a beach bum in Honolulu in three or four years.

Tom McAvity, head of

Lord & Thomas, hired me to write the "Evening in Paris" revue with Mark Warnow and his orchestra, the Pickens Sisters, and Odette Myrtle. That was my first job in New York in 1935. I was ambitious, and I was totally grabbed by the business. Coming from Hollywood, I was mad about movies. I never missed a movie at Dartmouth in the four years I was there. In New York City, I went to live theatre, and this, with the movies, really set me on the path.

In the thirties it was evident that radio was absolutely going to go through the roof. At the same time, talking pictures were revolutionizing the movie business, and you could foresee that we were in a mammoth move forward. I got a job at Young & Rubicam and worked hard for lots of reasons, which didn't include money. I always made plenty, but I never really thought much about it. A great mistake in my career!

I had the show with Tom McAvity, then I sold, through the CBS Artists Bureau, two-and-one-half hours a week on the Mutual Network for United Cigar-Whalen Drug Stores. I wrote and produced that show with Isham Jones, Woody Herman, Loretta Lee, the Eaton Boys with Ray Block, and Harry Von Zell. I gave the board a list of M.C.'s, and they asked me to do it. I said, "Fellows, I gave you a whole *list* of people; I don't like to perform." One of the directors said, "What if we gave you another $150 a week?" I said, "I'll do it!" So there I was in my white tie and tails at the New Amsterdam Roof for the next 26 weeks doing the show to a big audience. Just as I started that, Y&R offered me "The Fred Allen Show," the best show in radio. I said yes! and took the United Cigar account to Y&R so I could keep on doing that too. After a couple of years, I became Manager of the Radio Department at Y&R.

Fred Allen was marvelous. We worked out of Studio 8-H at NBC with an audience of 1,200 or more on Wednesday at 9 p.m. There was never an empty seat for the live midnight repeats to the West Coast, even on snowy nights. Fred was a great vaudeville and theatre performer, so it was nothing for him to convulse those people. He never played to the audience, but they just fell out of those chairs.

Fred was probably the best comedy writer in radio. The great writers and performers in show business never missed his show. Arnold Auerbach and Herman Wolf, just out of Columbia, both to become famous, famous writers, wrote stuff for him, but he rarely used it. I'd pick up the script at the Dorset every Monday, bring it down to NBC and go over it with Janet McCrory of Continuity Acceptance. The first night of my first on-the-air show for the 1935 season, a couple of guys were talking in the control room, and I asked them to leave. One of them was Deac Aylesworth, President of NBC, and the other was Lee Bristol, who owned Bristol Myers, the client. Off they went to the client's room where they should have been in the first place. When Fred found out about it, he was my pal. He hated NBC Presidents, Vice Presidents, agency men, sponsors, and almost everybody else.

I found myself working too hard at Y&R, seven days a week and going out to Hollywood all the time. Young & Rubicam had those marvelous shows in the top ten like Jack Benny, Burns and Allen and Kate Smith. Col. Stoopnagle and Bud was the best, but I finally decided I'd better, one, learn more by going to the client, and two, have a decent life with more time to think. I could see that war was coming; it was obvious that we were in for a terrible period.

In 1938, when I was 29, I went to American Tobacco. George Washington Hill, President of American Tobacco, had shows on NBC as well as CBS—"The Hit Parade," "Kay Kyser's Kollege of Musical Knowledge," later, "Information Please," on the Blue Network. Over a period of time, I got Mr. Hill to change his advertising policies. Lucky Strike cigarettes was in third place, and by changing the company's media policy of going to nighttime radio and weekly magazines only, 26 insertions a year, without going into his previous policy, and with basic copy changes, Luckies went from third to first place in two-and-one-half years. We spent less money than the competition in advertising, and the strategy was a great success. I was the fair-haired boy—up to a point. I had no trouble with Mr. Hill. He and I enjoyed our relationship mainly because his son, George Washington Hill,

Jr., was a very intelligent, strong-minded guy who kept his father from being too much of a monster.

In 1941, I took a leave of absence from Y&R. Nelson Rockefeller, a classmate of mine at Dartmouth, was a good friend. (When I first came here to do the NBC show, Nelson was in charge of renting 30 Rockefeller Plaza; indeed, renting office space in all of Rockefeller Center was his first job. I gave him the nickname Rags Rockefeller.) President Franklin Roosevelt appointed him Coordinator of Inter-American Affairs. He persuaded me to be head of radio for all of the Western Hemisphere.

Of course, we had short wave here at NBC and CBS, but I had to build a big organization to do pro-America shows in Spanish and Portuguese to the other countries in the Western Hemisphere. A lot of those countries down there were very, very authoritarian and could easily have been wooed by Hitler's people into Fascist thinking. It was a very important job. As soon as Pearl Harbor happened, I began to phase out of the CIAA and went into the Navy as a Lieutenant, j.g. I went through the Princeton training course, then through the Miami Sub-Chaser Training Center, and went out as Executive Officer and then Captain of an escort vessel in Destroyer Squadron Nine.

Tom Lewis, who had worked for me at Young & Rubicam, was running the Armed Forces Radio Service, and he asked me to go with it. I had married in the early part of the war, and this would be the first time I could be home in California. "Command Performance" was probably the best show ever in radio because we had unlimited talent, the list was incredible.

In nine months I did about 25 "Command Performance" shows. All the best radio writers in Hollywood were now privates and corporals, and, in addition, were still writing the "Bob Hope Show," the "Bing Crosby Show," and so on. They were all still making $2,000 a week, and yet they worked for AFRS. All the best musicians were still in town in uniform. In a single cast, we would have like, ten major names. Hope, Crosby, Sinatra, Dinah Shore, Judy Garland, Frank Morgan, Jimmy Durante were all on one show based on a comic strip: Dick Tracy.

After the war I went back as Advertising Manager of American Tobacco. Television was just becoming a reality, and, within a year, I went back to Young & Rubicam in charge of Radio, Television and Movies. I'd learned everything I could at American. In fact, I'd even stopped smoking and felt guilty about working there. In those days at Y&R, all the advertising was written in the radio-TV department, so that I ran a very big division with all of the radio shows, the new television shows, and all the advertising for both. I was on the Executive Committee, which meant I was a principal partner, so I was going to be very rich. Sig Larmon was head of Y&R, which had half of the top 10 shows in radio and television.

Remember, NBC was a facility, it was not a program operation. In radio, we bought the time from NBC and they had a censor, a sound effects department, and we had to use their musicians under certain circumstances, but they had no real program department. In the 30's and 40's, radio programming had been taken over by the advertising agencies, and that was true in television as well. Thinking about where television could go, and where it *might* go if we just left it alone, I was convinced that it should really be different from radio. The network should become a program company that sold advertising, instead of a facility that sold time to advertisers who put on their own shows. Was I prescient? Visions of the future engage my attention most. That's always been true. I've always been a futurist. Always.

Bobby Sarnoff and Niles Trammell wooed me. I was reluctant to leave an ownership position in a great agency. It was a risk, I knew, to go to NBC. The General was never totally popular in the financial world. When I went to NBC, RCA stock was about $10 or $11 a share. The Wall Street joke was that if General Sarnoff drops dead any night, RCA would hit $100 a share in the morning.

My terms were that I would be in charge of television. I wanted to run a program company that sells advertising; and the policies would be my policies, and they said okay. So I grasped the nettle, and I came over as Vice President in charge of Television in 1949 with my own comptroller and bookkeepers.

In my first week, I called Martha Dalrymple and told her to forget the cancellation she had just received from NBC for "Meet the Press," because it had been cancelled. The second was to see Fred Coe and say, "Fred, I want you to keep on doing 'Television Playhouse.' I know you've been promoted to be head of Drama; forget it. You don't want to be an administrative man; you want to be a creative genius. Now go back and create." He agreed.

There were no NBC shows or attractions. Milton Berle was a runaway hit, but he could have been moved by his client to ABC in the morning. We had no hold on him whatsover. There really wasn't anything there except for the farsighted radio affiliates who were building television stations. We had a good basic start. The next thing I had to do was to get great programming as fast as we could and try to explode the medium quickly. I was particularly worried about this because of the international troubles we were having, and I knew, if we got into a major war (we got into the Korean war), freezes would be imposed. We did get a station freeze, but I was afraid we might get manufacturing freezes so that the television set business would not explode like it could if my plans were carried out. We really made the business grow much faster than most people probably wanted it to. And we did that right away. I went in in '49 and "Broadway Open House" started that fall. I started Robert Montgomery early in 1950. "Show of Shows" and "Saturday Night Revue" started in February 1950, two-and-one-half hours.

"Show of Shows" was so extraordinary. When I was at Y&R I had gone up to the Catskills to watch Max Liebman put on a brand new comedy review every week for the guests at Tamarisk. It was a very, very, good show, and after talking to Max at great length, I recommended the show to General Foods for television. They bought the "Lamb's Gambol" instead. I kept in touch with Max because, although William Morris sold a 60-minute show to Admiral, it didn't really work too well. I wanted to make Saturday night a stay-home night. Max said he could handle 90 minutes as well as 60 minutes, so we had that as a main piece, and we had a lead-in comedy show with Jack Carter the first year.

Up until then there were no 90-minute shows. But this was really two-and-a-half hours and furthermore, when I originally sold it, it was to be sold in minutes, rotated; meaning that if, as happened, the "Show of Shows" was the runaway hit, and the first hour was "so-so," the advertisers would roll through it and all get the runaway hit part of the time. And, if that worked, then I could do it across the seven days in the week. In that way, I could have new shows all the time, with advertiser support. It was a *great* advertising idea, but the FCC blocked me because they said it forced the stations to clear the two-and-a-half hours and, therefore, with the limitations of many one-station markets, it was unconscionable. Television could have gone much faster and further if they hadn't interfered. However, the show was a great success.

Everybody in the agency business hated my plans, said I was a traitor to my profession. They wanted to buy time from NBC, put on their own shows with their own talent. They didn't want the networks to program; most of all, they were thinking of old values which I knew within two or three years would be gone. For radio, you bought a show, with one product sponsoring the program, and you had the gratitude factor. Eddie Cantor says if you like my show, buy toothpaste. There is great power in advertising to a great, huge public. I knew the minutes would work, the spot had worked beautifully. We sold minutes for the first time ever in network history at night in a great big show, and the minute-advertisers' business just went through the roof. It really broke the spirit of my competition because they had to admit, one, that it would work, and two, that it was true that as the TV business expanded, they would not be able to afford the radio formula within a few years.

Once that show was a runaway hit and sold out for 39 weeks firm, with a summer show, I immediately signed up the comics for the "Comedy Hour" on Sunday night, and I sold that to Frigidaire for Bob Hope (Mike Todd also did a couple of shows for us). The other three shows starred Eddie Cantor, Fred Allen, and Martin and Lewis for Colgate. I sold that basically on the idea of once-a-month marvelous shows; opulent, theatrical, great big audiences, and smash hits. The minute I sold that, I sold the exact show again with Danny Thomas, Jack Carson, Jimmy Durante and Ed Wynn, an all-star revue on Wednesdays, to three clients.

These NBC shows were done in a new form that had never been done before. The minute that money came back to me, I wasn't at risk anymore. I started the "Kate Smith Show," a big opulent five-hours-a-week daytime show to explode daytime as well. Everything worked, fortunately. "Broadway Open House" had already proved that we could get prime-time ratings at midnight with Jerry Lester, Dagmar and Morey Amsterdam five nights a week. All was going swimmingly.

In 1951 I was put in charge of radio and television. At the end of 1952, to my horror, in a reorganization, I was deposed, and, instead of running the empire I had built in four seasons, I became Vice Chairman of the Board, with nothing to do. I almost quit, and I should have, probably. Frank White became President, Jack Herbert was made head of Sales, and Bud Barry head of Programs. It was just a mess. When I finally agreed to stay as Vice Chairman, I took over the color TV problem as my main job because I wasn't to run radio and television anymore. The only reason the General gave me for not making me President was so ridiculous I can't bring myself to put it in writing. Oh, well—a close friend of his asked him not to make me President. Insanity.

One reason I stayed was that I knew those guys would screw it up and that my marvelous NBC structure that I built in the '49, '50, '51, '52 seasons would fall apart. It did. I knew that they'd come screaming for me to take over again, and the General did. When I

became President in 1953, I had a lot of new plans, but my foundations were a lot weaker than they had been because of nine months of mismanagement.

When the General announced that I was appointed President, he said, "I conclude that the President of NBC should have an awareness of high purpose, a sincere regard for public service, a proven capacity for showmanship, a thorough understanding of the advertiser's needs and problems, and an appreciation of the economic facts of life in the broadcasting industry. Mr. Weaver has a happy combination of the attitudes, talents, and experience needed for the job." That I had, for the three-year period I was President.

I thought that television news would be no good at first. Radio news was marvelous because we went from capital to capital all over the world. On the radio, we'd say, "Hello, this is London. The major story in England now is so and so." Then we'd cut to Paris, then to Johannesburg, then to Buenos Aires. Television had all kinds of problems. My solution to that was to do coverage of things that are part of the real world, but that really weren't news. So we did the "Wisdom" series. I got Bertrand Russell to kick it off, and Jim Nelson put 100 of the great greats on film.

I began to work on the "Today" show in 1951. Arthur Clarke was a friend of mine, the guy who was head of the British Interplanetary Society, of which I was a member. Arthur had told me that we were going to get the satellite for interconnection, so I knew that within a few years we would be able to go all over the world with our cameras; *then* we could have a real news service. But, in the meantime, we could begin with coverage of things that were not hard news. We explored various options like pre-empting time to do world coverage. For instance, the first event ever covered by a television network was when the Abadan Refineries in Iran were taken over. We had H.V. Kaltenborn and some of our other people report, and we just wiped out one hour and put on nothing else. The pictures were not live pictures from Iran. "The Martin and Lewis Show," which was the hottest thing on Sundays, we wiped out for a Summit Conference with Eisenhower and Khrushchev.

I had a big battle with the news people about pre-empting shows, particularly the "Today" show. Later, I put on a show called "Commentary" (that still ought to be on the air). I had Scotty Reston of *The New York Times*, and Marquis Childs, a famous columnist, and Alistair Cooke, *The Manchester Guardian* American correspondent, the Alsop brothers, each for four or five minutes, report the most important story of the week they thought the American public should see and hear. Our news guys all said, "Look, why don't you let us do that?" And I said, "Because you don't know anything. It's just that simple. When you're as smart as Scotty Reston, we'll put you on." They didn't like that.

In working on the "Today" show, I originally thought of an early rise-and-shine show like radio's Don McNeill's "Breakfast Club." A crazy gang show. As I saw that we wouldn't get a decent news show for a while, I thought we could do certain kinds of special things to get us ready for the day when news could be important on television with a two-hour coverage show of the whole spectrum, a magazine-of-the-air type of thing. It would have worked well for our magazine concept advertising if we sold minutes, because nobody could sponsor such a big operation.

"Today" started in January 1952. It was obvious that it would be a great service to the people at home and that we could handle it in such a way that it would be a success commercially. The biggest, hardest job in the "Today" show, besides making the news department get out of the way so we could do it right, was to get the stations to open up at 7 o'clock in the morning. I was able to do that, but it was probably the hardest job I ever had to do with the affiliates. NBC made a terrible mistake when they moved the show from the RCA Exhibition Hall because it could be viewed by passersby, a perfect spot. It should still be there.

I brought Dick Pinkham to NBC; he had worked with me when I was at American Tobacco. I put him in charge of what became "Today," "Home," and "Tonight." Mort Werner was a kid when he worked for me at a CBS station in San Francisco, then at AFRS. I thought Mort was a stubborn kind of a guy and he'd do what I told him so I left him in charge of the "Today" show. Mort had great rapport with Dave Garroway, who needed handling. We knew kids in the morning would turn on "Popeye" on WOR-TV, I think, and I said to the "Today" people, "This is a show for everybody, but it's got to be a good enough show so the adults will insist on control, but the kids won't watch unless there is stuff in it that the children will like, puppies and kittens and things. That would certainly help us."

J. Fred Muggs came in like a miracle, a great publicity gimmick for us. The canard that J. Fred made all the difference *was* a canard because, basically, what we had done to sell that show and make it successful was take the audience's view of the show, the unopened

mail, and dump it on the advertiser's desk, and say, "Open up the mail and see what Americans think of this show." And the mail was fabulous; our viewers understood the marvels that we were showing them. The critics all missed the boat in judging what we were trying to do.

When "Broadway Open House" fell apart, I began to think of a replacement show that was a little more structured. It was obvious that we could build a good show for the late night audience. That we had known from radio. Starting "Tonight" was easier than the others because I knew Steve Allen from his radio work and early TV. I knew that he had an Allen's Alley, like Fred Allen's Alley, and that he would be very happy to build it into a bigger Allen's Alley on the 90-minute late night show. Steve was perfect, he could ad lib, work with an audience, had a good personality to run a late night show.

From the early days, I learned not to be lured into the ratings trap from George Gallup, head of research at Y&R. He taught me that the cumulative ratings are the most important. They show you who isn't watching your service and who isn't watching advertiser's advertising in a given program project. I was very proud that the "Colgate Comedy Hour" had a 99% cumulative audience, meaning that everybody in the country watched one or another of the stars. Runaway hits usually get about an 80.

I decided to do a women's service show to get the money away from the women's books and magazines, to support our daytime structure, because half of the women in the country do not like soap operas and game shows and stuff like that. We finally developed the "Home" show with Arlene Francis and Hugh Downs. I found a designer to do the mobile that would be our "Home" show circular set. Each part of the mobile would scenically fit the department—beauty or cooking or child care or house decoration or whatever. It was a great show that should still be running.

"Home" was a success. The way I always figured it, as against RCA's way of figuring, was how much does the show cost, how much is interconnection, how much is the station compensation, and how much are we netting after the gross payments? When it hit $5 million rather quickly, by then we were already $1 million in the black. Now this is not the same way that the idiots would figure it out in the Accounting Department because they would figure out what you'd get if you sold the whole thing at full price, and, say, you're $3 million behind, but they're crazy. "Home" would never have gone off if I hadn't left NBC. That's part of the "after I left" story.

"Wide, Wide World" was part of the spectacular series, something we should talk about because they're the glory of the system. Having been influenced by Arthur Clarke and Norbert Weiner, I thought we could show people that television would be the end of privilege, that

privilege came through social history; first from blood, people born into the aristocracy, and then from money, which allowed people to go where they wanted to go. Suddenly, with television, everyone could be at the great hit on London's West End stage, could go to the Met, to LaScala, so it's a new world, a *whole* new world. How could we show people that? I said, "'Wide, Wide World' will show all the fascinating events going on in our country and neighboring countries." That was our range in the first stage. I built the show really for AT&T to sponsor because I thought if we could get them to see the vision of the future we see, then they'd beat their research people to give us better and better interconnection, faster and faster. We'd also have the inside with them. AT&T sales didn't buy it.

I went out to General Motors and sold it to them, I think, before we did the first show. "Wide, Wide World's" first show was a pick-up from Havana where we used an airplace with a relay system into Miami and then on to the coaxial cable. We had a pick-up in Canada and a pick-up in Mexico with the little Mexican comic, Cantinflas, doing his comedy bullfight routine. I remember segments where Kate Smith sang with the full orchestra in Yosemite with El Capitan mountain and the waterfall in the background, and Marge and Gower Champion danced in the Japanese Gardens in San Francisco. It was a marvelous show, everything *live*.

I used the word *spectaculars* in television to make advertisers realize that sometimes they were smart to spend all their money in one place, as in outdoor advertising. Douglas Leigh invented the name for his Broadway billboards. I said if we call our shows spectaculars, the artists may not like it because they know the critics will say it wasn't so spectacular. That's why Max Liebman would never call his spectaculars, even though I beat him with my stick. He still called his "specials." I knew the spectaculars would get a lot of publicity because they were absolutely new.

Everybody said they wouldn't work: this was a continuity medium, and nobody will know when they were on, and we'd interrupt the regular flow. There were 10 million reasons why it was a terrible idea. I had, for five years, tried to get the agencies to change the rule so that we could pre-empt without cost when we felt something should be pre-empted. The rules from the old radio days were that the network would pay the program costs and the agency commission when they pre-empted, and television couldn't do that; we'd go out of business. I wouldn't even sign contracts with our major clients, including American Tobacco, without our clause. I said to hell with them, we'd go without a contract. Finally, in the 1954 season, we withheld every fourth week from sale on Monday, Saturday and Sunday and set up these various spectaculars.

Leland Heywood was my original Executive Producer on "Producers' Showcase." He got sick so the Jaffe Brothers, his lawyers, and my lawyers set up "Producers' Showcase," and Fred Coe became the main creative genius behind them, although, again, individual shows were produced by individual people. That series was fabulous, shows like Humphrey Bogart's only television appearance in "Petrified Forest," by Robert Sherwood; "Peter Pan" with Mary Martin (which had 65 million viewers in 1955), "Lady in the Dark" and "Babes in Toyland." They were from Max Liebman on Saturday. The Royal Ballet dancing "The Sleeping Beauty" had 30 million viewers. Absolutely unbelievable. Fantastic.

The specs were great theatre, live, living Broadway theatre suddenly brought into the homes of people who never could get to Broadway or see great drama and hear great music. We did some experimental things too on "Producers' Showcase." One was Thornton Wilder's "Our Town," with Frank Sinatra, Paul Newman and Eva Marie Saint, as a musical!

I got Alexander Korda to make a deal with me. I persuaded him instead of spending all those millions promoting and opening a movie, let NBC put it on first, open it the next day and see the effect of the premiere. No matter how big our rating, three-fourths of the people wouldn't have seen it, and some who saw it on the small TV screen would want to see it again. He agreed to do it. The first was a Rex Harrison movie. We only did this twice, but, if I had stayed, we would have done it many times. But television was a whole new form, live, now gone forever. It really was the climax of great programming.

Did I know that my ideas would work? Not really. First of all, I brought in, in '49 and '50, the radio and television heads from about seven other agencies, who became my inner group. All of us were line guys, that is, we had all written and produced great radio shows. Fred Wile came in, but he was really different. Fred was my "do it" man. He would go and beat the guys, and they could come to me and wail and scream and yell, but Fred saw to it that they did what they were told. I had Tom McAvity, George McGarrett; top management guys who really knew the business. And I had Pete Barnum who did "All-Star," Sam Fuller who did "Comedy Hour," and Doug Coulter who did the late night show.

We really knew what we were talking about as far as the selling part went. We didn't pay any attention to the Sales Department because they only had sold time. I didn't change any of the NBC people when I came in. George Frey was my friend. He'd been on my account at Y&R and at American Tobacco, and I loved him. I knew that when Procter & Gamble screamed about what I was doing, they knew that George Frey would completely support their view, not mine. That was helpful to me, and I didn't have to take George out and give him another martini and say that's it, keep them happy, and we're going to do exactly what I say. The advertising side I knew very well and knew what I could get away with.

On the programming side, it was a matter of a long-range view that I'd had, that I was implementing with these different individual projects, which all fit into the same basic plan of building a cumulative total audience. We put on "Ding Dong School" for the little children, "Howdy Doody" for the older children, the sitcoms that appealed to adolescents. Then we wanted great programming for the enlightened viewers, college educated, affluent, intelligent people who can go and do things and have access to other things. We wanted them as regular viewers to our service, all of them. By 1955, we had 50 million sets, and I wanted to raise the level of American taste. I still do.

The attraction of most creative businesses is that you really have a lot more fun, laughs, than you do in conventional business activities. There's just no reason not to have a lot of fun when you're in this kind of a business. I had a sense of adventure because we were doing new creative things in the pioneering days of television.

My favorite program is probably the "Wisdom" series, but I was very much involved with "Victory at Sea." One of my favorite radio shows was "Monitor." "Monitor" grew out of what we learned in the first few years in TV and ran almost 20 years on NBC as the main revenue-producing activity that kept the radio network in the black. It started as an all-weekend 40-hour show in the vignette formula where we used entertainers and had a lot of comedy, but we also had a lot of coverage like in "Wide, Wide World." We gave people a feeling whether they were at home or in their cars that they were in touch with what was going on in the world, across a whole range of subjects. People still talk to me about "Monitor" as though it were television—they liked it so much. It was a wonderful show.

However, I was moving from attraction to attraction and plan to plan, and, once I got them going successfully, I was working on the next one. I still do the same thing. When I got to be President, I was already head of radio and television. The only new worry was the O&O reports. I didn't even look at the O&O reports, except to see if the guys who weren't making any money were fired. If there's any business where you can fall down and not get up and still make money, it's running the O&O's.

We always had problems with the affiliates. In general, I was able to persuade them to do what I wanted, and I enjoyed the affiliate meetings. They all knew I was one of them. I came from the boondocks too, just like they did. Los Angeles doesn't think of itself as the boondocks, but it's not New York no matter what they say. Walter Damm of Milwaukee always started every meeting asking for a middle station break in "Howdy Doody." After I got to be President, he said, "Now, finally, you've gotten to be President, when are we going to get a station break in 'Howdy Doody?'" I said, "Walter, when you get a new management at NBC, maybe."

Through those early years, I really had very little contact with General Sarnoff on a business basis. He didn't know what we were doing, and when we explained it to him, we could see he didn't know what we were talking about. Twice I had to see the General because a project cost so much neither Niles nor Joe McConnell would let me go ahead with it. One was to sign up Jackie Gleason, who had starred in the original "Life of Riley" on NBC. It had not been a success—the format's fault, not Jackie's. William Bendix starred in its revival for five successful years. "Bullets" Durgom, Jackie's manager, came back with a deal. When I outlined the deal, the General said, "But that's more than I make." And I said, "But, *General*, you can't do the fall." In those days, Jackie opened every show by taking a spill as he walked on stage. The General didn't know what I was talking about because I don't think he ever watched any of that stuff. He thought of himself as a man of culture.

He said to me once, going through the financial affairs of the company, that the network wasn't making as much money as the O&O's. I said, "Well, General, there's a very easy way for me to fix that. I can make $10 million more in the network if you really would like me to. Let me explain what I'm going to do. I'm going to walk over to your desk, pick up your phone, call Tom O'Neill (RKO Mutual) and say, 'Tom, we're moving the NBC franchise from our stations, which will become independent, over to your stations in New York and Los Angeles. We want you to promise that you will carry everything we give you, that you'll get no compensation whatsoever, *and* you'll pay us $1 million a year in each city.'"

I told the General, "Tom will say, 'I'll take it.' And then we'll have $10 million more in the network." He asked, "What will we do with our stations?" I said, "Well, General, the stations are the way we can make money, that's all. It's a phony." He really didn't understand that. I didn't have to see him that much. He said no to Disney; he said no to Gleason. But, basically, the only time he was a hurdle was when he would intrude in NBC's affairs and put in a new management team for no reason.

After I came in as President, we were making enough money, both at the network and the stations, so we didn't really have a problem, but radio was a problem, and "Monitor" was correcting that. We didn't have financial problems; I think, in 1955, we were making over $30 million, most of it from the network, but about $12 million from the stations. And it should have gone up $10 to $15 million the next year. The figures are not disclosed. I know about 1955 because the FCC made us divulge it. That's how I knew we made more than CBS did.

I didn't mind moving up to be Chairman in December 1955 as long as I could run the ship, and Bobby Sarnoff could be President. It was silly not to let me continue for a few more years and really build the programming solidly and then let Bobby run NBC. Then I thought I could go up to RCA because I had a lot of ambitious plans for the VCR, and for the Direct Broadcast Satellite, and other technological developments that I had put in writing in the early fifties. I wanted to leave broadcasting at a certain point without totally leaving it. But anyway, I had a big battle about that. RCA and NBC bought me with a new contract in which I couldn't be fired. They couldn't fire me if I'd stay. I was powerless but Bobby had promised that the guys who built NBC with me would not be thrown out into the cold without my approval, and unless I could see to it that they were taken care of.

I came back from a week's trip in the fall of 1956 to find that George Frey, Vice President of Sales, who had been with NBC for 30 years, had been fired; and Fred Wile, who was my pal and number two guy the first few years in programming, had been fired. And that was absolutely against our agreement, and I said to myself, "This is the beginning of Mr. Wrath's working on me to get me to quit, and it isn't going to be that hard." So I called up the Jaffe Brothers and said, "Get me out of here." So we negotiated a departure.

I left with real regret. I built the whole program structure, and I knew it would fall apart, which it did. I knew that the real trouble was that the new management would not understand where and how the money comes from—the advertising business; that they wouldn't understand show business either; that it was too late now to let the agencies do the programming again because I'd really made that change stick. I knew they would probably go back to the Hollywood studios who knew nothing about anything except the box office and story telling, and they would reduce the medium from a coverage medium which allowed everyone to go to the theatre, to attend the performing arts, to be energized by all kinds of creative experiences; and we would get the boob tube in the corner of the living room with programs done by Hollywood studios, which is about what happened.

One bright spot was the News Department. That was very helpful. I hired Chet Huntley in 1955. I heard him make a speech in New York. I didn't know his work because he was working on the West Coast. I'd been trying to get Ed Murrow or Eric Sevareid to come over to NBC until we developed our own people, John Chancellor, Ed Newman and others. In any event, I got Chet in and did a show called "Background." I was already working on a 25-minute news show that would start at 7:30 p.m. and end with a marvelous Bob and Ray animated cartoon. We would have done that probably in 1957 if I'd stayed. We didn't have tape yet so a half-hour news actually didn't happen until the early sixties.

Am I a visionary? Yes, if you mean someone who can foresee what probably is going to happen given what's going on right now. I've always been able to do that. I did it again with the pay cable business after I left NBC. The period of "Let's get Pat out of our system" resulted in cancelling the "Tonight" show to put on a terrible show called "Broadway After Dark." It was after that they put "Tonight" back on with Jack Paar. The "Today" show became the Dave Garroway Show, the Spectaculars became the Specials, the "Home" show was cancelled within a year or two, "Wide, Wide World" was not supported or it would have stayed on. NBC did not produce programs; they went to Hollywood studios for programs. You can't have too many chases and crashes live, so I was all for that, but the lack of control meant that they obviously went after what we called the heavy viewer center, the menace. By playing to the heavy viewer center, people who watch anything, you're in trouble, because your enlightened viewers will drift away. And that's true. A third of the American public probably looks at very little television these days.

When I found out nobody was going to hire me, I started a fourth network. After I started a fourth network, Henry Kaiser leaned on me to do "Maverick." At that time, Nelson Rockefeller said, "Pat, I'm going to run for Governor." I said, "You can't run for Governor. You've got a 20 rating in the polls and Harriman has 80." He repeated, "I'm going to run for Governor as a Republican!" I was his TV advisor for his gubernatorial campaigns and while he was Vice President. That was the second thing that took me off my focus, and the third thing was that McCann-Erickson wanted to do a "Wide, Wide World" show for Coca-Cola and would I be a consultant.

So there I was making all kinds of money as a consultant, but I couldn't run my network, and, as it begins to crumble and Nelson gets elected, I finally was persuaded by Marion Harper to become chief executive of the McCann Corporation (which was everything outside the U.S.) and M.E. Productions. Both were part of the Interpublic Group, and I stayed there five years. Again I was the second largest stockholder with Bob Healy and Emerson Foote; I was going to be rich beyond dreams, and along came the pay cable opportunity, and I just couldn't stand it because it had everything that I had envisioned years before.

I left McCann and went out to California to run that. I laid out the three-channel service, one covering movies and pop stuff, one covering the theatre and the performing arts, one covering sports and special interests, bridge, books, etc.; 50% of the people bought the service, which meant that there was no question that the timing was absolutely right as far as the audience and the market was concerned, but the broadcasters and the theatre owners were able to block us with vicious campaigning and unlimited money. They set back cable at least ten years.

Mary Wells persuaded me to come in part-time and run television for her new agency, Wells, Rich & Greene. As that began to phase out, I found that I could go back to California and still be a consultant, with the hope that maybe by now the bastards would let me back in the business. The studios wouldn't hire me because the minute Goldenson and Paley wouldn't hire me, that meant that the six idiots at the studio level wouldn't hire me either.

I developed and sold some shows. "The Garry Moore Mad Show" introduced Lily Tomlin and John Byner and several other people who made it out of our little comedy company. It was a success; it wasn't a real failure, but I could see the handwriting on the wall when Mary Wells asked me to work with her. In 1967 I again started a term with her and at the end of that, I moved back to California and did some other shows. I worked with Disney laying out Epcot Center, the World of Tomorrow stuff, and with Comsat, laying out what they should do, but they didn't listen. We still got the FCC approval with what I did for them. My main thing was called Subscriber Network. I'm right now on standby with a big deal about the World of Tomorrow with Sears that looks very, very promising. I have a company with Lou Harris, the pollster, and he says, "We're in." I don't believe it for one minute, you understand, but that's what he says.

My birthday wish for NBC's 60th is they keep on recovering and go back to some of the other marvelous things they could do, like covering the theatre, covering performing arts. Grant Tinker has already tried to upgrade the general taste and quality standards, and I think that shows, and I wish him well.

October 2, 1985

Tom Brokaw became the anchorman of "NBC Nightly News with Tom Brokaw" in 1984.

"I remember an assignment in Americus, Georgia, particularly because CBS had two correspondents and three camera crews, and I had one cameraman (not an NBC man), but we just beat the pants off CBS by staying up all night for two or three days running. We weren't afraid to go to Ku Klux Klan rallies…we were threatened and our cars were blocked…and they'd say, 'Where you from, boy?' I'd say, in a Southern accent, 'I'm from Georgia.' I was living in Atlanta at the time."

I was born in Webster, South Dakota, and, after my early schooling, I attended the University of South Dakota, graduating in political science. I thought politics and the politicians were, outside of athletes, the most fascinating life forms. As a young man, I was actively interested in news, perhaps because my grandfather paid attention to current events and talked about them. My family, although working-class, had a high level of interest in what was happening in the world. I had no role models for journalism. Our daily newspaper was poor, and we lived in such a remote part of the country that I didn't see television until I was about 16 years old, which is relatively late.

I wasn't bold enough to think I could make a living in journalism. It was all so unconventional. What I wanted to do and what everyone expected me to do was to go off to the University of South Dakota and then to law school, become a lawyer and settle down to law and politics in South Dakota. About that time Huntley and Brinkley started on NBC, and television news began to come of age. It was exciting to watch but still remote to me. There were no television stations where I lived.

While I was an undergraduate in college, I worked at KTIV in Sioux City, Iowa, an NBC affiliate, doing the weather and a little bit of everything. As the booth announcer, I said, "KTIV, Channel 4," every hour, and did my studies in between, but I had to keep an eye on the monitor at all times so I had intense exposure to NBC programming, eight, nine hours a day, all the news and all the specials.

My first grown-up city was Omaha. My first full-time job was with the NBC affiliate there, KMTV, as a general assignment reporter. Then I became the morning news editor. I went in at 5 o'clock in the morning to do the "Today" show cut-ins. I made all the assignments, processed and spliced the film, and went on the air at 7:25 a.m. and 8:25 a.m. I did a noon news program, and, if there was something going on in the afternoon, I'd help film it. NBC News correspondents came through regularly—Tom Pettit, Merrill Mueller (he came through a lot and we became good friends), Robert MacNeil and Sandy Vanocur. I was like a small boy with a baseball glove looking at Joe DiMaggio. They became my role models.

I didn't want to cover news in Omaha for the rest of my life, so I circulated my résumé to a few people. I didn't publicize it because the station would have probably fired me. Fortuitously, someone breached the confidentiality and told Ray Moore at WSB in Atlanta, a principal NBC affiliate, that there was a young man in Omaha he should see. He hired me in 1965. That was a heady experience. Atlanta was a bigger city, and they were doing a lot of reports for NBC on the civil rights movement, which was the major news story then. I spent a lot of time on that story. I anchored the 11 o'clock news, but, because NBC did not have an Atlanta bureau in those days, they often asked if WSB could get to, say, Americus, Georgia, if something was happening. We often represented NBC News at breaking civil-rights stories.

It was an important time in America, and in my life. I saw first hand the great players on the cutting edge of the moral issue of our time— civil rights. I think Martin Luther King, Jr., was indisputably one of the great Americans, not just of the 20th Century. When they come to write the history of our time, he'll have a very prominent role.

I was 25 years old, and I had *lots* of energy and a fair amount of resourcefulness. I remember an assignment in Americus, Georgia, particularly because CBS had two correspondents and three camera crews, and I had one cameraman (not an NBC cameraman, by the way), but we just beat the pants off CBS by staying up all night for two or three days running. We weren't afraid to go to Ku Klux Klan rallies in the middle of the night. We knocked on doors and got people to talk to us who'd never talked about the civil rights situation before. At one Klan meeting, we were threatened and our cars were blocked, but we kept talking and moving. Whenever they'd say, "Where you from, boy?" I'd say, in a Southern accent, "I'm from Georgia." I was living in Atlanta at the time.

Bob Schaefer, head of West Coast NBC News, called Ray Moore about me and Moore said, "He's been here *four* months." I flew to

California at NBC's invitation, spent four days and was offered an exciting job there, but I turned it down. I flew back to Atlanta. My friends in Atlanta had counseled me that it might be a fast move for someone as young and "green" as I was. I didn't like Los Angeles. It was smoggy, and crowded. My wife and I liked Atlanta. She was pregnant with our first child, and she was happy there. But California kept upping the ante, and Bob Mulholland and Floyd Kalber urged me to consider the position, so, in 1966, I took it.

That job was a wonderful mix of responsibilities. In those days, the News Division managed the Owned Stations' news. I was anchorman on the Sunday night news in Los Angeles which, at 26, was kind of overwhelming. I was the backup anchorman for everybody else, and the ready reserve for the network correspondents; Tom Pettit and John Dancy were there at the time. It was a great learning experience.

The people in Burbank were very tolerant, and my enthusiasm and determination got me over a couple of rough patches. I would do a story and think it was terrific, and they would say, "Hey, it had a lot of flaws." I'd stay until midnight working out the flaws.

When I arrived, I said I wanted to cover politics. I was told NBC had a lot of seasoned political news people in California, but they said, "There's this one guy, Reagan, an actor, who's running." People thought George Christopher, Mayor of San Francisco, would win the Republican primary for the gubernatorial campaign. So I spent a fair amount of time with Reagan in 1966.

I came to know him on a one-to-one basis, as well as some aides who are still with him. I thought then that he was such an ideologue but really one of the most effective communicators you could possibly imagine. He was a movie star, tall, handsome, and, in California, that's no small currency. The state was in an upheaval; it was going broke. The student rebellion at Berkeley was underway. Watts was still smoking. The Vietnam war was heating up and so was opposition to it. Reagan was hard-nosed and tough about it all, and he captured the middle-class working voters of the state. I've said to my Eastern friends all these years, never, *never* underestimate Ronald Reagan as a candidate.

At the 1972 Democratic convention in Miami, I was covering the California delegation, a big, important

delegation. I knew everything going on within it, and, as a result, NBC News benefited. At a party after the convention, John Chancellor said to me, "It's time for you to give up the good life out there in California, come East, and do some grown-up correspondent's work for us." It gave me something to think about. We had a wonderful life there; we'd built a wonderful house on the beach; the 11 o'clock news program was very successful, and I could do the network jobs whenever I wanted to.

My wife and I didn't want to leave all that. Bob Mulholland and Dick Wald, who had just come in as President of NBC News, talked to me about coming East to do national politics. They mentioned the appealing idea of going to London to get some "seasoning," and they talked about becoming a White House correspondent. Dan Rather was the CBS White House correspondent. Watergate had surfaced, and, I thought, "That's risky—throwing yourself into the limelight." I told Dick that London would be fine, or, Dick said, "Maybe you can do some national political reporting for a year, and then we'd move you into the White House." Mulholland said, "Let's put him in there now. He can swim; he won't sink. And we need the help there right away."

I was offered the job in part because I'd known most of the Nixon White House staff in California. Ron Ziegler did the advertising for KNBC at J. Walter Thompson. So I wasn't beginning with a 10-yard penalty. Julian Goodman and everyone at NBC encouraged me. With the handicap of coming in in the middle of Watergate, I thought the only way to do the job well was to work 20 hours a day. By then, a lot of the White House press corps was exhausted and a little jaded. I wasn't. I had to make my mark, and make it fast. I worked harder than I'd ever worked before. I came to New York on Saturday nights to do the Saturday Night News, then flew back and worked Sundays. I talked to everybody. If the President of the Texas Board of Realtors had a conventional audience with Nixon in the afternoon, I'd track him down that night and ask, "Did the President say anything about Watergate? Did you get any feeling about how he really looks?" I contacted the people I call "the moles," the people who worked in the White House basement who weren't so visible. I developed two or three good sources, honorable people who were really troubled by what was going on.

The Watergate story just got bigger and bigger. As a journalist, I arrived at the White House in time for the biggest political scandal in the history of the Republic and had a front-row seat. The Brokaw luck.

There were other items on the agenda, but Watergate was always there. I went with Nixon to Moscow, a strange journey for lots of reasons. He was desperate for a SALT II agreement because he thought it would help him with Watergate. Characteristically, the Russians read the American political situation extremely well, and believed they didn't have to concede in any discussions. We went to the Crimea, where the press corps was headquartered in an old health spa, and I roomed with Marvin Kalb of CBS, because the Russians, with their egalitarian attitude, put NBC in with CBS. It was fine; we had a good time. I remember vividly that the White House aides got roaring drunk on vodka almost every night. It was a catharsis. They were away from Watergate, and the Russian deal wasn't going well, so they thought they might as well have a good time. Then, the Russians turned Nixon down.

We came back to his resignation, and Ford's Presidency, a whole new atmosphere. Ford took office in August, and we traveled frantically all over the country so people would have a chance to see him.

It was impossible not to like Ford; that was part of the problem. He had been in American politics for so long, a member of the House of Representatives with its rigorous give-and-take, that you could maintain a personal relationship and still bang away at him as a correspondent. I once asked him live on the air if it bothered him that a lot of people in Washington thought he was too dumb to be President. Now, how many people can you do that with, especially the President of the United States? It didn't affect our relationship. A nice guy.

I handle stress by living with it, and I find physical exercise a good outlet for tension. But honestly, to be hokey about it, my life is so rich in many ways I never anticipated that it could be that I don't want to miss anything. I think, thank God, I'm fortunate to be here in this position, and why be casual about it?

I was flattered to be the White House correspondent. While I was, I came to New York to fill in for John Chancellor, and I liked that. But I loved the freedom of being a daily correspondent. The Nightly News anchorman has, in effect, a ball and chain and has to report to a parole officer every night at 6:30 p.m. As a correspondent, you are expected to do a single story well, and it's richly fulfilling if you have an interesting beat like the White House. That's not always true for an anchorman.

In 1976 I moved to the "Today" show, a major move in a very different direction.

When Frank McGee died, I was in the rotating cycle of people who filled in on the show. Then, Dick Wald became serious about my doing that job. I simply didn't want to do it. I was still the White House correspondent, and I wanted to see that through. They also wanted me to do commercials (that came with the territory), and I told Stuart Schulberg that I just couldn't do commercials. He asked me if I knew how much money we were talking about. I said I did. Jim Hartz had been a strong candidate, and the job went to him. Then, within a year Barbara Walters left, and the ratings had fallen, so they came back to me.

Dick Wald said, "Okay, no commercials, but this time you don't have a choice. We want you to do it." I'd been in Washington for three years; it was a very flattering invitation (read command). The "Today" show had always been important to me; I had a familial attachment to it because it was my mother's window on the world.

The "Today" show was fun, but it was also demanding, not just the early hours, but sitting there for two hours and not taking yourself too seriously, trying to keep ahead and do well in spontaneous situations. It was a great growth period. I learned a lot about myself, and a lot of other things. Curiously enough, I made friends with some of the guest authors and actors, and they are my friends to this day. Tom Courtenay, the very gifted British actor, was one; he was doing "Otherwise Engaged" at the time. I see him when we go to London. One of my closest friends now is a mountain climber who appeared on the show and said, "You ought to do more mountain climbing. I'll take you up the Grand Teton." We have just finished climbing Mt. Rainier. We do a mountain every summer. Those experiences enriched my life.

In 1978, I taught a course at Yale: "TV News in America: Effect of TV News on Decision-Making Processes." Some of the conclusions were obvious. One was that television indisputably has a major effect on the way politicans make decisions, because the process is instantly shared, examined and analyzed by the rest of the world. Then, we asked if television made it too difficult for people to make decisions. For example, what do we do about terrorists when the President wants to hit back at them and we have the hostages' families on the air weeping and saying, "Please, Mr. President, don't do that."

Some of my best memories involve the '76, '80 and '84 political conventions. In 1980, I was on the floor for our general coverage, then, after three hours of sleep, I did the "Today" show. Somebody asked, "What drives you?" and I said, "Ego. All that air time."

There were other memorable events, of course. Covering Prince Charles and Princess Diana's wedding was as much fun as I ever had. It's curious because I have very strong feelings about royalty. I'm not a fan. Yet the biggest single television audience I have ever played to was for that wedding. I must say, I did get swept up in it all, but I like to believe we brought a certain objectivity to the proceedings. One of our commentators was tart-tongued Tina Brown from *The Tatler* who now runs *Vanity Fair*. I turned to her when things got gushy, and she would snap it around.

Other experiences will always be in my mind's eye. I flew all night to Cairo to cover the assassination of Anwar el-Sadat after being on the air nine hours the day it occurred. I was struck by the way the American journalists had overplayed Sadat's popularity in Egypt. There was no national mourning going on, and we were all

surprised by that.

I have liked all of the News Presidents, some much better than others. There is no common thread, which is interesting. Dick Wald was the first one with whom I had an active, mature relationship. He is really one of the brightest people I know. He and Reuven Frank are in the same league, two exceptionally smart, deep people. Dick is a great non-stop talker as opposed to Reuven who speaks to you in moments of great silence. Dick did not have a background in television so we had to educate him. He has a wonderful, biting sense of humor, and, in spite of his facade, was warm and vulnerable.

Reuven is just a genius. We have an enduring relationship. He has profound insight about what we're doing, or what we should be doing. Reuven is the highest order of television animal, a producer who wants to use the medium as an outlet for his creativity and genius.

Each network's news has its own characteristics. ABC is flashier, more surface, and not quite as deep in their commitment to what they're doing. CBS is strong. Their great strength is their continuity of people through the years. They're not as good as they think they are, and it shows in the way they treat people at CBS. While NBC has always been a wonderful place to work, it wasn't when there were lots of top management changes. That period was like working in the Nixon White House or playing for the Cleveland Indians. It was traumatic for a proud company and a lot of proud people.

I did a major coverage of the anniversary of D-Day plus 40 years, and also in 1984 covered all the primaries. And I became solo anchorman, the first time NBC had a solo anchorman in a long time. Roger Mudd was gone from the show. When Reuven told me that I was going solo, I simply said I was grateful, I appreciated his confidence, and I would do everything in my power to make it a success. The first night, just before we went on the air, I suddenly had a head-snapping feeling, and I told myself, I have to go for it. There are fans out there who think Roger should have been given the job. I had worked for it; there's no question about that, but I also had been the beneficiary of good fate along the way.

I moderated the live debate between Mondale, Hart and Jackson. I thought the chance of Mondale's winning the election was a long shot. Reagan was the enormously popular incumbent; the most skilled national candidate in the use of television in a long time, and he had a well-oiled organization. Fritz Mondale went through a bloody nomination fight. He represented the past, not the future, and he was not a very exciting candidate.

If "NBC Nightly News" were an hour long, I'd do a lot of things. A good example would be tonight's show. We'd try to get viewers to understand the broader texture of the hijacking of the Mediterranean cruise ship, "Achille Lauro." We will do two full segments, two-fifths of our program, and we worry if that's too much. In an hour, you'd give the news, and at the back half of the program, interview terror experts, look at the political ramifications and the history of the Palestinian terrorist movement in a wider context. I think it could be a more exciting and less static program than I understand "The MacNeil/Lehrer Newshour" is. I would do cultural things, ranging from Bruce Springsteen to Zubin Mehta, Music Director of the New York Philharmonic. I had dinner with Mehta the other night, and we talked about his fascinating career and his astonishing schedule of concerts, from Jacksonville to Salzburg to Israel; the Conductor for Hire.

I keep a sense of proportion, in part because I never forget where I came from. My parents were the personification of middle-class working values. My dad was offended by anyone he described as a "blow-hard." He believed that your work should speak for itself. If you could do something, you didn't need to describe it or build a case for it. I've been driven by that.

The press is giving a lot of attention to NBC this year, and I am in a vulnerable and visible spot. I don't live week to week on ratings. I've been in this business long enough to know whether we're improving qualitatively or not, and I think we are. This is a rising tide. As I get better, and our product gets better, and the News Division becomes stronger internally, that will have an impact.

We have Larry Grossman as head of News now. He ran PBS, which did a lot of public service programming. He's not a naif. Sometimes when he's too serious, we say we're in the business of daily journalism; we're not rewriting history. I don't think news should be rated. On the other hand, I know the practicality of it; networks have to sell commercials and pay me this enormous salary and the other salaries, so they want a viable product. I don't mind the ratings; measuring circulation is fine. I do object to intense attention to the ratings, week-to-week. It's not fair to say Peter Jennings finished third because he was a tenth of a point behind us last week. It amounts to a dead heat.

What drives me crazy is that there is so little analysis of the quality of news, in newspapers especially. Some of the worst newspapers in America have the highest ratings. *The New York Daily News* has a much bigger circulation than *The New York Times*, and the *National Enquirer* is bigger than both of them. Do they win? That bothers me because news ought to be judged on merit, not numbers.

The rest of the network should treat newsmen with benign suspicion! But I regard the news as the most important thing the company does, not just because I'm here. NBC, for all its success in entertainment and everything else, is defined on the basis of its daily news, which touches people's lives directly. We're on the air two hours in the morning, half an hour in the evening, and do break-ins on other programs. As important as the entertainment programming is, it's essentially that, a distraction, whereas the News Division of NBC is the connection with the world.

We are involved in a very important process. We are obliged to do it with honor and integrity and serve the country well. I'm grateful to the rest of the network for the freedom and financial support they give the News Division. It absolutely broke my heart when David Brinkley walked out the door. That was a terrible time. I have an affection for him that is hard to describe, and we stay in touch. He has a wonderful style. He had the ear of the American people. David Garroway made the "Today" show what it is today. I don't know if it would have succeeded in those early years or become the institution it has without him. Pat Weaver thinks the "Today" show should be more serious now, but when I was named to host it, Pat thought it was a bad idea to put a serious newsman on it. That's full circle, isn't it?

I thought there was no one who covered space like Frank McGee who, with that timbre in his voice, had a quality of making you believe in it. Chancellor was a great foreign correspondent and a national affairs correspondent. I grew up in the era of the four horsemen: Vanocur, Newman, McGee and Chancellor on the floor, and Huntley and Brinkley in the booth. It was like growing up in the glory days of the New York Yankees. Chet Huntley, with that great Western style and that Mt. Rushmore face could make you believe *anything*. The strengths of all those people meant a lot to me. A young man could pick any one of them as a role model.

When Bill Small was President of the News Division, and Fred Silverman was President of the company, I was *very* tempted to move to another network. NBC wasn't the company I had been working for all those years. In my own mind, I felt this was more my company than it was theirs, and that persuaded me to stay and fight for what I believed in. I felt an obligation to other people here as well. I had worked very hard for NBC. I knew what I wanted to do in my life, and I wanted to do it here, not somewhere else.

I hope that this proud moment which recaptures the spirit of the past will continue and grow. It's very reassuring to go out to the public these days and see them look at NBC with respect. In the 70's, it was painful; now, it's gratifying to represent NBC and to know that the good feeling and the integrity have been restored. And the *morale* is very high. We're not only commercially successful, we can be proud of the programs we have on the air.

NBC is defining television again, not the other way around. That's my wish for our 60th birthday.

October 8, 1985

John Chancellor began as a broadcast journalist at NBC in 1950 and is, after 35 years, regarded by his peers as one of television news' most distinguished members.

John Chancellor

"At the convention in 1964...I thought I had every right to be where I was, when suddenly, two big, uniformed San Mateo sheriffs appeared...looking befuddled. They didn't want to touch me, and, I thought, I'm going to make them carry me out...Then Reuven Frank came on the little radio in my ear and said one word, *'Walk.'* And so I walked. The minute I got off the floor, the Chief Sergeant-at-Arms of the Republican Convention, looking grey, ashen, and out of breath, ran up, spun me around, and pushed me back on the floor because they knew they'd made a real goof."

I was born and grew up in Chicago, and I went to the University of Illinois where I majored in history and philosophy. I spent a couple of years, 1945 to 1947, in the Army, and came out without seeing any combat. I've never been graduated from anything except grammar school, not from prep school, and not from college. None of us wanted to be graduated from a university because a degree wasn't useful if you were going to be a newspaper man. Nobody had a degree.

I wanted to be a journalist, or a writer. I'd hoped to be a novelist, but the production of the first novel ended that conceit, and I realized that some kind of journalism was the easiest way to be paid for writing. This was just after the war.

On the staff of the *Chicago Times*, my first paper, there weren't four or five people with degrees. Some had gone to college, but not many. We had lost those years in the service, so the idea was to get to work. We took all the history courses available, and I took some philosophy and left. The history has been extremely useful. The logic part of philosophy helps in writing; it's good to have that background for clear thinking, or what passes for it.

In 1947, I joined the *Chicago Times* which then merged with the *Chicago Sun*. I started as a copy boy and became a reporter covering police, a good starting point for young reporters. It makes you face the realities of life quickly. It teaches you techniques about getting the right middle initial, the right address, things you need to know, so you never think about them again. A passion for accuracy. I loved it. I would not have left the newspaper business if there hadn't been an economy wave in 1950 when the *Sun-Times* stopped being a 24-hour newspaper and went back to being a morning paper. Sixty-nine of us, all editorial employees, were let go. We were out of work.

I called a friend, Len O'Connor at NBC, whom I'd met covering stories, and explained my plight. He gave me a chance to write an audition script as a summer replacement news writer at WMAQ-TV, an O&O station of NBC. That was April 1950. I was not hired because of my writing skill. I'd never written for radio before; I'd never really seen much television. There wasn't much television to see, except "Kukla, Fran and Ollie,"

"Garroway at Large," Studs Turkel's "Studs' Place," and, of course, some sports. All those programs originated in Chicago. It was the great age of television creativity at NBC in Chicago. From 1952 on, when the network requested news from WMAQ and other Owned and Operated news divisions, I was assigned to be the network's man in Chicago.

They needed a body, and I performed adequately doing various chores, among them, reporting for the network at the 1952 conventions in Chicago. For a long time, I was a NABET writer, and I charged them for overtime when I did all this reporting. In 1950's dollars, it was a healthy salary, but it was cut back considerably when they gave me the honor of becoming a network correspondent.

I had been on the convention floor in 1952 covering stories, but our equipment was cumbersome. (The idea of roving, independently targetable reentry reports began in 1956.) There were cameras around the edge of the auditorium, and, when we interviewed people, we had a long cord with a microphone at the end and took our guests over to those cameras. By 1956, we had mobility on the floor, and we started what came to be called "The Four Horsemen"—Frank McGee, Edwin Newman, Sander Vanocur, and myself. That team lasted for a while. The whole year, aside from the conventions, I was the chief NBC correspondent, and often the only NBC correspondent, with Adlai Stevenson, who was the Democratic candidate for President. Ray Scherer was the White House correspondent, and he and I switched for two weeks. I covered Eisenhower, and he covered Stevenson. It was standard operating procedure in those days for the White House man to go with the challenger if there was an incumbent in the White House, so in case of an upset, the correspondent would know the faces and the names of the people working on the campaign. I suppose if Stevenson had won, I would have become the White House correspondent. But we all knew there wasn't much chance of his winning.

At the 1964 convention, there was a virulent anti-press feeling. It surprised Eisenhower. I remember standing right under him when he made his famous comment about self-serving columnists and commentators. The Goldwater delegates were more Goldwater delegates than Republican delegates. Nelson Rockefeller was booed, and led the New York delegation off the floor, and the delegates roared with a throaty, Roman Forum "kill 'em" thrill in their voices. I looked up and blinked at Eisenhower's throwaway line. History has been written since about his surprise at the reaction in the convention hall.

The Goldwater delegates had little experience in politics. The 1964 campaign was the first one you could call a modern Presidential campaign because Goldwater and his team locked up delegates before the convention. Many of those delegates had never been to a convention before, and they felt the press coverage of Barry Goldwater was unfair, that it depicted him as a bumbler, a warmonger, and an antediluvian Conservative (which I think he was). Years later on the the Dick Cavett program, I was interviewed along with Goldwater, and I asked Goldwater about his supporters' feeling that the press had done him in. He said, "No, I think two-thirds of that problem was my own. We made a lot of mistakes in the campaign; made it up as we went along. We didn't check with our headquarters in Washington often enough, and we got a lot of facts wrong. Some of it was press hostility, but I think most of it was my own ineptitude." I nearly reached over and kissed him on the cheek. It was one of the most gentlemanly things I'd ever seen anybody do.

At the same convention in 1964, I was furious and wanted to be carried off the floor. I thought I had every right to be where I was, when suddenly, two, big, uniformed San Mateo sheriffs appeared next to me, looking befuddled. They didn't want to touch me, and, I thought, I'm going to make them carry me out. (To be carried out of a place then had more chic than it does now.) Then Reuven Frank came on the little radio in my ear and said one word, "*Walk.*" And so I walked. The minute I got off the floor, the Chief Sergeant-at-Arms of the Republican Convention, looking grey, ashen, and out of breath, ran up, spun me around, and pushed me back on the floor because they knew they'd made a real goof.

In 1972, 1976, and 1980, I was safe in the NBC booth with David Brinkley, an entirely different experience. On the floor, you don't have to be on all the time, and there are moments in every convention when there isn't a lot to talk about. Like fatigued runners, David and I occasionally "hit the wall" and had nothing left to say. It's a different kind of journalism. It is covering a story, but not a lot of little, discreet stories, the way it is on the floor of a convention.

I have mixed feelings about the cutback from gavel-to-gavel coverage. I believe that only once every four years can you capture the attention of the American people, and not all of them in terms of the civics lesson. So, I was all for gavel-to-gavel coverage, and more. But conventions now aren't really deliberative bodies. Unless they reform the convention process, I guess less coverage is probably not damaging to it.

I have been on-air every election night. I missed the 1960 conventions because I was in Moscow. In 1958 I was in Vienna. From there, I went to London, and from London to Moscow. Moscow in the mid-sixties was interesting. It was a very difficult cold-war period, and I arrived there about a month after Francis Gary Powers arrived in the Soviet Union. I was at the Summit Conference in Paris that June when Khrushchev broke it up. He was being his nasty best, or worst. The Russians set the U-2 plane up in a park in Moscow. There was a *very* strong anti-American campaign at that time, Khrushchev talked about wars of national liberation; Kennedy, who was running, talked about the missile gap and our need to catch up.

The Soviets were expansive and truculent in international affairs, and it was difficult to be an American resident there, not only hard on correspondents, but diplomats and business people too. On the other hand, Khrushchev was more accessible to the American press (a tiny group of, I suppose, 15) than any head of government in my experience, and I've covered a lot.

There were 130 or 140 countries with diplomatic representation in Moscow, and they all had a National Day party, to which correspondents, then on the diplomatic list, were invited. There were about three of these parties a week, and you had to go to them, but it was interesting because Khrushchev appeared at many with Gromyko, and Mikoyan, and others. We could talk to Khrushchev, and the senior members of the Kremlin hierarchy, sometimes only about the weather, sometimes about serious things. Khrushchev often gave us interviews, and I got to know him. He would not say, "Hi, John," but he did know the American correspondents. It was terribly exciting.

Llewellyn Thompson was our American Ambassador. Yuri Gagarin orbited the earth in a Soviet spacecraft, one of the most outstanding historical events I've ever covered. The Russians went berserk, a day I'll never forget: Gagarin in space, and we in Moscow, a long distance apart. We went to parades and celebrations all over the city. News copy leaving Moscow usually was severely censored; sometimes we waited 48 hours for it to clear. But when Gagarin was in space, they wanted news to go out, so censorship was cursory, and we sent thousands of words. I remember a mixture of things: the toughness of the official attitude toward us, Khrushchev's extraordinary ebullience and rascally character, and living in the Soviet Union when, for the first time since winning the war against the Germans, something good happened to them. It was a series of peaks and valleys.

I became host of the "Today" show in 1961, much against my will. Robert Kintner was boss. I had met him in Berlin, and we got along well. He was an old newspaper man, a terrible unapproachable tyrant at times, but that night he was feeling good. When the News Division took over the "Today" show, it was decided to replace Dave Garroway with a newsman. It had been an entertainment project with a lot of news until I came, but Kintner saw it as a vehicle for news. I was interviewed half a dozen times on it when I was a Soviet Union foreign correspondent.

Kintner decreed that Bill McAndrew take the program over. I was the Moscow correspondent working tempo-rarily in Vienna, consultant to Reuven Frank on "Our Man in Vienna" with David Brinkley, when Bill McAndrew called me and said, "We want you to take Garroway's place." I said, "I don't want to take Garroway's place. I'm happy as a clam. I'm your Moscow correspondent." He said, "You have to come back and talk about it." So I flew to New York, and in a week, they offered me a lot of money which seemed secondary to me at the time, but I suppose it was important then, and I did accept the position. My wife, Barbara, and I had planned to spend two more years in the Soviet Union, which would have been a total of four there, but we came back here in a hurry.

I just hated that assignment. It was an awful job, not just the hours, they were manageable, but introducing musical acts at 7:45 in the morning wasn't for me. Exactly six months to the day I began, I told Bill McAndrew I couldn't do it anymore. He said, "Don't tell a soul because the way this business works, they'll make it look as though you're being fired when you really want to get out. Trust me, and let me handle it." Bill was a father, or uncle, or brother to us all, and we adored him. He was the *best* boss I ever had in my life, and I knew I would get action. Then he got hepatitis, and was gone for a long time, so it took another eight months for me to get off the "Today" show. But it was a mistake from the very beginning.

We foreign correspondents get uppity. We've covered the state house somewhere, or an alderman in Chicago, and, suddenly, we're invited to briefings at the Prime Minister's house, and that's a heady experience. It's easy to tuck a handkerchief in your sleeve and wear striped pants. It's seductive, and I've seen it happen to many people going overseas. Some fellow who could hardly pay the rent back in Akron gets to be a foreign correspondent, and he assumes airs.

I came home in 1964 for the conventions, and politics in general. Then, they asked me if I'd be the White House correspondent (they had Brinkley call me), and I accepted. I had wanted to go back to Europe, not because I'm trilingual, or bilingual; I'm kind of nonlingual. I ought not to be trusted as a journalist in a foreign language so I rely on translators for covering speeches and reports. I get along reasonably in Russian; I get along fairly well in German and French, but

I use "pigeon" in Danish, and other languages you learn for a year then forget.

I had been at the White House less than a year when Johnson asked me to be Director of *Voice of America*. That was preceded by a big "courtship." LBJ invited Barbara and me to Camp David, and down to the ranch. I got to know him and all of his people extremely well. Then he sprung this job on me, and I didn't want it. I didn't want to be in government. The *Voice* was in trouble when Henry Loomis, the head, resigned, and it needed credibility. They made a great point of selecting me as the first working journalist to run it. In our last talk before I took the job, I told LBJ he'd given the press a hostage, he'd given them me. I said, if I am head of it, and this Administration starts to push it around, to damage its credibility, you know I'll have to go to the press with that. So I don't think your people will push the *Voice* around, because I am of the press and not a career government bureaucrat. I told Johnson he hadn't asked me because of my managerial or executive acumen. He looked out the window and didn't say anything, but that's really what I was, a hostage to the press. I ran the place credibly for a couple of years, got out with my whole skin, and was never asked to do a political thing. He kept his word.

We modernized the *Voice* a bit, and my tenure was productive, although I must say I'm remembered there today (talk about the first working journalist ever to run it) as the man who put the newsroom in the basement. They have never forgiven me for that.

When I took the job, I came to New York to ask NBC for support. In our first meeting, Kintner looked at the ceiling and said, "Gee, that might not be bad for your career, John." And I knew that the fix was in. I started at the White House when the Vietnam war began to build. I think Lyndon Johnson made a deal with Kintner. I don't know what it was, but it paid off because when Kintner was fired from NBC, he became the Secretary of the Cabinet. I thought Kintner and LBJ used a private back channel when they talked to each other. I can't prove it, and I don't think it changed any news decisions at NBC. Kintner liked LBJ, and felt it was useful to be the President's pal. Frank Stanton was around the White House giving away little three-set television consoles, so it wasn't an unusual relationship. Kintner was extraor-

dinary. He expanded the News Department, and it probably has never been as healthy or as frightened, frightened of a boss. The ratings were wonderful.

One night at a convention, Huntley and Brinkley were in the booth, the four of us on the floor, and a lot of other good reporters covering stories, when Kintner called us in after the broadcast. Joe Derby, a press agent, showed me a little piece of paper with a number, 71, I think, on it. I said I didn't know what it was. He said, "That's the share." I remember I said, "Share of what?," and he looked as though I was from outer space. The shares of the audience would be worth looking up in the files of the political conventions' coverage, but I never, until then, knew what they meant.

Kintner was a great salesman. He and Julian Goodman persuaded Gulf Oil to buy a series of instant documentaries without Gulf knowing what those documentaries would be. The News Department was an exciting place, and Kintner was very hard to work for. I never worked for him, but on election nights, it was Bill McAndrew's job to talk to Kintner when he called on the phone. We felt sorry for Bill to have to take the abuse he did from Kintner during eight hours on the air. Kintner was bad in many ways, but he was brilliant, and he helped the News Division a lot. Huntley-Brinkley didn't hurt it, and the general excellence of the place under McAndrew helped, but it all came together under Kintner. It was never as good before, and it's never been as good since. There was a revolving door policy for NBC News Presidents when it began to go downhill, and, then, the financial relationship between the News Division and the network itself changed. The network began to see news as a profit center. In the early days, when Reuven Frank and I were hired for television, radio people would not work on television. The fees weren't big enough, and they were, I think, afraid it would go nowhere. Our first television generation came from the newspapers primarily, and some magazines and wire services. It is interesting to me that we had been trained in print, which I still believe is a different set of dynamics in approaching the news and describing its function. Not that there weren't good journalists on radio. God knows there were, but we gave news something never effectively charted in history, a professional attitude different from radio.

When television began to take off, it was too late for the radio people to go in because they didn't know enough about the techniques.

We, a relatively small number of us, were given the incalculably valuable gift of being asked to invent a new medium when we were young and eager. We thought there was considerable social usefulness in our documentaries, that the news was fun, that the whole world was interesting. It was the 1950's, an exhilarating period. It was something very few journalists have ever gone through.

In the beginning, I think Reuven Frank had a lot to do with setting standards for the news. McAndrew talked to him about ethical questions, and Reuven's role was less appreciated than it should have been. McAndrew was a wonderful organizer and father figure. He could "fix" things because he was so well-liked at the network (an important lesson for any NBC News President to learn, and many haven't). He knew where the bodies were buried in the News Division, knew how to keep people out of trouble or get them out of it gracefully. He was a strong executive, but he consulted Reuven and Julian Goodman on purely editorial things.

They worried more about the effects, the impact, the ethics of the things we were doing than Bill did. Bill arranged his life so he didn't have to worry; he had these interesting people worrying for him. I thought he was a wholly admirable man. He was, in a sense, the smartest alderman you ever met, and I say that with respect, and affection, indeed, with love.

When McAndrew died so unexpectedly, Reuven had to take over. We all talk about taking jobs we didn't want to take, but Reuven was thrust into that job twice, and it was hard on him both times. An excess of sentimentality did it. Julian Goodman was fitted by God, handcrafted, for the job. He should have been identified in his crib as the perfect president of the News Division, but because he was president of the company, he was not available. Reuven had been McAndrew's good and special friend, and, I guess, Julian thought he could keep an eye on the News Division, and so a combination of events made Reuven president. It happened again a few years later, sentimentality triumphant, and it shouldn't have been. Reuven is the smartest person, and in some ways, the most gifted producer, who ever worked for

NBC News. Just tremendous.

When you have been here as long as Reuven and I have, you come to a plateau where the youthful urgencies of ethics and ideals are perhaps not as important as they once were. Reuven and I now tend to look at the place, not so much be a part of it. We watch it. Each of us, in our own way, has found a job that he designed. In looking back on it, I think we both specified that we didn't want too much involvement with NBC News, operated now by a new generation of people with world perspectives different from ours. I don't say the flame has burned out; it just has a different quality.

Julian and Reuven brought in Dick Wald. Reuven was extraordinarily fond of Dick, and groomed him to be his successor. Wald is an effective, thoughtful executive, but, again, from a different generation, with different dynamics for the network. I think Wald would have been a good head of News if he had stayed. He accurately predicted that Herb Schlosser's desire to make Barbara Walters an anchorperson would not work. He saw that it did *not* work when she went to ABC. Dick felt other things were wrong for the News Division that Herb Schlosser felt were right. In the end, after a series of events, there wasn't any comity left in that relationship.

I was spoiled by Bill McAndrew, and the rest of the presidents of News didn't look as good to me, including Reuven, and Reuven is a great, close friend. After I'd walked to the top of the mountain with Bill McAndrew, everybody else was down in the foothills. He had a wonderful hold on us all.

What were my Presidential interviews like? Gerry Ford's was the easiest Presidential interview by far. He was fun to be with. I still talk to him from time to time. He was pretty much at peace with himself, or at least gave that impression. He had less "side" than the others, except maybe Kennedy. There is a line in Congreve (and I seldom quote Mr. Congreve) about a woman affecting to be unaffected. That may have been true of Kennedy. Aside from a few people like Ben Bradlee, and maybe Joe Alsop, I don't think Kennedy let his guard down as much as history likes to say he did. He was wonderful in many other ways, but you felt there was a little bit of plexiglass between the two of you. You never felt that with Ford. You always felt it with Nixon. You always felt that Carter was on his best behavior, very much "on" all the time. In formal interviews, and televised interviews, they're all nervous as they can be.

Tom Brokaw, then White House correspondent, and I interviewed Gerry Ford live for an hour upstairs in the White House. After the interview, we took off our microphones, and walked down that long corridor on the second floor of the White House, and Ford said, "Let's have a drink." I said, "Terrific idea. I thought the interview went very well." He ordered a scotch and soda from the waiter as we walked along, and the waiter scurried off. I said, "How in the world do you stay so calm? I had butterflies. It's live and all that." He said, "It's just being yourself, just being comfortable with a couple of nice guys like you." When the waiter arrived with a big scotch and soda, he downed it in one long gulp. He wasn't nervous at all.

I was the Contributing Editor on Huntley-Brinkley after I left the government when the Six Day War in the Middle East broke out. That was the fastest exit from government on record! I was one month short of the 24 months I'd promised Lyndon Johnson I would serve. The day the war began, I spent about 18 hours at the *Voice* to be sure the coverage was what I wanted it to be. Then I called Jack Valenti at the White House, and said, "Can I get out of the next 30 days? I want to go and cover that war." Valenti was nice enough to arrange the whole thing in about four hours, including my request that I wanted to say goodbye to Johnson, whom I had not seen much while I was in the government. I went to the White House for one of those little photos, and a hand-

shake, and then ended up in the Sinai Desert.

CBS sent Bill Small to see me when I was in Washington with the *Voice of America*, to ask me to become a CBS commentator. It was very tempting, because I had the desire to get out of the executive suite and into the field again. NBC looked like the best, most logical place, so I told CBS no. I called Reuven

Frank, and said, "Can I come back?" They took me back on the basis of that phone call. I was not obligated to go back to NBC. I had made a complete and legal break with them because of conflict of interest—the *Voice* rented several RCA transmitters.

I ask myself what would life have been at CBS? I was 40 when they offered me the job as commentator, and 40, I thought, was too young to be a commentator. I didn't know enough, and I didn't want to do it. By the time I was 50, eight years ago now, I thought seriously about accepting their offer to replace Eric Sevareid, a going job which appealed to me. In negotiating that, we wrote the job description of the commentary job I have now. I had some stiff negotiations at the time with Dick Wald. I wasn't sure how long Wald was going to last, and things at NBC weren't as peaceful as they had been some years before, so I wanted any deal locked up and written out. When you begin to mature at a place like this, you do that. In his day, McAndrew would have put his arm around my shoulder, and said, "I'll fix it, kid. You just go to the war, and everything will be all right." And it would. But now, it has to be legal.

McGee, Brinkley, and I started in 1970 to anchor "The Huntley-Brinkley Report." In 1971, I took it over by myself. Then Brinkley came back for a year and stayed in Washington. It drove us all crazy. It's a bad way to do a program. Writers had written the show with Huntley and Brinkley for 16 years. But business had changed, and that method became difficult. I was the sole anchorman from 1970 until 1982, except for the year with Brinkley.

I do commentaries three days a week, Tuesday, Wednesday and Thursday. If I get to my office by 8 o'clock in the morning and know what I want to write (many days I don't), I may be able to do the reading, and make the calls I need, and finish writing the commentary by 4:30 in the afternoon. It eats up about three 10 or 11-hour days a week. Then, there's the mail, and all the other "Mickey Mouse" stuff. It's a busy job.

It takes so long to write a White Paper that you begin to ask yourself if it's worth it. "A Portrait of the Press: Warts and All" was the first one I've done in a long time, and I'm not anxious to do another because it takes about three months. I enjoyed doing this one with my friends. It was fun seeing and interviewing people I've known for years.

"Warts" was a family project with a small staff: Arax, my assistant, and I working as a unit, Laura Waltz, a researcher, Thomas Tomizawa, the producer, and two working for him. We had one camera crew, and two very good editors, which brought it to about 12. I didn't want a bigger group. On the program, Creed Black, a former President of the American Society of Newspaper Editors, said the public perceives print newsmen as the guys in the white hats, and the television newsmen as the guys in the black hats. While he was president of the society, he made a speech saying that the excesses of television journalism were ruining the reputation of the rest of the people in journalism. I put that on because it's a widely-held view.

In doing our research for the program on the press, we found that there was less glitz and hype in local television news than we had expected. It is getting much better in many places. But we also found that television news, network and local, does antagonize a lot of people with interviews of victims of tragedy. Television should be much more careful about invading privacy.

One very important reason for the bad reputation of reporters in general is that television allows the audience to see the process of journalism, see reporters working. Before television, during the radio days, we never saw reporters doing what they were supposed to do: asking hard, tough questions of accountable public officials. The public never went through those experiences, so when they see the press ask the mayor of their town tough questions, they think press people are rude. This reaches its apogee at the Presidential press conferences when they see the President being treated roughly sometimes by reporters. Viewers say, how dare they? He's the President of the United States. I think that's given all of us a bad name.

On a Fred Friendly seminar, when James Schlesinger said there are no more Ernie Pyles, that really got to me. I looked around that table. There was Charlie Moore, a *New York Times* correspondent who had saved a number of wounded Marines in terrible street fighting in Vietnam. He and another reporter were given the Bronze Star by the Marine Corps, a rare honor for civilians. I looked over at Sydney Schanberg of *The New York Times* who had done all that wonderful work in Phnom Penh when it fell after the Vietnam war. I looked around at Morley Safer, who has taken his chances. I don't think these are unpatriotic people. For Jim Schlesinger, an old pal of mine, to accuse us of being unpatriotic, was too much to take.

I closed the White Paper with "You say your mother loves you? Check it out!" That's a quote from a man named Dornberg, a legendary City News Bureau Editor in Chicago. I wanted to use it as the title of the program but was dissuaded.

I haven't received many awards I really liked. I honestly don't care much for them. Often, they're not given for merit but for other reasons. I've always been nervous about television and radio awards because I think some politicking goes into them. At this stage of my career, they look down their list, and say, "We never gave him one. Why don't we now before he dies or retires?" And, there is an *incredible* array of awards given because they want you to make a speech. We are getting pretty good in our dotage, we turn those down. We say thanks very much.

Dear NBC, I hope you'll be as good in your next 60 years as you were for much of the first 60.

October 7, 1985

Former President of NBC News and now Executive Producer of NBC News, Reuven Frank's achievements in broadcast journalism are distinguished, diverse and many times brilliant.

"Everyone had to crawl the whole 40 yards in a 3½ x 3½ shaft [of the tunnel]. First her head (it was like a birth), and then she came out, stood up, reached back and someone handed her her baby. Klaus Dehmel put down his light to help her. I thought I'd kill *him* because he was supposed to be taking pictures. I remember her, with the silk stockings with the great big hole on one knee, just sitting there, exhausted physically and emotionally. I first saw it in negative, and it still just knocks me right off my chair."

I was born in Montreal and attended the University of Toronto with a major in economics. I thought it was a pretty good background for news. I realized that I wanted to be a newsman when I was in high school, which prompted me, when I was in college, to work on the college newspaper instead of going to class.

I came to New York in 1943, where I finished my degree at City College. I spent four years in World War II as an Army prisoner-of-war guard in Huntsville, Texas. That was interesting duty, different.

When I was discharged, I enrolled at Columbia's School of Journalism and graduated in the Class of 1946. I wrote to every paper in the country looking for a job. When the *Newark Evening News* asked me to come over for an interview, I brought over all these things that I'd written in school. I had nothing else. The City Editor looked at them and said, "Oh, that's fine. This is very *good*." I said, "*Really?*" He then replied, "You have *no* idea how difficult it is to teach people to triple-space." So I got the job because I had learned how to triple-space at Columbia.

I started in June of 1947. I was doing all bids around Newark, and being sent out when somebody jumped into the Passaic River. Usually, by the time I got there, he'd been fished out. Then I was moved to the newspaper's Elizabeth Bureau in Union County. For a while, I was a court house reporter, which was a marvelous experience. That's news coverage. You're covering about four or five courts, all the way from murder to divorce, learning how to get a story. You learned the clerk of the court is more important to you than the judge and things like that. How to have a drink with a defense lawyer. Why you don't take gifts at Christmas. All those things. Court house training is even better than City Hall. They found out I was a pretty good editor and moved me inside.

In 1950, I was very close friends with one of my classmates at Columbia Journalism School, Gerry Green (who later became known as a writer and dramatist and novelist). He was, interestingly enough, the last member of that class to get a job, and that job was at INS, International News Service, of blessed memory. A terrible place to work. They really squeezed their employees, so Gerry was one of the first to change jobs. His second job was at NBC Network Television News, which was at 106th Street and Park Avenue, in the Pathe Building. They built the studios there because they had to be near the film processing lab. A dozen of us in that class were close, and we made fun of him and the funny new medium. He got very angry because he's one of those people who is always angry.

One day, he called me and said (by that time I was Night City Editor, and a brand-new father), "There's a job up here, do you want it?" And I said, "No." And he got really angry, blew his top. "You've got nothing to do all day; you work at night; you sit around the house all day and listen to a baby cry, the least you could do is come up here and look at it." I thought that was a good idea so I went up there, and it was fascinating. I went into what I thought was a theatre; I learned they called it the screening room, and some men were looking at negative film, negative movie film. A guy was saying, "I want 10 seconds of this, 15 seconds of that."

I thought that was the best way to live I'd ever come across. The guy in charge said, "You want to try it?" I said, "Okay, I'll try it." I wrote scripts for what has since become the NBC A-News. It was the beginning of syndication. And some sports stuff, whatever, for two weeks while I was working at night in Newark. I gave the paper two weeks' notice, and for four weeks I held two jobs. At the end of it, I asked Art Lodge, "How come you hired me? This is a *big* news organization. I'm a friend of Gerry Green, but to you I'm a guy who came off the street." He said, "Well, I'll tell you. All those guys in radio won't come up here. They don't think television is going to last." This was 1950.

Anyhow, I decided that was for me. So I said, "Okay, I'll take the job. How much does it pay?" He said, "It pays $100 a week." I told him I was already getting $100 (which was a lie, I was getting $90). He said, "Okay, I'll give you $110." The newspapers were paying $175 even then, 1950 Guild salary in New York. In those days, there was some jealousy when newspaper reporters looked at television salaries. It depends on who's looking at whom. They look at Brokaw—in fact, so do *we*!

Television and radio news were separate operations then. When they were reunited, Davidson Taylor came over from CBS to head the department. He brought Bill McAndrew up from Washington to merge radio and television news at the very end of 1950 or early 1951. The news studios moved to 30 Rock about '52, but the film editing rooms stayed at 106th Street. The film editor would be up there, and we'd be down here, and we had a closed-circuit system that started in '52, until the film editing operation moved down to 727 Seventh Avenue. The New York City fire code and building code hadn't caught up with the fact that film was no longer flammable, so the film unit couldn't join the rest of the news department here. Oh, that was a terrible pain. And we'd still have to use the closed circuit for news. For instance, when I was working on the weekly show ''Outlook,'' every time I wanted to look at a piece of film, I'd walk over to the film studios, come back and write the story. A terrible nuisance!

When News moved down here in '52, Bill McAndrew was my boss. My whole career depended on him. He and I had a very unusual relationship; he trusted me and I trusted him. He ran the place, and I did the stuff. I did most of the shows in those days; hours, half hours, as well as the news. The term producer wasn't used then. We got along very well personally. For a man in that position, he was a very quiet and painfully shy man if you didn't know him. He had a terrible time making a public speech, but he had a very great commitment to the news business. It's all that ever mattered to him. He'd get very fierce if he found encroachment. Within the company, everybody wanted to encroach. There's no business that has more outside experts than news—more so than show business. Everybody is a news consumer, and everybody knows how to do it better.

Let's face it. There is no such thing as journalism without journalists. Although there's nothing arcane about journalism, it's something you have to learn. It's a discipline, a simple negative code of ethics, things that you mustn't do. It never tells you what *to* do. You mustn't lie, you mustn't steal. All those things that you should have learned a long time ago, or that your mother and father taught you. Or should have. Or used to. Everybody was always getting in the act, and we were trying to do a reasonably good job of presenting the news. Any kind of communication has what is pejoratively called a show business element, because if it doesn't have a show business element, nobody pays any attention, in any medium. This is just as true of print.

The terrible problem is how do you keep the presentation from taking over the content. And all this business about anchorpersons. It's all the same stuff. So there were a lot of battles. Bill insisted that people who gave the news be trained in the news. That took a long time. In those days and for a *long* time, the network news department, as it was then, was responsible for the local news on the network-owned stations. We felt that we had to apply the same standards to the local news, and the fact that other stations not owned by the network had their own set of rules did not relieve us. There were a lot of fights about that.

Pat Weaver was President after we moved down. Bob Sarnoff was higher on the news than Pat. Pat was the guy who ran programs, and every now and again, Bobby would come in and rescue us. He rescued me about three times. Pat wanted to cancel ''Outlook,'' and Bobby stopped him once. ''Outlook'' was a very early magazine show that we did with Chet Huntley on Sundays. It was a period when budgets got squeezed and squeezed and squeezed, and we pared the show's cost to where we couldn't do it for less, and they said okay, cancel it. Bobby saw something he liked, and said no, you can't do that. That saved us. Later on, I believe Bobby was responsible for the fact that ''The Tunnel'' finally got on the air.

When the ''Today'' show started, Pat approached Frank McCall in News, specifically, to run it, and News turned him down. He brought in someone from outside, and then there was a question of who ran it. These were the very early days of network television. Lines were not very sharply drawn and precedents didn't exist. So there was a Producer of ''Today,'' and then a Managing Editor. The first and longtime Managing Editor was Gerry Green, who worked for McAndrew, so ''Today'' news was part of the total news output. They did news four times during the two hours, and some news stuff the rest of the time, and the rest was just kind of collegial. I heard later that there were all kinds of executive fighting, but I wasn't an executive.

Bill McAndrew was a professional newsman of great integrity. Later, Kintner hired some people with impressive credentials to do big blockbuster documentaries. Bill looked at one on organized crime after it had been all but finished, and he noticed one spot that he thought would have been very difficult to get with a camera. He probed the producer and found out that he really helped it along a little, and he threw the whole damn thing out. It had already been announced and scheduled.

As I was given more responsibility, the John Cameron Swayze show for a couple of years, the 1956 conventions and the "Huntley-Brinkley Report,"

I found only one thing: you've got to make decisions, a lot of decisions, particularly if you're *the* producer, what we now call the Executive Producer. (On movies, the Executive Producer is really a chief accountant. He's like the guy in Hollywood in charge of the books. They don't let him near the set.) If you're doing that on a regular five-day-a-week news program, you spend all day long making decisions because all you do is say "yes, no, yes, no." I found out the hard way—by trying to bring along people I felt were talented and skilled—that making decisions scares people. I'd rather make the wrong decision than none.

In 1954, Pat Weaver started a program, "Background," with Joseph C. Harsch. This was the very beginning of magazine programming. Pat picked a producer from his Chicago gang, Ted Mills, who had no news experience. McAndrew was upset, and he twisted my arm to be the number two man to keep the faith. That program ran for almost a year until it went under, and I was a producer without an assignment. I started working with Chet Huntley, whom I'd never heard of, on "Outlook," which started on Easter Sunday 1956. Nobody watched it, not even my mother. My wife said she watched, but I never believed her.

Bill asked me to organize for the '56 political conventions in Chicago. Four or five very talented people had worked on "Background," and that small team tried to figure out what is a convention. At the '52 convention, I was the writer on the Swayze program, and after 8 p.m. I had nothing to do but go to the control room and watch

all those things that were done wrong. So when '56 came, I decided how to do it. It was very simple: a convention is a news story, and the only way to cover a news story is to put a reporter where the news is, and the only way to get it covered on television is to put a camera where the news is. We surveyed that terrible place, the International Amphitheatre down in the Chicago stockyards, to figure out a place to put the cameras. We didn't have permission to put in cameras, except for the pool cameras covering the podium. We wanted our reporters on camera.

I got a lot of my information from Joe Meyers who ran NBC's radio coverage of the '52 conventions. NBC Radio News had the best coverage of any medium or any organization. Joe had floor reporters with these enormous radio-operated mikes (they called them beer mugs—they had beer-mug handles). I remember spending hours on the phone with Jack Chancellor, a young kid in a subordinate position on radio in Chicago in 1952, asking, "What did you do here and what did you do here and here?" I figured out that we'd do the same thing, only with a camera on it.

For example, the television anchor booth for the 1956 convention was not even in the hall, it was *downstairs*, but there was a radio booth; the frontage was about six or seven feet, at most. Radio was anchored by Pauline Frederick, who was in the booth with Chet Higgins, the radio producer, notes, microphones and an engineer.

We put in two cameras, one on either side of the booth, which didn't please Pauline. Now we had two cameras on those four guys, and all we needed was one or two more, and we *finally* got them. We invented coverage.

On the technical side, my director, a marvelous young fellow named Jack Sughrue, had been a fighter pilot, and we designed the control room (where the pictures came in and the way they went out) based on the communication system of an aircract carrier. Jack taught me that those elements that were not on the air had to come into "the filter center." Everything has to come to the same place and then go out. In 1984, in San Francisco or Dallas, all four network setups, including CNN, were based on what we did in 1956. Everybody assumes that's the way it is, as if this came from some textbook. Jack Sughrue and I had to figure out what to do with X people and Y dollars and a story to cover.

Chet Huntley and David Brinkley were made after the conventions. Huntley had made a reputation on the West Coast working for all three networks. He was a large, Montana-type fellow who wrote pretty well, a little too resonant, but okay for those days. A great debate arose in the news department because we had no outstanding candidate to anchor. Bill McAndrew wanted to use Bill Henry, who'd done a marvelous job for us in '52, and I opposed Henry, even though I liked and respected him, because he was not a full-time member of the organization. I was torn between Huntley and Brinkley. When someone then suggested two other people I couldn't stand, I said okay, that solves our problem—Huntley *and* Brinkley. Then Bill had to sell that idea to the top executives of the company. We had no idea that the interplay would be super. The idea of two people spelling each other during long stretches of gavel-to-gavel coverage seemed to be a good idea. They were both very conscientious; they tried to make it work, and it did.

Ben Park, Dave Taylor's assistant, suggested Huntley and Brinkley do the Nightly News. I thought it was a terrible idea. The decision to replace Swayze was a year-and-a-half old.

I can remember the second convention, the Republican convention, which was a renomination of Eisenhower. It was duller than the renomination of Reagan; it was terrible. It was just *awful*. I was sitting back there in the filter center, and Monday went by and Tuesday went by, and I had a show to do with Huntley on Sunday. We had arranged to do the show in Los Angeles; with that tight budget, I couldn't get back to New York. I told the guys at the convention, "Okay, I'm going to Los Angeles and do this show. I have to edit film, I have to do all this stuff. We have to get on the air Sunday, somehow." I ducked out early, and the convention ended on Thursday, and Huntley came down to Burbank airport. I said, "Hey, we've got a recording tomorrow at 10 o'clock so we can get on the air on Sunday." On the way to the hotel, he said, "By the way, Ben Park again asked me what show David and I could do together." And I said, "Tell him the 1960 convention. Now here's the schedule for tomorrow."

And I just brushed it out of my mind. With the success of Huntley and Brinkley at the conventions, a lot of people thought they should replace Swayze, and so they, and I as the producer, began a 14-year collaboration which made the "Huntley-Brinkley Report" Number One. The closing, "Goodnight, David…Goodnight, Chet," was my idea. A show has to end somehow, and that was the shortest ending I could think of.

I produced the show until in 1965 I couldn't stand it anymore. I first left in April 1963. I was bored to death. It was too easy. On an August morning, I read that CBS had announced that Cronkite was going a half hour. I drove in, parked my car, and there was Shad Northshield. I told him I had to get to the office in a hurry because McAndrew would be on the phone asking me to come back and take the show to a half hour. About 10:30 a.m., McAndrew called, "You got a minute?" And there I was back again. That extra 15 minutes made a *big* difference. My deal was two more years and out. "Huntley-Brinkley Report" won ten Emmys and two Peabodys.

Did that show subsidize NBC News? Part of my deal with Bill was that I had nothing to do with income. I had an operating budget and tried not to go over it unless there was a good reason. Is it unfair or accurate to say that news people think of themselves as a sacred priesthood? I think it's unfair and accurate.

The documentary "The Tunnel" in 1962 was the story of some young men at the Technical University in Berlin, who had a classmate who lived in East Berlin with his wife and kid. He couldn't come to school after the Berlin Wall went up in '61. The *very* important thing that gets lost sight of is that the program itself was a function of NBC News as an organization. It's not something that even the most brilliant producer could have thought of and, even with unlimited money, done. It took place because NBC News existed; because we had a bureau in Berlin staffed by competent journalists, and it grew out of that.

I had been involved in reports both on Huntley-Brinkley and on "Outlook" about the various pressures causing people to come from East Berlin to West Berlin. Huntley and I had done an hour's program called "The S Bahn Stops at Freedom" (the first time Americans had ever seen Willy Brandt). By a *very* strange coincidence, Brinkley and I were in Berlin the weekend the Wall closed, and we had the only television reports of it. Because of my interest, (and because I was doing, besides everything else, a regular five-day-a-week news program with a nice fat budget), before Brinkley and I Vienna I sat down with the correspondent Piers Anderton, and with Gary Stindt, the head of the bureau, and I said to them, "The closing of the Wall will build pressure which will need a safety valve. Whatever you can get about that, grab it and charge it to the show, and we'll cover it."

We got all kinds of little stories, most of which were unusable: people swimming the canal, jumping over the Wall. Escape attempts continued during the fall and *all* winter. Many people tried many ways to escape. There were little short tunnels that a man and his wife, a man and his son dug very close to the Wall, maybe ten yards one way, ten yards the other, and we'd get there too late to film them. The East Germans put up big heavy grille fences in the sewers. Big city sewers, like the sewers of Paris. *Les Miserables*. I saw miles of film, which were interesting in a Sunday rotogravure way, but there was no story.

Most of the subversive activity was being done by students at the Free University and the Technical University. A young stringer working for us, Abe Ashkenazy, a former second lieutenant in Army Intelligence, had taken his discharge in Berlin (his wife was an opera singer) and was going to school. Speaking perfect German, he went around asking everyone if they knew of any activity. And nothing happened. Winter came, and somewhere around March or April, two Italian engineering students walked into Gary Stindt's office and

said, "We understand you're interested in filming a tunnel." They had started one and had run out of money.

Remember the big issue about whether we paid money? We said, "We're not going to give you cash. We're going to buy your supplies." So it was wires, light bulbs, rails and shovels and lumber. They were, after all, engineers. They wanted to dig a subway, not a rabbit hole. We were trading equipment, supplies, for the right to film. More than anything else, we didn't want to know what they were doing until they did it. We didn't want to be in on the plan. We told them, you go dig your hole; we'll take the picture. That's all. It was supposed to be done in a month, but they ran into water main-breaks, and it took over three months. By the time we got to it, they were already to the Wall, and they were going to the other side.

A German student who lived in East Berlin with a wife and kid couldn't come to school. That was the trigger. They found other kids who had family or friends who signed on to dig with them. They thought it would take them several weeks, and, in the end, it took them all summer long. They started in the spring; they did not break through until late August. They were digging underground and ran into water-main breaks. They were afraid to report the breaks for that would bring the police, and to whom should they report? To the East or the West?

Time and expense got to be an issue, and I flew over to Paris and had dinner with Piers and Gary (secrecy was all-important), flew back to London, and home. The tunnel was supposed to be like a highway for hundreds of people to get out. The tunnel was down roughly ten feet, and at either end there was a vertical shaft. We did not go into the tunnel during the escape; Peter and Klaus Dehmel worked for Gary Stindt and were at the head of the West Berlin shaft, and suddenly they could see, with one battery-held light pouring down this dirt shaft, totally unlined and reasonably straight-sided, a woman who couldn't have been much older than 30, on her hands and knees. Everyone had to crawl the whole 40 yards in a 3½ x 3½ shaft. First her head (it was like a birth), and then she came out, stood up, reached back and somebody handed her her baby. The light man, Klaus Dehmel, put down his light to help her. I thought I'd *kill* him because he was

supposed to be taking pictures. I remember her, with the silk stockings with the great big hole in one knee, just sitting there, exhausted physically and emotionally. I first saw it in negative, and it still just knocks me right off my chair. Two and a half days after the breakthrough the tunnel filled with water again and had to be shut down. Less than 40 people got out of there.

After it was closed and after the people were out, there was kind of a press thing done by the government of West Berlin, and none of the escapees talked about the filming; they talked about the engineering students and about the tunnel and about the people who came out, including the German student, his wife, baby and mother-in-law. We were then the only organization of any importance to use film made by du Pont. Everybody else used Eastman Kodak. Somebody from CBS saw a little du Pont box in which a 100-foot reel of 16mm film comes and knew NBC had filmed it. And *then* the trouble started. The West Berlin government decided that we should not have filmed it, and started to bring pressure on the State Department. One reason was that it would expose people to danger. We kept saying it's all over, and we've done this great thing. I've always thought that one of our competing organizations got hold of a member of the German Senate (their City Council), and he got very loud. (Our State Department has special relations with Berlin, completely separate from its relations with West Germany. Even today, we're still under the Occupation Statute with Berlin. That has never been resolved in 40 years.)

Going in there and filming without official permission or recognition became a very big issue. There were so many organizations involved: the State Department, the West Berlin police, the State police, the Intelligence police and the Border police. It got to be a very loud campaign. They never said that we could not put it on the air. Bill McAndrew and I went to see Dean Rusk and others with Elie Abel, then our State Department correspondent. We asked him, "Do you want us not to run this?" They said, "No, we'd never say that."

Yet this kind of drumfire went on and on and on. The original air date was in October, and Kintner decided to postpone it. I said he's never going to put it on, and Bill McAndrew said yes, he is. I said if he doesn't put it on I'm going to quit, and I put it in writing. Oh, very, *very* bitter days. We finally put it on on December 10th. Other than the wear and tear on my gut, the biggest result of the State Department campaign was that we had an enormous audience. Dick Pinkham told me it was the only Monday that NBC beat CBS that entire season. CBS had that tremendous Monday lineup with "Lucy" and "Andy Griffith" and I forget the third one, and we went on for 90 minutes and beat them.

I'm proudest of that and the 1960 convention coverage. I believe we taught American television how to cover a convention in '56, but in 1960 it really came together, and from then on (before the beginnings of the big space age), conventions were *the* thing for network news organizations to make an impact. We really did it that time. We killed our competitors. In '56 we learned how to do it, and in '60 we did it.

To cover a story you put a reporter where the story is. You give him something to talk into, you get some way to get his picture back *and only the story matters*. That is very simple. On camera before, there were a lot of politicos, commentaries, interviews. But here you follow the story. You don't know what you're going to do until something happens. Journalism is not an active process, it's a reactive process. Somebody else does something, and you tell people about it. You don't do anything. You're not supposed to. It's not your function. That's all we did. Jack Sughrue organized the communications system in 1952. In '60 we refined it so that there was one producer in charge of the four people, Edwin Newman, Frank McGee, Merrill Mueller and Martin Agronsky, on the floor.

In 1964, at the Goldwater Convention in San Francisco, the air guys were Huntley-Brinkley. The booths were just above the seats, and Chet told me that after Eisenhower made his scathing remark about the press, all those people turned, and he thought they were coming through the glass. He was never so scared in his life. I told Chancellor, when he was arrested, not to be carried out of that convention hall. I said *walk*. Dignity. In '68 we made an 80-something share! Everybody else had the 16 or 17; I think Brinkley still has the little telex that came in from New York.

The Young Republicans had a big tent outside where they sold souvenirs to raise money; the hottest item there (they had to have a reprint of them) was a button, "Stamp Out Huntley-Brinkley." I still have one at home. It was a terrible period for us; professionally, it was very good. Nobody had done that before. CBS took Walter Cronkite off between conventions, remember that?

In 1984, all three networks and CNN were using *that* way of coverage. It has not changed because it was logic, very simple logic. We don't care what had been done; we're here to cover a news story; it's the only thing we do, the only thing we know, it's what we get paid for. Everything falls into place once you know what you're setting out to do. But nobody had done it. 1952 was a shambles, mostly the pool coverage. The pool coverage is not the convention; the pool coverage is the rostrum, and everybody knows that the rostrum is a fraction of what goes on at a convention. These days it's all changed. What goes on at a convention is set before the convention starts. And they're not worth covering.

Gavel-to-gavel is an imposition on the audience because today it's nothing but a political commercial that doesn't end.

Bill McAndrew and I complemented each other. He understood the company and the organization. He was totally dedicated to the news business, but he understood the business. I was only interested in doing programs; I had no other interest. I was the producer. I had more fun producing news than I could possibly have had doing anything else. He and I generally agreed how one faces life and conducts oneself. Up until '65, Bill took all the heat from Bob Kintner, and there was a lot of it. Kintner was a man to be feared. Bill shielded us from Kintner, and I used him as a model both times that I was in administration. People who were out doing shows were not supposed to be worried about budget problems, administration problems. Management is there to do that.

Kintner was a total autocrat. People who *never* saw him knew that he was President of NBC. He certainly made all the difference. The day that he became Presi-

dent of NBC he changed his reporting structure, which sounds like a simple and a dull bureaucratic matter, but, from then on, the Vice President in charge of News reported to the President of the company. To be able to go to the top with no intermediate steps makes all the difference in the world, because the essence of a news bulletin is time, speed. He didn't understand how things got done, he just said do it. Even before Bob Kintner, Bill would fight for time and lose many times; he was absolutely dedicated.

He was the first one I knew who saw what the combination of television and news would mean in terms of impact on audience. He used to say to me, and I'm talking now about 1952, "We've got to be careful, the power we're working with is tremendous. First we must figure how to do it, and then we're going to do it very, very well." He stressed the responsibility we had all the time. A dead body on television is different from a dead body on the radio or in a newspaper. Vietnam was an absolute example. If we hadn't known how to use television, we'd still be there.

My biggest failure as a manager was not sending any reporter to Vietnam who did not volunteer, so our best reporters didn't go. The other networks did not take that position. I thought of what would happen if somebody told me to go. I think it was an unprofessional judgment.

We can get an awful lot into a two-minute, 40-second story. For the reporters who came out of print journalism, used to having time and space to write a full story, excerpting was a new art. It damaged their ego a lot. The print guys by and large haven't done badly. My early years were a time when radio guys were trying to move into television. Very few of them made that transition gracefully. Because radio is only the voice, it's only me. Television is a team effort, and maybe the voice is secondary to the impact of the picture. Some guy who doesn't shave very often, doesn't clean his nails, is the guy who is really doing that picture, and you're the guy with the trench coat, and you're secondary. A lot of them took it very badly and never made the transition. Some of the biggest names in radio who had plenty of working years left, really never made it. Just like John Gilbert and the talkies.

Television prompted a cosmetic approach as to whom should be on camera. That's a management decision, and strong managements resist and weak managements don't. Parenthetically, strong managements, networks and affiliated stations, resisted pressure from Washington during the Watergate period. We told them to go to hell and found that, if we stood our ground, Washington would back down. There are plenty of egos in television, but a foreign correspondent is not such a big deal any more. Remember the days when the foreign correspondent was somebody who had dinners with the foreign ministers? It's just a reporting function now, because they can fly in and out of countries.

When Bill McAndrew died unexpectedly, I was asked to be the President of NBC News. Bill and I started working together in early '52; he died Memorial Day weekend, '68. Whatever the organization structure said on paper, I was working for Bill and he and I accepted that, and that was fine. Although I didn't want the management when he first asked me to get into it three years before, at the time of his death the prospect was that I would work for somebody else, and I didn't like the idea. So I would have been very upset if I hadn't been offered the job.

The landing of the Apollo 11 on the moon with Neil Armstrong was a major organizational thing; getting people in the right place, but the technical part had all been taken care of, and a lot of it by NASA. They provided the pictures of Armstrong jumping up and down and taking his first step on the moon. Programming was a little difficult because there was originally planned to be a long period, something like six hours between the time the capsule got to the moon and the time we'd get the first pictures. George Murray organized a six-hour parade of guest stars because we knew people wouldn't leave their sets, and we had nothing to show them. It was a great time for television.

Do I think that news should be rated at all in the ratings? Absolutely, we're part of television. We survive on the basis of advertiser support. The advertisers are going to buy ratings because they're trying to sell. They'd rather sell to somebody than nobody.

I brought in Dick Wald, who is a very, very bright, good journalist. He had to learn the television business and he learned fast. In those days, the News Division was responsible for news on the owned stations, and that's one of the things I put Dick in charge of. That's a very

rough school: pressures of money and budget, production and very savvy station management. Ray Welpott was a good teacher. License renewal applications then were so complex; it's now a postcard. A rough training ground.

Dick Wald left, and Les Crystal followed Dick, followed by Bill Small from CBS. Bill did not get along well with the organization. A lot of people didn't like him. The term "corporate culture" applies. NBC News differs from CBS News and NBC differs from CBS. Bill believed that the CBS News structure and the inter-relationships with the people in charge were the right way to do it. He denigrated the people here, and NBC News was not in very good shape. It had been starved and kicked around a little.

I was ready to leave in 1980 because I was very upset. I was doing a program called "Weekend," and it was doing pretty well until Silverman got his hands on it. It was pretty successful, it was a lot of fun, it was different, and it was well accepted. No program has ever gotten that kind of press, and this was at the time when NBC was getting *terrible* press, but they got their dirty little hands on it and before you knew it, it was dead. Lloyd Dobyns is an excellent writer, one of the greatest. Reminds me of Brinkley, and I still believe writers make the difference.

Small asked me to stay on and do documentary. I gave him a list of about ten ideas. One was "American Productivity is Falling," and he said do that one. I started poking around. I had done some economic subjects years and years ago for Julian Goodman. I did one with Jack Chancellor on the Common Market. I went down to the dean of the business school at American University. I've known him for a hundred years, and I said, "Do you know anything about productivity?" He said, "Funny you should ask." He called the head of the Productivity Institute at the university. I was told to see Ed Demming. When I asked why, I was told Dr. Demming serves the best martinis in Washington and he's an expert on Japanese productivity.

F. Edwards Demming is primarily a statistician. He had been in Japan with the Occupation trying to help Japanese industry get back. He had evolved a system of checking the productivity of machines. By very careful statistical control, which I don't understand to this day, he developed a system of keeping meticulous records of what it's doing; the theory being if that machine doesn't produce right, it's not the fault of the man, it's the fault of the machine. This revolutionized Japanese productivity. To this day,

1985, once a year, there is The Demming Prize, given by the Japanese manufacturing industry, to a manufacturing company in Japan for record productivity.

We showed Demming's operations in a paper company up in New Hampshire. The program was "If Japan Can, Why Can't We?" It was absolutely *fortuitous* timing! That program has had a life after television unlike anything. They are still using it in graduate schools of business. We still get requests for copies. This is now five years later, and it keeps going and going and going. A very, very smart, nice man, Bill Abernathy, who was a professor at the Harvard Business School, told me he used that program in class. I told him that was intended for a general audience, and if he was using it in the preeminent graduate school of business in the United States, we were in even more trouble than I thought.

I wanted to do a documentary on the decline of management. Abernathy and a man named Hayes, also on the Harvard faculty, had done an article for the *Harvard Business Review* which had more requests for reprint than any other in the history of the *Review*. It's called "Managing Our Way to Economic Decline," and it went along with a pet theory of mine: that one of the evils of the American economy, one of the things that is going to drive us into the ground and back to the caves, is the theory that a trained manager can manage anything without knowing the process that's involved. I will make speeches denouncing MBA's at the drop of a hat. I think they're a blight; they will ruin us.

I don't know to this day why Bob Mulholland asked me to replace Small in February 1982. I thought about it for a long time and decided that I ought to do it. I had had a lot of fun, bought a house, raised a couple of kids, all on NBC. I would have felt funny if I hadn't done it. I felt an obligation, but I wasn't too happy about it. Morale was low when I took over. You'll always find somebody to tell you the morale was low, but the results were not good.

It's like muscle tone, and we had a lot of trouble on those incidents that are such a trial for a news organization, which require you to put all your resources on the line immediately and publicly—the shooting of the Pope, the killing of Sadat, the Air Florida plane going into the Potomac—which was not the fault of the NBC News organization, or the success of the ABC or CBS News organizations, because all three mostly depended on their local stations. By the time we got on, everyone was sure that NBC News had fallen apart.

To wind, up, I've been very lucky. Larry Grossman, the new News President, who took over in 1984, has me back to being an Executive Producer. That's what my card says. I think the best of television is what's now, because now I don't care what's ahead. There's nothing like it. I learned by doing in the early days, which were exciting. And nobody knew I was wrong. I've worked for NBC for 35 years. It's a very amiable company. People are not pushed around as much. There are legends about people who've been let go who have been seen on the second floor years later. It wouldn't happen any other place. NBC News is always trying to do with not quite enough even in the best days. This is an organizational factor. Some of the results are bad. One of the good results of that is that individual ingenuity is given a higher value here. It's not a massive, Teutonic organizational approach, and I tell you, I've flourished under it. I've got no complaints!

I think that my principal wish for NBC's 60th birthday or any other day, is to keep in mind the business it's really in.

September 26, 1985

Edwin Newman's career as a distinguished broadcast journalist at NBC spanned 34 years, from 1949 to 1984. The number and variety of his assignments outnumbered his years with the network. He has rightly been called NBC's "Instant Renaissance Man."

"When you are on the air, the idea is not simply to emit a sound that can be recognized as having something to do with news, the idea is to communicate information... choose words with some care, some discrimination..."

Edwin Newman

I was born in New York City and went through high school there. Then I went to the University of Wisconsin. I intended to study journalism, but, after a year, I decided to major in political science and economics. I remember that Henry L. Smith, my advisor in the Journalism Department, said to me, "Mr. Newman, do you want to work for a small-town paper?" I said, "No." He said, "Then you don't want to be in this department." That was in 1936, 1937. Schools of journalism are different now in their ability to get jobs for their graduates, but I think it was excellent advice.

I suppose because I was from New York, I had romantic notions about working in Washington, in a big city or overseas. I had no idea of working in radio. There wasn't any news to speak of; you'd get an occasional news summary in between programs like "The Cities Service Hour" with the soprano, Jessica Dragonette, who always wore evening dress for her broadcasts. That brings to mind that in the early days of television in England, BBC announcers wore dinner jackets but the trousers were ordinary trousers. The female announcers often wore slacks under their evening dresses.

At Wisconsin, I thought of becoming a lawyer. Then I decided that would take too long and take too much money that we didn't have. Then I thought I ought to become a teacher, with any luck a professor. So I got a fellowship at LSU, and went there to get an M.A. While I was there, I was offered a job in Washington with the Department of Agriculture, as a result of having taken a Civil Service examination when I was still at Wisconsin. After training, I would be sent to an Agriculture Department research laboratory as a personnel officer. I took it because it paid around $1,620 a year, which sounds ridiculous now, but was not bad beginning pay, far more than my first news job.

I quickly saw it was not something I wanted to do. It took them a little longer, but not much, so after a couple of months, I resigned. Richard Davis, a friend from Wisconsin, then on the Washington Bureau of *Newsweek*, told me about a job opening for a dictation boy at International News Service, and I took it. My duties there were to take the stories the man covering the Senate wrote and dictate them to the dictation boy in the office. After a couple of months, they moved me into the office because I was a fast typist. I had been

there six months when I heard about an opening at the United Press, and I became a dictation boy there.

Working as a dictation boy was excellent training. You admired the way people under pressure dashed out of a news conference, a trial or a hearing, picked up the phone, shouted "Bulletin," and dictated the story as smoothly as anyone could want it. You learned not to waste time or words, and get to the point.

In the Navy during World War II, I was commissioned because I had a college degree. I had the grand title of Communications Officer, which meant, literally, that I could type, and operate coding and decoding machinery. I was stationed in Trinidad in the West Indies for a couple of years, before being transferred to the Brooklyn Navy Yard. That was my war. The only enemy I saw was an Italian prisoner in Grand Central Station. The only time I went to sea was as a passenger on a ship to Trinidad. I was seasick, a great naval officer.

I returned to the UP in Washington as a reporter at the State Department. R.H. Shackford, who later became a columnist, was there too. Shack was important in my life; I learned a lot from him. I worked the "overnights," assigned to low people; I was the third man at the State Department. I had the great and fortunate experience of going to the White House when they needed help there occasionally.

I stayed at the UP for about a year after the war. Then I worked for a couple of months for I.F. (Izzy) Stone in the Washington Bureau of the newspaper *PM*, now defunct. It was considered liberal, and it was full of political factions. If you wrote a story straight, it seemed suspicious to them.

Then, my old friend, Richard Davis, found me a job with his friend, Esther Van Wagoner Tufty, a celebrated character called "The Duchess," who ran a bureau in Washington. She supplied regional coverage for newspapers and material for a service called Transradio. This job brought me in contact with members of Congress, and gave me valuable experience on the Hill. (I remember we took a streetcar to the Hill; we never took a taxi.) After I had been there for a while, I worked for two years for Eric Sevareid, helping to write a weekday-night 15-minute news radio show sponsored by The Metropolitan Life Insurance Company.

I was fortunate to learn about writing for radio from Eric, who took the news seriously and wrote about it seriously with as much skill and care as anybody in the business. Winston Burdett also gave me invaluable advice. The pay in radio then was better than in the press, and that made a difference.

My wife, who is British, and I were married in 1944, and we decided to try our luck overseas on the continent or in England. I had two possibilities in Paris: one was to work for UNESCO, and the other was to take courses in international relations and French at the Sorbonne on a Fulbright Fellowship. My French was fair because I had studied it in college and had taken a course at Berlitz under the GI Bill. We went to London. I went to see Shackford, then head of the London Bureau of the UP, and he said that NBC needed a stringer. Merrill "Red" Mueller, NBC correspondent, told me they needed somebody to do a couple of broadcasts a week, not a staff member, but somebody who would be paid by the broadcast. I made a recording and went off to Paris to the job with UNESCO. (I decided not to take the Fulbright, and incidentally, Ed Murrow was on the first Fulbright Committee, which may have had something to do with my getting it.) I'd been at UNESCO about an hour when I got a telephone call. I could have the stringer's position in London. So we went back to London. That was going home for my wife, and it meant that our daughter could be educated in English.

Bill Brooks was President of NBC News. I was a nobody then so I had very little contact with him. I can remember I was told to buy a bottle of whiskey when he was coming to London. I didn't pay attention to the British early closing hours, and barely got under the wire to get it. If I hadn't, I don't know what would have happened to my NBC career.

Between 1949 and 1952, I did some broadcasting for NBC, and, in December 1952, I became a member of their London staff. In those years, I also went to Greece, Turkey, and Western Europe as a writer for the Marshall Plan, and did some work for the BBC. The first television I ever did was for the BBC, a series of programs called, "An American Looks At Britain." In those first days of television, I remember memorizing the script and working under very hot lights, uncomfortable compared to radio broadcasting.

To make a living in those days I wrote for British and American magazines. I wrote for *Punch*, and for a magazine called *Everybody's*. I had pieces published in *The Atlantic*, and *Esquire*. Most of what I wrote was humor, or so I believed.

In 1956, I became head of the Bureau in London, and in 1957, I was moved to Rome. Those days you traveled a lot; if the Pope's health were good, you were not in Rome. I did enjoy the traveling.

When you were overseas it sometimes seemed that nobody at home understood the stories you were doing. They seemed to have preconceived notions picked up from the wire services. And who can blame them? It was perfectly understandable. Eventually, Joe Meyers in the News Department issued an order: if there is a conflict between what the NBC man says and the wire services say, go with the NBC man. I admired Joe, and he was very kind to me and important to me. I remember being on the circuit, saying what I had and being told that wasn't what the AP said. I'd say, with annoyance, "I don't give a damn what the AP says."

This impatience came about because you depended on circuits which often failed, and gave you the feeling that you were way off alone somewhere, nobody loved you, and nobody was there to sympathize. You'd be in Turkey, you'd come up on a circuit, they couldn't hear you in New York, you didn't know whether you were getting through, you'd do your piece blind. You did it three times, and you went away not knowing if you'd ever made it. There were many people in New York in those days who had not had experience overseas, and did not understand it was possible to feel a long way from home working with difficulty against heavy odds.

Bill McAndrew as President of NBC News was the buffer between the administration and the news, and there must have been times when that wasn't easy, especially during Kintner's presidency, although Kintner did a tremendous amount for the News Department.

After about a year in Rome, I was transferred to Paris. I was happy about that, and my French certainly was a lot better than my Italian. I'm devoted to Italian opera, so I had some fluency in Italian. I could speak a kind of operatic Italian. If phrases from "Vesti la giubba" or another aria sounded relevant, I could throw them in.

Pat Weaver was at the Savoy in London when Stalin was in the process of dying (which, of course, was a tremendous story), and Pat said, "I wouldn't want to be that cold."

I spent a good deal of time in North Africa, because Tunisia was seeking its independence from France, and because French settlers, who felt that France was getting ready to let Algeria go, staged an uprising. There was trouble between Turkey and Syria; we did some stories about that. I went to Israel for the first time. When I was in London I had worked in Egypt to fill in for the NBC correspondent, Wilson Hall, while he was on home leave, and also filled in for his wife, Lee Hall, who was stringing for *The Daily Mail* of London. Lee had trouble getting back into Egypt because of some cartoons in *The Mail* about Nasser. I also went to Kenya to do a story about the Mau Mau. In Egypt, I did a story about whether the British could stay in the Suez Canal, for a program called "Background," produced by Reuven Frank and Ted Mills. It was a weekly half-hour show, maybe the first of its kind. Another story I did for that program was about a Czechoslovakian ice skater who defected while competing in Vienna, so I went to Vienna, and several towns in Germany.

In 1961, when NBC sent me back to New York, it did mean some separation from our 16-year-old daughter, who, we decided, should stay and continue her education in England. There was sadness in that. I was brought back to anchor some programs, take part in others. I often took a turn on the "Today" show. For six months I did the news on it when John Chancellor was the host. Just the other day when I was speaking in Utica, New York, a woman introduced herself to me and said she was Robin Bain, the "Today" girl in those days. It was 25 years or so since I'd seen her, and it was a great pleasure.

From time to time, I would get assignments that kept me in one place for a while: a few weeks on "Nightly News," one summer filling in for Brinkley in Washington, and then doing some of the four daytime news programs

that NBC did at one time. Then I began doing documentaries at quite a clip.

I was able to do a variety of things. I had, even when I was overseas, done many things, and I was glad to go on that way. In those days, we also did many programs known as "Instant News Specials." Gulf Oil sponsored some of them. Frank McGee used to do them, and I used to do them.

Frank and I became friends; we liked each other. Frank was different from most of the news correspondents. He had a harder time as a boy and a young man; he was poor, and he had less education. He served as an enlisted man in the National Guard, and, I think, he was stationed in the Aleutian Islands during World War II. His reports from a local station on the troubles in the South attracted NBC's attention, and they hired him. We worked well together, and I wish Frank were here to tell you so. I'm sure he would have.

Frank had an unusual quality which I recognized during Democratic and Republican Conventions. John Chancellor, Sandy Vanocur, Frank and I were the Four Horsemen at many conventions. There were two circuits open to us; Sandy and John shared a circuit, and Frank and I shared a circuit. When he was on, I could not broadcast or communicate with the booth because the circuit was occupied, so I listened to Frank, and I noticed that delegates asked *him* questions. If I interviewed a delegate, he would answer me. With Frank, it was different. If he interviewed somebody about a dispute on the floor, that person would ask, "Isn't that a reasonable position, Mr. McGee?" as though he were an authority, appealing to him as though he were a judge. The people he interviewed had confidence in him. I think it was his clear sincerity, and a sympathetic quality he had. People got the idea that this was a nice man; he must surely understand what we're getting at.

Frank set an example for everybody when he was dying. I can't tell you how many times I was called and told, "We don't know whether Frank is going to make it. Be ready." And he would come out of the hospital to do his shows. He was brave indeed.

There was a series on Channel 4, WNBC-TV, called "The Open Mind," and they asked me to do some substitutes for it. "Speaking Freely" came out of that. The title was mine, but I think the idea came from Jack Reynolds, then a Channel 4 executive, and Ted Walworth, who ran Channel 4. Jack and later, Joe Michaels selected the guests.

Joe and I traveled together to do "Speaking Freely" with the Shah of Iran and all kinds of people. I would like to say it was a combination of NBC and my name that opened doors to us, but it was something else. The program was unedited; anybody who came on the program knew that what he or she said would be on the air. If somebody wanted to ventilate ideas, this was a way to do it. It was a serious program, it wasn't banter and badinage. The result was that we put people on the air who would never have been on American television otherwise. We had a very, very substantial following. We won Emmys every year. It was the kind of program that couldn't *not* win one. It was available to the NBC O&O's, and given to educational stations around the country.

People who came on the program knew they weren't expected to be solemn, but they knew it was a serious program, that I had read a great deal and prepared for it. If the questions I asked indicated this, the guests were grateful, opened up, and talked. If the conversation went off in a particular direction, if that direction seemed to me to be a useful one, I'd let it go and not insist on asking the next question I happened to have on the sheet. People tried to get on the show, and they thought it was a compliment to be invited.

We had about 250 people on it, and we did it for nine seasons, until I just couldn't do it because I was doing other things and I had started to write some books. I didn't want to do it without being properly prepared. It's an awful feeling not to be familiar with the subject the person is talking about. If you interview Claude Levi-Strauss about ethnology and haven't read his books, he will find out very quickly. If you interview B.F. Skinner, and know the points he is making, his attitude changes. I don't mean Skinner particularly. I found this with Mohammed Ali. We went to Cherry Hill, New Jersey, to interview him after his first fight with Joe Frazier, the one he lost. I asked him questions that showed I knew something about boxing, and his attitude changed immediately. He stopped kidding and began to talk seriously about his fighting technique. I asked why he never punched to the body, never threw punches in clinches. As far as I know, nobody had ever asked him those questions. He said to himself this man knows *something*, and he answered that it was a waste

of time and energy. I was lost in some subjects, like astronomy. But we put on people I was proud to put on.

We put on authors, playwrights, politicians, athletes, and musicians like Zubin Mehta, Seiji Ozawa, Beverly Sills, Aaron Copland. I can't help thinking that it was worthwhile, but it took a tremendous amount of work.

The Instant News Specials are the old "tear out the front page" idea, the romantic view of news as a way to make a living in which there is some excitement. When you were on the spot, you found out quickly how good you were, if indeed you were. Although the stories were almost always things you wished had not happened, you were pleased to be one of those selected to meet the challenge. When doing a network interrupt, you rarely have time to go to the typewriter; you usually ad lib. Most of the time, it is a matter of getting in position and getting going, often without knowing what is to follow or how long you'll be there.

The day President Reagan was shot, Richard Hunt told me to get in the position and go on the air. When I went to the camera in the news room with which we can go on immediately, two NBC executives were discussing whether we were to go on from Washington or New York. I said to them over and over again, "Break in, break in, break in." The point was to get on the air. CBS and ABC were on. We were not.

I started at 2:38 p.m., and I did not know how long I would be there. I didn't know Hinckley's first name, but during a lull Sumner Weener, the editor on the desk, told me. When I got there, there was no one else in position, no one set up in Washington, which was the reason we went on from New York. We relied on the wire service copy which was handed to me as quickly as possible. It was an unorganized day. I sat on two telephone directories because the chair in the studio wasn't high enough. Jim O'Gorman, an experienced floor manager and a friend, came to the news room on his own, got those telephone directories, and a make-up artist, and kept people from walking between the camera and me. When the producer, Joe Angotti, arrived, my communication with him was relayed through Jim Plante, who was standing next to me holding a telephone to Joe. Later in the afternoon, Joe said to me, "We're going to handle this from Washington. We don't need you any longer." I sat there because I wanted to hear what was said from

Washington, and I suddenly heard myself being cued back on to the air and I stayed there until 6:30.

At a time like that you have to think fast, but there are people around who want to help, like my secretary then, Katherine Meehan, now Katherine Ryan. I asked her for the World Almanac, the 25th Amendment to the Constitution, because that governs the transfer of power if the President has been incapacitated. I asked someone to telephone my wife and tell her I was on the air, but I gave our London telephone number instead of the New York number. The woman who answered naturally denied that she was Mrs. Newman. By chance, my wife had the television on and was watching.

There's a tremendous feeling of satisfaction in doing the job well. In my first job in the news business with INS when I asked the boss for a raise, he changed the subject, and I've never forgotten what he told me. He said, "Anybody in the news business must have a great fund of miscellaneous information." I think it's true, but because of the teleprompter and because of the specializing among the reporters, a great many people in the business now are never called on to ad lib, so they never find out whether they can do it, which I think is too bad. The first ad libbing I did for NBC was at the funeral of King George VI. It seemed to me that I was ad libbing forever. I suppose it was a few minutes. Somebody in New York, I think it was Joe Meyers, listened and said, "This man can ad lib," which was important to me later on.

I was in the studio for days when Martin Luther King, Jr., was killed, when Robert Kennedy was killed. I felt as though I were living there. The training and experience of working in many places is invaluable. There are times when you have to be ready to call on information you didn't even think you had. You never know when, but you can bet the time will come when you will need it.

My career didn't progress steadily upward. When it comes to assignments, the question is, are you better off spreading yourself around or having one, more lucrative

assignment. You may be fragmented and you do not get the plum, the single anchor Nightly News, but that's confining. I'm not saying it's anything I would have gotten anyway. I took my turn doing it from time to time. But somehow there's more prestige associated with it.

Reuven Frank had a good deal to do with many of the documentaries I did, either directly, or because he was in charge generally. But I think I have worked on more documentaries than anybody else in the business, and it was with Reuven, Al Perlmutter, Dick Wald, Nigel Ryan and Les Crystal. "Pensions: The Broken Promise" was highly acclaimed, aroused a good deal of controversy, and became a Fairness Doctrine case. I was proud of that one. "Fair Trial—Free Press" was a good program about the conflict between the First and Fifth Amendments. "A Soviet/American Debate" was a tricky one we did at Georgetown University, a debate between two Americans and two Soviet citizens about human rights.

In 1961, when I returned to this country, NBC assigned me to a regular debate program, "The Nation's Future," produced by Lucy Jarvis. We went on live on Saturday night, which is now hard to believe. One of the debates was between Alexei Adzhubei, Khrushchev's son-in-law, editor of *Pravda*, and Pierre Salinger, with one other man on each side. I think there is a good deal to be said for such a program, but, of course, I don't meet the payroll.

The subject of "I Want It All Now" was life in Marin County, California, which seemed to us to be highly sybaritic, all summed up in the title Joe DeCola, the producer, gave it. It was not admired very widely in Marin County, and the NBC San Francisco station didn't like it. They showed it in advance of its air time to local news people so that the morning of the day that the show was going on, there was an unfavorable story in the San Francisco paper. My wife and I laughed later because we have very close friends in San Francisco, and about six months after the show went on, they said, "We want you to know that it is now safe for *us* to go to Marin County again."

I've done a number of programs for NBC about drugs, and the most important one probably was "Reading, Writing, and Reefer," produced by Bob Rogers (who also produced "Fair Trial—Free Press"), about marijuana use among young people, children. I have rarely worked on a program that shook me more than that one did. I found it frightening, and depressing. That program was so effective that NBC put it on a second time at a time when schools could show it, and gave anyone who wanted it permission to tape it and use it. We received a tremendous amount of mail on that program from parents, policemen, chiefs of police, from teachers. Those that made the greatest impression on me were written by parents who said their children watched because it was on television. They had never been able to get through to them before on the subject. In some of those letters you could see where the ink had been stained by tears. When something like that happens, you know you have done a good thing.

I have never believed that having an hour of news in itself was necessarily desirable. News could have more time on the air, yes, but I don't necessarily believe that it should take the form of a one-hour program. I think the time ought to be used experimentally in a variety of ways until we see what works best.

In the summer of 1960, I filled in for Chet Huntley on "Chet Huntley Reporting." It was an election year, and I was called back from Paris to help. Reuven was the Executive Producer, George Murray was the Producer, and Reuven and I often had healthy disagreements, not about whether we ought to do a particular story but about its significance and how it ought to be done. Reuven was a newspaper man, but television was his metier, made to order for him, because he was one of the first people to understand that television was not the same as newspapers, that the story has to be told in a different way. In the early days, when Reuven and Ted Mills produced the series "Background," we were all learning. Reuven learned quickly. He had his own ideas and could see how other people's ideas could be adapted. Chet and David had a great deal to do with the tremendous success of "The Huntley/Brinkley Report," but I think it can be argued that Reuven had as much to do with that as anybody.

Then Julian Goodman and Reuven brought in Dick Wald, whom I had known before when he was with *The Herald Tribune*. When NBC hired Gerald and Betty Ford, and Henry Kissinger, Dick didn't think it was a very good idea, and he was absolutely right. You have no business hiring people you may have to be reporting on.

In the early days, I think Joe Meyers set the tone with his high standards of accuracy and correctness for the news department. Joe was intelligent and could not be fooled at all. He was a good guy, but he liked to send out toughly-worded messages: heads will roll, winds will howl, that kind of message. I was just a stringer, but when he heard that I had had articles accepted by *Punch*, which was very unusual for an American in those days, that mattered to him. Here was someone who could write. He had great respect for the ability to use words clearly, succinctly, and, if possible, with flair.

There were many good writers at NBC. Bob McCormick had a particular knack for writing for radio. You had to learn in this business that you couldn't write the way you did for the wire service. I was lucky to have worked for Sevareid, a very good teacher. I wish the difference between writing for radio and the newspapers were sufficiently understood. It often is not. It isn't just a matter of not writing long, convoluted sentences for the air. It is also not writing everything in the same way, not using tired words.

Some words are so tired, they're useless; *controversial, massive, meanwhile,* can all be tossed aside. It isn't their fault. *Incredible.* The word *incredible* is being destroyed before our eyes. If it means anything now, it means slightly interesting. We have to be careful not to overuse words. When you are on the air, the idea is not simply to emit a sound that can be recognized as having something to do with news. The idea is to communicate information, to get something across. To do that you must choose words with some care, with some discrimination, some sense of proportion, which means that you have to leave out a great deal. In the nature of things in wire service work, a tremendous number of stories are written the same way. They have to be straight reporting. On the air you're much more free to back into stories, get at them sideways, to put them in a different order, and that ought to be used.

I've been approached by a number of institutions of higher learning, but I would not like to teach. I once filled in for two days for Elie Abel at Columbia. I've been tempted because one feels perhaps one has a duty, but apart from that, no.

I have published three books: one, a comic novel, *Sunday Punch*; two about language, *Strictly Speaking* and *A Civil Tongue*, for which I did at least some of the work on NBC's time, and certainly gathered a great deal of material while I was on NBC's payroll. They were very successful, best sellers. I didn't expect they would be. I suppose everybody cherishes a hope or a dream that a book will be a great success, but when it comes along, it's tremendously satisfying and surprising. When you actually see your name on the best-seller list, the first time, it's a tremendous thrill. Then you begin to become angry with the publisher because he hasn't printed enough copies, and some store says it doesn't have them in stock.

I was ready to retire, but I was not entirely ready for the amount of work that I would be asked to do after I left NBC. I write a column for King Features, and I lecture a great deal. Once you become prominent in television, you are asked to lecture. In my case, the number of invitations was multiplied by my books. Then I do television sometimes, cable, PBS, and sometimes NBC as well.

What is my wish for NBC's 60th birthday? I have many friends there, many kind, good people and I wish them well. I truly do. Not only in news; people in other departments have been kind to me as well. I worked with Sports, and on "Saturday Night Live." And I always feel when I come back here that I am among friends.

October 10, 1985

Harry Coyle is the most respected sports director in broadcasting. He has won many distinguished awards, including two Emmys—the first sports director so honored. His Pioneer Award from the Directors Guild of America was only the second in the Guild's long history. Film great D.W. Griffith took the first.

Harry Coyle

"There's nothing obvious about baseball. A little, teeny ball, thrown at 90 miles an hour, being hit, taking three seconds to go from home to third to first, being caught...runners going around scoring...simultaneous action. You can't take one camera and follow the action. You could cover football and basketball with one camera, but not baseball. That's why we say it's a director's sport."

I'm Coordinating Producer of Baseball and a TV Director. Mike Weisman is Executive Producer for Sports, and, under him, there are producers in charge of each sport. Basically, my career has been that of a TV Director, but this is my fourth season as a Coordinating Producer, and I spend most of my time in that role.

In the early days, being a director was like being a whole ball of wax; there weren't a lot of them. I started with DuMont and worked on everything, first as part of a crew then as a director. That was the beginning of television and nobody specialized. On a freelance basis, I did the 1947 World Series between the Brooklyn Dodgers and the Yankees for NBC. That was the *first* televised broadcast of a World Series.

I was born in Ridgewood and grew up in Paterson, New Jersey. I played a little baseball in high school. Then in the late thirties, I went to New Jersey State Teachers College, and worked nights at Wright Aeronautical.

When World War II erupted, I became a pilot in the Air Force and went to Europe as commander of a B-24 bomber. I was with the Eighth Air Force and flew 35 bombing missions over Germany. After all the combat, I was not ready for an office job when I came back. My buddy, Bob Jamison, was 4-F and hadn't gone to war. He worked for The Allen B. DuMont Television Lab in Passaic, New Jersey, where they built television sets. They had a TV station in New York, experimental, not commercial, as all TV stations were during the war. When I came out of the service, Bob told me I could work for DuMont. By that time, television had call letters; DuMont had Channel 5, NBC had Channel 4, and CBS had Channel 2. I went with Channel 5 on a crew as a cable pusher. In those days, it was an expansion industry and advancement was very fast. I became a so-called director in about a year and a half. Then, you could choose your own vocation, your own profession, keep your nose clean and just ride along. At first, I did a little of everything. I did Johnny Olson's "Rumpus Room," a ladies' participation show. I did "Twenty Questions." And I did the sports. I liked sports, and I chose it because I felt it would be the kind of show to go on continuously, with no highs and lows. There would always be sports shows on television through depressions and booms, through country breakdowns and successes. Thank God, I was right!

It had its financial advantages. In those days, a guy would go on the air for four weeks with a so-called dramatic show and receive a nominal amount of money. I'd do a baseball game or a football game in two days and make almost as much. I felt it was going to be solid. The only sets on the market at first were 7-inch sets, then 10-inch RCA sets and DuMont 12-inch sets, and they were all in bars; almost nobody had them at home. The Joe Louis fights, the Army-Navy game, and the World Series sold television sets. The sale of TV sets went along normally, until after the World Series was televised in 1947. Then the demand for sets went crazy. No matter what anybody tells you, I was there. Sports were the main reason television got off the floor.

NBC was the prime network, a class outfit, and I can say that without prejudice because I wasn't working for them then. They didn't televise baseball in its first two years—DuMont televised the Yankees locally. The rights to the World Series in 1947 were owned by the Mutual Radio Network, which was very heavy in sports. They sold those rights to the Gillette Razor people who hired NBC to do the World Series. Then NBC hired DuMont to make the pickup. The "Cavalcade of Sports," and most everything Gillette did, was on NBC. Gillette demanded the NBC network, but they didn't believe their crews had enough experience, so they used the local pickups. That's how I got involved.

Equipment then was very primitive compared to today's sophisticated electronic gadgetry. Today, we do a World Series with 16 cameras, a blimp, zoomar lenses, equipment for visual effects, instant replay, and as many as 12 tape machines. (I was one of the first to use zoomar lenses.) We have computers for special effects or still pictures; we go all over the world via satellite, to the complete NBC network of some 200 stations in the United States, as well as Europe and Japan. An average crew is over 100 people, and NBC will have 250 people on the site including clients, sales people, and station affiliates.

The original World Series was done by a crew of seven people without zoomar lens or tape, and only three cameras, two at first base and one at home plate, very high home. A fourth camera did live commercials. We made a horrendous error once and showed a twist-open razor which would not open. After that, Gillette

ordered that all commercials be on film.

In the early days, we were the poor kids on the block. We didn't have any power; it was all experimental. This isn't saying anything that isn't known by now. The press hated us when we began showing baseball on TV because it meant they could not build up a game in their news reports. A writer could leave the game in the 6th inning, and write whatever he wanted after just looking at the box score. There was a rough feeling toward the TV boys because we stole the glamour of the press event, though we did not have credentials or pins, and we weren't allowed in the press box.

When we first worked at Yankee Stadium, we had a hanging cage at first base where we stood and held cameras over our heads to catch the good light. We finally asked for a room. They put a door upstairs on the top deck over an opening between an elevator shaft and the men's room, and that was our control room. In a double header, men would line up to go into the men's room, and those who couldn't wait sent a stream under the door toward us. They raised the floor but that didn't take the smell away. In those early days, we weren't concerned with finesse. Our first worry was to keep the equipment going so we could stay on the air. We felt the equipment had a brain because every time we said "We're on," one camera would fail, which meant a third of our cameras gone; or the microwave at the Empire State would go down. Then we'd worry about the coverage and just try to cover the play. It was very crude.

I could never have broken into NBC without Tom Gallery. At DuMont, we had a lower level of TV strategy than the people at NBC, the class network, the high rider in the early days. ABC-TV wasn't even heard of. CBS was there, but NBC had the great shows, Milton Berle and "Victory at Sea" and all the top sports events. Tom Gallery is a man with a tremendous, tremendous background. Very famous. He was a sports promoter on the West Coast; he sent out Red Grange in the first pro-football, became General Manager and head of the New York Yankees with Dan Topping, and ran the Brooklyn Dodger Football Club. He went from the Yankees to DuMont as Sales head and Sports head, where I worked for him. When he moved to NBC, he took me with him. In those days, the Sports Department was part of the News Department, but the news dominated.

In 1955, there were four in the NBC Sports Department: Tom Gallery, Lindsey Nelson, his assistant, an announcer in town named Perry Smith, who was Producer and ran the office, and I was the TV Director. There were also two girls in the office. Today, there are about 170 people in the Sports Department. I think the burst came in the sixties and it just kept growing and growing.

Since that first World Series telecast in 1947, I have done 32 Series, 12 NCAA Basketball Championships, 12 or 13 World Series of Golf. I did The U.S. Open about eight or nine times, and the Rose Bowl for almost 30 years. I've received most of my Emmys for baseball. NBC won Emmys in 1975, in 1978, and another one in 1980. The Director's Guild gave me the Pioneer Award. There have only been two and I'm very honored to say the other was given to D.W. Griffith. The Emmy which really made me feel good was the one given in 1978, because I received that as a Director. It was not for the show in general, but for me, Harry Coyle, nobody else. After only three, they stopped giving that award, so I'm extremely proud of that one, and I have it in a special room at home. People in production at NBC, CBS and all the others may want to win one once in their career. It's nice to win 12 or 13, but with winning one, you've reached the ultimate in awards. It puts you on a certain level in your own mind.

I worked in unexplored areas back in the forties covering the World Series games. There were no guidelines, but I can't say I did it myself. The greatest innovators were the boys in that first TV. We invented everything. We achieved a split screen by putting an ordinary cardboard cone, like a thread spool, over a lens, making a little round spot in the corner, then superimposing that over another camera. It looked silly, but that's how we did it. We put four lenses on a turret, split a turret halfway and split another one halfway and got a split screen.

I've also taken ideas from local stations, the affiliates; the backbone of television. One of the fallacies about television is that people around the country think that network personnel look down on local operations. In sports, we certainly don't. When I go around the country to do our shows, I get into the hotel and turn on the local stuff to see if I can steal any ideas. I'm not ashamed to admit it because local stations are a part of the family. They supply the people. Very few people start in New York. Top people work up through the local stations.

You ask about my heroes along the way, and I don't want to slight anybody. I've had the privilege of working with almost everybody, and they've shown greatness all the way through. I even worked with Ted Husing, and there were many others. I worked a lot with Dennis James on wrestling at DuMont. And Tom Slater, a great guy, whom nobody knows today. The first big-time announcer to impress me was Mel Allen. We worked together on the Rose Bowl, the World Series and the New York Yankees.

That started a stream of giants like Russ Hodges, Curt Gowdy, Lindsey Nelson. Today there's Al Maguire, Joe Garagiola, Vin Scully, Merlin Olsen. Mel dominated my thinking in the early days. He was so good; he had a great, great voice, but so did a lot of others. There are many fine announcers today: Tony Kubek and the young guys coming up, like Costas.

Beside the changes in equipment, as we went along we acquired knowledge about what made television exciting. We were helped as much by letters from the public as by our own ideas. In the early days, they wrote letters like mad. Today a show for 30 million people might bring 10 letters. Then you would do a show watched by 1,200 people and receive 100 letters. People were a real part of it. To this day, the public is not aware of how they have molded television. If they'd only realize their power and write more! They asked questions like, "Why are you shooting this so tight? Why don't you make it wider?" "Why do you give us this kind of shot?" "Why does the announcer talk about this? We'd rather hear that." Announcers came to TV from radio, where they had talked a lot, and they refused to subjugate themselves to pictures which told the story better than their words. They wanted to remain the stars they had been in radio. One problem was simulcast, which meant the radio announcer did both radio and the TV audio.

I'm very proud and pleased to have been involved in the development of the outfield camera. There's a story behind my idea. I grew up in Paterson near a softball park. In those days, there was only one umpire in a softball game, and he stood behind the pitcher. I remembered that and thought, what a great place for a picture. We couldn't put a camera there, but we could simulate it by putting a camera with the right cable lens in center field. It was tremendously well received. I have a book of press releases and stories about how people went crazy over it. Today it's a staple, basic shot in every telecast of baseball.

Then came tape and color. After them, the big thing was instant replay, which seemed to open up the whole ball of wax for advancement in sports. From the instant replay, we went to chyron and visual electronics and all the other special effects.

There is a danger that the director who calls the shots with so many possible capabilities will lose some of the excitement of the game. I think that's the biggest problem a new director has today. The main reason we're out there is to tell the story, to report the ball game. We are not there to tell how many cameras we've got, or how we're going to spin the picture. How much he can use these gimmicks without interfering with coverage will be the real test of a good director. NBC baseball has a fine reputation because our first effort is to show the play, then think about all the electronics.

My World War II experience piloting those bombers did help. I had a crew of 10; we had head sets, and worked on a split-second operation exactly the way the original crews in TV did. I was decorated in combat with the Distinguished Flying Cross, but I feel I wasn't exceptionally brave, because as a pilot I had so much to do on a bomber I couldn't think about being scared. All the poor gunners had to do was sit there and think. I say they are the heroes. Traveling all over the world for the Air Force was no different from traveling all over the world for NBC.

To reach a high level in television production, you've got to have a natural flair for the business and a natural ability. I feel that it's a God-given quality, not a developed quality. From the first minute I sat in a director's chair, I felt comfortable. I'm not saying I'm a genius; I just felt comfortable. I've never had to ask, "What am I going to do next?" Worrying about the 50 million people out there would drive you up the wall. A director must learn that if he's doing a one-minute spot, or a World Series, he's got to attack it the same way. I'm not implying there's pressure, but the ego is a big factor with anybody. If you make a mistake in front of 100,000 people, it's not like making a mistake in front of 50 million. If you're a professional, that might enter your mind as you're waiting to go on the air. Once you hit the air, I don't think you can worry about it.

The most difficult major sport to televise is baseball. We have a saying in the business that basketball and football are a cameraman's sports and baseball is a director's sport. In football, all the men are together, going one way. It's all there in front of you and the ball is big. Basketball is the most obvious sport, confined to a small area, a great big ball, five big men on each side, going back and forth.

There's nothing obvious about baseball. A little, teeny ball, thrown at 90 miles an hour, being hit, taking three seconds to go from home to third to first, being caught, or flying in the outfield or on the ground, runners going around scoring, nothing obvious, simultaneous action. Is the man going to run at first base, is it going to be a bunt? You can't take one camera and follow the action. You could cover football and basketball with one camera, but not baseball. That's why we say it's a director's sport.

NBC Sports did a football game without announcers a few years ago. It was innovative, but it didn't get a true test because the effort to get the sound of the action on the field was too great and it defeated itself. It proved to me that announcers are needed, but that's proven every time I sit in the stands by myself without the announcer. I mean it's an entirely different ball game. Although these days, I spend the least possible amount of my time in stadiums!

I must finish by saying that I consider Art Watson one of the finest executives I have ever worked for. Not only is he a top executive, but he is a gentleman. He is one of the reasons I have such high hopes for NBC in the years ahead.

My 60th birthday wish for NBC is to achieve the dominance of the industry they had in the beginning. They're leading up to it, and I hope it's the start of an era that will send NBC soaring. NBC's prime time didn't do so well for a few years, but NBC's sports has always been tops. Everybody at NBC is a fighter, and so are all our stations and affiliates. NBC is coming back strong, *strong*. Let that be the beginning of a new era which will last for a long time.

August 27, 1985

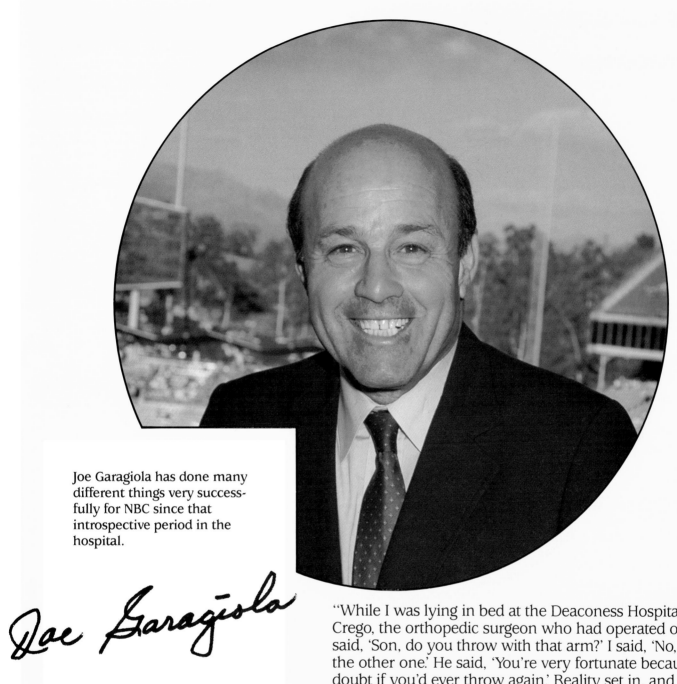

Joe Garagiola has done many different things very successfully for NBC since that introspective period in the hospital.

Joe Garagiola

"While I was lying in bed at the Deaconess Hospital, Dr. Crego, the orthopedic surgeon who had operated on me, said, 'Son, do you throw with that arm?' I said, 'No, I use the other one.' He said, 'You're very fortunate because...I doubt if you'd ever throw again.' Reality set in, and I told myself, hey, I can't play baseball forever, and when I can't, what will I be able to do?"

I grew up in a landmark section of St. Louis, Missouri, permanently etched in St. Louis' history as "The Hill," an Italian neighborhood. In fact, I wonder where I learned to speak English because when I first went to school, I spoke Italian; that's all we spoke at home.

Frank Crespi of the Cardinals lived on The Hill for a while. Jack Juclich of the Pittsburgh Pirates lived pretty close to The Hill, but I was the first big leaguer actually born and raised there. Yogi Berra came to the big leagues in 1947, but his older brother, Lefty, who could *really* hit, was our big hero. We had other heroes growing up, good ball players who lived on The Hill, but who never had the opportunity to go even to the minor leagues because it was tough to convince our fathers we could get paid for playing baseball. We never had equipment. Our clothes were hand-me-downs, and our fathers wouldn't buy us shoes with nails or spikes sticking out of them because we couldn't wear those to church.

I remember when I signed my first professional baseball contract, the biggest thrill I had was asking for a $500 bonus from the Cardinals, which was like the millions of dollars ball players get today. Mr. [Branch] Rickey just about went through the ceiling. He screamed, "What are you going to do with all that money?!," and scared my brother and me half to death. I asked for $500 because that's what Pop owed on our house, and I'll never forget giving him that check, which meant the house was his.

My mother went to only one baseball game in her life, a game in which the people from the neighborhood had a special night for me at the ball park on September 5, 1946. They collected money and presented me with a Nash Rambler. I didn't even know how to drive!

My mother hardly ever left The Hill. She went downtown twice a year to register as an alien. (My father became a naturalized citizen.) But when she went to that night game at the ball park and saw the lights on, she wanted to know who was going to pay for all the electricity. My brother told her the 30,000 people in the stands had paid at least $1 a piece to come in, and she said, "Then the guys who own it can afford it." My father went to two games, that one and one other. They knew that I, as a professional baseball player, was doing something different, but they never really understood, which is sad. It really got to me.

Yet you can turn it around and see another side of it. A couple of years ago, when Tony Kubek and I did the College World Series, I remember a kid on the Texas team whose father wanted him to be a big leaguer, and his father built a batting cage in the basement of his house for him. Tony and I thought that was wonderful. In this great country of ours, the rich kid may have a little better start than the poor kid, but everybody's in the race. Persistence helps.

Yogi's father didn't know third base from the coach's box, and yet Yogi ended up in the Hall of Fame. In this country you have a chance, you are given an opportunity. I preach that all the time, because I know what happened to Yogi, and I know what happened to me. My father never took me aside and said you have to hold your elbows away from your body when you swing a bat. We just went out and *played*, and the results speak for themselves.

I was a major-league ball player for nine years, from 1946 through 1954, first with the Cardinals, then the Pittsburgh Pirates, the Chicago Cubs, and the New York Giants, the old Giants.

In the 1946 World Series, my rookie season with the Cardinals, I had a .316 batting average, 4 RBI's, and a four-hit game that tied a World Series record for most hits in a single game. It is almost unfortunate to win a pennant and play in a World Series your first year, because you never really appreciate it. I was 20 years old, just out of the Army. World War II was over, and like other young guys, I felt that Eisenhower, and MacArthur, and I, had won the war. I was really on top of it. I went into the big leagues, and I played against guys whose pictures I collected on bubble gum cards.

I had a severe injury in 1950 when I had a collision at first base with Jackie Robinson. It was probably the best start I ever had; I was hitting .356 the end of May. The first of June when we played the Dodgers, Preacher

Roe was pitching for the Dodgers, and Eddie Dyer, our manager, told me I was going to start. My first time up, with a man on first and second, I bunted the ball. It was a rainy night. Robinson, playing second base, came over to cover first. The throw was low, and he stretched out on the ground to reach for the ball and clipped me across the shins. I landed hard on my shoulder, and suffered a shoulder separation and cracked ribs. After an operation I was out most of the year. I came back in September but couldn't do anything.

While I was lying in bed at the Deaconess Hospital, Dr. Crego, the orthopedic surgeon who had operated on me, said, "Son, do you throw with that arm?" I said, "No, I use the other one." He said, "You're very fortunate, because if it had been that arm, I doubt if you'd ever throw again." Reality set in, and I told myself, hey, I can't play baseball forever, and when I can't, what will I be able to do?

That was 1950, and Gabby Street and Harry Caray did the games on radio here in St. Louis. Gabby Street was friendly on the train trips. Harry Caray encouraged me, and that started me thinking about his kind of job, but not too seriously. I was traded to the Pirates first, then to the Chicago Cubs. I was only making $12,000 a year, and after maintaining a house in Pittsburgh or in Chicago, while still living in St. Louis, I never had any money left at the end of the year. I didn't think that was the way it should work. I made speeches, as all ball players did in those days, at Cub Scout banquets, men's clubs, and groups like that.

Then I made one key appearance, a dinner honoring Stan Musial, where I was asked to be Master of Ceremonies. Afterwards, a man named Al Fleishman said, "I've never seen you before, but if you want to work when you're through with baseball, I'd be very interested in you." So I filed that, thinking it was nice, but I didn't know who he was, or whom he worked for.

Then I was traded for the third time, to the fourth team, the Giants. The first time you're traded, you think the other team made a mistake. The second time you say this is a second chance. But when you're traded the third time, you better take a good look at yourself. I was 28 years old. I finally said to myself, I'm not going anywhere. Then, Al Fleishman came back into the picture. I learned that he headed the company which handled the P.R. accounts for Anheuser-Busch. I went to see him.

Ultimately, Anheuser-Busch was accused of tampering. I was subpoenaed to testify in Washington, and that's how I got my first national attention. When I was on the stand, Senator Edwin Johnson of Colorado asked what would happen if Anheuser-Busch came to Roy Campanella and said, "Put down your glove. We'll give you a job." I said, "You can't compare me to Campanella. I'm a .250 hitter." And that statement got all kinds of publicity.

Harry Caray kept encouraging me. I started doing half-time football scores on KMOX. The next spring I did color in St. Louis for the Cardinal games, and I had a tough time. Al Fleishman and Dick Meyer, Anheuser-Busch Vice President, were my backers, and said, "Hey, give the guy a chance." As a third-string catcher I really had no name, like a Stan Musial, or Enos Slaughter, or Red Schoendienst.

A lot of people say I am somewhat of a pioneer in broadcasting regarding the former athlete in the booth. If I am, I'm a pioneer for third-string catchers. Bob Uecker came way after, but it's usually the marquee guy like Sandy Koufax, or Joe Namath in football, who gets the job. Al Fleishman convinced me that people were more interested in *what* I said, not *how* I said it. That encouraged me and bought me time to improve how I talked about the game.

That's how I got started. I still did a lot of banquets. A microphone can't do anything to me that hasn't happened to me on the banquet circuit. At one banquet, after five or ten minutes with no reaction, I looked at the program and discovered that I was advertised as Joe Giardello, the boxer. Everybody expected fight stories. Another time, I made a speech to deaf mutes. Nobody told me that they were, and *that* was an experience!

The way I got started with NBC is interesting. When they were looking for a Game of the Week broadcaster (I was told this story), it was a choice between Ted Williams and me. The network tried repeatedly to reach Williams, but they couldn't. Finally, Tom Gallery, Sports Director at NBC, who had heard me in St. Louis, said, "I know if I tell the affiliates I got Ted Williams, they'll be ecstatic, but if you give this unknown kid a chance, he'll do the job." He said he would have to sell me. And he did. He gave me my start with baseball broadcasting.

237

Tom Gallery had the guts (that's what it took) to say he believed in me. I'll never forget it; I'll always be indebted to him. It's easy for the network to say they knew all along. That's garbage, they didn't know all along. Tom convinced the network powers-that-be to take a chance, and they don't like to take too many chances.

The TV talk-show circuit began for me in a number of different ways. My book, *Baseball Is a Funny Game*, opened many of those doors. Writing a book was a new experience. I always felt, and couldn't understand why, the authors of baseball books kept writing about how to make the double play, how to throw the curve ball and so on. People 40 years old couldn't care less. They want to know what a catcher says to the pitcher, what the players say to the umpires, and what happens in the clubhouse.

Then the New York writers asked me to do their dinner, and a neighbor of Jack Paar's was in the audience. The neighbor told Paar, "Hey, there's this bald-headed baseball player, you got to get him on your show." In those days, Paar's show was real hot, but he was leery of sports people, and he knew very little about baseball. Jack realized that this must be the guy Tom O'Malley (Paar's talent coordinator) had been trying to get him to have on the show. (Jack is a good friend now, we visit him all the time.) Once I did "The Jack Paar Show" the floodgates opened, and I've been on the Carson show more times than I had hits in the big leagues. I've hosted the "Tonight" and the "Today" shows, and game shows.

I began appearing on "Today" in 1960. I remember being on with Jack Lescoulie when the Pirates beat the Yankees in the World Series. When Shad Northshield was producer, he put me on after my book was published. He introduced me to Dave Garroway. I stood there, a scared kid in my best Sears Roebuck suit, and Garroway said, "I don't know anything about baseball. Let Lescoulie interview him. I don't want to talk to him."

And I said to myself, good God, what am I into? When Garroway walked away, Northshield said, "Look, there's only time for two questions: what does a catcher say to a pitcher, and what do players say to umpires when thrown out of games, with a commercial in between. You just keep going, keep going, don't let him back in." That was Northshield. I did exactly what he said, and Garroway was great after that. He asked me to stay on to repeat the hour. Northshield put me on as a once-a-week regular, and when John Chancellor had the show, I was a regular guest, almost a fixture.

Al Morgan asked me to come on "Today" as a regular while I was doing Yankee games. I could only be on three times a week. I was also doing "Sale of the Century," a game show. I finally decided to give up broadcasting the Yankee games. When Stuart Schulberg became producer of the "Today" show, he was great to me, put me in other areas besides sports. I'd ask him, "Stuart, what are you doing to me?" He'd say, "You're going to be all right." I reviewed the play, "Hair." I interviewed Martin Mayer when he wrote his big, thick book, *The Lawyers*, and I interviewed poet Marianne Moore. I became a regular with Hugh Downs, Frank McGee, and Barbara Walters.

To me, the "Today" show was like postgraduate work in college, great on-the-job learning and training. Even now, I use my "Today" show habits in interviews. We did not have the luxury of asking, "How have you been, what are you doing?" We had to go right to the jugular.

I still have great love for the "Today" show, and if they called me right now, and said, "Joe, can you get on a plane and do the show?" I'd say, "I'll be there." I owe it that kind of loyalty. But I found, after 35 years of marriage, it was either the show or my family. There was no choice; my family comes first. I adjusted to the unusual hours—up 3:30, 4 o'clock in the morning, going to bed early, 9:00, 9:30 p.m.—but it's difficult when you have kids growing up. The kids tried to be quiet, my wife tried to keep the television down, but it was hard to sleep. After the show was over at 9 o'clock in the morning, I had to work on the next day's show until 2:30 or 3 o'clock. When I'd get home, I'd be pretty tired, still have to do some things, and try to have dinner with my family around 5:30, 6 o'clock. After you've been up over 12 hours, you're not very bright, or crisp at conversation.

Social life from Monday through Friday—forget it. I'd say to my wife, "We'll go out Friday night, 'cause I can sleep late Saturday." Then, on Friday night, I'd say, "We'll go out tomorrow night because I can sleep late Sunday. I'll go to 5 o'clock Mass." Saturday night when I'd take her out to dinner, my mind was on the book, or whatever was coming up Monday. I was not a part of family life. I felt my wife and I were drifting away from each other only because I was going down one road, and she was going down another.

Being part of the "Today" show is very heady wine. When Bryant Gumbel asked me about the pitfalls of doing it (Gene Shalit did, too), I told him to keep in mind: it's the show, it's not you. When I was on that show, the phone in my office rang off the hook. It wasn't unusual to have the White House, a Senator or some powerful person call. I was invited to state dinners, and premieres. When I left the show, I thought it would go off the air. How could it possibly stay on the air without me? It did, but the invitations stopped. And I thought, gee, I'm still the same guy. You really have to put it in focus. It's a marvelous show, but its high mortality rate is understandable. People still ask me why I left it. They don't realize that the most important thing in my life is my family.

"The Baseball World of Joe Garagiola" was a pre-game show. It bothers me that people think a pre-game show is nothing more than a vehicle to sell commercials before the big event. We're proud of the Peabody Award one of those programs won because, in working on it, you could create something interesting. It was a prison show; baseball was just the backdrop. It was the story of Gates Brown, who happened to be a baseball player for the Detroit Tigers, how he overcame being in prison and what it was like in prison. We showed how they doctor infields, how they throw a spitball, how they steal signals, not just how they put their fingers on the ball

to make it curve. We took pre-game shows out of "Lower Slobovia," and elevated them.

Our theory was simple. We took three or four minutes, called "hunkers," made them the most interesting pieces we could think of, and surrounded them with today's game. A big show for me was the one about the lady umpire. We didn't just take a film clip. For two days we followed her around, listened to people heckle her and saw some of the emotional rides she had to take.

My emotions show, and that can make some interviews very interesting. The Archie Bunker image really took a beating when we took a picture of the pre-game show crew. There I was with my Producer, Ginny Seipt, my Associate Producers, Carla Engelman and Linda Johnson, and the rest. My staff was five women, and I said "You guys are ruining my image!" But, you see, these gals did the best job. Some people will say the word "gals" is sexist. Baloney, spumoni! I know that they did the best job, and that's why they were there. It was so funny when I saw the picture. There I was, old Archie Bunker surrounded by a harem.

I've had other mentors besides Tom Gallery. Bob Wogan brought me into radio, and Marion Stephenson was very strong, very honest. I could take problems to her. She didn't tell me what I wanted to hear, sometimes it would hurt a little, but, I must say, she was almost always right. She had her finger on the pulse of the radio affiliates. Carl Lindemann, very good. Arthur Watson is my boss now, and he and I go back to the days when he was in Cleveland. One of my "things" about being at NBC is, when they mention a particular person or a city, chances are I've made a speech, or I've done promos in that town.

Many times in my life I've needed what I call a "confidence shove." Somebody has got to say, "Hey, do it. Be yourself." My wife is my best bet for that confidence shove. But it all boils down to getting a chance. A lot of people at NBC gave me the chance.

There are other people I don't want to leave out. Craig Fischer put me on the show, "Sunday." I worked with Bud Grant, then head of daytime programming, and Larry White, former Vice President of Programming, at the game shows. I remember the day I did a commercial on tape; two days later it showed up on the screen, and I'd blown a line, made the famous blooper, and I had to go and apologize. I thought, oh, man, they're going to fire me now. But Larry White and those guys hung in there. It was so good working with them.

I remember when I told Julian Goodman and Bill McAndrew that I was going to leave to broadcast the Yankee games. They sat me down and said, "Don't leave. We're going to get baseball back. Just stay right here, be patient." When I told NBC I was going to leave the "Today" show, Julian was President of the company, and he said to me, "Don't say anything for another week. Think about it. Let's talk about it." Every time I see him I kid him, "Julian, I'm thinking about coming back to the 'Today' show," and he always laughs. Now there's a beautiful guy! When you talk about networks, sometimes it's very impersonal, but it isn't at NBC.

I have so many wishes for NBC's 60th birthday! I wish that NBC's people would get back just one tenth of the happiness they have given me. When I tell somebody I work for NBC, it says a lot. Sixty years is a long time, but the world needs at least another 60 years of NBC.

October 15, 1985

Bill Cosby co-starred in NBC's "I Spy" from 1965 to 1968. The first "Bill Cosby Show" came next, then a series of innovative specials. With "The Cosby Show" in 1984-85, there came the ultimate success of being Number One.

"We're working to make the show better for the people.... Those numbers don't have feelings, but there are feelings behind all those numbers. When I'm in the street, and a woman comes up to me and says, 'Very seldom do we talk to each other in our family, but on Thursday night at eight o'clock, we all sit around the television.' Or some woman tells me she and her husband became more romantic again after watching how Cliff and Clair Huxtable feel about each other. In that 62 share in Detroit, there's *one* family that comes together to watch the show. That means that there are feelings."

I was born in Germantown, Philadelphia, where, after finishing high school, I went into the Navy. I found I had to adhere to certain rules. The Navy was in charge of my life. When I was living with my parents, I was very good at not adhering to rules. I'd been told early on by my teachers that I had a good mind and, like so many kids, that I wasn't working up to capacity. I'd been in the Navy for all of two weeks when I knew I could be a wonderful student. I realized that if I had, earlier in my life, gotten a formal education, paid more attention to doing what people suggested—using my mind to become a better student—that I could have been more in charge of what I wanted to do, rather than doing what I was told by other people. Inner-directed.

There was nothing boring about the Navy. It was quite exciting. It was a good experience. I put in three years, eleven months and two weeks not wanting to be in the Navy. A long time!

I was determined to go to college. I wasn't academically qualified to get into Drexel or LaSalle or the University of Pennsylvania, but there in Philadelphia was a great university, Temple University. Temple is set up to handle people who've done a turnaround in their life. Late bloomers. I was very, very proud to go to Temple. They have a great reputation. They had a great basketball team; the football team wasn't that great, but they were making inroads. I realized that a degree from Temple was just as good as any other, depending upon my grades and whatever it was I was studying. And, more importantly, they gave me an opportunity to get a good education by giving me an athletic scholarship.

I majored in education. I wanted to become a school teacher, because I felt I was equipped to tell children like myself why they ought to study. Before I finished my B.A. in education, I took a very long sabbatical. I left to do some nightclub work because I decided that, if this thing of show business was on my mind, I could not put my time into my subjects. I didn't want to try to float through and get a degree.

When did I discover I could make people laugh? By doing stand-up comedy in coffee houses. Greenwich Village. The Gaslight at 116 MacDougal Street. My career took off from there, *but* my whole career is based on people who gave me the opportunity, and then my fulfilling their and my expectations. Being ready. Thanks to my days in college, when I studied journalism, sociology, psychology, and some history, and the fact that I was a good and prolific writer, I was able to apply all that to my stand-up comedy routines. That is what I mean by being ready. To work in the coffee houses at a time when you were not allowed to curse, or verbally pull your pants down, or take the easy laugh by alluding to sexual parts of the body, was wonderful training. When I was coming up, you couldn't say certain words, nor could you say them on television.

People came to see me and didn't give me a chance. People came to see me and gave me a chance. People in charge come down and judge a person and walk away, and they say, "I think that person will work," or, "I think they won't work." So Mike Douglas, Allan Sherman on the "Tonight" show, and then Jack Paar, in that order, were the people who gave me the breaks. Those were the jobs that I got from my start at the Gaslight club.

I've always wanted to get my degree. I felt that it was very, very important. I'm still basically a teacher. I've always wanted to say things about human behavior in terms of education. I was doing a lot of nightclub appearances and television shots, a lot of different things, but I got my B.A. in 1961, at Temple.

I was very pleased to receive an honorary doctorate from Brown University this past May, and the only thing I said to the graduating class was what my grandfather told me: "*First* comes reality, *then* comes philosophy. *Now* we start with the rent."

In 1965, a great thing happened. Sheldon Leonard, then one of Hollywood's most creative television producers and under contract to NBC, heard about me, called Carl Reiner to check me out, and got me the part of Alexander Scott, one of the two American agents in an adventure/espionage series, "I Spy," co-starring with Robert Culp on NBC. I didn't have to audition for it or anything. For Culp's cover, he played a top-seeded tennis player competing in worldwide tournaments. My cover was to act as his trainer and traveling companion.

There were two firsts connected with "Spy." It was my first serious acting role, and it was the first show to co-star a black actor in a starring role on American television. In those days, and now, producers and directors watched the new talent on the "Tonight" show, and

many times booked them. For beginners, an appearance on "Tonight" often was an open sesame. The big chance. Steve Allen, Jack Paar and Johnny Carson have helped hundreds of youngsters get their first big break in show business.

"Spy" was a well-written show; cool, witty and sophisticated, because of Bob Culp. After the first few awful weeks we had fun doing it. The writers were excellent, and our producer allowed us to be ourselves. The opportunity that I was given with "I Spy" was just the opposite of my philosophy: my credo is that you have to be *ready* to handle a big break when it comes. My opportunity was extended on that show, but *not* because of my ability or readiness. It was extended on my potential. And it was extended because Sheldon Leonard and Bob Culp, after they watched my first horrible performance, said that I should be given time. One of the NBC executives suggested, "Why don't we pull this guy Cosby and get somebody like Rafer Johnson. Cosby is godawful."

That was true. I *was*. No excuse, I was *horrible*, and I knew it. Word went out to get rid of Cosby. Culp and Leonard said, "Look, if he goes, we go." You've got to weigh and measure what these men were saying! I mean, their careers! And the money involved with this show. It wasn't a matter of get us a white guy to replace the black guy. It wasn't a civil-rights situation. Sheldon and Bob were really talking about giving up that show because of *me*. We hadn't been together that long to develop a relationship to the point that they were protecting their *friend*.

But something happened. The second performance was better, the third was better yet. And I began to grow. I hadn't had any acting experience, but it doesn't make any difference. You give a bad performance, you give a bad performance. People in the business of selling air time, putting programs on the air, can't tolerate inept or inexperienced actors, nor should they have to. There was one thing in my favor; it was the first time, other than

the show that George C. Scott had done, where he had Cicely Tyson as his secretary, that people had a chance to see a black American every week. I still think that "I Spy" caught on because people were curious the first couple of weeks.

And so it wasn't a matter of pass or fail for me that first week. By the time we got to air, we were able to throw the best Cosby performances up, and those episodes made good shows. When the horrible performances were put on air, about two or three when I still didn't know what I was doing, the television audience knew I could be *better*. They had already seen that.

I began to feel comfortable solely because of the wonderful support system. Support not only from Sheldon Leonard and Bob Culp, but everybody. Everybody! Mort Fine, David Friedkin, the head writers, the camera operators. Have I ever been that unsure of myself since? I don't think so. I couldn't even call myself an actor in those days. I was given on-the-job training. It was good training because I won an Emmy at the end of the first year for Best Dramatic Actor.

That's why I think if anybody can find any fault with me as a producer, yes, as a producer, it will be that I always see myself whenever I see anybody with a natural potential, floundering. I want to give that person more than the benefit of the doubt. I'll work with them more than the others. Sheldon used to take great pride in telling me that he felt that nightclub performers, if one wanted to do a comedy or variety show, were probably the best performers to select. His example was Danny Thomas. He produced and directed "The Danny Thomas Show"

for years. He cited people like Phil Silvers and Milton Berle as other examples.

"I Spy" was never that successful. I saw it as a show that was hanging in there. We were around Number 30, where you keep a show alive. If it had been really successful, they wouldn't have closed it down in 1968, in its fourth year. But it was a show we and NBC were proud of. It had class; it was a good show. It's still remembered.

My next venture was in 1969 with "The Bill Cosby Show." I played Chet Kincaid, athletic coach in an L.A. high school. His character was based on a wonderful man, a football coach I met in the service—Harry Jefferson. He was outgoing, gregarious, and I enjoyed his con-manship. I had a two-year guarantee for the show's run. In the beginning, I had a few arguments with some individuals at NBC. I hated laugh tracks. The people at NBC were very angry because I wouldn't put a laugh track on it. I felt that tracks were put in for writers, not for the audience. I wanted to do a show where the viewer at home could laugh anytime the *viewer* wanted to.

We preceded Disney, and we did the show on film. It was a failure in terms of numbers. I kept saying to the network people, I don't care. *But* the greatest thing that came out of that show, which went off in 1971, was the money. I used it to set up apprenticeship programs for black Americans, Asian Americans and Hispanic Americans, and we did some very nice things.

I am still proud of that show. It plays in many places. Chicago is one of our greatest markets. That show has been playing there over and over and over, at hours like three and four in the morning. We had Quincy Jones doing the music for the show, along with many other great musicians.

During that run there were other big projects. The first, "The Bill Cosby Special," went on in March 1968. I won my fourth Emmy for that. "The Second Bill Cosby Special" was aired in April 1969. That was the first time I did my Noah's Ark monologue. In June 1969, on an NBC

Children's Theatre Special, George Heinemann, June Reig and I did "As I See It," an exploration of the minds of kids we found in different parts of the country. That same year, in November, "Hey, hey, hey… It's Fat Albert," was the first animated special on television, peopled with all the kids from my neighborhood, Old Weird Harold, Dumb Donald, my brother Russell, and Mush Mouth. From that, the Saturday morning series, "Fat Albert," developed. We won Peabodys for that. I *love* that series.

The following year, April 1970, "The Third Bill Cosby Special" was produced. In December, "Dick Van Dyke Meets Bill Cosby" was put on. It wasn't until 1973 that we did our second animated special, "Weird Harold." Two more specials in 1975 were "Highlights of Ringling Bros. Barnum & Bailey" and the "World of Magic," with Doug Henning. In '75, I also went back to doing a lot of live shows.

I got into trouble again with NBC on another special. Again, I wanted to do a special with no audience, no laugh track, and no big names. And word came down that NBC would be *very* happy if I had some name people, so I got upset, and I went out and got who *I* knew were name people. I got Billy Eckstein and Nancy Wilson. That wasn't a good show. That last sour note was the end of NBC's happy relationship with Bill Cosby, until later we, NBC and I, were able to do a special called "Top Secret." Sheldon Leonard was the boss on that one. It was filmed in Italy and I played a government agent posing as an art dealer. Good show.

To come to what I'm doing now. A couple of years ago, I said to Tom Werner and Marcy Carsey (Carsey/Werner Productions) at the dinner table, what can we do next? We agreed on the kind of show and how it should be done. And they went out to find a network. Around that time, Brandon Tartikoff, I understand, was watching the "Tonight" show with his sleepless baby and saw me do a monologue on parenting. He thought, Gee whiz, this guy, judging from the monologue, could star in a good series built around a father with Cosby's kind of attitude. I was *ready*. I was receptive, because I was tired of what I saw on TV—the situation comedies that I was looking at. I didn't like the fact that the parents were losing all the time.

I never felt that, because you put a child in an environment—with the same parents, the same brothers and sisters, the same economic level of the family, whether upper, middle or lower class, the same house with all the variables—that each child in that family will turn out the same. The child *chooses* to do what he or she does, depending on his or her physiological and neurological mix.

That's the foundation, and then you start with parenting. Would I call myself a behaviorist at this time? No, I call myself a concerned parent right now. But, as we all know, if you have children, it doesn't make any difference what you say a lot of the time. I can't say that my kid doesn't want to study because I didn't dry her off in 30 seconds, and she remembers that and is what she is today, a slow thinker. There's just too much emphasis put on early childhood traumas, and too much time wasted wondering if those were the causes of poor behavior, when we should be getting on and trying to deal with the person.

I asked Dr. Alvin Poussaint of Harvard Medical School to be our advisor for the show. It may seem that I've made some disparaging remarks about psychiatrists, but I respect all of them. It's the *people* who take what they say and begin to meander down the road. The

same people with the 1984 mentality who said, "Television is going to become Big Brother." And I say, "That's not necessarily true." We are able to say to all the negative people, "Look, there are positive things that can be done. There's always going to be TV. There are always going to be pornographic materials. But what are the positive things?" The pessimists can

say, "Well, the light at the end of the tunnel is another train coming." And the optimist will say, "Well, maybe the light is the hole that we're going to come out of."

That's my point. I want to use this behavioral scientist so that we, who use humor, who are the biggest defenders of disparaging remarks and disparaging behavior towards human beings, will, even if the joke is very funny and people are going to laugh, will care about the people we trample on. Who cares who's hurt if there's truth to it? I want Dr. Poussaint to tell me and tell my writers, "Look, this is wrong, this is not today's attitude, this is not an attitude that you want to perpetuate. There's a certain behavior that would be nice to see in 1985." That's why Dr. Poussaint is our advisor.

It's challenging. We're working together to make the show better for the people, and it's showing up. I mean those numbers don't have feelings, but there are feelings behind all those numbers. I'm talking about when I'm out there in the street, and a woman comes up to me and says, "Very seldom do we talk to each other in our family, but on Thursday night at eight o'clock, we all sit around the television." Or some woman tells me that she and her husband became more romantic again after watching how Cliff and Clair Huxtable feel about each other. That means that in that 62 share in Detroit, there's *one* family that comes together to watch the show. That means that there *are* feelings. And some of that has to do with Dr. Poussaint's theories about touch, feel, good sexuality. Some people don't know how to do that tastefully in a show.

I have high standards for what I do for TV. In real life, sometimes, I had a very low taste level. Sure I made mistakes, but I've never resorted to smarmy stuff. I don't have to. I'm doing this program with a serious purpose in mind. I was tired of what I saw on TV, and I wanted the parents to win, because they deserve to win. On some programs, too many times they don't get to graduate from high school. Many parents, when they watch their child graduate, feel that they want to up and get the diploma with the kid. Same with college. It's not just the money; it's the mental input. It's the fatigue, it's dealing with these people called your children. Even with the brightest and the best behaved, there's an *awful* lot of work and an awful lot of love. And parents deserve more. I'm trying to get people to see people love, feel and relate to each other, and to be good parents.

When the show was in formation, I was hoping that I'd get enough viewers to keep me alive, also enough viewers to keep the grey suits and the paisley ties off my back. What have I got against paisley? That's the way they (the network people) love to dress. The "they" are the ones who have executive positions of retrospect. They look at numbers *after* the shows are off the air. You don't hear people tell you when you're failing to not do things that you wouldn't do early on. You say Grant Tinker doesn't have a paisley tie in his closet? It's not Grant Tinker. Grant Tinker is quite all *right*.

Before the show went on, we thought it was going to take time to build. I don't know the public. I just know what I'm serving up, and I hoped that I'd get enough people to like what I'm serving up to keep us alive. If the show started to fail, we knew people would tell us to do something that would draw the viewers, to hype it up.

I never took it for granted that we would be given time for the show to build. Grant Tinker never promised me that. The show struck an immediate and a responsive chord, but we certainly didn't expect it to zoom. We have good writers. It's a different show. We break an awful lot of rules. But, like the people who are working with the inner ear, we're getting great results. In 1984, when we left to go on Christmas break for a couple of weeks, I had a guy take all the pictures down in my office and put them in my New York house. I wasn't taking anything for granted. I don't know these people. I don't know the

audience out there. I don't know when or if, tomorrow, whatever, NBC might decide to take the show off. That is why I work as hard as I can to get my viewpoint across, not thinking about a 62 share or a 34 share, just thinking about what can I do that will make "The Cosby Show" do that best.

When I went on hiatus this summer, I left these pictures up. On this wall are the people whom I really appreciate: jazz musicians. On that other wall is a *big* picture of Sidney Greenstreet and Peter Lorre autographed to me. Sidney's inscription says: "I love your show. Keep cooking!" Peter Lorre says: "I would watch your show, but I watch 'Magnum, P.I.' instead." There is that big picture of Basil Rathbone because he played the mad doctor in quite a few movies, and if you look at what Basil played and what exists today in medicine, we've got people doing things today that Basil, as the mad doctor, was doing. I think it's funny. There was a small problem with the autographs since they were long gone, so I helped them out a little. On another wall are pictures from some of the shows (Robert Culp is in many of them) and some sports pictures. The fourth wall has my pictures of my family.

To get back to the show. I'm doing a very serious show in a funny way. But sometimes the intentioning and the stress are not caused by the seriousness of the situation. We may already have the seriousness of the situation down pat in the story. Now we have to try and make it funny, but we don't want to take the easy laugh. We don't want to drop our pants. We don't want to use the children. Some of the critics, negative critics, complain that these children are cute. Perhaps they say that instead of saying they don't like the show. They are not cute. I'm not talking about racial undertones. I can't find "cutesy" in these kids, because it's the one thing I'm determined not to allow. And I think I've succeeded.

I will *always* keep my fingers crossed because every Thursday night is a new night. It's like going off the high board every Thursday night with one's fingers crossed. Each show should be a wonderful show, because who knows when a new viewer is going to decide to tune in, to give it a chance this week. So each time is never a throwaway.

The commercials were not an unexpected development in my career. I did think ten years ago that I would do commercials. I sure did. They're very valuable. I've always felt that a strong 30 seconds is better than a weak 30 minutes. I've always felt that if they gave people humor and something to laugh at, something they enjoy, they'd remember a commercial as much as an hour's special that you did.

What do I like doing best? I'd rather do the show now than do the commercials. I enjoy live performances every once in a while. The show takes an awful lot out of me, and I'm much older now. When I was 30, I could rehearse this show, fly to Miami, do two shows, fly back, get four hours sleep, and come back here. But now, at 48, I can't do that; I get tired. When I'm tired, I don't like anybody. I get mean, and everybody seems stupid to me. So I like to get a lot of sleep. I'm beginning to pace myself. I have to or else I'm going to self-destruct.

I object that the networks (I'm talking about paisley tie people) still have cars skidding on two wheels into buildings; they still have people dropping to their knees firing 357 magnums, and they still have socio-documentary series that are laid out so that somebody can pull out a breast or call people names to sell some commercials. We haven't set aside the basic time to say, let's help to educate American viewers to love each other, to raise a caring family. I'm talking about *quality*.

I sure would give Michael Landon an "A" for effort. He succeeds in writing scripts with good people who have to deal with good and evil. *But*, there's a way of doing what I want the networks to do without being namby-pamby good. You don't want to have people look at the show and say, Oh, *God*, who wants to be that way! That's sickening. I want the scripts to be real. If someone has a real but ugly attitude, then you ought to straighten that person out.

I never had to introduce myself to the audience to say, I'm the same guy. Everybody knew about "I Spy." How *wonderful*! I mean, in one's lifetime, that this kid from a housing project, with total rejection by the white society—intelligent black Americans know about what Caucasian people want to put on, and what color is supposed to be right (they want to get one black in a pack of seven)—that *this* one, that all of the white ones that they had, that *this* one turns out to be the one that saves them.

How many people are going to learn from that? We've still got a long way to go. We don't have native Americans, we don't have Hispanic Americans, we don't have Asian Americans writing, directing. These Americans have things to say.

I think *you* have to understand (all this other stuff that we talked about is fine and good) that this is a *marvelous*, wonderful story—that here he *is*, the guy in "I Spy," *and* the same guy today in "The Cosby Show." It reminds me of Aesop's fable, "The Lion and the Mouse." The lion, the king of the beasts, shows mercy to a mouse who woke him up and lets the mouse go. The mouse thanks the lion by saying that she hopes some day to do *him* a favor. The lion falls into a hunter's trap sometime later, and the mouse gnaws the net, setting him free. The fable ends by saying no one is so unimportant that he may be unable to repay a good turn.

"The Cosby Show" is my present to NBC on its 60th birthday.

November 4, 1985

Bob Hope brought his comedic gifts to NBC radio 49 years ago as Sunday night star of "The Rippling Rhythm Revue." Because of his wholehearted gift of self, he has made millions laugh and has raised millions for a multitude of causes. His *joie de vivre* is infectious.

"Hey, can you believe I'm into my 36th television year on NBC? Really. I started out doing TV shows for 'em way back in 1950—B.C. That's 'Before Cosby.' It's been a long time. I can remember way back when 'Miami Vice' was jaywalking in Florida…the 'Hill Street Blues' were the Keystone Cops… and 'Highway to Heaven' was the road to Hedy Lamarr's house. A lot of people get nervous in front of a camera. I get nervous when I'm not in front of a camera. My agent does, too."

I was born in 1903 in Eltham, England, and christened Leslie Townes. My mother, Avis Townes, was a concert singer, and my father, William Henry Hope, was a stonemason. I was the fifth of seven sons. The Hope family came to Cleveland in 1907; 13 years later, we became U.S. citizens. I took any job I could get when I was in high school, a delivery boy, soda fountain clerk and shoe salesman. After I graduated, I got a job with a motor car company.

I became a boxer as a gag. My buddy and I went to box at the YMCA regularly. He signed up as Packy West for the Ohio State Amateur Boxing Championship. I went down the next day and registered as Packy East, to the delight of everybody in our neighborhood. I was pretty bad and pretty careless. Didn't train too much. Unfortunately, I won my first and

drew a bye, and, in my second fight, I met the 135 lb. champion. I lasted two rounds. He hit me so hard that I bounced right into dancing school.

That was a big leap from boxing to dancing school. A friend at school was taking dancing lessons, and he showed me the buck-and-wing, and I said, "*Where* did you learn that?" He said, "Down at Sojacks in Cleveland." I said, "Well, how do I get there?" And I went down there and loved it. After studying for a year, John Root, the fellow who ran it, had to go to California for his health, and I took over the school. So I taught dancing after that.

I started dancing around Cleveland with my sweetheart, Mildred Rosequist, my first girl, as my dancing partner. I went to Mildred's mother and said, "I'd like to take her on the road," and her mother said, "I've got to see the act." She saw the act, and she said, "No way. You're not going on the road. I'm taking my daughter right out of that act." Mildred came to NBC about 15 years ago to see me, and she said, "If my mother was alive today, I'd slap her right in the mouth."

In 1924, I found another partner, George Byrne, and he and I got our first break doing an act, only in Cleveland, in Fatty Arbuckle's touring show. He got us booked into "Hurley's Jolly Follies." Two years after, we broke into vaudeville in Detroit. We auditioned for Eddie Dowling and Kate Smith, Ruby Keeler and Smith and Dale for a vaudeville show, "The Sidewalks of New York," at the Knickerbocker Theatre. When the New York run ended, we quit and went back into vaudeville. A short time later, George and I split up, but by then I had started doing a comedy monologue.

I was literally starving to death until I got a booking for three days at the Stratford Theatre in Chicago as emcee. I stayed six months. From that time to this, I haven't stopped working. In 1932, I was the emcee of a show at the Capitol Theatre in New York City with Abe Lyman's orchestra. The singer's name was Bing Crosby. That was the beginning of a lifetime of jousting and clowning with each other in public and the start of a wonderful friendship. Every time I played the Capitol, I appeared on Major Bowes' variety musical show on Sunday mornings.

From 1932 to 1936, I had major roles in the musicals "Ballyhoo," "Roberta," "Say When," "Ziegfeld Follies," and "Red, Hot and Blue." It was during the "Roberta" run that Dolores and I married.

In the early thirties, June 8, 1933, to be exact, I began in radio as a guest on Rudy Vallee's show on NBC. When I was given a check for $750, the guest fee, I just stared at it. I couldn't believe I had made that much money for *one* brief appearance. I appeared as a guest four more times on it. I had to work out a format for radio. I tried one on the Atlantic White Flash show (CBS, from December 1934 to September 1935); I experimented on another show for some other product and used the same format, experimented further on the Bromo Seltzer and the Woodbury soap shows for NBC. I really started to get a little idea of a format, a successful format, on the Woodbury soap show. When I came out for "Your Hollywood Parade," I knew what I wanted to do.

From January, 1935, to April, 1935, I appeared on Bromo Seltzer's "The Intimate Revue," with James Melton, Jane Froman, Al Goodman, and Honey Chile Wilde, who was a Southern gal. Her opening line always was, "Does the Greyhound bus stop here?" That was our lead into a comedy routine. I met her in my agent's office, and she was so charming and beautiful that we put her on the show as a regular. I also signed her up to make personal appearances with me for quite a while. Now she's Princess Hohenlohe, and she lives in Marbella, Spain. She did *very* well. I wasn't exactly a surefire success. I tried several times to get my own show.

In 1937, I was signed for the Woodbury soap shows, "The Rippling Rhythm Revue" on Sunday nights, from May to September 26th, with Shep Fields and his Rippling Rhythm orchestra. I was making motion pictures in Hollywood, so I arranged to do my first remote monologue for the Woodbury show at the NBC studios in Hollywood. I discovered that John Swallow, head of NBC programs on the Coast, had not planned on a live audience. I knew I'd die without one, so he had velvet ropes put up which channeled the Edgar Bergen (Bergen with Charlie McCarthy was Number One then) audience across the hall. Minutes before the show went on the air I did a speedy warmup, "Folks I only have *one* minute. If you don't understand the jokes, laugh anyway, and I'll explain them later!" I did my vaudeville routine—contemporary format taken from the newspapers. In those years, NBC had Sunday night locked up.

Next, American Tobacco signed me for "Your Hollywood Parade," from December 20, 1937, to March 23, 1938.

The start of 12 wonderful years for Pepsodent on NBC radio began in 1938 when I was signed to do "The Pepsodent Show Starring Bob Hope." When Lever Brothers acquired Pepsodent in 1944, the title of the show became "The Bob Hope Show." That affiliation was affectionate as well as contractual. In the Pepsodent show were Skinny Ennis and his orchestra, Bill Goodwin, Frances Langford and Jerry Colonna.

On the Pepsodent shows I did a fast monologue to open, almost like Winchell talking, then put a guest star in the second spot, and, in the third spot (it was a half-hour show), I would bring all the regular characters, like Jerry Colonna and Brenda and Cobina, and the guest star, back for the finale. The format worked and the show, right from the start, went boom, boom, boom! It took about half a year, and we started to go big. And, I think, before the end of the year we were Number One in radio, and stayed there for a long time.

For the Pepsodent shows, I assembled a tremendous staff of writers. Mel Frank, Norman Panama, Mel Shavelson, Milt Josephberg, Jack Rose, Norman Sullivan, Al Schwartz, Sherwood Schwartz, and a lot of others. They used to come over to my place in Burbank and read the scripts. We'd all sit there and listen. Writers don't laugh at other writers, you know. So if *they* laughed, we knew damn well it was good. The good ideas that we decided not to use were put up on the board so we could use them later. The show was previewed on Sunday night, and it was a riot, because it was all ad lib. Everybody wanted to get into the studio to see it because of the ad libbing. I had all manner of guest stars, movie stars, and it was such a ball!

After the show, we'd go up to the Lord & Thomas agency and cut the hour's script to half-an-hour. We'd number the script; the big jokes were 3's, then 2's, then 1's. That's how we put the script together. Stapled and numbered. And then the writers would put it all together, and we'd take a look at it. It worked out great because it was a different style, it was all boom! boom! boom! In all, I did about 1,145 radio programs on NBC.

Some years ago, Dolores and I were invited up to Pocantico Hills in Tarrytown by Governor and Mrs. Rockefeller. When "Happy" saw me, she came over and hugged me and told me, "You don't know what this means to me. I would never miss your radio show for anything in the world. I would take my little radio to bed and listen to you. My mother didn't know it."

Radio was something! It was magic, absolutely magic. It was all in your imagination. Everybody had his or her own idea of Amos 'n' Andy's Fresh Air Taxi Company, for instance.

In 1941 my radio producer, Albert Capstaff, told me we were invited to March Field, the Army Air Corps base at Riverside, California, to do our show. I said why, because there was no war, and we were doing great at NBC in Hollywood. He wouldn't take no for an answer. And the next Tuesday, I found myself on a bus going down to March Field with a whole mob to do the show. He never told me he had a brother in the service down there. The audience was so fantastic, so exciting! I asked everybody, "How long has this been going on?" Pepsodent saw the show, and I was told, "You can go anywhere you want, and we'll pay the expenses."

In December 1941, war was declared. Bing Crosby and I were offered commissions with rank of Lieutenant Commanders in the Navy, but President Roosevelt sent us a message not to join *any* service. Traveling to the military bases really became dramatic, heartwrenching and exhausting, *but* we felt that we were making a difference. Everybody who was asked to be in any of the radio and television shows fell in line if their schedules allowed, and we didn't stop until 1972, 31 years later. It was *wonderful*; it's been one of the most emotionally satisfying things in my life. Talk about being appreciated!

Have those experiences made me a pacifist? Yes, but I'm still a semi-hawk as far as keeping our defenses strong. Anyone who has seen as much as I have of war and the kids who fought them has got to hate war. I don't want us ever to get in the position where we have to fight another war. The only thing that will keep us out of that is strength. And good thinking.

I was asked by Secretary of the Air Force Stuart Symington to do a Christmas show for the servicemen involved in the Berlin airlift. We all flew over to Berlin and put on a show: December 28, 1948. That was the first. For 24 consecutive Christmases, our troupe was in Alaska, the Pacific, England, Iceland, North Africa, the Caribbean, the Far East, and South Vietnam. I finally decided to spend Christmas at home in 1973 with my family! On Christmas afternoon, nurses, Marines, and soldiers from San Diego came up to the house because they thought I'd miss them. I was completely surprised; they just showed up in our back yard. I think someone had alerted Dolores. I *tell* you, we got a kick out of that.

Pepsodent was with me for a long time. I worked a lot for Chrysler and Texaco, of course, over a 20-year period. They were all beautiful. They were fine sponsors.

I want to get all my radio shows together, and I want to present them to certain colleges so the students can study them. My daughter, Linda, had them taken off the big records and put on tape last year. She's into show biz in a major way. She worked for me for quite a while; now she's working with another gal doing pictures. Their latest effort is one on Alzheimer's disease. She's presently working on a story of my young life.

Have any of the other three children gone into show biz? No. Tony, my oldest son, was a producer on the show about an attorney called "Judd." He's a lawyer; he met and married a woman lawyer, and now they live in Washington with two little briefs.

Back to September 7, 1937. I left for Hollywood and Paramount Pictures. In my first film, "The Big Broadcast of 1938," I sang what was to become my theme song, "Thanks for the Memory," written by Ralph Robin and Leo Ranger. It won an Oscar. How did I feel when I went to Los Angeles? After all, I had had a lot of experience in vaudeville, on Broadway and radio, but, nonetheless, it was exciting to begin my first motion picture. I was lucky. In those days Hollywood and the studios were a country club. There wasn't the running around, the schedules and the pressure. All the studios owned their own picture houses. When they made a picture, they knew it was going to be distributed.

Doing a film was a casual, wonderful thing. And if you came out from Broadway and did a picture, the studio heads thought that was wonderful, but they didn't care if you stayed on the West Coast or departed. Thanks to "Thanks for the Memory" and the stars in the show, "The Big Broadcast of 1938" was successful enough so that Paramount decided to give me three more pictures. The third picture was "The Cat and the Canary," which made money. It was a box office hit, and then they signed me for seven years.

The road pictures started in 1940: Bing Crosby and Dorothy Lamour. That was my first film collaboration with Bing Crosby. He was something else. We had so much fun doing those pictures. They made millions for Paramount. Incidentally, I stayed with that studio for 19 enjoyable years!

During that period, Bing was on CBS radio, and he and I used to double back on each other's shows. We had a little theatrical feud going about everything and anything. I was on his show maybe five, six times a year; he was on my show five, six times a year. I'd meet him and say, "You owe me two." He'd say, "No, you owe me three."

For many years Bing and I played a lot of exhibition golf. During World War II, we sold millions of dollars of War Bonds. For years, the annual Bing Crosby Open and the Bob Hope Desert Classic raised a lot of money for good causes. As you'd expect, we had a hilarious time playing in those golf tournaments.

Over the years I've taken great delight in taking comedy potshots at the Motion Picture Academy because I was never given an honest-to-God Oscar. Did I deserve one or two? I think that I should have had a chance at it with a couple of the pictures I made. "The Seven Little Foys," "Beau James," and also the one I did with

Lucille Ball, "The Facts of Life," which got *raves*. There was a full-page review in *Time* magazine. Their movie critic just raved about that picture.

I've received two Honorary Oscars from the Academy. Years ago, Cecil B. deMille gave me a little Oscar as a gag. I was given a plaque which was inscribed: "For Unselfish Services to the Motion Picture Industry." I feel awfully lucky the Academy has honored me in the way it has.

In 1950, when I signed a five-year television contract with NBC, I defected from motion pictures. (I had made my first television appearance on "The Ed Sullivan Show" on CBS.) People don't remember how the big studios feared, hated and scorned television in the early days. I had a great start in television because I had been making pictures for so many years. (I think I was Number One at the box office in the world at one time.) So when I went there, NBC made me awfully happy. They made my estate *very* happy.

Barney Balaban, President of Paramount, told me that I would lose my status in the business if I went on television. The movie people were very hostile. It was either/or for performers. I told Barney, "You give me the same deal that NBC is giving me, and I'll stay with you." I never heard from him. So I've been solid NBC up to this date.

I wasn't apprehensive about going into television, as so many radio stars were, because I had done Broadway musicals. Some of my radio friends didn't make the transition to television. Benny and Burns and those who'd been vaudevillians, with experience of traveling around the world and working to audiences, knew what people laugh at. That's the *big* thing. That's the most important part of our business. On all of my television shows I've done monologues, as I had on radio.

I was on NBC radio for 15 years before I appeared on television. Of course, when I started, I had the highest ratings ever known. Many things account for that. If you look at my record—where we've been, and what we've done, how we've traveled, the different shows we've done—it's pretty exciting. We've given the people different kinds of shows from all over the world…Russia, and even China.

On Easter Sunday, in 1950, I did my first TV show for NBC, the first of my own series of comedy specials, the "All Star Revue." Everyone had to learn how to do everything in those early years of television. We were pioneers in a new medium. The lights were so hot, and the cameras so heavy; all the equipment was primitive by today's standards. We had to learn a whole new technique—how to move on stage within the limits imposed by the cameras, how to act for television.

Two years later, in 1952, we went to New York to do "The Colgate Comedy Hour," our first color show, with Fred MacMurray and Janice Paige at the Colonial Theatre. The producer didn't like the way it worked there so we finished the show at the RKO Theatre. The Colgate show had rotating hosts: Eddie Cantor, Martin and Lewis, Fred Allen, Donald O'Connor, Abbott and Costello, Jimmy Durante, Gordon MacRae, and Robert Paige. Incidentally, it was the first show to compete successfully with Ed Sullivan's Sunday night show on CBS.

I alternated variously with Milton Berle, Martha Raye and Steve Allen on the Buick-Berle show from 1954 to 1956. Again, rotating stars were hosts for "The Chevy Show," which was on the air from October 1955 to September 1956. In the years that followed, I had many guest shots on most of the big variety shows. Starting in September of 1963, I was the host of "Bob Hope Presents the Chrysler Theatre," until September, 1967, when it went off the air. Reruns of that were done on "NBC Adventure Theatre" in 1971.

I've jumped ahead in recapping some of the television years. Joe McConnell, then President of NBC, signed me for the original five-year contract, and I've finished seven of them. I knew the Sarnoffs best because I was with them for so long, and I admired them so much. General Sarnoff, Robert Sarnoff, and Tom Sarnoff. They were like family. About five years before he died, I was at a big dinner for NBC in New York and General Sarnoff got up and said, "I can't imagine NBC without Bob Hope." And he really meant it.

John West, Vice President of NBC on the West Coast, died recently. John West! I was at Sunset and Vine doing the shows when NBC was building Burbank, and John invited me over to look at the new television studios. He asked me what studio I thought was best and how I would like it outfitted. I said, "You know something? The best theatre in the world is the Palladium in London, because they have the tunnels where the people come in. If you put the cameras in the tunnels and just wheel them in and out, the audience won't be aware they're there because they'll be looking at a live show." They never bought the idea, and they put the audience up high. In 1952, I guess, I made them put bleachers in so the audience would be much closer to the action. The idea of bleachers caught on and now most studios are built that way.

Speaking of NBC vice presidents, Fred Allen made a specialty of harpooning them. He was something else. Just a great, great guy. He lived on 58th Street and 6th Avenue in New York City in an apartment with Portland Hoffa. Do you know that Fred would greet you, say hello, and then go back to his typewriter and type, and *then* talk to you? You'd have to take him out to dinner to get him away from the typewriter. He worked all the time. Those scripts would then go down to NBC for final approval by Clarence Menser, the Censor.

I've done my share of jokes about not only vice presidents, but everybody at the network. One time we put a joke in about a vice president, and just about that time NBC issued an edict which said no more jokes about vice presidents. We loved this joke. Before we went down to Whittier College to do the broadcast, an NBC executive, John Swallow, asked (read told) us to take that joke out of the script. I said, "I'm *not* taking that joke out. I'm allowed to do that joke. Fred Allen does it, and I'm going to do it." We go all the way down to Whittier College, and here comes John Swallow, who pleaded with me, "Do me a favor, I'm in *such* trouble, take it out." I said, "John, if you drove all the way down here to ask me, I'll take it out." And we did. That hurt because I thought it was a *very* funny joke.

I've enjoyed most of the NBC executives. I have. They're all talented people. In fact, I've enjoyed all of them. I've known them all. It's like presidents, they don't get into that position unless they have some kind of talent. I'm a combination of actor, talent, businessman and golfer. I have to spend a lot of my time being a businessman, so I appreciate the responsibilities executives in any corporation carry.

I'm so proud of the writers and producers of the TV shows which entertain this country and the world every week. I think all of them should be decorated, I really do. They've done and do such a job! I'm from vaudeville where we did the same act over and over. You do the same act for 25 years, and it was a great living, but in television, you've got to have the savvy to put a show together every week. You've got to know a little something. And talent, and a way to utilize your talent. That's the important thing. And taste, and most important, good writers.

When I started in '38, I said I've *got* to get great material. And I had the best staff of writers who ever lived. One time, say, about 20 years ago, the Writers' Guild honored me, and the toastmaster said, "Would all the writers who have worked for Hope stand up." Forty writers stood up. I liked that.

I didn't take a walk from NBC over to CBS like Benny did. I felt it was a great distinction to be on NBC. I stayed with NBC for many reasons. We were doing well. NBC was big; NBC was *the* Number One network at that time. The class act. They never knew the humiliating third position that they've had for about ten years—up until this year.

I established, early on, on radio and television, the type of comedy I wanted to do, comedy that would appeal to families. I set my own standards. I didn't want to have anything to do with shoddy or smutty comedy. No! First of all, even if we had wanted to, we couldn't get away with anything like that. The censors were real rough in those days. I just can't believe that sophisticated shows like "Dallas," "Dynasty," and many different kinds of shows can get on the air today! And cable is unbelievable. I'm not judgmental—I don't approve or disapprove. I think that there is something for everybody, and people pick the things they want to see.

However, Bill Cosby comes out with the greatest show last year with the love within a family as its theme, and he's Number One. So that's a message to the networks and studios. And it's so beautiful. I hadn't seen it, and Dolores told me I *had* to see his show. She loves that show. I agree, it's wonderful. And look at its rating.

Grant Tinker is one of the major reasons for NBC's success. I think there has to be an awful lot of talent, but I also think there's an awful lot of luck connected with network ratings. I may be wrong in that. It's a matter of picking the right shows. Here "The Golden Girls" comes on the air, and it gets a nice rating. Marvelous casting.

You suggest that my monologues over so many years have been perceptive and witty commentaries on what's happened in this country and other countries. Do I think it's a social history? Certainly, they were/are politically acute. Some critic said that I pricked but didn't draw blood with my pointed satirization of events and governmental officials of our times. I think they might make a good book.

In 1981, we had a 30th anniversary show with clips from three decades of the best comedy sketches from 200 Bob Hope Specials with outstanding guest stars. By the end of this year, I'll have done 325 Specials. Putting that show together brought back so many memories. It was hard to believe that 30 years had gone by.

Hey, can you believe I'm into my 36th television year on NBC? Really. I started out doing TV shows for 'em way back in 1950—B.C. That's "Before Cosby."

It's been a long time. I can remember way back when "Miami Vice" was jaywalking in Florida...the "Hill Street Blues" were the Keystone Cops...and "Highway to Heaven" was the road to Hedy Lamarr's house.

A lot of people get nervous in front of a camera. I get nervous when I'm not in front of a camera. My agent does, too.

A lot has changed. What they used to do to my face before a show was called makeup...now it's called special effects.

But I'm still with NBC for three simple reasons: the creative atmosphere, the fine working conditions, and the pictures I took at the 1950 Christmas party.

To this day, I'm re-energized by the next thing on my agenda. Is the public persona the real Bob Hope? I think so. I might have a big comedy star reputation, but that doesn't mean a thing unless you come up with good shows. We work, struggle, think and really beat ourselves to get the best possible show every time we go to bat. We've done something like 436 hours on television. All over the world. We did the first television show ever filmed in China, a three-hour special. The logistics were difficult, but it's great.

How do I remain enthusiastic? I get such a kick out of doing shows and hearing an audience laugh. Oh, Westbury Music Fair was wonderful this summer. I loved it. We've been there for about six years. We have fun, and when I introduce Dolores, the audience is so surprised and delighted when she comes out. She's a great singer and they really buy that.

Friends among my peers? Jack Benny and Bing, of course. Who makes me laugh? A lot of guys make me laugh. Jackie Gleason makes me laugh. Red Skelton, Johnny Carson, Sheckey Green. I was a godfather (figuratively) to Carson and to many other young comedians when they were starting out. I love most comedians.

Why have I lasted longer than everybody else? *Work*. Working at it. I work all the time, because I enjoy it so much. I take on extra chores, such as the commercials. I know they're an additional commitment to a heavy schedule, but they're so lucrative. The plans I have, I need all the money I can get, believe me. I want to build a museum and an entertainment center. That takes big stuff, big money.

Speaking of money, in 1985 the new USO building was dedicated to me in Washington, and I said I thought it should have been the IRS building!

In between all the benefits I do, I want to make more money to do what I've planned. I have so many places for it. I have a lot of charities that I have been supporting for years. I hate to talk about my charities; there are so many it's hard to pick out a few. I've been honorary chairman of the National Parkinson Center for 25 years in Miami. The Cradle in Chicago is one of my favorites. Also, SMU—I built a theatre there for them. The Port Arthur Crippled Children's High School. The Eye Foundation. I'm honorary chairman of Cerebral Palsy. The Bob Hope International Heart Foundation in Seattle. The Bob Hope House in Cincinnati for delinquent kids. The list is long, but these are all organizations which need support every year. I'm very much a "count your blessings" man. So it keeps me busy!

I don't know what the count is up to now, but, as of 1974, I had received over 1,000 awards. I have a warehouse full of memorabilia: all my movies, all my radio and television shows. And a trophy room in my office. I'm going to put them in a building which I won't call a museum because the word museum has a stuffy, slow sound to it. I want people to be able to come and hear and see all those shows. I wish General Sarnoff could be at the dedication when it's completed.

Some awards stand out. In the 60's, I was in the White House one very special day. I thought back to when I was standing alone in front of the Wood Theatre in Chicago in 1928, *starving*. I couldn't get a booking, and here I was receiving this honor. While they were preparing for the ceremony, I was standing alone in the Oval Office in the White House. President John F. Kennedy was about to give me the Congressional Medal of Honor, the third civilian at the time to receive it. I thought then that show business is pretty great!

President Eisenhower gave me the Medal of Merit and President Lyndon Johnson awarded me the Medal of Freedom; I was given the George C. Marshall Award, and the Distinguished Service Medal from the Navy. It's hard to single them out because they all came from distinguished groups of Americans. I was honored by every service, Army, Marines, Navy, and Air Force. I'm very proud of the statuette for the Distinguished Public Service Medal which is in the Smithsonian Institution. Fifty civilians received one for helping the nation during World War II.

We've all had a marvelous time doing the birthday shows; 1983 was the big one—my 80th birthday. I was given a whole year of birthday parties. One of the 1985 Specials was "Bob Hope's Happy Birthday Homecoming: A Royal London Gala," for my 82nd birthday. Somebody said if I had my life to live over again, I wouldn't have time for it. That's exactly right.

I loved that Special, "Bob Hope Buys NBC?" I didn't buy NBC this fall because they wanted money, they wanted a down payment. The timing was perfect because of Ted Turner's attempt to take over CBS. Absolutely perfect. However, we got a tough break on the rating. "Family Honor" was a two-hour special on another network, and they plugged the hell out of it. It went on against us at 9 o'clock. Along came President Reagan on

Tuesday night for a half hour. Then we followed "The A-Team," which shoved us back to 9:30, but ABC didn't do that. When the President talked, they pulled out one of their half-hour shows, put it on at 9 o'clock, and I had to battle them from 9:30 on. So they got a half-hour head start. But we caught up to them anyway.

I'm booked all the time for television and personal appearances. The message I got last week from Dolores was *don't* book *anything* else. It's a little silly to be so busy because we've got a beautiful place in Palm Springs, and I love to play golf, and I don't have a chance to get there. I was there for all of 41 days last year. I am going to take her advice. Starting now. It's a safe promise because I'm booked so far ahead that I won't have to stop for a long time. These shows, benefits, tournaments, are things that I want to do. I enjoy doing everything I do because I select them. It's not slave labor!

Backing me up is a staff of about 50 people in the Bob Hope Production Company, my television office and my home office. I have to use my time well; I can't waste it. I'll work in the afternoons I'm home, but I sneak off. As I get in the car, my secretary will run out the door and say, "What about…?" "Yeah, I'll tell you when I come back." I just go off to the club, which is right around the corner, and play nine holes of golf and come back. That's how I relax.

It's been a ball being on NBC radio and television. It's the only network I know. It's my boarding house. Forty-seven years ago, I never dreamed that NBC radio would grow the way it did and be around that long. And television was unknown! Here I am with another first—an NBC made-for-television movie, "A Nice, Pleasant, Deadly Weekend" with Don Ameche. It's being filmed in a gorgeous estate (very high class, tony murders), in Vancouver, but it's raining so much that I think I've grown an inch. It's been great. How lucky can you get! Only in America.…

My birthday wish to NBC's 60th—now that I'm not going to buy it—is that I'll celebrate the birthday with them 60 years hence.

October 21, 1985

Michael Landon, producer, writer, director and actor, has brought his talents to four of NBC's most successful series during his 26-year association with the company: "Bonanza," "Little House," "Father Murphy," and now, "Highway to Heaven."

"In 'Bonanza,' none of the Cartwrights could really ride a horse when we started the series. You'd get on a horse, but that didn't mean you could ride. It's just desperation; you pray. We'd ride studio horses, and they know where they're going. When one horse leaves, they all leave, and you just ride along with the pack with that silly grin on your face, *dying*."

I was born in Forest Hills, New Jersey, but grew up in Collingswood, New Jersey, where I went to the local schools. In my senior year of high school, I became the All-American Javelin Champion.

I was one of only two Jewish kids in a school where there was a certain amount of anti-Semitism, as there is everywhere. As one of that small minority, I fell back on my religious background to the extent that I began to believe that I was like Samson, because in the summer when my hair grew longer, I threw the javelin further than in the wintertime. My parents never really understood *what* I was doing. Back in the early fifties, I became one of the first hippies, with hair down to my shoulders. I don't think my father even noticed how long my hair was.

He worked *all* the time. He never came to any of our meets, but when scholarships were offered to me, he finally watched a track meet the day I set the New Jersey State record. He didn't come into the stadium, but I saw him peering through the fence when it was my turn to throw. He looked for a minute, shook his head and got back in his car. He couldn't figure out why anyone would *pay* my way through college for throwing a long stick.

I had scholarship offers from about 46 colleges. I accepted an athletic scholarship to the University of Southern California. (I've been in California ever since.) I injured my arm at a meet in my freshman year at Southern California and was given cortisone every other day for the pain so I could compete in meets. I was in such pain that I decided not to go to the university doctor but went instead to a doctor not connected to the school. He told me I was going to ruin my arm so severely that eventually I wouldn't be able to write my own name or tie a shoelace.

When I told that to the coaching staff, they humiliated me and called me "chicken" because I wouldn't continue to throw. They made it so difficult for me to remain in college that I left. They had only so many scholarships, and if they got me to leave school, they could give my scholarship to someone else. In a way, it was very fortunate for me, because if I had stayed in college after 1954, I would have missed the "Bonanza" series.

How did I turn to acting? When I went to high school, guys never performed in a play in their own school.

Your classmates would kill you! My sister went to read for a part at a prestigious playhouse (for that area), the Haddenfield Plays and Players. She was so scared that I said I'd go with her. She didn't get a part, but I did. I was about 14 years old at the time, and, on a lark, I tried out for the role of a Japanese house boy in "The Bat" and got it. I did all my own makeup and received very, very good reviews. I was a shy kid, but I found that I was not shy once I was on the stage. I was someone else. That was wonderful.

After leaving college I got a job unloading freight cars at J.J. Newberry's warehouse in North Hollywood, where I met a guy who wanted to be an actor. I did a scene with him when he tried to get into Warner Brothers' dramatic school (no salary, but a chance to learn how to act). He didn't get into the school, but I did. To make a living, I opened a carwash across the street and washed all the Warner Brothers executives' cars. About five months later, when I was washing Jack Warner's car, he asked what was going on across the street. He didn't even know about the dramatic school, but when he found out about it, he said, "Close it." He just didn't want to spend money for it.

I hounded all the agents' offices and did scenes in the parking lot when they were going for their cars. I was *very* tenacious, and eventually, I got a break. By the time I was 18 years old I was doing a lot of the live shows, like "Playhouse 90," and the William Morris Agency signed me. "I Was a Teen-age Werewolf" was my first picture, which started my brief recording career. I toured the country for a couple of months doing record hops with Jerry Lee Lewis. After I did that picture, we recorded at the same record company. I'll tell you, that was an experience! We were two, green, slightly crazy 19-year-old kids at that time. You'd have to be crazy to do that. You see, I could only sing one song, "Give Me a Little Kiss, Will You, Hon?," an easy song when you're not a singer, but I sang it over, and over, and over again. One time, I sang it nine times at one record hop.

The three weeks of filming my part in "The Legend of Tom Dooley" turned out to be disastrous for me personally. My father died the second day of rehearsal. Then I broke my foot. I was cutting a guy off a horse in a scene, and I was afraid of hurting him, so I cut toward myself. The knife wouldn't cut, and when I asked the prop man for a better knife, he gave me one like a razor. In the middle of a very emotional scene, I yelled a line of dialogue, and the knife went through my face to the other side of my cheek, almost cutting my tongue off and leaving a huge hole. Because I didn't use the studio doctor (a gynecologist), that nullified the studio insurance policy. I went to a plastic surgeon, had 58 stitches in my face,

and ended up paying the bill. It's hard to believe that I starred in a movie and came out in the red. That wasn't a winner.

Mort Werner, head of NBC programming at the time, and one other guy, put on "Bonanza" in 1959. It took up 14 years of my life. I had been doing "Playhouse 90" and "General Electric Theater" with writers like Reginald Rose, and I wasn't making a great deal of money. I knew this series would be very good for me financially.

It was fun to be a hero; no two ways about it, it was exciting. All of a sudden people noticed me, which had never happened before. I thought the pilot was dreadful, embarrassing. I was fighting people with an umbrella, sword fighting! We sang a terrible song which sounded like a car commercial at the end of it. The show, I'm sure, would not have gotten on the air except that RCA wanted to sell color television sets, and it was an hour in color on a Saturday night when department stores were open, and people could watch the show on those new color sets.

We were so fortunate to be part of that show. In "Bonanza," none of the Cartwrights could really ride a horse when we started the series. You'd get on a horse, but that didn't mean you could ride. It's just desperation; you pray. We'd ride studio horses, and they know where they're going. When one horse leaves, they all leave, and you just ride along with the pack with that silly grin on your face, *dying*.

By the time the show was moved to Sunday night, the real "Bonanza" time slot with Chevrolet, it had im-

proved, and people felt that Lorne Greene, Dan Blocker and I could do a better show. The three of us got along well and had one heck of a time. It was a party. We worked hard, but we played hard together. A *lot* of laughs. I think when people get along well personally, it shows up on a screen, more on a TV screen than a motion picture screen. We spent a lot of time together, shooting 39 or 40 shows 11 months in a row, with a two-week hiatus in the summer.

"Bonanza" was the best school in the world. I learned how to do things right. I learned how to do things wrong. And I learned that if you really want to make yourself feel good at the end of the day, you have to do things the way you want to do them, not the way they've always been done or the way that pleases everyone else. I had a different feeling about the whole look of television. In the early days when I first started directing the show, there was no textured lighting in television. We used flat lighting. If I'm remembered for anything, I think one of the things should be how much I did to alter that. I got together with Ed Ancona and the other color experts at NBC who were convinced that we could make a motion picture instead of a television show. We did just that. We brought arc lights on the stage for the first time and gave pictures deep shadows and definite moonlights, making them visually what they should be.

I directed my first "Bonanza" in 1965, six years after it started. Before that, I had written some of the episodes, but I was always considered Little Joe Cartwright, the young, wild, crazy kid. Little Joe certainly did not have the savvy and background knowledge to direct. At one time, we went to shoot at Lake Tahoe, where there was a big press party on a riverboat. David Dortort, the Executive Producer, gave a long speech and introduced me by saying, "Here's a man who is young, he's growing up on the show. He's learning, and he has written several very good scripts for us, and who knows, maybe someday he'll direct." The minute he said that, the door was open, and I got up in front of 200 members of the national press and said, "When?" He said, "Er, ah, I'll have to check the schedule and find out when we have an opening." I said, "We have no one for show 17. I've got a script for it. Why don't you announce it now?" That's how I got my first shot.

I started writing several years before that because I needed money. I'd gotten a divorce, and with no money saved, I needed money for alimony and child-support payments. The first one I wrote was when we'd run out of scripts for the show, as we did very often. They were going to finish the current episode on a Tuesday and shut down on Wednesday to get some new material. I couldn't afford to shut down. So I went home that Friday night, wrote a script in longhand over the weekend, a friend typed it, and I brought it in on Monday. They bought it, and we continued to shoot.

I like writing when it's cooking, but like anything else, when it's not, it's dreadful to sit there and stare at the blank page. I don't write story outlines. I write the screenplay. I have no notion of how it's going to come out. I pick some of the characters, and when they begin to talk to each other, I begin to write rapidly, because I want to see how it's going to turn out, whether it's a happy ending or a sad one.

My ambition stems from necessity, a powerful spur. I worry that my kids will be robbed of that need, the feeling that, hey, I've got to get a job. They know they'll never starve. I love to work and I do work very hard, but sometimes, to justify it, I buy something and convince myself that it's an extravagance when it really isn't. I tell myself that I'll write a certain number of shows to cover it if my income from acting doesn't. Recently, I bought a whole interior of a gymnasium and put it in my house. All the equipment! It looks like a Jack LaLanne health club without all the bodies.

I always wanted to have a little more control over the product than I had in "Bonanza." Acting wasn't enough for me. I was interested in the whole process of making a film and not having anybody tell me how to do it. I think you have an idea or vision of what you want when you've got the script in front of you. Perhaps the way I want to do a script is not better, but it is the way I see it. I don't think you can make a film the way somebody else wants it to look. You don't get your own self into it,

and it doesn't mean anything. Not everybody is going to like my kind of product, and I don't expect them to.

The "Bonanza" series was shown in almost every country in the world. In the Japanese film of it, the actor playing Hoss had a rather high voice, which made us all crack up. Dan Blocker told me when he was in the service, the Japanese didn't care for him because of his size and his hairy chest. They gave him a nickname which meant "akin to the apes." Dan was something! The show was no fun to make after he died.

During the "Bonanza" years, I supported a lot of family and relatives, so I wasn't loaded when the series ended, just comfortable enough to have some freedom. NBC wanted me to do a series right away, but I wanted to take a year and think about it, and I wanted to do some other things. I wrote and directed, with George Schaefer, the first of a 1973 NBC series, "Love Story." It had a great opportunity to be a hit but wasn't. Perhaps today, when anthologies have a better chance, it would be.

"Little House on the Prairie" came about in 1974. I had written one pilot (on another theme) that I was thinking about doing when Ed Friendly approached me with a "Little House" script and all of the Laura Ingalls Wilder books. Of course, now I've read them all, but then I hadn't. I gave one of the books to one of my daughters to read. She liked it, thought it was fun for kids to read. I read the screenplay and thought it was possible to make the show for adults too. We made the pilot in this area (Calaveras County); it tested very highly, and the show got on the air. It did very well for a couple of years, and then "The Bionic Woman" was put on opposite it.

Any soft show opposite a gimmick show has a good chance of getting hurt, but not for long.

I met with Larry White and others at NBC, and they wanted me to change the look and the format of the show. They wanted me to make it an action show. I mean, after all, I had seven people living in Walnut Grove, and once I'd grabbed their collars for seven weeks,

I couldn't beat the same guys up again. That would be monotonous. So I told them I felt they should drop the series because I couldn't make the show into something it wasn't. They said we'd wait and see. Then they moved the show to Monday night, and it skyrocketed. "Bionic Woman" was on and off in a short period, proving that gimmicks don't last.

I wanted to do "Little House" because it explored people's relationships with each other, a subject no one else was touching at that time.

I wrote and directed one of the shows about bigotry. "The Wish," with Ossie Davis, which caused a furor. Chevrolet was very upset because they had tremendous pressure from their Southern dealers about that episode, and it was taken from the schedule. When I found out the reason for the cancellation, I asked to meet with NBC in Burbank to pick the air date and discuss the publicity. (Chevrolet had seen the script because the script had gone to their ad agency.) I told the guys at NBC that if the show didn't go on, I'd go to the press, because I was furious about the sponsor's reaction. NBC gave me the air-date I wanted, did one hell of a publicity campaign, and the show received extraordinary reviews. We were bad-mouthed in certain states, and the show was not shown in Mississippi.

I learned a lot during the "Little House" years. Almost every scene in the loft (where the kids slept) was based on a scene of something that happened to my kids. I know it's probably wrong, but I eavesdrop on the children. I love to hear their conversations. I don't tell them about what I hear, nor can I berate them if they say something they shouldn't, because it's none of my business to be eavesdropping. On the other hand, how else am I ever going to find out what really goes on?

I want viewers to feel an emotion when they watch a television show, and not just be immune and insensitive to people being shot down. I mean to make people laugh or cry or get in an argument with each other over what we're talking about, so television isn't just a night-light you watch with interchangeable acts. The scripts are always different. Around Christmas I may do a very sad show. People don't think that's good for the holiday time, but a lot of the people out there with dire troubles are more depressed around the holidays than the rest of the year. It's good for them to be able to look at something and say, "Hey, we're alive, we're all right!"

NBC has always been terrific with me about one thing: I never had anybody looking over my shoulder. In the nine years "Little House" was on, we, NBC and our production group, didn't talk on the phone about any problems more than three or four times. There may have been a conversation about the use of a word like "bastard," but never creative interference. That was and is unheard of! It is a wonderful feeling, just terrific.

It nearly changed when Silverman came in. Fred was a workaholic. He got involved in all areas of everybody's shows. That's all well and good, except when someone dictates from the position of president of the company, I question why I have been hired for my creative talent when that talent is being usurped. The first major thing that bothered me was that I was told that all of my guest stars would have to be videotaped, the tapes sent to New York so Fred could pass on whether or not they were the proper people for the shows. On several other shows, he looked at certain actors even after they were shooting and said he didn't like them, and they had to re-shoot those scenes.

Once NBC sent the people from casting over for a meeting at my office. Not Jay Michelis. Are you kidding! He's a great asset to NBC. Anyway, they all came over. Perry Lafferty was there as a liaison for the new casting people that Fred had brought in. I knew what the meeting was going to be about so I just prefaced the meeting by saying, "Look, before you say anything, I just want you to know I've had a good run with 'Little House,' and I've really enjoyed it, but I'm pooped. I wasn't going to tell you at this meeting, but when I thought about it, I thought this is just as good a time as any. I just don't want to do the show anymore. I'm going to wrap it up." It was the Number One show on NBC at the time. The NBC guys were absolutely stunned. We never discussed casting. We talked about airplane flights and maybe taking a vacation and stuff like that. The meeting adjourned, and I never heard about casting again. I wrapped it up four years after that. We went to '83 with it.

One of the things that I love about this business is that it *is* a business, and I don't want to be over budget. I don't want to spend more money than is needed. That's part of the challenge. If you have a great script and

$24 million, you can make a pretty big picture. If you've got a great script and $750,000, you've got to work. You've got to figure out how to make that look like a bundle. That's why the Michael Landon Production Company gets along as well as it does and has a reputation of coming in on budget.

What did we do next? Paul Klein and Brandon Tartikoff knew that Merlin Olsen had a good following. They asked me to think up a series for Merlin, who was a big, soft guy like Dan Blocker, and do something with kids. With no more suggestion than that, I wrote the screenplay for "Father Murphy" in a couple of weeks. Klein and Tartikoff read it and liked it. It tested extremely high, but it started out slowly. It held its own with "Laverne and Shirley," and the numbers picked up gradually. They tried it on Sunday night against "60 Minutes," and it got slaughtered. I felt very badly for all the people involved.

I don't want to do two shows at the same time again because I do not delegate authority well. I was trying to rewrite 48 scripts a year then. That's very, very tough. I couldn't devote enough time to make the show as good as it was originally. It ran for two years but didn't have the strength to stay on longer. If it had come on during NBC's upswing, it might have been different. A network on the rise is like something crackling through the air. Suddenly, everybody says, "Hey, that must be the one to look at."

I starred in two NBC movies, "The Loneliest Runner" and "Comeback." I wrote and directed "The Loneliest Runner" during "The Little House" run and before "Father Murphy." I was very proud of that little 90-minute movie we made for peanuts. It came in at $360,000, but we had a great production. I phoned Carroll Rosenbloom, owner of the Los Angeles Rams, and said we needed an Olympic Stadium for five minutes at half time to film me as I won the marathon. Could we film that in the Los Angeles Coliseum during a Rams half time? I told him I knew he was a busy man and asked him to hear me out for one second. I said I was a terrible bed-wetter as a kid, that I had a movie which would help kids with that problem. They'd find out that a lot of people wet their beds, and some of them are big people.

There was a pause on the phone, and then he said, "Send me the script. I guarantee you I wet the bed a hell of a lot more than you did." He did a terrific thing—he pushed an NBC movie during a game televised by CBS. We did a number like the raid on Entebbe. With five cameras, we practiced all day to be precise, because we had *five* minutes, and that was *it*. I prayed that the crowd and the weather would be on my side. The minute the whistle blew at half time, the poles of Olympic flags went up, and I made a quick announcement to the audience about cheering when I came in. First they booed me, but I dropped to my knees and pleaded, and the crowd was wonderful. It really looked like a spectacular event at the end of that movie. I'm terribly proud of that movie because there was an incredible response—very moving. Parents realized, "My God, my kid doesn't wet the bed to spite me. I feel awful about that. I've got to tell him I'm sorry."

Now I'm back with "Highway to Heaven." I've always had a production company, but I really never ran any shows through it until "Highway." I got used to being with NBC Entertainment, and, in many ways, that was very comfortable. They had a hands-off policy, but I never loused them up. I was never over the budget on "Little House" in all of the years we did it.

I like to act, to produce, and I'm a businessman, but really a very bad one in terms of what a businessman is considered to be. I think I know as much about this business as anybody in the world. I've done all aspects of it for so long. The group around me in my production company knows business. Kent McCray is my right arm (I just happen to be lefthanded). He is sensational. He's efficient at running the company well, keeping the unit of about 112 or 115 together, and knows how to handle it without a separation of church and state.

We don't have any "biggies" on the show who live in motor homes. If I have a guest star on my show, his or her agent will insist on the same accommodations as Michael Landon's. When they come to where we're filming the show, they discover my dressing room is in a honey wagon. A motor home separates you from the rest of the people. I'm not comfortable as an actor on the set unless there's a feeling of camaraderie with the crew—they're our only audience. That's what makes it work. This crew will walk across the river for us because they know we'll all be walking with them. As you can tell, I'm an egalitarian with a passion.

I got the idea for "Highway to Heaven" when I was driving from Culver City through Beverly Hills to pick up my children and was stuck in bumper-to-bumper traffic. Everyone was angry; they honked horns and cursed at each other out of their car windows. I thought, *gee*, I'd like to do a show where people could see that if you're nice, even slightly nice to each other, everybody's going to be happy. Example: people don't treat waiters like human beings, and then they don't like the way waiters treat them. People react to what they're given. I'm not saying everybody. There are probably a hell of a lot of rotten people in this world, but there are a lot more good people than we realize.

I've always had a feeling, more in recent years, that there is something else, something different, that I'm supposed to be doing. And I don't know what it is. It's a very strange feeling, but a very strong one. I know I could very easily spend half of each year of my life in Africa. I've never been to a place I've enjoyed as much. I'm like a different human being there. I'm no longer hyper; I don't bite my nails; I can sleep a long time. And no one knows who I am. It's an *extraordinary* feeling. I've only been to Kenya, and I would have gone this past year, but we have a new baby, and I want to wait until she's able to handle the rigors of Africa. It's rough. We stay in a tent because staying in a lodge is not seeing Africa at all. You miss the animals' beauty, their whole social life, and the chance to see all the remarkable things they do. I love animals.

My wish for NBC's 60th birthday is that I hope I'll still be with them on the 70th.

October 22, 1985

Photo Index